Psychological Management of the Physically Ill

Dedication

For
Emma, Ben and Joffy Lacey
and
Ellen and Kiki Burns

Psychological Management of the Physically Ill

EDITED BY

J. Hubert Lacey MD, MPhil, FRCPsych
Reader and Head, Adult Psychiatry Section,
St George's Hospital Medical School,
London, UK

Tom Burns MA, MD, MRCPsych
Consultant, Honorary Senior Lecturer,
St George's Hospital Medical School,
London, UK

CHURCHILL LIVINGSTONE
EDINBURGH LONDON MELBOURNE AND NEW YORK 1989

CHURCHILL LIVINGSTONE
Medical Division of Longman Group UK Limited

Distributed in the United States of America by
Churchill Livingstone Inc., 1560 Broadway, New
York, N.Y. 10036, and by associated companies,
branches and representatives throughout the world.

First published 1989

ISBN 0-443-03601-2

British Library Cataloguing in Publication Data
Psychological management of the physically ill.
  1. Man. Diseases. Psychological aspects
  I. Lacey, J. Hubert (John Hubert)
  II. Burns, Tom
  616'.001'9

Library of Congress Cataloging in Publication Data
Psychological management of the physically ill.
  1. Sick — Psychology. 2. Behavior therapy. I. Lacey,
J. Hubert. II. Burns, Tom, M. D. [DNLM: 1. Behavior
Therapy. 2. Disease — psychology. 3. Patients —
psychology. W 85 P974]
R726.5.P792   1989   616'.001'9   88–18075

Produced by Longman Singapore Publishers (Pte) Ltd.
Printed in Singapore.

Contributors List

G. H. B. Baker MD, FRCPI, FRCPsych
Consultant Psychiatrist, Westminster Hospital, London, UK

Gary Bell BA, MBBS, MRCPsych
Lecturer in Psychiatry, University College and Middlesex School of Medicine, London, UK

Tom Burns MA, MD, MRCPsych
Consultant, Honorary Senior Lecturer, St George's Hospital Medical School, London, UK

John Anthony Cotterill BSc, MD, FRCP
Consultant Dermatologist, Leeds General Infirmary, Leeds, UK

Chris Evans BA, MBBS, MRCPsych
Research Fellow and Honorary Therapist, St George's Hospital Medical School, London, UK

Charlotte Feinmann MD, MSc, MRCPsych
Consultant Psychiatrist, Eastman Dental Hospital; Senior Lecturer in Psychiatry, University College and the Middlesex School of Medicine, London, UK

Maurice Greenberg BSc, MPhil, MRCP, MRCPsych
Consultant Psychiatrist, University College Hospital, London, UK

J. J. Groen FRCP, FRCPsych
Emeritus Professor of Medicine, Hadassah Hebrew University, Jerusalem; Professor of Psychological Research, University of Leiden, Netherlands

Heather Humphrey
Research Assistant, Department of Psychiatry, St George's Hospital Medical School, London, UK

Michael Humphrey MA, PhD, FBPsS
Reader in Psychology, St George's Hospital Medical School, London, UK

Janice A. Kohler MRCP
Senior Paediatric Registrar, Southampton General Hospital, Southampton, UK

J. Hubert Lacey MD, MPhil, FRCPsych
Reader and Head, Adult Psychiatry Section, St George's Hospital Medical School, London, UK

Geoffrey G. Lloyd MA, MD, MPhil, FRCPE, FRCPsych
Consultant Psychiatrist, Royal Free Hospital, London, UK

Andrew J. Macaulay LRCP, MRCS, MBBS, MSc, MRCPsych
Clinical Research Fellow, Urodynamic Unit, Department of Obstetrics and Gynaecology, St George's Hospital; Senior Registrar, Department of Psychiatry, St George's Hospital, London, UK

Peter Maguire BA, MB, BChir, FRCPsych, DPM
Senior Lecturer in Psychiatry, University of Manchester; Consultant Psychiatrist, University
Hospital of South Manchester; Director, Cancer Research Campaign Psychological Medicine
Group, Manchester, UK

Richard Mayou BM, MPhil, MSc, FRCP, FRCPsych
Clinical Reader in Psychiatry, University of Oxford; Honorary Consultant, Fellow of
Nuffield College, Oxford, UK

Keith A. Nichols BSc, MSc(Clin Psych), ABPS
Lecturer, Department of Psychology, University of Exeter; Principal Clinical Psychologist,
Renal Unit, Exeter, UK

H. E. Pelser MD
Former Head, Endocrinological Outpatient Department, University Hospital, Amsterdam,
Netherlands

Martin Radford MD, FRCP
Senior Lecturer and Consultant Paediatrician, Southampton General Hospital, UK

Ingemar Sjödin MD, PhD
Senior Lecturer in Psychiatry, Department of Psychiatry, Sahlgren Hospital, Göteborg,
Sweden

Andrew Steptoe MA, DPhil
Reader in Psychology, St George's Hospital Medical School, University of London, UK

Peter Storey MD, FRCP, FRCPsych
Honorary Consultant Psychiatrist, St George's and Springfield Hospitals, London, UK

Jan Svedlund MD, PhD
Associate Professor of Psychiatry, University of Göteborg; Assistant Chief, Department of
Psychiatry, Sahlgren Hospital, Göteborg, Sweden

Christopher James Thomas MBBS, MSc, MRCP, MRCPsych
Consultant Liaison Psychiatrist, Leicestershire Health Authority, UK

Jenifer Wilson-Barnett BA, MSc, PhD, SRN, FRCN
Professor and Head of Department, Department of Nursing Studies, King's College
London, UK

Contents

Introduction

Virtually all contemporary physicians would accept the sentiment that there is an emotional component to physical illness. Most would agree that mental matters may determine, or be implicated in, the aetiology of illness, or, at least, may influence the course of it. Few, however, would have the confidence to square the circle and attempt usefully to harness feelings, both declared and denied, in treatment. This volume is intended to be a source-book for the few and an encouragement for the many.

In clinical practice, physical and psychiatric disorders commonly occur together. A number of surveys have shown that between a third and a half of patients, both when attending the surgery and when admitted to a ward, have a co-existing psychiatric illness or concurrent emotional distress.

With the proliferation of medical books it is reasonable to question the need for another. However, we believe that there is a gap in the literature, which can be filled by a volume that delineates in greater detail the treatment approaches currently being advocated for certain physical illnesses. In particular, there is a need for a book which enables the reader to compare and contrast various methods within the covers of what is a brief volume. We have been very fortunate to be able to assemble a group of distinguished clinicians and researchers who have been at the forefront of recent treatment innovations. They have been required to give descriptions of their treatment methods in sufficient detail to allow critical examination and, if the reader so wishes, replication.

This book aims to provide a practical manual of treatments. Whilst it is intended primarily for the practising clinician, the scientific orientation of the contributors has resulted in scholarly presentations which should make it of interest to the academic also. Certainly, we required our contributors to declare their treatment philosophies but overall we emphasised that the predominant theme of each chapter should be the practical implementation of treatment. Most chapters have been heavily punctuated with clinical vignettes and case examples, which promise to be valuable to the practitioner faced with patients suffering from these disturbing disorders.

This, then, is a pragmatic book. Certain books in this area require the acceptance of a specific medical or psychological perspective. Most readers, if they are unprepared to accept an author's faith as received wisdom, become irritated, put the book on one side and recognise that psychosomatics is a house hopelessly divided. This book attempts to be different. Each contributor has successfully practised the treatments described and all have been warned against painting on a broad canvas models of treatment designed to encompass every disorder. Readers can assume the efficacy of treatments even if they doubt the theology.

The chapters of the book reflect variations in psychiatric convictions and treatments. Unsurprisingly, this results in diverse emphasis and at times conflicting recommendations on fundamental issues. For example, some of the behaviourally orientated programmes might be considered to sit uncomfortably with treatments which emphasise the counselling role or take a purist psychodynamic approach. Some contributors try to de-mystify the doctor by, for example, advocating group treatments; others lay stress on the curative power of the traditional clinician, enshrined with wisdom and care. These discrepancies stem from different models of aetiology. Rather than apologise, the editors would emphasise the advantages of bringing together authors operating from diverse theoretical perspectives.

The book highlights a number of unanswered questions and issues for future debate. Certain methods of treatment have been covered by more than one author, thus enabling the reader to exercise some selection in the methods he or she wishes to use. The perceptive reader may also detect a relative lack of objective evidence in support of particular treatments. He should, perhaps, refrain from harsh judgement in view of the necessary embryonic nature of the subject; but, none the less, it should be registered.

Despite this air of diversity, the impression the editors gained, from reviewing the chapters, is the remarkable accord on so many facets of treatment. The procedures described in this book are the result of many years of observation and research. Whilst they may have developed from very different medical or psychological positions, there are large sections in each chapter which read in uncommon harmony. Most contributors appreciate that there are many aspects of their subject, not least the recognition that certain symptoms may be unrelated one with another and do not fit easily into a simple syndrome. There is agreement that not all treatments will help all patients. This has led, perhaps, to the tendancy to recommend the integration of treatments: family, group and individual therapies occurring contemporaneously; or, mixed cognitive, psychodynamic and pharmacological approaches managed by multi-disciplinary teams. The trend towards the systematic application of strategies, albeit empirically derived, has been argued to have a more powerful curative potential than treatments stemming from one theoretical position.

In summary, integration and eclecticism seem the watchwords.

London, 1989   H. L.
                                                                                T. B.

Peter Storey

Brain damage and strokes

INTRODUCTION

This chapter is concerned mainly with the long-term psychological and psychiatric aspects of brain damage from closed head injury (CHI) and stroke (cerebrovascular accident, CVA), considering the family as well as the patient. Acute disturbances, including confusional states and delirium, are not covered, nor is progressive multi-infarct dementia, despite its great importance.

Brain damage, in the sense of neuronal death, can be caused by very many agents, but, as is discussed later, the principles of assessment and management apply whatever the pathology.

Primary disturbances. Unlike the conditions considered in other chapters of this book, the main psychological and emotional disturbances arise as a direct result of the organic pathology, altering the nature of the individual, often changing profoundly and for ever his perceptions, thinking, feeling, and communicating. Life becomes much more difficult to cope with, but the very cerebral equipment which he must use in order to cope is impaired.

Secondary disturbances arise from his own reactions to his disabilities — which may include complete or partial paralysis of a limb, sensory losses of various types, epilepsy, impotence, ataxia, deafness, and many more, as well as those psychological and perceptual impairments considered in more detail in this chapter. The term *tertiary disturbance* could perhaps be used for the problems which arise consequently in the family and in society.

Although these conditions are so common, causing immense disability and suffering, many doctors and other professionals involved are uncertain about some of the specific intellectual, perceptual, and personality changes which commonly occur, and do not know how to assess them, or sometimes even what to look for. Much of the first part of this chapter is therefore devoted, after briefly considering some background epidemiology and pathology, to the commoner forms of impairment. It is hoped that this will help professionals to understand the experiences and problems of the patients and their families. The later sections are devoted more to management issues, but the divisions are not rigid.

UNDERLYING FACTORS

Both strokes and head injuries are extremely common. The former cause more severe disability than any other illness in our society, with about 120 000 new cases per annum in England and Wales, and with about 250 000 survivors alive at any one time. Of those who survive 1 month the average length of life is about 3 years, ranging up to 10 or more years (Marquardsen 1969).

Closed head injury is also a common condition, and there are about 1000 severely damaged new survivors each year in England and Wales. Most of these are young, with a life expectancy little short of the normal population.

Open head injuries, with fractured skull and torn dura mater, are much less common than CHI in peace time, but are not rare.

In addition to strokes and CHI, very many other conditions can lead to permanent brain damage, for example: tumours before and after surgery; infections such as meningitis, encephalitis or abscesses; toxins such as lead; metabolic disorders or hormonal insufficiency such as hypercalcaemia or hypothyroidism; genetically determined neuronal degeneration as with Huntington's chorea. A very long list could easily be compiled. There are however certain basic principles which apply to all patients with brain damage, which can be used to understand the impairments from which the patient suffers to which he reacts, and to which the family and sometimes the rest of society also reacts.

Before moving to the main subject of the chapter it is worth briefly considering the role of psychological factors in the causation of strokes and CHI.

Emotional factors in causation

1. Strokes

This subject has recently been reviewed by the present author (Storey 1985). The main known antecedent causal factor of strokes is hypertension and the author concluded that the evidence which links emotional factors *directly* with hypertension is not completely convincing. It is however interesting and suggestive. In addition, and probably more importantly, other factors in the genesis of strokes, such as obesity, diet, smoking, and excessive alcohol intake, are obviously largely determined by psychosocial factors. There seems little doubt that the incidence of strokes could be brought down more rapidly in this country, as it has in the United States and elsewhere (Evans 1986) by measures which would be simple if they did not involve changes in people's attitudes.

The only form of stroke illness in which emotional factors clearly have a major role seems to be the relatively uncommon form of subarachnoid haemorrhage (SAH) in which there is no aneurysm or angioma (Storey 1969). There are no ways of avoiding the sudden severe emotional turmoil of the type which plays a part in that illness, and which indeed has always been known to precipitate strokes on occasions. The evidence which links stroke illness to emotional factors such as 'giving up/given up' or repressed hostility, is unconvincing (Storey 1985). Studies of life events before strokes (other than SAH) do not seem to have been reported.

2. *Closed Head Injuries (CHI)*

Again, the incidence of these is obviously affected by complex psychosocial factors, because the main causes of CHI are road traffic accidents (RTA), assault, and falls. Alcohol plays a part in each of these categories, and personality factors associated with alcohol abuse and violence are common in drivers in RTA. There is also evidence that some accidents occur when drivers are emotionally disturbed, as after a serious quarrel. Aggressive, risk-taking behaviour, and criminal records for violent offences are common in these drivers, at least in the USA (Selzer et al 1968, Shaffer et al 1974). British reports suggest similar factors are at work, perhaps less markedly (Fahy et al 1967).

Young men are those mainly injured as drivers in RTA, and are more likely to receive head injuries in fights. Children, the old and alcoholics are most likely to sustain them in falls.

FACTORS AFFECTING IMPAIRMENT OF FUNCTION AFTER BRAIN DAMAGE

As indicated earlier, the term 'brain damage' can properly include all cases in which there is permanent neuronal death from any cause. In this chapter, from now on, only head injury and strokes will be specifically considered, although, as already stated, the principles apply to other cases.

1. Rate of onset: the more acute the injury or damage, the more likely is consciousness to be disturbed. Thus a punch on the jaw can lead to unconsciousness, which will probably leave no sequelae, whereas a slowly growing tumour can destroy a large area of brain without disturbing consciousness at all. Confusional states including delirium and subdelirium develop when consciousness is impaired, but are not considered in this chapter.

2. Extent of damage: the greater the volume of brain damaged the greater the effects, depending also on the site, although there is much individual variation.

3. Site of damage: this is important because of localisation of brain function, including lateralisation to right and left hemisphere, frontal as opposed to parietal, and so on. This is considered in more detail in the appropriate sections later.

4. Pathology: the pathology is relevant, in that it determines site, extent, and rate of onset, but there is no difference in the mental state resulting

from surgical removal or from an infarct, if the same piece of brain is affected.

Closed head injury

1. Pathology

In CHI there is diffuse damage, largely due to shearing strains on the neurones as the brain, which has a semifluid consistency in life, swirls about in the cranial cavity after the usual RTA deceleration injury, stretching and tearing neurones and small blood vessels, causing oedema and then compression and consequent ischaemia. In addition to the diffuse damage there is also often direct contusional damage ('coup') and damage on the opposite side as the brain bounces back and hits the skull ('contre-coup'). In CHI from RTA the subfrontal and anterior temporal regions suffer most from direct contusion, so the characteristic disturbances of frontal and temporal damage are commonly added to that of diffuse damage, as described later. Focal damage of a different type develops quite frequently when a haematoma forms after CHI, if it is large enough and is not evacuated in time. The enduring impairments of CHI therefore are due to diffuse brain damage with or without focal damage from contusion or haematoma. (See Jennett & Teasdale (1981) for pathology and many other aspects of CHI).

In open head injuries, caused either by penetrating missiles or by some blow which fractures the skull and penetrates the dura mater, the extent of the lesion obviously depends on the size and velocity of the object, and the characteristics of the skull. The damage, and consequent impairments, are principally focal except when complications such as infection or haemorrhage occur; there may also be a deceleration element with diffuse damage in some cases (Lishman 1987).

2. Assessment of severity of injury and outcome

In CHI the outcome, particularly in terms of impairment of personality and cognitive function, is, overall, proportional to the severity of the injury as measured by the duration of post-traumatic amnesia (PTA), although there are exceptions to the general rule. PTA is defined as the period of time from the injury to the return of continuous memory (Jennett & Teasdale 1981). During that period, for which the patient will later be amnesic, he will be clouded in consciousness to some degree, and possibly will have florid disturbances such as delirium.

The duration of disturbed consciousness is naturally also an indicator of severity and there is a clear relationship between the duration of coma and severity of impairment. Various methods of defining and assessing coma are in use; perhaps the most widespread is the Glasgow Coma Scale (Jennett

Table 2.1 Relationship between duration of PTA and outcome after CHI

PTA (days)	No.	Severe impairment	Outcome (%) Moderate impairment	Good recovery
<14	101	0	17	83
15–28	96	3	31	66
>28	289	30	43	27

From Jennett & Teasdale (1981).

& Teasdale 1981), in which it is defined as: 'eyes not opening, not obeying commands, and not uttering recognisable words, no response even to pain'. Coma of more than 6 hours is regarded in that system as indicating a severe head injury, and about two-thirds of survivors will have permanent mental impairment. Greater age increases the severity of impairment, and shortens the time over which improvement takes place.

The most severe injuries lead to death, or to the living death of the so-called 'vegetative state'. 'Severe disability' indicates 'conscious but dependent' (for all activities); 'moderate disability' indicates independence in daily living activities, but disabled; and 'good recovery' includes those with mild disabilities but capable of work and normal social life. Many of those in this last category will in fact have quite marked intellectual and personality changes and psychiatric disturbances.

The relationship of PTA and outcome has often been studied. The Glasgow group published typical results as in Table 2.1.

Even after a mild head injury, with a minimal or no PTA, there will be some slowing of mental function apparent to the patient and family, or on subtle psychometric testing, for some time after the injury in many cases; if there is a PTA of more than 21 days there will usually be some permanent cognitive impairment.

It is helpful for those dealing with patients with head injuries and their families to be familiar with these aspects, in order to offer more accurate prognoses, and help to plan for the future.

Most recovery is made in the early weeks and months, as cerebral oedema lessens, and as damaged but living neurones begin to function again. Later recovery is largely due probably to using new neuronal pathways, and 'relearning'. Children, with greater cerebral plasticity, can continue slowly to improve for years. In middle age most recovery has been made after 6 months, but can go on for up to 2 years or so. The old have a much shorter period, perhaps only a few months.

3. The family in the acute stage

This is perhaps the best place to point out that although there are no particular psychological aspects to the care of the truly comatose patient, the family is almost always extremely distressed, bewildered, and often troubled by feelings of guilt — with justice or not, depending on the circumstances. They find it difficult to take in what doctors and other professionals say to them; they need clear and if necessary repeated information. Everyone concerned should tell them the same sort of things, and they should be given the facts with a reasonably optimistic tinge, and told that it will probably be several months before the future can properly be assessed.

There is a role for counselling and support with the relatives, but this is often difficult to arrange in a busy neurosurgical unit. Typical problems include the guilt which uninjured survivors feel, whether or not they were responsible for the accident, when they see the injured patient and realise what they have been spared. Many relatives want to sit day and night by the bedside in hospital, feeling that their presence is essential to recovery, talking and encouraging endlessly. If the patient does not respond they become, naturally, very despondent, and often feel guilty that somehow this means they have not done enough. Obviously, the nature of their previous relationship, and any problems there may have been recently, play a part here, as well as underlying beliefs and attitudes.

Those involved are mainly parents and siblings; boy or girlfriends play a peripheral role, and relatively few are married. The situation is very different from that found by the bedside of the typical patient with a stroke.

Strokes

1. Pathology

Most survivors of CVA have had an infarct in the territory of the middle cerebral artery, affecting motor and sensory cortex and the anterior temporal and temporoparietal areas. Other arterial territories with their characteristic pattern of impairment may also be affected (Lishman 1987, Ch. 2). Cerebral haemorrhage has many fewer survivors. Subarachnoid haemorrhage (SAH) from aneurysm or angioma affects mainly young and middle-aged people and has a very high recurrence rate in the early stages; the fear of recurrence engenders great anxiety in patient and family.

Compared to the pattern of mainly diffuse damage with some focal impairment common in CHI, these strokes lead mainly to major focal impairment with some added diffuse element.

2. Assessment of severity and outcome

There are various systems of assessing the overall picture, taking proper account of perceptual deficit as well as motor ability, and assessing cognitive, social and emotional aspects. A well known one is that used by the Frenchay Stroke Unit (Wade 1986).

3. The family in the acute stage

Much the commonest family situation after stroke is that of the elderly spouse. She, or less commonly he, faces either the death of the patient, with all that means in terms of loss, or has the bleak prospect of a disabled survivor. The implications of that are well known to most older people — incontinence, paralysis, loss of speech, the need for a perpetual watch to prevent falls, and so on. All these burdens then must fall on someone old and possibly frail herself, often in a house poorly designed for such a purpose, perhaps far from bus stops and shops. The alternative is of course that he may never leave hospital, but will be in a geriatric ward, with all its attendant humiliations, while the survivor stays alone at home, with an obligation to visit regularly, and guilt about leaving her husband in such a place.

All these feelings and fears can overwhelm the spouse. If there are adult children nearby, and if — which is often most important — the patient and spouse have been on good terms with them and with the neighbours, then of course it is not quite so bad. If the family has not been close, perhaps largely because of the temperament of one or other parent, then although the adult children visit in the early stages they often soon drift away again. The elderly dread strokes with good reason.

Counselling and support of the spouse in this acute stage, while the patient is still in an acute ward, as well as after he has left, is inseparable from helping with practical planning for the future. In the early weeks there is often the emotional numbness seen after any catastrophe, but the anxiety, tension, and later the depression which follow are based on reality, and are best helped by mobilising services in the community, trying to involve the wider family, and by inducing a justified confidence that she is not going to have to cope entirely on her own. An opportunity to express her feelings and fears is always valuable, as are careful and repeated explanations. Many hospitals have specialised stroke teams which offer this form of help.

IMPAIRMENT OF MENTAL FUNCTION AFTER STROKE AND HEAD INJURY

Patients suffering from brain damage from any cause may experience similar impairments, depending on the site and extent of damage as described above. Because perceptual impairment occurs mainly after moderate or large parietal or temporoparietal lesions, it is commoner after strokes than after CHI, in which the damage is mostly diffuse, but it also occurs commonly after open head injury or with tumour.

1. Perceptual impairment

This is put first because too often it is not considered as a possibility unless there is something really obvious, like neglect or denial of a paralysed limb.

Perceptual loss is in fact common, occurring to some extent in most people who have parietal damage, and it should be carefully examined for in every patient. (See Lishman (1987) for details of assessment.) Adams & Hurwitz (1963) showed that perceptual loss can be the main cause of failure to improve after stroke and is more important even than paralysis in this context.

All senses may be impaired in complex ways. The most disabling kinds are those which affect the patient's awareness of his own body, mainly caused by lesions in the parietal lobe. These range from a slight loss of the attention paid to the impaired limbs, to a failure to recognise that the limb is actually his, or to a denial that it is paralysed.

In the visual fields there may also be a similar lack of attention in one half field, so that events are not recognised if there is something happening at the same time in the other half field. This means that a patient may become suddenly functionally blind in one half field if, for example, a car flashes its headlights on the opposite side. If someone is trying to cross the road visual inattention of this type can lead to a frightening experience. The problem is made worse because he cannot explain why he did not see the vehicle coming from the other side, as he is *not* blind on one side when he tests his vision by looking to right and left. His family may feel that 'he is not trying', and become critical and rejecting. Discussion with someone who can explain the problem is often very helpful in relieving the tensions and conflicts that can develop.

Related difficulties occur when there is visuospatial memory loss, or difficulty in understanding visuospatial relationships. People become muddled and anxious in their homes because they can no longer organise household goods, or they get lost in familiar places, and so on. Loss of right–left orientation similarly leads to all sorts of puzzling difficulties in and out of the home.

All of these impairments have to be suspected and examined for if they are to be detected, and careful explanation to the family as well as to the patient is necessary. They are bewildering and frightening, not just academic indicators of the site of the lesion, which is how they may appear from a text book.

There are other difficulties, which may be classified equally as perceptual or cognitive, that arise from the inability to cope with a series of stimuli in rapid succession. For example, in a busy street at night there may be flashing pedestrian crossing lights, traffic lights, vehicle lights, and so on. Most of us can process this information rapidly and without effort, but many brain-damaged people cannot. To them it is chaotic, leading to fear, tension, headaches, and to retreat — into the safe quiet of the home, from which they may be reluctant to venture out again.

A similar failure of 'information processing' happens with the sense of hearing. A brain-injured person may be able to have a normal conversation with one person, but if another joins in, or the radio is switched on, he seems suddenly 'deaf'. He is unable to sort out the different threads and make sense of them. If he tries, the usual result is failure, with tension, headache, anxiety and, again, withdrawal.

All of these minor-sounding perceptual problems have the effect of making life more difficult to comprehend and to deal with. They often affect people who look outwardly normal, and are not obviously impaired when in quiet conversation or pottering about at their own speed. The sudden 'breakdown' in communication is incomprehensible, often leading to anger and rejection in the family unless explained.

2. Cognitive impairment

This is a subject in which a vast amount of important research has been done over the years, and it cannot usefully be reviewed in detail here. The reader is referred to the survey by Brooks (1984).

The main clinical disability is of impairment of new learning, most obviously for verbal information, less obviously (unless tested for) visuo-spatial and other information. It has been suggested that underlying the memory difficulties is a slowness of 'processing' information (Van Zoemeren et al 1984), which affects all kinds of familiar and unfamiliar material. It is suggested that this affects the way in which the patient 'decides' to attend to something, affecting speed of thought, concentration, and judgement, as well as memory.

Certainly patients with organic cognitive impairment are slow. They can often function happily and well if given enough time, but if put under pressure to keep up to a certain rate can perform very badly, and develop a 'catastrophic reaction' (described later). The inter-relationship of cognitive and personality change is strikingly illustrated in these aspects.

After strokes and open head injuries, or other more focal lesions, the same slowness may be present, but it seems to be mainly due to more diffuse damage, and in those conditions perceptual problems are often dominant.

Methods of trying to cope with memory impairment are mentioned later (see Cognitive Retraining).

3. Communication difficulties

These are of two main types: dysarthria due to impaired neuromuscular control of speech; and dysphasias — expressive (motor), receptive (sensory), and mixed. In some unfortunates dysarthria and dysphasia coincide.

Severe dysarthria is more common after CHI than after stroke, because of brain stem damage, and can be very distressing and frustrating, and outbursts of anger and despair are common, as is more settled depression.

Expressive dysphasia is obviously frustrating, and it is easy to empathise with the patient in his efforts and distress. More damaging to rehabilitation prospects, and common after more posterior-dominant hemisphere strokes, is receptive dysphasia, in which comprehension of the spoken word is impaired. It is easy to be misled by a patient who looks alert and who responds socially in an appropriate way. It is easy to believe that he understands the meaning of what is being said, but cannot answer fully because of expressive dysphasia. Often he is only responding to the non-verbal cues: tone of voice, smile and gestures. It is quick and easy to test for receptive problems, using household objects, coins and so on, by asking the patient to arrange objects in order of length, value, etc., or to put 'the biggest object over the smallest one' for example, in increasingly complex ways. More formal psychometric testing is also available (see Lishman 1987). If receptive dysphasia is not recognised then no sensible plan for the patient can be constructed, but sadly it is often missed.

Communication difficulties intensify the isolation and misery which many brain-damaged people experience. Their friends soon lose interest in laborious and superficial exchanges, and only the most dedicated family members, mostly wives or mothers, keep it up for long. Although the therapeutic effects of speech therapy are often difficult to demonstrate on speech itself, there is no doubt that regular speech therapy has a great effect on morale, and a decision to end it, because no progress is being made, is often a severe blow to patient and family.

4. Personality changes

These put a greater strain on families than does physical disability, intellectual deterioration, or impaired communication, and the longer the family has to cope the greater the distress and frank psychiatric morbidity they show (Rosenbaum & Najenson 1976, Thomsen 1974, Carnwath & Johnson 1981, Panting & Merry 1972, Wade et al 1986).

It is essential, if these changes are to be properly understood, that the family is seen without the patient on some occasions; otherwise the relatives may be unwilling, even frightened, to describe them in the patient's presence. It is also essential that professionals involved should realise their own limitations and be aware that interview alone does not allow a proper assessment of personality and behavioural changes. It is a good rule that if one can identify evidence of personality change at interview it must be *severe*, and that there will probably be problems in the home arising from it. Another useful rule is that most people with any CNS signs after a stroke or CHI will probably have some personality and cognitive changes, and so will some who have no CNS signs.

The changes may be of several possible types, which can overlap.

a. Exaggeration of previous personality traits

This is common and extremely important. Although major personality deterioration can and often does occur in people of perfectly normal previous personality, especially with frontal lobe damage, in most cases where there are major problems after the damage there have been some problems beforehand.

The previously impulsive and aggressive become much more so; the previously fussy and meticulous become overtly obsessional, and check endlessly; the previously suspicious and touchy become difficult and paranoid, and so on. A healthy and stable personality tends to protect against the worst developments.

b. More irritable, anxious and withdrawn

These features, combined usually with lessened energy and easy fatigue, are the most common of all personality changes with brain damage. In the present author's study of brain-damaged patients after SAH it correlated roughly with the severity of neurological signs, and occurred in more than half of those with CNS signs (Storey 1970a). Similar changes occur after CHI (Bond 1984).

Anxiety is an extremely important consequence of brain damage, often related to an inability to cope with some task, more often intellectual than physical. The anxiety is at times overwhelming, and in the *catastrophic reaction* the patient bursts out with angry irritability, often with tears, shaking, even with incontinence or a near-faint. This happens particularly when he feels he is under pressure to do something well or rapidly, as described earlier. The task concerned may be a seemingly simple physical one, like washing dishes and putting them away, perhaps rendered difficult because of right–left disorientation and visuospatial loss, so that he cannot work out where to put them.

The task is more often a social and emotional one, as when a grandmother, home from hospital after a stroke, is talking with a grandchild, quietly and successfully, until others come in. The noise level rises as television is switched on, and she is soon unable to cope with the noise and the 'information processing' needed. She suddenly becomes tense, shaky, and may then explode into a little burst of irritable shouting, followed by weeping. The effect of this sort of behaviour is that very soon grandmother is not asked to cope with such things, the children tip-toe round the house, and grandmother enjoys the peace and quiet of the front room on her own, while the life of the family continues elsewhere without her. The 'catastrophic' behaviour can be seen to lessen and stabilise the demands made on her. In the short term this is welcomed, and is in fact appropriate, but it can lead to increasing withdrawal and isolation, with grandmother spending her days alone in a silent room, because no-one ever properly works out how to grade the stimulation and demands appropriately. Obviously, previous personality and the pre-existing relationships will profoundly influence these interactions. (See Lishman (1987) for more detail on this important aspect.)

Rehabilitation of any patient with any condition must match demand and stimulus to the capacity to respond. This is easy to see and to manage when muscle strength is involved, but more difficult in the psychosocial field. Without accurate assessment of the disability, as for example of visuospatial or body image disturbance, or of the level of anxiety, a proper balance can never be achieved.

c. 'Organic moodiness'

This term was used (Storey 1970a) to describe a common pattern of personality change after SAH which can also be observed with other brain damage. It is a combination of chronic shallow depressive mood, often lifting briefly in response to some new stimulus, but rapidly falling back with apparent boredom, loss of interest, and fatigue. This 'organic moodiness' merges into the pattern of irritability, anxiety, and withdrawal already described, into more severe depressive states which often come and go, and into the predominantly apathetic mood described later.

d. Frontal lobe syndrome

This syndrome has been recognised for many years as a clinical entity, developing after damage to the frontal lobes. It is independent of the other types of organic personality change, and can develop in people of perfectly normal and stable temperament, although the results are usually worse in those whose premorbid personality was already lacking in control.

It is much more commonly found after CHI, or with penetrating lesions of the frontal lobe, than after strokes, as the territory of the anterior cerebral artery is less often infarcted than that of the middle cerebral. It is however not uncommon after SAH if there is rupture of an anterior communicating artery aneurysm. The frequency after CHI from RTA is due largely to subfrontal contusion.

The most striking change is the disinhibition of sexual and aggressive impulses, especially in the early months after the injury. Most of the patients are young men, their sexual drives are at their peak, and of course many of those who have head injuries in RTA are to some extent self-selected for poor impulse control and other psychopathic traits (Selzer et al 1968; Shaffer et al 1974). At times these patients present very great management problems, because of a kind of sexual frenzy — continually interfering with women and even children, completely without insight and disinhibitedly aggressive when others resist or complain. In a hospital or rehabilitation centre they can be unmanageable except by the use of neuroleptics such as chlorpromazine, as nurses and other female staff are repeatedly assaulted. Being without insight the patients deeply resent being controlled by medication with its attendant side effects. At home they are even more difficult.

After a few weeks the intensity of the disturbances usually dies down, and there is a return to more normal social behaviour in public and away from the family. At home however excessive and inappropriate sexual demands are one of the main factors leading to the breakdown of marriages and other relationships.

Aggressive impulses are also disinhibited, but the patients are not usually spontaneously aggressive. It is more that aggressive responses are more readily released, so that a man might lash out at his crying child or complaining wife whereas he might previously only have spoken sharply or muttered an oath.

Of the other changes in the frontal lobe syndrome perhaps the most important is a loss of foresight. The affected individual has a concrete and limited response to everything. He cannot think or plan ahead; he does not say to himself 'if I do such and such the likely consequence will be so and so'. Everything is done as an immediate reaction. A very striking example was of a patient expecting a home visit by the present author. He had mislaid his key (being also forgetful), and not wanting to keep the doctor waiting, he took an axe from the garden shed and smashed down his own front door. His wife and children had left him years before, just after his return from hospital after SAH from a ruptured anterior communicating aneurysm. He had attempted to rape his teenage daughter in front of his wife and other children, and had broken his wife's jaw when she tried to stop him. That early 'frenzy' had died down, but he still had severe residual personality change years afterwards.

Those with the frontal lobe syndrome tend to be rather fatuous, shallow and joking in their affect, easily excited, interfering, incapable of serious thought or prolonged concentration, and very egocentric. All this may co-exist with normal intelligence and cognition as measured by standard IQ psychometry. There are some tests, however, which are of some value in assessing these higher functions, as for example the Wisconsin Card Sorting Test. (See Brooks (1984) for a review of this subject.)

The individual with a frontal lobe syndrome of this type does not usually complain of suffering. He has no insight into the disabilities he has, although he may complain of the way he has been treated. He is often quite content, and even euphoric, if left alone and not thwarted. At times the clinical picture resembles hypomania, but without the pressure and rapidity of speech and action characteristic of that illness.

The effect on the family is devastating, and few marriages survive if the changes are severe. Parents find it easier to cope than does a spouse because they can see him, and respond to him, as their child; but to a wife he is so changed as to be a different person. A common problem that develops between parents and adult child resembles the dependence/independence conflicts of adolescence, but in a caricatured way, from which there is no escape by emotional maturation or by leaving home, as the brain-damaged individual does not develop beyond a certain stage. The parents remain fixed in their fears of what this unpredictable and poorly controlled 'child' might do if allowed to do as he wishes, and they can easily seem over-protective to the onlooker. If it is a girl they dread particularly promiscuity (which is common in the disinhibited) and pregnancy or that she might be assaulted or raped, as the characteristic loss of foresight and self control can easily lead to taking serious risks. The brain-damaged individual, usually a young adult, or even middle aged, rarely has insight into the situation, feels competent to manage his own affairs although usually is very demanding of attention and help, and can be impulsively aggressive and even violent, often to ageing parents, continually resenting the constraints they try to impose.

A wife may continue looking after a severely affected husband, especially if they have had a number of good years together, so that there are reserves of duty, pity, and love to draw on. It is also easier if the patient has been slowed up by his injuries, either physically or mentally, so that the impact of the personality change is blunted. A frequent problem in the marriages which do survive is that the wife can cope only by regarding her husband essentially as a child, which for most women means that they cannot respond sexually. This conflict is often described openly and directly by the wife, but in others is beneath the surface, only coming out during the course of an interview in which there is time to explore problems and feelings in detail.

e. Apathy

In some patients with predominantly frontal lobe damage, and in a smaller number with damage elsewhere, a profound lack of motivation is the main problem, rather than disinhibition, although this may also be present. This change seems more common after penetrating lesions of the frontal lobes, and is akin to the apathy which sometimes resulted from too extensive prefrontal leucotomy as originally practised.

DEPRESSION AFTER STROKE

Serious depression is common after strokes, as many studies have shown. (For example, Murrell et al (1983) found that 64% of women and 43% of men were depressed after strokes, compared to 16% and 13% respectively in their controls.) Everyone who has been involved in the care of patients after stroke can sympathise and empathise with that depression. In fact the very empathy, and the feeling 'if I were like him I'd be depressed too' can be a disadvantage to the patient, as it is easy to assume the depression is inevitable and unalterable, and to offer sympathy but no active treatment.

Holbrook (1982) is one of several authors to have given an illuminating account of the stages through which many patients pass after a serious stroke.

1. Shock and confusion, with dread and anxiety about disability, and the threatened loss of so much that makes life worth living.
2. Hopes are high that treatment will succeed, as fears and despair are pushed aside or denied.
3. The dawning realisation that little improvement has taken place, and that these disabilities and this new way of life are permanent. This brings frustration, anger and despair; serious depression often follows.
4. Many never reach this stage — acceptance and adjustment.

In her series, and it is not atypical, 41% of patients could not walk out of doors, and two-thirds never or rarely went out. There is loss of strength, mobility, intellectual sharpness, loss of income, of role, of friends and of social status. These things are grieved for, and it is not easy to come to terms with such loss. Many other authors have written in a similar way, emphasising different aspects, but all recognising the central role of loss and disability. Some patients have written movingly about their own experiences (Ritchie 1960).

People who had had depressive states before, or who had always found life difficult, seem more prone to depression after stroke. Another group who seem to do badly in this way are striving and very active people, especially those who have been physically fit, involved in sports, and have taken pride in their skill and strength. They find it particularly difficult to accept the clumsy shambling wreck they have become.

Site of lesion

In recent years a number of studies have considered the relationship of depression to site of lesions, independent of 'understandable' reactive factors. Certainly it has been a puzzle why some patients, even though severely disabled, escape depression and yet have apparently similar personalities and circumstances to others who do become depressed.

Cerebral laterality and its relationship to psychopathology has been increasingly studied since Flor-Henry (1969) described a link between right frontotemporal lesions and depression, and between left frontotemporal lesions and mania, euphoria, and paranoid states (see also Gruzelier 1981). Robinson and his colleagues in a series of publications concerning patients after strokes (e.g. Robinson et al 1984) claim that patients with left anterior damage are more likely to become depressed, and that the more anterior the lesions the more frequent and marked the depression. They observe that right anterior lesions lead to a cheerful apathy, but that right posterior lesions may be associated with depression.

Another recent approach, contradictory in some respects to the above, is that of Ross & Rush (1981), who put forward observations and theories about localisation of brain function and the experience and expression of emotion. They see a parallel organisation of left and right hemispheres.

They claim that posterior lesions in either hemisphere lead to a failure to recognise meaning (of words on the left and of affect on the right) and that anterior lesions lead to a loss of expressive ability (again of words on the left and of emotion on the right). They call these disorders of recognition and expression of emotion 'aprosodia' — sensory and motor respectively. They see them as analagous to the dysphasias, again sensory (or receptive) and motor. A recent paper (Gorelick & Ross 1987) provides a more detailed analysis of the concept and a further case study. It is thought-provoking and calls for replication.

Assessment of depression after stroke and head injury

On the whole we have to rely at present on the clinical assessment of depression in brain-damaged people, because the questionnaires and rating scales commonly used to assess and measure depression have been designed for physically healthy people. The Beck Depression Inventory (Beck et al 1961), the General Health Questionnaire (Goldberg 1972) and numerous others, very naturally contain items about dizzyness, tiredness, memory, concentration, involvement in customary activities, and so on. In brain-damaged people, or even those with other serious physical illnesses, impairment in these fields is often the direct effect of their illness, and may be unrelated to mood. Even the Hospital Anxiety and Depression Scale (Zigmond & Snaith 1983), although an improvement on the others, is not suitable for stroke patients. The Wimbledon Self-Report Scale (Coughlan & Storey 1988) is aimed at assessing depression and anxiety in a more pure form in the physically ill, especially in the neurologically disabled.

Psychological management

The main aim must be to create or maintain morale and hope in both patient and family, so that it seems to them to be worthwhile continuing to make an effort.

It is not that people should be misled into expecting more improvement than is possible, as that only leads to disillusion and loss of trust. Rather there should be a feeling that if something cannot be achieved in one way, it is worth trying another. As a simple example, if the right hand is paralysed, you must learn to write with the left. These principles and attitudes are at the base of any good rehabilitation programme. When a demoralised patient first enters a specialist rehabilitation unit, begins to realise what can be done, and picks up the positive spirit of the place, there can be a transformation. Sadly all can collapse if after discharge there is not enough stimulus and encouragement.

Treatment of depression

This can be considered under the three main headings which apply to all emotionally disturbed patients: environmental change, psychological methods, and physical treatment. As was emphasised in an earlier section, accurate assessment of perceptual and cognitive deficits as well as of physical disability is necessary if the patient's situation and experiences are to be properly understood, and also to be able to discuss matters realistically with the family and patient.

1. Environmental change

In its broadest sense this is the most important element. It includes not only housing conditions, or the nature of the ward, but the feelings and attitudes of family or staff, themselves of course subject to change and support through counselling or psychotherapeutic means. Whether or not someone is visited, can be taken out in the car to see relatives, can attend a day centre, have speech or occupational or physiotherapy, can find some necessary task and therefore useful role in the home, and many more factors are involved.

The range of possibilities is wide. At one end is the patient with a comfortable home, well adapted for his disability, with a caring but not smothering family, good local services, and an interested family doctor. At the other is a run-down nursing home, where residents sit endlessly, wearing incontinence pads, unvisited. It is easier to identify what is missing than to provide it, but a specialist stroke team, or a particularly interested and dynamic doctor or nurse, can make a big difference.

2. Psychological methods

In the usual formal sense of the word this is rarely appropriate, but there is an important need for support, explanation, and counselling, for both patient and family. The latter comes under great pressure, and references to their morbidity are given in the section on personality change, as it is from that change and consequent behavioural problems that the main stress arises, and not the physical burden of care. The longer they have to cope with it the more they themselves suffer. Practical measures, including holiday admissions to hospital, attendance at day centres and so on, can be a great help, as can stroke clubs (where patient and family can go together) and voluntary organisations.

The patient himself can benefit a great deal from the opportunity to talk through some of his problems. If he has a speech disability this can be practically impossible, especially with dysphasia, but with patience and time even severely dysarthric people can unburden themselves.

3. Physical treatment

Little has been published on trials of antidepressants in stroke patients, although Lipsey et al (1984) found nortriptyline significantly better than placebo. In the author's experience antidepressants can be extremely effective, but must be used carefully. The more the depression resembles that of the so-called 'endogenous' pattern, with altered sleep and appetite, loss of concentration and interest, and guilt feelings (patients not uncommonly feel that a stroke has been a punishment for evil deeds in the past) the more likely it is to respond to medication. Any patient with severe depressive mood, weepiness, or marked apathetic withdrawal, in whom there is clearly a change from a previously better level of well-being, should be considered for drug therapy.

The tricyclic drugs often cause marked side effects — constipation, retention of urine, and unsteadiness from postural hypotension are the most troublesome. It is best to start with very small doses, such as 10 mg twice daily of amitriptyline, and build up gradually to the maximum which can be comfortably tolerated, as high as the usual maximum recommended (150 mg daily of amitriptyline). Sometimes a less sedative tricyclic such as protriptyline (usual maximum 60 mg daily) is more suitable. Mianserin is often too sedative for stroke patients, but can certainly be effective. Monoamine oxidase inhibitors are not contra-indicated, and can have a useful stimulant effect, but stroke patients are often forgetful and diet must be carefully supervised. Electroconvulsive therapy (ECT) has been used after strokes, but not by the author for some years. The careful, persistent, and methodical use of antidepressants is often very rewarding, and serious depression, even of several years' standing, can sometimes be seen to lift.

PSYCHIATRIC DISTURBANCES AFTER HEAD INJURY

The psychiatric complications of CHI are much more complex than those of stroke, in which depression is predominant. When considering the subject one must bear in mind the way in which the damaged individual is reacting to his physical, cognitive and perceptual impairment (through the medium of his personality, itself damaged) to his family and to others, and to the demands put upon him. The subject is reviewed by Bond (1984).

1. Post-traumatic personality disorders

These have been outlined earlier in the section Personality Changes. They can lead to such marked behavioural problems that a psychiatric referral is made.

Aggression

This is of several types, occurring particularly in the frontal lobe syndrome, but also with temporal lobe dysfunction, and less seriously as part of the 'irritable, anxious and withdrawn' personality change.

a. Frontal lobe syndrome. Disinhibited violence, often associated with *sexual disinhibition*, tends to be at its worst in the early weeks or months after the accident, and medication such as phenothiazines may be necessary (e.g. chlopromazine in doses ranging from 25 mg two or three times daily up to large doses of the types used in florid schizophrenia of 800 mg daily or more in divided doses). The sexual disinhibition may also be helped in the short term by medication, such as benperidol 0.25–1.5 mg daily in divided doses or cyproterone acetate 50 mg once or twice daily.

Counselling of the patient is useless in these states, but a calm, supportive, non-judgemental and non-provocative atmosphere is needed, as well as occupational therapy and nursing, preferably by men, which continually diverts and if possible pleases, while waiting for spontaneous improvement. As mentioned earlier, marriages rarely survive when these features persist, and it is neither kind nor practical to intervene to keep such families together, except that in the early stages it must be made very clear that a great deal of improvement will probably occur in the first few months, so that the distressed spouse should not take irrevocable steps too soon.

b. Temporal lobe dysfunction. Persisting epilepsy occurs in about 5% of people who have serious head injuries. The focus is in the temporal lobe in about 25% (Jennett 1962). Although most epilepsy makes itself known within 4 years of the injury it may be delayed for many years. It is commoner if there has been a depressed fracture or a haematoma, and much commoner if there has been a fit in the first week after injury.

In some patients 'formes frustes' of temporal lobe epilepsy (TLE) occur in which there is no convulsion, and none of the characteristic symptoms of TLE, but only episodic behavioural disorder with aggression. In others there is not even an episodic quality, but merely continuous moody aggressive behaviour, often associated with depressive feelings. An EEG will obviously be needed as part of the assessment. Anticonvulsants, particularly carbamazepine, can be extremely helpful. Carbamazepine should be built up slowly and the dose ranges from 200 or 300 mg daily to 1.6 g daily (in divided doses). Therapeutic blood levels as for epilepsy should be aimed at (20–50 μmol/l).

c. 'Irritable, anxious and withdrawn' syndrome. Sometimes, especially in those of previously irritable or aggressive temperament, the outbursts of irritability which are a sign that the individual cannot cope with the demands made on him (as described in an earlier section), are so venomous and aggressive that the family are seriously distressed, even without physical violence. In these cases it is worth carefully considering the circumstances in which the outbursts occur, and attempting to modify them, by explanation and counselling of both family and patient. In some cases the irritability is worse when the patient is depressed, and lessens as that improves.

Depression

Depression is common in the brain injured, fluctuating in severity often for years. Suicide is also common, occurring in 1% of a large series reported by Vaukhonen (1959). The biological symptoms of depressive illness are less frequent in these patients than after stroke, and they are more reactive and variable in pattern, often very severe for brief periods, and characterised by intense frustration and angry misery. Some studies have demonstrated what is also apparent clinically, that the most depressed tend to be those in whom the cognitive and personality impairment is *not* very severe, so that the patient can seem reasonably normal when unstressed. Such patients try to lead a normal working life, but unfortunately cannot cope with it and become frustrated and hopeless (Hillbom 1960). When the damage is so severe that work is obviously out of the question, there is less hope and drive, and therefore less frustration and disappointment.

Site of lesion and depression

Lishman (1968) found that in patients with open head injuries depression was commoner with right-sided lesions, although overall mental changes were commoner with left-sided damage. In CHI, however, with a preponderance of diffuse damage to the brain, such effects are less easy to study. Nevertheless *manic* disturbances, which are sometimes early complications of head injuries, do seem to follow left frontal lesions in particular (Bond 1984).

Schizophrenia-like and paranoid states

There are contradictory reports in the literature on this subject, perhaps mainly because of different diagnostic criteria. Occasionally typical schizophrenic illnesses, without any organic impairment, seem to be precipitated by head injury. More commonly schizophrenia-like disturbances occur, with some organic impairment of cognition and/or perception, when the temporal lobe, especially the left, is damaged. The EEG often shows epileptic or quasi-epileptic disturbances in these cases (Achte et al 1969, Davidson & Bagley 1969).

In the acute stages of confusion after CHI schizophrenia-like symptoms are quite common, more so in those with a family history of schizophrenia. In those acute stages one should remain alert to the possibility that alcohol withdrawal is playing a part in worsening and prolonging delirium, and intravenous vitamins should be given if there is any likelihood of that.

The mainstay of treatment in the schizophrenia-like illnesses is medication, combining anticonvulsants, especially carbamazepine, with neuroleptics such as phenothiazines, as in schizophrenia.

Non-psychotic paranoid developments are quite common, especially in those of previously touchy and suspicious temperament, as part of the exaggeration of previous personality traits so common after any brain damage. The patients are continuously hostile and wary, seeking and finding evidence that people are rejecting them in the familiar paranoid way. There is often an admixture of depressive mood, and if this can be lifted the paranoid attitude may become less marked.

Psychological management and treatment after closed head injury

The principles here are the same as those set out previously for stroke patients, with an even greater emphasis on the role of the family, and the stresses on it, as mentioned earlier. In these families there is even more distress and psychiatric morbidity than in the families of stroke patients, and again it is the personality and consequent behavioural changes which are more burdensome. The fact that it is a young person affected, with a lifetime of disability and often of suffering ahead, causes parents the greatest anguish. At least a stroke can be seen as a finish, rather than as a beginning.

Those who have suffered a CHI are predominantly young and physically active, and often with previously poor impulse control. Combined with the complex personality changes already described there is very often a characteristic physical state: all four limbs are spastic, and there is a clumsy, jerky gait; the face, tongue, and other muscles of speech are also spastic (because of brain stem damage), and the voice is loud, monotonous in pitch, and jerky in quality. Not only can there be a hostile and frightening quality, especially in the early stages, but the loss of normal facial movement and of normal speech modulation make it very difficult to empathise with the patient, as his words are not reflected in his tone of voice or gestures. In the family and among others involved, there is a tendency to cut short or to avoid conversations, and thus to ignore the emotions or problems described. All this intensifies the isolation and rejection the patients feel. Unfortunately this in turn leads often to a vicious circle of frustration, anger, greater rejection and sometimes on to violent outbursts.

As with stroke patients treatment can be considered under three main headings: environmental change; psychological methods; and physical treatment. The first two overlap a good deal. Often all three are necessary.

1. Environmental changes

The patient's main complaint is often of loneliness, combined with loss of physical and mental ability. Help in creating and maintaining a social network, using day centres, social clubs, volunteers and so on, can be very helpful. Helping the family to cope by both practical and counselling methods, and by offering long-term support, is also important. Often a hostel is in the end a more suitable place than the parental home, because of the conflicts, frustrations and tensions which are so commonly present, some of which have been outlined earlier in this chapter. In the most disturbed, or in those whose families cannot cope for other reasons, admission to a mental hospital or mental handicap hospital is sometimes necessary. Behavioural techniques used at times in these patients are described later.

Active physiotherapy, work and other rehabilitation, and the company of others, have profound psychological as well as physical benefits. If a patient has to leave a rehabilitation programme there is often a catastrophic fall in morale.

Voluntary organisations, and in particular Headway (The National Head Injuries Association) have a great deal to offer. Headway has a central office at 200 Mansfield Rd, Nottingham NG1 3HX, telephone (0602) 622382, and dozens of local branches with which enquirers can be put in touch. They offer local groups for discussion and support for both families and the head-injured themselves, with social, educational and self-help activities; they issue leaflets on a wide range of subjects, give advice on housing and accommodation problems, and help with assessment of disability and capacity. All patients and families should be given their address and telephone number. (Branches of Headway have now been established in several other English-speaking countries).

The particular social problems of the head-injured patient have been more studied recently (e.g. Weddell et al 1980). In the more severely damaged, who are not working, there is indeed a striking loss of social contact, pleasurable activities, sports and hobbies, confirming the loneliness of which so many patients complain.

2. Psychological methods

a. Psychotherapy and counselling. Very often the patient has too little insight and/or is too forgetful to benefit directly from these approaches, and it is to the family they must often be directed. As in so many situations in life, it is a relief to be able to unburden oneself to someone who understands, but in addition more focused therapy can be offered. For example, in the field of the sexual activities of the head-injured, it can help to discuss contraception with the family, and to try and put the patient's sexual drives and needs in a less troublesome context; the voluntary organisation Sexual Problems of the Disabled (SPOD) may usefully be approached. Wives, when still involved, can gain relief by discussing the sexual conflicts generated, for example by the child-like qualities in an injured husband as described earlier, as can parents by discussing the problems resembling prolonged adolescent conflicts which they are having. More important than simple relief, changes in interaction can sometimes occur, with benefits all round.

b. Cognitive retraining. For many years attempts have been made to help patients cope more effectively with their memory and learning problems, and more recently there has been much objective research.

Several methods are used. One is the so-called 'Peg-List' technique, first used by ancient-Greek students, in which each item to be remembered is linked in the mind with a place, for example a well known room or building, and the sufferer tries to associate a vivid and familiar visual image with each item. Another method is *behavioural*, based on reward for success. A schedule of activities is drawn up, for example when to rise from bed, to clean teeth, get to the occupational therapy department, and so on. Each successful act is rewarded, either by praise, a cigarette, or whatever has been agreed as appropriate. In others there is emphasis on the use of diaries, wristwatch alarms and the use of computers to store important names, addresses, items for the shopping list, appointments and so on. Mnemonics and other strategies are also developed, trying to find out what helps any given individual most.

These techniques are also used in stroke patients. Descriptions and reviews include those by Brooks (1984), Siev and colleagues (1986) and Wade (1985).

c. Behavioural regimes (behaviour modification) after head injury. A few individuals present such severe and persistent problems of aggression and violence after CHI that they cannot be coped with except as inpatients in psychiatric units. Unfortunately, although most such hospitals have to take patients like this, they are often poorly equipped to cope. Some units have developed special programmes of behaviour modification for them. They use techniques such as tokens and other rewards for good behaviour, 'time out' for undesired behaviour, and sometimes even controversial punishments, such as the smell of ammonia. In combination with carbamazepine or other drugs these units can be very helpful, and lead to improved behaviour and well-being, which persists after discharge.

Similar types of programme can also be developed to help motivate the predominantly apathetic, in whom it is so difficult often to find anything which acts as a reward or re-inforcer. (The subject is reviewed by Wood (1984).)

3. Physical treatment: medication

There is little role for ECT in the treatment of depression or other major mental illness in the brain-injured, but medication has a great deal to offer. The use of antidepressants is affected by the same factors mentioned in the section on treatment of depression after stroke, and the use of carbamazepine alone and combined with phenothiazines (or other neuroleptics) has also been described earlier, in the sections on temporal lobe dysfunction and paranoid states.

Drugs to lessen sexual drive (benperidol and cyproterone acetate) were mentioned in the section on the frontal lobe syndrome.

It must be remembered that the brain-injured are more prone to suffer from drowsiness, and from worsening of concentration and memory, when given sedative drugs. The benzodiazepines are particularly likely to do this, and also to worsen ataxia and unsteadiness. They can be very useful in the short term to lessen tension and anxiety in some acute situations, but should not be given for more than a few days at a time.

Sedative tricyclics and neuroleptics can also cause similar worsening; brain-injured patients are more likely to develop physical side effects than are the neurologically intact, especially extrapyramidal disturbances. If anti-Parkinsonian drugs are then added, there is an extra hazard of muddling or confusion developing.

If these drugs are given carefully, in small doses, building up with close supervision, maximum benefit with minimum side effects is more likely.

Neurotic and other reactions to closed head injury

So far we have considered only those cases in which some permanent brain damage has been sustained. In many cases of course the injury is trivial in that context, and yet there can be far-reaching effects.

Quite minor head injuries, with concussion and momentary clouding, or a few seconds or minutes of PTA can nevertheless generate great anxiety, especially in those of anxious or hypochondriacal disposition. Anxiety states can be triggered off, particularly if the doctors involved express much concern, or fail to reassure the patient. These states usually settle with reassurance, perhaps after some further physical examination (examination of the fundi seems very reassuring) or even a skull radiograph.

Depressive illnesses, and manic illnesses, can both be triggered by head injuries, and the pattern can be either reactive or markedly biological. A family or previous personal history predisposes, and these illnesses do not seem related necessarily to anxiety about the effects of the injury. They need treatment as for any other similar affective disorder.

Any pattern of neurotic syndrome can be triggered by head injury, including obsessive–compulsive disorders and, quite commonly, hysterical disorders. It is well known that people with hysterical fugue states rather commonly have a past history of head injury with PTA, as though the experience of that amnesia is used as a model in the fugue; head injury seems common in the history of many with other hysterical disorders (see Lishman (1987) for a review of this subject).

In the management of these conditions, which can all lead to severe invalidism, early mobilisation and active rehabilitation are needed. It is in the early days and weeks after minor head injury, when there are some organically determined symptoms — slowness of thought, impaired memory, giddiness — that the anxieties of patients and their families become entrenched.

Post-traumatic neuroses

There is uncertainty about the naming of this syndrome, for which the terms 'accident neurosis' and 'compensation neurosis' are also common, which reflects uncertainty about the role of neurotic and compensation factors.

It is a common condition, severely disabling at times, and medicolegally important. It can last for years, and does not necessarily clear up when the case is settled, as so often believed (Merskey & Woodford 1972).

The symptoms are relatively standard — headache, dizziness (rotatory only early on usually), impaired concentration and memory, irritability, labile anxiety and depression, poor sleep, easy fatigue, and intolerance of noise. These, or many of them, occur in almost all patients after concussion, but settle in a few days, but in these early stages vestibular dysfunction can be demonstrated (Toglia 1969) and slowed cerebral blood flow has been claimed (Taylor & Bell 1966).

As many authors have pointed out (e.g. Miller 1961), these prolonged states do not seem to occur in those who sustain the injury in sport, and they do not occur in those who have sustained head injury with unequivocal brain damage. They are much commoner where compensation is an issue, or in people of anxious and vulnerable personality.

It is probable that the transient organically determined postconcussion state is prolonged and intensified by various factors: the possibility of compensation; resentment and a sense of injustice about those responsible; an already anxious and vulnerable personality; secondary gain arising from the avoidance perhaps of unpleasant responsibilities or work; and others. Family attitudes seem very important, and disability can be too easily accepted and even encouraged: it is not uncommon to have the feeling that a spouse is more interested in the compensation than is the injured person.

As with the simpler reactions briefly mentioned before, it is surely in the early stages that intervention is most likely to help. Firm reassurance after careful examination and history taking, active and optimistic rehabilitation, an opportunity to discuss anxieties, and involvement with an explanation to the family, would seem the most useful approach. Gronwall & Wrightson (1974) did indeed find that early rehabilitation for all patients led to better results than waiting to see who was doing badly, and then offering help.

REFERENCES

Achte K A, Hillbom E, Aalberg V 1969 Psychoses following war brain injuries. Acta Psychiatrica Scandinavica 45: 1–18
Adams G F, Hurwitz L J 1963 Mental barriers to recovery from strokes. Lancet 2: 533–537
Adams G F, Hurwitz L J 1974 Cerebrovascular disability and the ageing brain. Churchill Livingstone, Edinburgh

Beck A T, Ward C H, Mendelson M, Mock J, Erbaugh J 1961 Inventory for measuring depression. Archives of General Psychiatry 4: 561–571

Bond M 1984 The psychiatry of closed head injury. In: Brooks N (ed) Closed head injury. OUP, Oxford

Brooks N 1984 Cognitive Defects after Head Injury. In: Brooks N (ed) Closed head injury. OUP, Oxford

Carnwath T C M, Johnson D A W 1987 Psychiatric morbidity among spouses of patients with stroke. British Medical Journal 294: 409–411

Coughlan A, Storey P 1988 The Wimbledon self-report scale: a questionnaire for the appraisal of emotional state and the detection of mood disturbance suitable for use with neurological patients. Clinical Rehabilitation (in press)

Davidson K, Bagley C R 1969 Schizophrenia-like psychoses associated with organic disorders of the CNS. In: Herrington R N (ed) Current problems in neuropsychiatry. British Journal of Psychiatry Special Publication No 4: 113–184

Evans J G 1986 The decline of stroke. In: Rose F C (ed) Stroke: epidemiology, therapeutic and socio-economic aspects. International Congress and Symposium Series No 99: 33–40

Fahy T J, Irving M H, Millac P 1967 Severe head injuries: a six-year follow-up. Lancet 2: 475–479

Flor-Henry P 1969 Psychosis and temporal lobe epilepsy: a controlled investigation. Epilepsia 10: 363–395

Goldberg D P 1972 The detection of psychiatric illness by questionnaire. Maudsley monograph No 21. OUP, London

Gorelick P B, Ross E D 1987 The aprosodias. Journal of Neurology, Neurosurgery and Psychiatry 50: 553–560

Gronwall D, Wrightson P 1974 Delayed recovery of intellectual function after minor head injury. Lancet 2: 605–609

Gruzelier J H 1981 Cerebral laterality: fact or fiction. Psychological Medicine 11: 219–227

Hillbom E 1960 After effects of brain injuries. Acta Psychiatrica et Neurologica Scandinavica (suppl) 142: 1–195

Holbrook M 1982 Stroke: social and emotional outcome. Journal of the Royal College of Physicians, London 16: 100–104

Jennet W B 1962 Epilepsy after blunt head injuries. Heinemann, London

Jennett B, Teasdale G 1981 Management of head injuries. Davis, Philadelphia

Lipsey J R, Robinson R G, Pearlson G D, Rao K, Price T R 1984 Nortryptiline treatment of post-stroke depression: a double blind study. Lancet 1: 297–300

Lishman W A 1968 Brain damage in relation to psychiatric disability after head injury. British Journal of Psychiatry 114: 373–410

Lishman W A 1987 Organic psychiatry, 2nd edn. Blackwell, Oxford

Marquardsen J 1969 The natural history of acute cerebrovascular disease. Acta Neurologica Scandinavica (suppl) 45: 38

Merskey H, Woodford J M 1972 Psychiatric sequelae of minor head injury. Brain 95: 521–528

Miller H 1961 Accident neurosis. British Medical Journal 1: 919–925, 992–998

Murrell S A, Himmelfarb S, Wright K 1983 Prevalence of depression and its correlates in older adults. American Journal of Epidemiology 117: 173–185

Panting A, Merry P 1972 The long term rehabilitation of head injury with special reference to the need for social and medical support for the patient's family. Rehabilitation 38: 33–37

Ritchie D 1960 Stroke. Faber and Faber, London

Robinson R G, Kudos K L, Starr L B, Rao K, Price T R 1984 Mood disorder in strokes. Importance of localisation of lesion. Brain 107: 81–94

Rosenbaum M, Najenson T 1976 Changes in life patterns and symptoms of low mood in wives of severely brain injured soldiers. Journal of Consulting and Clinical Psychology 44: 881–888

Ross E D, Rush A J 1981 Diagnosis and neuro-anatomical correlates of depression in brain damaged patients. Archives of General Psychiatry 38: 1344–1354

Selzer M L, Rogers J E, Kerns S 1968 Fatal accidents: the role of psychopathology, social stress and acute disturbance. American Journal of Psychiatry 124: 1028–1036

Shaffer J W, Towns W, Schmidt C W, Fisher R S, Zlotowitz H I 1974 Social adjustment profiles of fatally injured drivers Archives of General Psychiatry 30: 508–511

Siev E, Freischtat B, Zoltan B 1986 Perceptual and cognitive dysfunction in the adult stroke patient (Ch. 10). Slack Inc, New Jersey

Storey P B 1969 The precipitation of sub-arachnoid haemorrhage. Journal of Psychosomatic Research 13: 175–182

Storey P B 1970a Brain damage and personality change after sub-arachnoid haemorrhage. British Journal of Psychiatry 117: 129–142

Storey P B 1970b Psychiatric aspects of sub-arachnoid haemorrhage. Unpublished MD Thesis, University of London

Storey P 1985 Emotional aspects of cerebrovascular disease In: Trimble M (ed) Advances in psychosomatic medicine Vol. 13. Karger, Basel

Taylor A R, Bell T K 1966 Slowing of cerebral circulation after concussional head injury. Lancet 2: 178–180

Thomsen I U 1974 The patient with severe head injury and the family. Scandinavian Journal of Rehabilitation Medicine 6: 180–183

Toglia J U 1969 Dizziness after whiplash injury to the neck and closed head injury: electronystagmographic correlations (ch. 6). In: Walker A E, Caveness W F, Critchley M (eds) Late effects of head injury. Thomas, Springfield, Illinois

Van Zoemeren A H, Brouwer W H, Deelman B G 1984 Attentional deficits: the riddles of selectivity, speed and alertness. In: Brooks N (ed) Closed Head Injury. OUP, Oxford

Vaukhonen A 1959 Suicide among the male disabled with war injuries to the brain. Acta Psychiatrica et Neurologica Scandinavica (suppl.) 137: 90–91

Wade D T 1985 In: Wade D T, Langton Hewer R, Skilbeck C E, David R D. Stroke: a critical approach to diagnosis, treatment and management. Chapman and Hall, London, Ch. 10

Wade D T 1986 Assessing disability after stroke. In: Rose F C (ed) Stroke: epidemiology, therapeutic and socio-economic aspects. International Congress and Symposium Series No 99: 101–114

Wade D T, Legh-Smith J, Langton-Hewer R 1986 Effects of living with and looking after survivors of a stroke. British Medical Journal 293: 418–420

Weddell R, Oddy M, Jenkins D 1980 Social adjustment after rehabilitation. Psychological Medicine 10: 257–263

Wood R L 1984 Behaviour disorders following severe head injury: their presentation and management. In: Brooks N (ed) Closed head injury. OUP, Oxford

Zigmond A S, Snaith R P 1983 The hospital anxiety and depression scale. Acta Psychiatrica Scandinavica 67: 361–370

Neurological disorders

INTRODUCTION

The relationship between neurology and psychiatry has been an intimate
one. Historically many psychiatrists have trained primarily as neurologists
(the most famous, of course, being Freud, whose investigations into the
nature of hysteria gained their impetus from Charcot's demonstrations at
the Salpêtrière). In some European countries it is still necessary to train as
a specialist in both neurology and psychiatry to practise as a psychiatrist.
Whilst the closeness of this relationship has varied over the years, the
central aspects remain.

At the simplest level both disciplines are often concerned with disorders
of behaviour — and the evidence of the patient's disorder may be not what
they complain of but what they do — for example the overactive, intrusive
behaviour of a hypomanic patient or the disinhibited inconsiderate behaviour of a patient with frontal lobe damage. Apparently inexplicable changes
in behaviour are in one case clearly linked to structural brain damage and
poorly understood in the other.

The inexplicability of behavioural change has led to shared social
responses to many of the disorders. Behaviours which are unpredictable or
hard to understand in a given society tend to be lumped together and
treated similarly. How such behaviour is understood (e.g. divine possession,
deviance, mental illness, etc.) will of course vary from culture to culture.
The strength of the forces binding such disorders together is illustrated by
the continued inclusion of epilepsy as a psychiatric disorder in much of the
Third World.

Even where the dominant model for understanding such disorders is
medical (and therefore theoretically distinguishes the neurological from the
psychiatric), problems of differentiation still arise. We distinguish as neurological those disorders of behaviour and sensation which are secondary to
identifiable CNS damage. Those which are not secondary to CNS damage
are assumed to be a manifestation of either constitution or previous experience and therefore psychiatric. The clinical differentiation, however, can
be extraordinarily difficult. The misdiagnosis of the early signs and symp-

toms of space-occupying lesions as psychiatric disorders has always attracted attention. Virtually any neurologist can recount a long list of such cases he has treated. It may be that with the advent of more sophisticated, non-invasive, investigative techniques, such as computed tomography and nuclear magnetic resonance imaging, that such mistakes will be fewer in the future. Similarly, psychiatrists regularly see patients with quite obvious psychiatric disorders who have been extensively neurologically investigated and even treated before a psychiatric opinion has been sought. The most dramatic of these disorders are the hysterical conversion and dissociative states. Just as improved diagnostic techniques in neurology will hopefully reduce mistakes in one direction, the increased acceptance of psychiatric assessment with the waning stigma attached to it will hopefully decrease mistakes in the other direction.

The development of a substantial component of secondary gain as an important feature of both psychiatric and many neurological disorders also contributes to the relationship. Primary gain is the avoidance of conscious conflict (e.g. from having to acknowledge unacceptable sexual or hostile feelings) obtained by symptom development. Secondary gain is the benefit accruing to patients because of the changed behaviour towards them of other people. This includes both the practical caring and nursing of patients and the reduced social expectations we have of the ill (i.e. time off work, taking it easier etc.).

Whilst secondary gain is a normal aspect of all illness, it appears to play a prominent role in many neurological disorders. There are no comparative studies of the extent of secondary gain in different medical populations but clinical impression is clearly suggestive of it being most widespread in long-term fluctuating disorders. This may be partly due both to the 'invisible' nature of so many neurological conditions as well as to their fluctuation. The absence of any external evidence of the pathological process with which to identify the patient's symptoms (as for instance swollen joints and pain in rheumatoid arthritis) couples the family's response solely to the patient's subjective report (as in the varying exhaustion of the multiple sclerosis (MS) sufferer or the sadness of the depressive). The fluctuating nature of the disorder is itself an aspect which can lead to confusion. Many of the symptoms in neurological disorders are exacerbated by fatigue or tension. They can sometimes be assumed therefore to be 'just nerves' or even more disastrous for the patient 'just attention seeking'.

Inasmuch as some neurological conditions can cause direct and unpredictable changes in mood or behaviour (e.g. temporary euphoria in MS or postictal irritability) they share, with psychiatric disorders, the capacity to undermine profoundly the patient's sense of self. Control over our thoughts and understanding of our own mood is central to the core experience of our individuality. Whilst most patients come to terms with this experience and construct a protective understanding of it, for some (especially where the disorder starts early) it can lead to poor self-esteem, even in prolonged well periods. It will be obvious that where low self-esteem develops it enhances the attraction of the 'sick role' and hence the likelihood of entrenchment of secondary gain.

Many of the psychological issues in dealing with different neurological conditions relate to the specific features of structural damage and their prognostic implications. Effective intervention requires adequate knowledge and understanding of the disease process. Psychiatrists asked to help with such patients must acquaint themselves with the patient's physical state. Undoubtedly the best way to do this is to speak to the referring physician. I always ask for the diagnosis, the prognosis (as accurately as this can be given), the symptoms and (often forgotten but increasingly important) the side effects of any treatment and its importance to the course of the disease. Neither the patient nor those treating him will take the psychiatrist's advice seriously if they feel he has not fully understood these problems. Quite apart from the issue of credibility, however, many of the psychological aspects of management are impotent if not carefully tailored to the combination of 'this patient and this illness'. Reassurance is quite useless unless specific. Just saying 'don't worry, it'll be all right' is of no help unless the patient feels you know their specific worries and that your reassurance is based on informed judgement of the likely outcome.

Most physicians and general practitioners using this book will be familiar with the natural history of the disease but be less sure of the common patterns of emotional response to these diseases and how to meet them. Multiple sclerosis will be discussed in greatest detail as it is the neurological disorder most frequently referred to the author. The problems encountered with Parkinson's disease and root pains will also be touched upon. The psychological management of rapidly progressive degenerative disorders such as motor neurone disease (MND) are skills being developed in the hospice movement. The psychological management of stroke patients has been dealt with in Chapter 2.

MULTIPLE SCLEROSIS

Introduction

Multiple sclerosis is the commonest of the demyelinating diseases. It affects about one in 2000 of the population in Britain. The distribution is uneven both globally (comparatively rare in the tropics) and locally, between different parts of the country. It affects women more than men by a factor of nearly two to one (Shapiro et al 1985) though is often more severe in the latter. Differences in racial vulnerability and the predominance of certain human lymphocyte antigen (HLA) types have been demonstrated. Despite these epidemiological clues and pathological examination of the placques there is as yet still no established aetiology.

The clinical features of the disorder are extremely variable, involving both motor and sensory disturbance. Considerable clinical experience has accumulated to give indications of prognosis based on age at the first episode, the specific symptoms during that episode and its resolution. The long-term course of the disease is equally variable but can be usefully classified into the following five groups (Shapiro et al 1985).

Benign sensory	10%
Benign relapsing and remitting	20–30%
Chronic progressive	10%
Chronic relapsing progressive	50–60%
Acute rapid progressive	10%

The commonest group (chronic relapsing progressive) constitutes those patients whose illness progresses to significant physical disability over a long period, often 10–20 years, characterised by marked temporary fluctuations.

Just as there is no clear understanding of the aetiology of multiple sclerosis there remains no effective curative treatment nor any viable prophylactic measures. Treatment aimed at hastening remission is most commonly by short-term, high-dosage anti-inflammatory agents such as dexamethasone. In severe progressive cases attempts to slow the course of the disorder with immunosuppressive drugs can be made (Rosen 1979). Symptomatic treatment for spasticity, incontinence, pain etc. are a most important aspect of the management of MS patients. Similarly, ensuring adequate provision of physiotherapy and physical aids to ensure maximum mobility are important contributions to the patient's health and well-being.

Imparting the diagnosis

Breaking the news to a patient that their disorder has been confirmed as MS is a difficult aspect of management. Whilst some patients may genuinely not want to know, most do and the evidence suggests that adjustment is better if more is known about the illness (Counte et al 1983). Certainly, patients who are not told often feel cheated. They have often assumed that they are suffering from something even more serious (MND or more often cancer) or may have made decisions (e.g. starting a family) which would have been profoundly affected by proper information. The situation can be even more complicated if the family know and are adamant that the patient should not. Whilst it is virtually impossible to over-ride a family's wishes, the issue of who rightfully owns information needs to be faced. The family needs to be informed about the problems which arise for patients who become isolated behind a wall of 'protective' silence. The family member may say 'I know what she would want' but the clinician must bear in mind that this is a unique experience for the patient and not accept too readily the family's insistence (comfortable though it might be for him).

In this department the neurologist usually tells the patient when the diagnosis is confirmed and the MSW makes an appointment to see him

2 or 3 days later. As many GPs may find themselves precisely in this latter position, the MSW's approach will be dealt with in detail.

The first step is to see the patient in an unhurried, private setting and ask him what he has been told. Make sure the term MS is introduced early so that you both know what is being talked about. The next step is to ask the patient if he would like you to tell him some more about it. Few patients refuse such an offer. In telling patients about MS it is important to be prepared to explain what may seem obvious or what has already been discussed. Remember that the breaking of the news was almost certainly a very emotionally charged experience and that recall is notoriously poor in such situations. Explain what the tests were and why they were done. Remember to point out what the patient does *not* have — it's not cancer, it's not genetic nor is it infectious etc. It is also important to talk about aetiology — if for no other reason than to allow the patient to bring out their own worries about causation. They need to be reassured that they have not brought this upon themselves by stress or faulty diet etc.

Prognosis needs to be discussed. Point out that the course of any disease is particular to the individual who has it and that much of the information he will come across will not be relevant. I find it useful to give two varying examples — Mrs X still well after 15 years with only minor symptoms and no discernible handicap and Mrs Y diagnosed only 3 years ago and now in a wheelchair. You are unlikely to make things worse by citing this poor outcome as few people are unaware of the serious consequences of MS. Talk concretely if you can about how the respective families are adjusting to the practical problems.

It is not uncommon at this stage to encounter some anger from the patient about perceived evasiveness by their hospital doctors. It is important to see this for what it is and not to simply side with the patient. They are going to need to trust the hospital in years to come. Point out that doctors are used to dealing in facts and during the investigation of their disorder it is not realistic for the hospital doctors to start discussing possible problems until the diagnosis is confirmed.

It is difficult to do much more than this in one interview. It is best to round off the interview in a less charged atmosphere by spending time explaining to the patient who are the various 'actors in the play' — occupational and physiotherapists, social workers etc. Save introductions to the MS Society until a second interview, which should not be more than a week away and does not need to be quite as long as the first. Say that you know it has been a lot of information to take in in one go and that you will clarify any confusing issues at the next interview. Point out that people cope with bad news in different ways — some want to take just one day at a time and others want all possible information. Reassure them that they will be in charge of the information flow from now on.

At the second meeting misunderstandings can be rectified and gaps filled. An introduction to the national MS Society is valuable and the patient should be encouraged to join; members receive a newsletter, learn about benefits, holidays, research etc. It is best to get to know your local organisation before recommending it. Whilst these are invaluable for many patients they may be counterproductive for others. Usually the Patient Care Officer will come and advise about the atmosphere of the local group.

The follow-up interview is often invaluable for its opportunity to talk about the feelings liberated in the first interview. Patients will often talk then about the strong emotions they have experienced. They need acknowledgement that neither they, nor their families, are expected to feel saintly and mature all the time. They need to know that feeling conflicting strong emotions simultaneously does not mean that they are going mad. Rage and bitterness, when they occur, need to be channelled towards the disease and not between partners.

Associated psychiatric problems

The main psychiatric problems associated with MS are often poorly dealt with in medical textbooks. The old saw about the frequency of euphoria is often repeated and the commoner and more important issues, depression, lability of mood, fatigue and, in advanced cases, dementia (Schiffer et al 1983) neglected. The higher incidence of depression in MS sufferers compared to equally handicapped matched neurological controls (Whitlock & Siskind 1980) suggests that it is, at least in part, 'a manifestation of the disease not a response to it'. Severe depressive episodes requiring antidepressant medication are common in MS patients. They must not be ignored because the physician can so easily identify with the patient's situation. Treating the depression requires the correct use of antidepressants, plus all the support and tactful encouragement which any seriously depressed patient needs. Organising the provision of adequate support in MS patients is dealt with more fully below in 'Adjustment to MS'.

Fatigue is a common feature of MS — in particular in the afternoons or after a warm bath. Whilst this is almost certainly organic in origin it can so easily be confused with depression or neurasthenia that it is mentioned here. Its fluctuating character can confuse carers and family. Whilst there is no specific psychological treatment it is important to distinguish it from depression so that both the patient and family recognise it for what it is. This will prevent them over-reacting to it as a sign of incipient depression and also help them to make realistic rescheduling of tasks and duties to minimise it.

The euphoria in MS which seems so bizarre in the hospital ward is hardly a problem at home. Apart from the rare patient who may have a co-existing manic depressive disorder the euphoria rarely results in distressing over-activity or disinhibited behaviour. Rather, it is characterised by a denial of handicap and an unrealistic optimism. Both patient and family usually view these episodes as welcome relief when discomfort and pain are temporarily discounted. The only serious worry is that the patient will exhaust himself. Ensuring adequate sleep with a suitable hypnotic is usually all that is required.

Adjustment to MS

To provide adequate support to the MS sufferer requires some understanding of the process of adjustment undergone by those with chronic diseases. Matson & Brooks (1977) used 'self-concept' as a measure of adjustment in a controlled questionnaire study of 174 MS sufferers. They found that, on the whole, self-concept was not demonstrably lower in the MS group. Looking at the pattern of adjustment they drew some important, if not particularly startling, conclusions.

Firstly, poorer adjustment was associated with increasing physical disability. Secondly, adjustment improved over time (despite increasing disability) up to about 10 years after which little further adjustment appeared to take place. Examining coping strategies adopted by their patients Matson and Brooks noted considerable variation and drew up a league table of their efficacy. Religious stoicism was the commonest defence (the study was carried out in Kansas) but only the second most successful. Self-reliance, taking a pride in coping, was most positively associated with good adjustment. After that came religious belief, reliance on the doctor, reliance on the family and, lastly, acceptance of their fate, in descending order of success. Not surprisingly, 'fighting it' was more commonly reported in younger patients. These findings are reminiscent of Greer et al's (1979) work with breast cancer patients where an ostensibly mature acceptance of the disorder may in reality reflect a sense of helplessness and 'giving up'.

This certainly reflects our experience in London. Depression and despondency are often seen when the patient withdraws, or is withdrawn by well-meaning family members, from taking responsibility for the running of their lives. Even fairly trivial decisions passing out of the patient's hands can intensify feelings of hopelessness.

A woman inpatient was tearful and dejected just before Christmas. She had stopped eating and even stopped getting out of bed into her wheelchair. In interview with her it became clear that her husband's well-meaning insistence that he would choose and buy their daughter's Christmas present was the precipitant of her present state. Helping her to insist on being involved, so that the husband brought in catalogues to choose from, etc., rapidly restored her characteristic energy and drive.

Supporting MS sufferers requires striking a balance between keeping sight of the realities of the disease and yet encouraging as much self-determination as the patient can manage. Meeting family members is particularly important in this context. Family (particularly men) often need guidance in finding practical ways of helping the patient, e.g. passive exercises, reading to them when they are tired etc. This is important in countering any tendency to a despairing withdrawal which can leave the patient lonely and isolated. At the same time, however, they need to learn not to over-protect the patient. They need to recognise that family life for everyone involves conflict and disappointment as well as shared joy and fulfilment. Depriving patients of their role in the running of the family not only deprives them of the satisfaction of achievement (or even just the closeness which comes of mutual distress) but also of an external focus for concentration and activity to distract them from debilitating introspection. The MS patient needs to be allowed to live in the present, not continuously obliged to contemplate his handicap and his prognosis.

In setting up these supportive structures for MS sufferers the chronicity of their disorder must be recognised. Given this, it is important that dependence, which of course must be tolerated, should be on the institution rather than on any one individual. Sharing the responsibility of supporting the patient between team members fulfils a dual function. First of all it protects individual team members from becoming overwhelmed by the patient's distress. Secondly, and more importantly given the way health care is organised at present, it minimises the disruption and distress which is caused by the inevitable moving on of personnel because of promotion etc.

PSYCHOLOGICAL PROBLEMS IN PARKINSON'S DISEASE

The issue of finding the balance between accepting the realistic limitations imposed by the disease and yet maintaining maximum self-sufficiency often needs addressing in Parkinson's disease (PD). Obviously there is no external reference for determining such a balance — it depends upon the patient's temperament and his family. Some individuals go to enormous lengths to fight their disease, often exhausting themselves and their families in the process. Others, the majority, display an outwardly calm acceptance of their fate, often developing a quiet humour (Bernen 1986) to put their companions at ease. In the past it has been suggested (Todes & Lees 1985) that there is a characteristically controlled, industrious, premorbid personality found in PD sufferers. They are reputed to have a lower use of tobacco and alcohol than the general population. Whilst originally there were speculations that this control may have caused the disease, more recent research suggests that there may be a long prodromal period in the disorder in which 'pleasure-seeking' behaviour atrophies somewhat as a consequence of decreasing serotonergic activity (Harvey 1986a).

Courage and stoicism are regularly encountered with PD patients. Often the physician or social worker needs to help counsel the family, in particular, with the issues of allowing the patient to attempt things in the home which might more easily be done for him by the spouse or children. The tendency to do everything for the patient arises both out of sympathy for him and from the frustration of having to slow down to his pace. Allow family members to acknowledge this frustration with you 'I suppose you must get really frustrated, especially when you have got such a lot to do to help him, and yet have to hang around while he takes ages to put his coat on'. Such openings can help the family members to feel less ashamed of their irritation and learn to obtain appropriate relief from it, e.g. in discussing it with their friends rather than bottling it up thereby either wearing themselves out or, even worse, eventually exploding at the patient. Families need help to understand the heightened importance that attaches to remaining competence, no matter how laborious, for individuals with serious long-term disability.

Despite the courage and determination found in PD sufferers, depression is common. Different studies report a prevalence of between 20% and 60% for depression in Parkinsonian clinic attenders (Harvey 1986a). The depression is normally mild to moderate (Santamaria et al 1986) and its relationship to the degree of disability is weak (Celesia & Wanamaker 1972). Like MS and epilepsy the incidence of depression in PD is higher than that found in equally neurologically disabled controls. This higher prevalence, the frequency of endogenous features and the suggestion that the depression often develops before the clear clinical manifestations of the disease have led to speculation that the depression in PD is part of the disease rather than a reaction to it.

Placebo-controlled trials of tricyclics have shown them, despite concerns over their cholinergic side effects, to be effective in depressed PD patients. This is so both with imipramine where mild dopaminergic effects also improve the physical state and with nortriptyline where there is no physical improvement (Andersen et al 1980). Similarly, in severely depressed patients, electroconvulsive therapy has been shown to help without any impact on the physical state.

Schizophrenia has been reported in PD (Crow et al 1976) and while this of theoretical interest it is treated in the routine manner with major tranquillisers. Organic psychotic states are common (Harvey 1986b) and are usually due to the combined effects of failing cognitive function and the side effects of the pharmacotherapy. Adjustment of the treatment regime with symptomatic use of major tranquillisers is usually rapidly effective.

ROOT PAINS AND WEAKNESS

Neurology clinics are regularly referred patients with persistent complaints of pain thought to originate from nerve roots. Many of these patients have associated complaints of weakness, sometimes leading to falling or even a reluctance to maintain mobility. There is some overlap with patients with chronic pain but the major similarities are often with hysterical conversion. While there is often no clear evidence against the existence of the lesion the patients' apparent handicaps are often grossly in excess of their disabilities and may be seen to fluctuate markedly or be inconsistent over time. Unlike the belle indifférence commented upon in classical conversion hysteria, these patients often display overconcern with their problem and may be demanding and dramatic. This behaviour is described by Pilowsky (1969) as 'abnormal illness behaviour'.

There is little (or even no) successful primary gain but the disorder often seems to be maintained by secondary gain. To the outsider it is often pitifully obvious that the patient is exaggerating his symptoms. In rare circumstances, most often with prisoners, this may be due to conscious deception. With most patients, however, the issue of whether the whole process is conscious is an academic nicety of little value in resolving the situation. My assumption is that there may be times when the patient is consciously aware of how he is contributing to the situation but that usually he is not. I also assume that when he is aware of it he either lacks the resources to change or else has 'painted himself into a psychological corner' from which he does not dare move.

The first approach with such patients is to take a full, free-ranging history. If there are major stresses revealed in their lives one can dwell on these and explore them. I specifically avoid making any direct association between these issues and the pains, falls, dizziness, weakness etc. Occasionally an area of conflict is revealed which leads to cathartic unburdening of considerable distress and this may in itself lead to rapid symptomatic relief.

A 44-year-old dustman had been admitted for severe incapacitating left-sided pains in his head, neck, back and arm. He had been off work for 3 months. During the interview he talked of the problems posed by his 'tearaway' 15-year-old stepson. The boy had recently bought a motorbike with what the patient could only assume was stolen money. He was continually challenging his father, who felt powerless to assert himself or maintain discipline. Much of his powerlessness stemmed from a fear of revealing his illiteracy in the event of a confrontation with the police. He had been trying vainly to conceal this illiteracy from his new wife and stepson for the 6 years of his marriage. Helping him tell his wife about it (she of course knew and was relieved that it was acknowledged) and encouraging them to start devising a joint strategy for dealing with their son resulted in the evaporation of his symptoms. He never recognised the link between the interviews and his improvement, preferring to see his illness as having 'just got better anyway'.

Usually the results of such intervention are not so rapid (although Balint's work, (1964) with GPs suggests it can be more successful than most hospital-based doctors believe). Where exploration and ventilation of problems produces no effect a procedure has to be evolved to help the patient relinquish his symptoms. This needs attention on two fronts — the patient himself and his carers (family or physiotherapists, nurses etc.).

The patient

The patient needs to be reassured that the disorder is benign. This has to be spelled out: 'it is not cancer, it is not a progressive degenerative disorder' etc. The main purpose of this reassurance is to introduce the concept of remission. It needs to be acknowledged that the patient has been ill but that it now looks as if things are likely to start *gradually* getting better. Do not link the symptoms to emotional problems as this will undermine the patient's trust in you and most likely cause resistance to your treatment. The 'gradually' is important as it relieves the patient of the anxieties associated with rapid change and the loss of familiar, comforting routines. It also gives him a chance of taking some responsibility (and pride) in the rate of recovery.

This initial reassurance should take place, or be repeated, with the patient and family together. The purpose is to make sure the patient knows his family are expecting some change and that the doctor has acknowledged the reality of the illness. This ritual, in which 'licence to change' is given, is used extensively by family therapists. Patients whose chronic illness has been a major burden to their families may otherwise fear that improvement without obvious cause will be seen by the family as evidence that there was never anything seriously wrong in the first place and thus be angry with them.

Having reassured the patient and predicted a start to improvement one should predict that there are likely to be good days and bad days. 'Set backs are inevitable after such a long illness, but if you keep at it I'm sure you will begin to notice the improvement'. A programme of graded mobilisation or physiotherapy is worked out and put into operation. Progress is rewarded with praise and set backs treated in a matter of fact but sympathetic manner. Expect set backs when important goals are being reached. The patient who says that his main goal is to get back to work 'but for this weakness' is likely to have conflicts about his work place. Exploration of these areas as they are confronted is often useful but leave it for the patient to draw the conclusions.

These patients (like the chronic pain patients, Ch. 5) can irritate their carers. It is important to acknowledge this and allow your coworkers to do so also. Frequent short contacts are better than infrequent longer contacts. The patient needs to know that his emotional needs will be met (Pilowsky 1969) and that he is sympathetically viewed. This structure also uncouples reward from the symptoms and protects the carer from irritation and impatience.

The carers

It is highly likely that the care and attention received by the patient are potent factors in prolonging his disorder. His carers may either know about this but not know how to break the pattern or they may be quite oblivious to the part their behaviour plays. If it is the former it needs to be openly discussed. More often the carer may know what to do but need emotional and cognitive support in doing it.

A woman knew that her husband's weakness and repeated 'collapses' in the local supermarket were his mechanism for evading contact with the outside world after a disappointment at work. She was aware that fussing over him in these situations made things worse but she found his reproaches hard to withstand. Even more difficult were the comments of the other women in her block of flats — 'What sort of wife is she, letting that poor man struggle all the way to the shops?' With a regular fixed outpatient appointment she was supported and encouraged to maintain her stand, which was eventually successful in helping her husband relinquish his symptoms and confront his supervisor.

Construing the required behaviour in its most positive light can help support the carer. Give them an explanation of why they should behave in the desired manner that is phrased in *positive* terms. Talk of 'helping him preserve the strength he still has' and 'exercising his muscles back to fitness' rather than 'leave it to him to do it or he'll never learn'. Imparting a vocabularly to those involved which characterises their activities without any moral overtones or any loss of face for the patient is invaluable both as an internal support and also in paving the way for attitudinal and expectation shifts in the patient's social network.

A man in his mid-sixties was repeatedly admitted for falls and weakness in his legs. A psychiatric consultation was requested because of the disparity between the physical findings and his symptoms and concern that he might be depressed. He showed no signs of depression but was angry and openly critical of his care. Vigorous physiotherapy produced considerable improvement and he returned home still complaining but mobile and independent within 2 weeks. He sought re-admission, as bad as ever, within 10 days.

On this occasion his wife was seen at home with him. She felt that life had changed profoundly after he had failed to be elected to a Masonic office he had expected shortly after his retirement. He had resigned from the order and was now no longer out every night as previously. Their relationship had never been close and spending so much time together was clearly intolerable. He complained of weakness and was now bedridden, with her bringing his meals to him on a tray and even helping him wash and shave. It became clear that neither of them knew how to get on with each other. Her guilt at being glad that he spent all day in bed, freeing her to carry on much as before, fuelled her oversolicitousness.

Treatment was brief and involved structuring a graded mobilisation plus a fairly unemotional joint discussion about the nature of marriage. Their lack of involvement in each other was relabelled as 'admirable independence' and it was agreed that one could have a good marriage without necessarily falling into one another's arms on retirement. According to his family doctor he regained his mobility, remained grumpy and critical as he always had been, but became an active gardener.

ACKNOWLEDGEMENT

The author acknowledges his debt to the Neurology Department of Atkinson Morley's Hospital and in particular to social worker Barbara Monro for the section on imparting the diagnosis in MS.

REFERENCES

Andersen J, Aabro E, Gulmann N, Hjelmsted A, Pedesen H E 1980 Antidepressive treatments in Parkinson's disease. Acta Neurologica Scandinavica 62: 210–219

Balint M 1964 The doctor, his patient and the illness. 2nd edn. Churchill Livingstone, Edinburgh

Bernen R 1986 Subjectively speaking: a patient's view of Parkinson's disease. Royal Institute Medical Journal 69: 313–317

Celesia G G, Wanamaker W M 1972 Psychiatric disturbances in Parkinson's disease. Diseases of the Nervous System 33: 577–583

Counte M A, Bieliauskas L A, Pavlov M 1983 Stress and personal attitudes in chronic illness. Archives of Physical Medicine and Rehabilitation 64: 272–275

Crow T J, Johnstone E C, McClelland H A 1976 The coincidence of schizophrenia and Parkinsonism: some neuro-chemical implications. Psychological Medicine 6: 227–233

Greer S, Morris T, Pettingdale K W 1979 Psychological reponses to breast cancer: effect on outcome. Lancet 2: 785–787

Harvey N 1986a Psychiatric disorders in Parkinson's disease. 1. Functional illness and personality. Psychosomatics 27: 91–103

Harvey N 1986b. Psychiatric disorders in Parkinson's disease. 2. Organic cerebral states and drug reactions. Psychosomatics 27: 175–184

Matson R R, Brooks N A 1977 Adjusting to multiple sclerosis: an exploratory study. Social Science and Medicine 11: 245–250

Pilowsky I 1969 Abnormal illness behaviour. British Journal of Medical Psychology 42: 347–351

Rosen J A 1979 Prolonged azathioprine treatment of non-remitting MS 1979 Journal of Neurology, Neurosurgery and Psychiatry, 42: 338–344

Santamaria J, Tolosa E, Valles A 1986 Parkinson's disease with depression: a possible subgroup of idiopathic Parkinsonism. Neurology 36: 1130–1133

Schiffer R B, Caine E D, Banford K A, Levy S 1983 Depressive episodes in patients with multiple sclerosis. American Journal of Psychiatry 140: 1498–1500

Shapiro R T, Van den Noort S, Scheinberg L 1985 The current management of multiple sclerosis. Annals of the New York Academy of Science 436: 425–434

Todes C J, Lees A J 1985 The premorbid personality of patients with Parkinson's disease. Journal of Neurology, Neurosurgery and Psychiatry 48: 97–100

Whitlock F A, Siskind, M M 1980 Depression as a major symptom of MS. Journal of Neurology, Neurosurgery and Psychiatry 43: 861–865

3   *Charlotte Feinmann*

Facial pain and headache

INTRODUCTION

Facial pain and headache are common. Such pains include tension headache, neckache, facial arthromyalgia (temporomandibular joint dysfunction syndrome or myofascial pain and joint dysfunction syndrome), atypical facial pain, atypical odontalgia, and more bizarre disorders such as a burning tongue or a phantom bite (Feinmann et al 1984). These pains differ from classic neurological disorders in that they appear to arise from blood vessels and nerves rather than as primary disturbances of the sensory nerves (Miller 1968).

Headache and facial pain are rarely the patient's exclusive problems, nor are the symptoms mutually exclusive as they recur sequentially or simultaneously in the same patient (Berry 1978, Feinmann et al 1984). The variety of symptoms may, however, not be elicited by specialists unfamiliar with the variety of the disorders. Eighty per cent of patients who report such symptoms also complain, when asked, of other recurrent symptoms such as chronic neck pain, low back pain, migraine, pruritic skin disturbances, spastic colon and dysfunctional uterine bleeding (Gold et al 1975, Berry 1978, Feinmann et al 1984). The prevalence of these symptoms in this group is much greater than is found in the general population and indicates that facial pain and headache are features of a more generalised disorder. The pains are commonly associated with stressful life events and the variety of symptoms experienced suggests the existence of a 'pain-prone' patient with a vulnerable neurochemistry.

Central to the psychological management of these patients is the concept that patients who are emotionally disturbed frequently present with physical symptoms, and that recognition of the emotional disturbance benefits both the individual and the health service (Bridges & Goldberg 1985). Recognition and appropriate treatment can, however, occur only when a common understanding is reached concerning the classification of facial pain and headache. Unfortunately, these disorders tend to be separated by their clinical presentation, so that the patients with oral and joint and muscle pain are seen and treated by dental specialists and the rest by neurologists, ear, nose and throat surgeons and psychiatrists, with very little genuine collaboration between the specialties.

PREVALENCE AND INCIDENCE

The prevalence of headache and facial pain in the general population is much greater than the incidence of patient referrals would suggest (Waters & O'Connor 1971, Helkimo 1976, Kent 1985). In clinical populations women outnumber men by three to one, but in the general population the sexes are equally affected (Lipton & Marbach 1981, Gross & Gale 1983). Headache and facial pain are not unique in having a high prevalence and a low incidence of referral. There is a large 'symptom iceberg' for most psychological and physical illnesses, suggesting that the decision to consult a doctor or a dentist is not simply a question of the presence of symptoms (Kent 1985, Watson 1985). Different symptoms are more likely to lead to consultations. For instance, Banks & Keller (1971) found that people were more likely to see their doctor if they had a sore throat than if they had a headache. There are obviously several factors and many intermediate steps which may be involved in the decision to seek help.

Personality

One explanation of why one group of headache and facial pain sufferers consider their symptoms severe enough to obtain treatment concerns personality differences. There is no consistent evidence, however, that headache and facial pain are associated with any characteristic personality traits (Feinmann et al 1984, Merskey 1985). Such a correlation would not imply causality anyway since the disorder itself may have an effect upon personality, for example through the punitive attitude generated in clinicians towards patients with chronic pain. Merskey (1979) described the typical patient with atypical facial pain as a 'lower class married woman, who probably once was, but no longer is pretty, has never been keen on sexual intercourse, a sad tale of a hard life.' Miller (1968) described the typical patient as: 'female, middle-aged, edentulate, haggard and importunate.'

The concept of a long-standing and relatively immutable personality structure exerting a major influence on disability or treatment outcome is difficult to sustain. Costa & Mcrae (1985) have shown that the personality dimension of neuroticism is closely related to the number of medical symptoms reported. Thus neuroticism-related complaints are best viewed as exaggerations of bodily concerns. Some people persistently under-report medical symptoms while others have frank hypochondriasis. No doubt these patterns reflect the two ends of a continuum. Neuroticism leads to complaints and complaints lead to diagnosis. Neuroticism influences the perception of health rather than health itself.

Psychiatric disturbance

In contrast to measures of personality trait, measures of current psychological distress in the forms of depressive symptoms and somatic anxiety have been helpful in defining psychological management. Any associated psychiatric disturbance must also be identified (Merskey 1979), a task which is complicated by the difficulty of defining pain (Beecher 1959) and in quantifying and diagnosing psychiatric illness (Kendell 1975).

Headache

There is an extensive literature referring to the importance of emotional factors in headache patients, although few studies have used standardised psychiatric rating scales. Headache is a prominent symptom of depression (Merskey 1982). Blumer & Heilbrom (1982) have proposed a 'pain-prone' disorder as a variant of depression, based on the observation that the patient's pain responded to antidepressants. 'Pain-prone' is a diagnosis similar to 'masked depression', carrying the implication that pain must be accompanied by psychiatric illness. It seems more plausible that mild depression should give prominence to a pre-existing trivial headache. Worry about possible causes for the headache could easily lead to further depression, and a vicious circle of pain and anxiety arises.

Facial arthromyalgia and atypical facial pain

Psychiatric studies have been mostly concerned with descriptive accounts of the patient's psychopathology and until recently few have used standardised psychiatric assessments. Merskey's (1985) study of new referrals with chronic facial pain found that patients resembled a general practice population on measures such as the general health questionnaire (GHQ) (Goldberg 1972). This led him to conclude that at least some of the 'psychiatric illness' he had previously detailed in chronic pain patients was a selection phenomenon caused by emotionally disturbed patients consulting more frequently. In a prospective study, 93 patients with facial arthromyalgia, atypical facial pain, or both, were examined using standardised psychiatric rating scales (Feinmann et al 1984). Forty of the patients were not considered to be psychiatrically disturbed. Of the 53 who received a psychiatric diagnosis, 33 had a depressive illness, and 20 received a diagnosis of mixed neurosis (mostly hypochondriacal). Sleep or appetite were rarely disturbed, and few patients had taken time off work because of their pain. Most patients, however, reported that their enjoyment of life was adversely affected by pre-occupation with pain.

In general, the patients with psychiatric diagnoses were more neurotic and more socially isolated. The depressed patients more often had lost or were separated from their parents in childhood, or had an unhappy childhood — both characteristics are said to increase the vulnerability of women to depressive illness in later life (Brown & Harris 1982).

Summary

These findings suggest four groups of patients who suffer from facial pain and headache:

1. the 'emotionally fit' individuals who are under stress,
2. those with transient emotional illness, such as an anxiety state or depression in addition to pain,
3. patients with persistent hypochondriacal traits,
4. the uncommon patients whose pain develops as a manifestation of psychosis.

Most patients do not merit a psychiatric diagnosis as their emotional problems are of short duration and are not severe.

Between 50% and 70% of patients presenting to general practitioners complain solely of pain and deny emotional disturbance, which may only become apparent when examined by a psychiatrist. The complaint of pain often leads to specialist referral. However, the specialists consulted often have neither the time nor the training to discuss emotional problems and frequently a number of investigations are carried out before a diagnosis, or more often non-diagnosis, of organic disease is made. Clearly, the investigation and management of such patients takes an inordinate amount of time and energy. Not only do negative investigations cost money, they also demoralise both patient and doctor. What is required is some means of identifying emotional disturbance and therefore restricting the number of physical investigations. Nabarro (1984) has suggested that all hospital inpatients should initially be screened with an instrument such as the GHQ to identify psychological disturbance. Patients identified could then be referred for psychiatric assessment. It would be difficult for psychiatrists to provide this service and it may not always be in the patients' best interests. Not all patients who complain of facial pain and headache are psychiatrically disturbed. Psychiatric diagnoses may not be appropriate to patients with somatic symptoms, as they are designed to classify patients with more severe psychiatric illness.

Several investigations have implicated stressful events in facial pain. Unfortunately, almost all of these studies have been retrospective, introducing a range of probable biases. Patients may be more likely to remember and report such events, or, more simply, to find such events stressful because their coping resources are reduced by illness. Nevertheless, there does seem to be a relationship between the experience of life stress and the incidence of facial pain. Moodey et al (1982) found that the severity of life events (measured by the Holmes & Rahe scales 1967) was higher than in control subjects. The higher the score, the more frequent were the number of symptoms. Using a more sophisticated approach, Speculand et al (1984) found that patients reported more than twice as many events for the previous 6 months than did dental control subjects. In a third study (Heloe & Heloe 1978) patients were more likely than controls to report a range of distressing conditions in their daily lives, and in a fourth (Feinmann et al 1984) 80% of patients with facial pain reported a life event such as bereavement or a family illness within 6 months before the onset of pain.

It seems that many people consult a dentist or doctor not simply when the symptoms become more severe, but when their symptoms begin to interfere with their daily lives. Whilst this can be due to an increase in severity, it can equally be due to an increase in social demands (such as a new job or having to look after an ailing relative). Prior to these new demands, the symptoms could be coped with. Negative life events could also have a demoralising effect, making it more difficult to contain the symptom and leading to an increase in illness behaviour. This view highlights the indirect effect of the life events (not necessarily their effect on severity) which 'triggers' the decision to seek help. This contention is supported by studies showing that many patients have experienced their symptoms for several months or years before seeking help (Heloe et al 1977, Feinmann et al 1984).

It seems clear that many headache and facial pain patients do not experience psychological disturbance severe enough to warrant psychiatric diagnoses. The pains appear to develop as a response to stress but in patients made vulnerable by a deprived childhood, a neurotic personality or poor social adjustment, mild psychiatric symptoms may also develop alongside facial pain.

Psychiatric disturbance detected in these patients is often mild, of brief duration and is probably better considered a normal distress syndrome (Williams et al 1980). Such a classification would free the patients from the stigma of psychiatric diagnosis and may allow them more appropriate treatment.

A number of selection processes affect the psychological profiles of patients undergoing treatment for headache and facial pain.

PRESENTATION, AETIOLOGY AND MANAGEMENT

A patient's management is frequently dependent upon the clinician's opinion of the aetiology of the pain.

Headache

Tension headache is a steady, non-pulsatile band-like ache. The pains radiate to the forehead, temples, back of the head and neck. They may be unilateral or bilateral and may involve the temporal, occipital or parietal regions or a combination of all these areas. Until recently it has been assumed that the pain resulted from muscular contraction. However, Philips (1978) was one of the first to question the traditional assumption that these headaches are caused by sustained contraction of the skeletal muscles of the shoulders, neck and head. She found considerable overlap between EMG levels during headache and non-headache periods and suggested that other variables besides muscular spasm affected the presence or absence of tension headache (Philips & Hunter 1981).

As muscle tension has become a less popular explanation for the aetiology of pain, attention has unfortunately foccused on other mechanical explanations, such as the way teeth meet. Malocclusion in the form of abnormal teeth contact has been suggested to be an important factor in pain development, although there is no evidence to show that patients with malocclusion complain of tension headache more frequently than those with a normal occlusion (Feinmann et al 1984, Gross & Gale 1985).

The diagnosis of 'craniomandibular dysfunction' implies that tension headache, migraine and backache all develop because teeth do not meet symmetrically (Pinkham 1984). The dental profession, perhaps because an improvement in dental health has led to a decreasing workload, has adopted the concept with enthusiasm. Teeth are ground and occlusions 'rehabilitated' without any scientific evidence to support the treatment (Ayer 1983, British Dental Journal Leading Article 1984).

Several authors have discussed the efficacy of relaxation methods in reducing tension headache, and they have generally been found to be effective in reducing both intensity and frequency (Nigl 1984).

Turner & Chapman (1982) reviewed all interventions for chronic pain and concluded that EMG biofeedback was no more effective than muscular relaxation for the treatment of headache. Relaxation was far less costly as no equipment was required and more efficient as it could be taught in groups.

Supportive psychotherapy or other, more directive therapeutic interventions designed to reduce psychological stresses have always been an important part of treatment. Wolff (1963), in a review of methods for managing tension headache, concludes that the greatest therapeutic benefit was likely to result from teaching the headache sufferer to 'recognise his faulty attitudes, to change them and to adjust to what had been intolerable or hopeless situations'. Cognitive behaviour therapy involves such strategies as relabelling sensations, relaxation and imagery with the intention of helping the patient avoid or deal more adaptively with pain-increasing events. Turner & Chapman (1982), having reviewed all major studies, concluded that cognitive behavioural approaches show potential to alleviate headache pain more effectively than EMG biofeedback.

Facial Arthromyalgia

The presenting symptoms facial arthromyalgia is a dull ache, which may be unilateral or bilateral, with occasional severe attacks affecting the temporomandibular joint and its musculature, and radiating down the back and up to the top of the head and neck. It is associated with disturbance of joint function such as clicking, sticking, trismus, deviation of the mandible, and, occasionally, aural symptoms such as tinnitus and a sense of fullness in the ear (Harris 1975). The dental profession see and treat the majority of these patients and usually attribute the disorder to both bruxism (teeth grinding) and malocclusion (teeth meeting together in malalignment). Hence the pain and dysfunction are treated by a variety of physical agents, including heat, exercises, bite-raising appliances or grinding teeth to improve the functional occlusal relationship. However, the incidence of malocclusion is no higher in these patients than in the general population and occlusal adjustment has not been shown to be effective (Thomson 1971, Laskin 1969).

Surgical intervention has never been shown to be successful, and interference with the joint in other ways, such as injection of sclerosing agents, has been shown to be detrimental (Kydd 1959). Greene & Laskin (1972) failed to demonstrate that occlusal therapy was any better than placebo in patients with facial arthromyalgia.

Those authors who consider muscle disturbance to be of primary aetiological importance have claimed success with a variety of treatments. Muscular exercises, biofeedback, electrical stimulation, corticosteroids and muscle relaxants have all been used. The evidence that muscle relaxants and exercises are ameliorative (Schwartz 1959) is mainly anecdotal — most studies are not controlled and the results, therefore, are not conclusive.

There have been relatively few attempts to assess the long-term outcome of any form of treatment. Greene & Laskin (1983) reviewed the major published series with good outcome in 66–97% of patients: three were telephone interviews, two involved follow-up by mail, four were unstandardised reviews and only one study involved a standardised examination. Mechanical forms of treatment have not withstood close scientific scrutiny; in fact several authors have found that such treatments lead to the development of intractable pain (Feinmann et al 1984). The American Dental Association has now directed its membership that only conservative reversible forms of treatment can be recommended and stresses that a warm, positive and reassuring attitude on behalf of the clinician is an essential part of treatment (Ayer 1983).

The evidence for the efficacy of psychotherapy has been equally inconclusive, although several authors have reported some success (Moulton 1955, Fine 1971, Gershman et al 1977). Moulton (1955) claimed that the problems were better managed when the psychiatrist was familiar with the physiological mechanisms and recommended a practical approach, with reassurance rather than waiting for insight to relieve the physical symptoms. Fine (1971) reported that some of his patients improved with antidepressants, but did not state how many, and Gessel (1975) stated that five of eight patients who failed to improve with biofeedback improved on a tricyclic antidepressant.

Atypical Facial Pain

Atypical facial pain differs from facial arthromyalgia in that it does not specifically affect the temporomandibular joint and its musculature. It can usually be differentiated from the pain of neurological syndromes, such as trigeminal and post-herpetic neuralgia, because it does not conform to a cranial nerve distribution and tends to be diffuse, vaguely described and felt deep within the soft tissues or the bones and in the teeth, tongue or oral mucosa (Lascelles 1966, Harris 1975). It is further distinguished from trigeminal neuralgia by its chronic non-remitting nature, although the conditions can co-exist (Weddington & Blazer 1979). The pain is usually experienced as a constant dull ache, sometimes with boring or throbbing exacerbations. It may persist for long periods and most patients have had it for months or even years by the time of presentation. The pain is often attributed to some dental or other trauma. It rarely disturbs sleep and does not usually respond to simple analgesics. It may be clinically valuable to subdivide atypical facial pain into atypical odontalgia and oral dysaesthesia; both diagnoses imply the absence of detectable underlying pathology.

Atypical odontalgia

This is a continuous or throbbing pain in the teeth, distinguishable from that of a pulpitis or periodontitis. Additionally, the teeth may be hyper-responsive to all stimuli. One or more teeth or quadrants are involved for variable periods of time. There are no detectable signs of dental pathology although previous attempts to diagnose and treat the condition may have led to extractions, pulpectomies, root fillings and apicectomies. The pain frequently moves to another tooth or remains in the tooth socket following dental treatment (Brooke 1980, Harris 1981).

Oral dysaesthesia

This group of symptoms consists of a burning tongue (glossopyrosis, glosso-dynia), 'dry mouth', salty taste, 'salivary sand', and gripping dentures. One feature of importance is that the burning tongue is usually relieved by eating or drinking, whereas organic lesions are aggravated by food and drink. All these disturbances of taste or intolerance to denture-wearing persist in the absence of clinical, haematological, biochemical and immuno-logical abnormalities (Harris 1981).

Wilson (1932) commented on the lack of relief afforded by various attempts at surgical intervention in seven cases. He suggested that intrapsychic conflict in some way upset the sympathetic nervous system and caused pain.

Engel (1959) noted the enthusiastic investigation of allergy, endocrine disturbance, autonomic disturbance, vasomotor factors and functioning of the sphenopalatine or Vidian ganglion and trigeminal nerve, with only meagre results. Despite thorough investigation of 20 cases, Engel demonstrated no physical disturbance. He considered that the pain represented serious underlying psychological disturbance.

Despite early recognition of the failure of operative treatment, almost every study comments on a long history of unsuccessful dental and surgical interventions, including extractions, explorations of sinuses, etc. Fourteen out of 20 of Engel's (1959) patients had submitted to '52 surgical attacks'. Lascelles (1966) states that of 54 patients, 31 had some sort of dental operation, 3 had nerves resected, 9 had operations on noses and paranasal sinuses and 3 had tonsils and adenoids removed.

Psychological approaches to treatment have become more widely accepted. Wilson (1932) recommended psychotherapy to resolve the intrapsychic conflicts and reported improvement in five of his seven patients with such treatment. Engel (1959) reported dramatic relief of symptoms after a few sessions of psychotherapy, but warned against intensive 'insight therapy' because of the danger of precipitating psychosis or suicide. Neither of these studies attempted a controlled trial or long-term follow-up of patients. Moulton (1955) advised reassurance with minimal dental and surgical intervention and commented that such reassurance was better received from a physician because of the patients' reluctance to accept psychiatric help. Lesse (1956) similarly stressed how unacceptable psychiatric help was, with all but one of 18 patients refusing help or refactory to all techniques.

It is obvious that patients presenting with symptoms of atypical facial pain are often misdiagnosed as having an organic disorder and so receive inappropriate and irreversible treatments.

Mechanical and surgical treatments are inappropriate and unsuccessful in providing relief of facial pain and headache. It seems likely that counselling provides more effective relief than muscular relaxation. There are not, however, sufficient well controlled studies to be dogmatic.

DRUG TREATMENT

There is increasing evidence that tricyclic antidepressants, monoamine-oxidase inhibitors and phenothiazines can relieve headache and facial pain, and there is some evidence that this may be through an analgesic rather than antidepressant effect (Feinmann 1985). Indeed, it has been suggested that gross pharmacological similarities exist between the tricyclic antidepressants and the centrally acting analgesics and that clinical pain and depression share a similar biochemical aetiology. Furthermore, the discovery that certain endogenous polypeptides (such as leu-enkephalin, met-enkephalin, and the endorphins) possess 'natural' analgesic activity has prompted some authors to argue that pain and depression are chemically linked (Lee & Spencer 1977).

Drug treatment is not recommended in isolation. A pragmatic treatment approach is recommended in which the patient is first thoroughly assessed, counselled in terms of life style and reassured that no serious physical disorder is present. A strong association with adverse life events and other long-term problems indicates the need for a thorough clinical assessment of the patient's problem and conservative forms of management. The patients who do not respond to reassurance should then be treated with antidepressant medication in slowly increasing doses. However, it must be borne in mind that in some cases this must be maintained for at least a year to prevent relapse.

It is vital to emphasise to patients that pain is real and not imaginary, arising in cramped blood vessels and muscles as a response to stress. Failure to respond to treatment requires psychiatric examination and exploration of other therapies.

PSYCHOLOGICAL ASPECTS OF TREATMENT

Facial pain and headache have been considered separately, but there is overwhelming evidence that the symptoms occur recurrently or simultaneously as a response to stress. It is not possible to define precisely the aetiology of pain, although the association with other recurrent symptoms such as backache, irritable colon and pruritic skin disorders suggests that headache and facial pain are part of a psychophysiological response to stress. Referral to different professional specialties, lack of familiarity with symptoms and unreliable classification have all contributed to an arbitary separation of the disorders.

The patients have been described as reluctant either to see psychiatrists. (Moulton 1955) or to accept a psychological explanation for their pain (Lesse 1956). The lack of motivation for psychiatric treatment may even be an essential part of the disorders, since a poor capacity for insight to psychological problems may lead to the genesis of somatic symptoms (Salminen et al 1980).

By the time the patient sees the psychiatrist, he will probably have received a variety of treatments, and will probably consider himself to be beyond therapeutic help. The fear of being stigmatised as a psychiatric patient is still considerable and referral may imply to patients that their pain is imaginary (Salminen et al 1980). The distrust of psychiatric therapies shown by physicians (Miller 1968) may contribute to the lack of a combined approach. In addition, these patients present themselves to doctors with no knowledge of dentistry, or to dentists with no training in psychological disorders.

Patients with psychogenic facial pain present the dentist, the ENT surgeon, the neurologist and the physician with a difficult problem. The pain resembles organic pain, but fails to improve with surgical intervention. Doctor and patient are then caught in a variety of different trials of treatment until referral to another specialist is suggested.

The style of therapy described below has emerged as a result of the author's experience as a liaison psychiatrist at the Eastman Dental Hospital.

Aims of therapy

The main aims of treatment are to persuade the patients that their belief that they suffered a physical illness is false, to allay fears about physical illness, to increase understanding about the nature of the symptoms and to relieve symptoms of pain as well as any associated anxiety and depression.

Treatment strategies

Setting for treatment

The manner in which a patient is referred for treatment is important. Too often patients are told that there is nothing wrong with them and that a psychiatrist will take over their future care. This leads patients to believe that they are imagining their pain and also implies that psychiatry has little to offer (Pasnau 1982). To be successful the psychiatrist must be seen as a member of the health care team. To fill the role, he must be identified as someone who has the interest and expertise to solve behavioural or mental problems. The psychiatrist should be called in earlier, rather than later, and the patients should be told that for some kinds of problems psychiatric consultation is routine. It is essential that the physician, surgeon and psychiatrist work together so that psychiatric referral is not seen as an abandonment. Obviously a close working relationship between the referring physician or surgeon and the psychiatrist also leads to mutual informal and formal learning. The psychiatrist functions best working in the department from which the patient is referred rather than in a psychiatric clinic. The majority of patients with headache and facial pain are seen as outpatients, though occasionally a short period of inpatient stay is necessary to cope with crises.

The following vignette illustrates the management in a general surgical setting.

Case 1
A 38-year-old woman was referred to the oral surgery department because she was convinced that a lump in the floor of her mouth, which had been present for 16 months, was malignant. No physical abnormality was found and she was referred for a psychiatric opinion. She claimed to be unable to swallow and described a sensation of not secreting saliva from one side of her mouth. She was extremely agitated,

unable to sleep, eat or indeed remain on her own for any length of time and had given up her job as a hospital clerical officer because of her condition.

Her personal history revealed that she had an 18-year liaison with a married man by whom she had one child. Shortly before her symptoms developed she had made plans to leave her parents' home for the first time. Coincidentally a friend told her the details of her mother's death from oral carcinoma; 6 months prior to this a cousin died from leukaemia.

The patient was admitted to a surgical ward with a diagnosis of oral dysaesthesia and agitated depression and was sedated with dothiepin (Prothiaden) 225 mg daily. She gained considerable relief from the joint attentions of surgeon and psychiatrist. Her symptoms receded and she was discharged after 2 weeks, but maintained on medication and reviewed in the outpatient department at weekly intervals for the next 5 months. She gradually accepted the association of the stress in her life and her problems with her mouth. At follow-up 2 years later there had been no return of her symptoms.

The patient developed her symptoms at a time when she was emotionally vulnerable, leaving home for the first time, and her attention was focused on her mouth, presumably because of an awareness of malignant disease. Her case illustrates how a difficult psychological problem can be managed by a liaison psychiatrist in a general surgical setting. However, a short period of inpatient care and intensive follow-up were needed to maintain improvement.

STYLE OF TREATMENT

First of all, the psychiatrist must establish a long-term empathic relationship with the patient and aim to become the only therapist but *not* the only hope. Constant 'doctor-hopping' is countertherapeutic. With one doctor managing the disorder, unnecessary diagnostic procedures can be avoided. However, the patient must be encouraged to seek emotional support from other agencies. It is essential to understand that any new symptoms presented are an emotional communication rather than new disease. A further benefit from working in a medical or surgical clinic is that consultations and physical examination can be carried out with ease and the patient quickly reassured.

Patients should be seen initially at *regular or frequent intervals* so that they *will not* have to acquire new symptoms in order to see a physician. Visits can in some cases be brief and thereby minimise any negative feeling that may otherwise develop in psychiatrists caring for such patients.

The following case illustrates how a patient's anxieties can be contained by specialist co-operation.

Case 2

A 31-year-old woman was referred to the oral surgery department for an opinion on her further management. She complained of severe pain in all her teeth. No organic cause for her pain was found and she was referred for psychiatric help, aged 16. She was an only child, who was not very close to her mother. She was unable to complete her second degree because of her dental appointments, but she was able to maintain a full-time job. She had been engaged for 5 years but was unwilling to marry because of fears for her teeth and a reluctance to consummate her marriage.

She presented in an extremely agitated state, convinced that she would lose all her teeth, and said she was unable to resist attending dental casualty departments, where she felt she could be helped. Her pain was a constant dull ache with occasional sharp exacerbations which moved from tooth to tooth. She was extremely depressed and felt she could not continue living with her teeth. The patient also suffered from headache, backache, spastic colon and pruritis.

She was first referred to a psychiatrist when still at school and was described as obsessionally ruminating about various diseases, including venereal disease. She was treated with diazepam (Valium) but did not remain in psychiatric care. The following year her father died from carcinoma after a long illness, and the patient began to attend a dental hospital complaining of pain in several teeth. She even failed to attend her father's funeral because of a dental appointment. Dental interventions failed to relieve her pain and she was again referred to a psychiatrist but declined any further help. For the following 9 years she had a variety of dental treatments, including root canal treatment, occlusal rehabilitation and several crowns, none of which permanently relieved her pain, although she experienced the typical 3 weeks of placebo relief.

A diagnosis of atypical odontalgia was made and the patient was initially treated with dothiepin (Prothiaden) 150 mg daily to which trifuperazine (Stelazine) 5 mg three times daily was later added. She was seen at weekly intervals for 1 year for extensive exploratory psychotherapy and during this time was provided with essential dental care by a tolerant dentistry department. Her pain-free intervals became longer and after 18 months she felt confident enough to marry.

At 8-year follow-up the patient is more or less free of pain but still pays occasional visits to the psychiatrist and a conservative dentist. She is on no medication.

The patient's symptoms developed at a time of emotional stress and, possibly because of the large amount of dental treatment, persisted over many years. She had a number of other symptoms for which she had not sought help but which improved as her pain resolved. The co-operation of dental and psychiatric therapist were necessary to contain her impulses to gain constant dental treatment.

Initial consultation

As a result of numerous negative investigations the patient is often in a state of anxiety and fairly hostile in the first interview. To perform successful consultations psychiatrists must be able to recognise, contain and dissipate anxiety. It is essential that patients realise their pain is being taken seriously, and to this end a full medical and psychiatric history should be taken to identify other chronic pain disorders such as neck, back, pelvic pain, spastic colon or pruritis, which frequently accompany facial pain and headache. It is also important to identify any adverse life events and a history of emotional or psychiatric illness. During the first interview the psychiatrist has to overcome the patients' reluctance to accept a psycholog-ical explanation of their symptoms. By making an association with unhappy events such as bereavement or ill health in the family, the explanation becomes more acceptable to patients.

Furthermore it must be stressed that pain is real and not imaginary, arising in 'cramped' muscles and dilated blood vessels and an overloaded joint in response to stress. The identification and comparison with other somatic symptoms helps the patient understand the nature of the pain. Giving patients a diagnosis and assuring them that they are not unique often assists the consultation.

The patient must be given accurate information about pain development and an explanation of the principles of selective perception. A patient who blames all his pain on a tooth extraction or previous trauma should be able to understand that concern about a part of the body will make this point the focus of attention. He can then be encouraged to 'unlearn' the habit (Kellner 1982). Terms used by previous physicians to label minor discomforts (such as sinusitis, allergy, rheumatism) are often misunderstood. These conditions are regarded by patients as the causes of current symptoms even when totally unrelated. These relationships must be explained and clarified. Since patients frequently forget information or remember it inaccurately, information must be frequently repeated and different aspects of the phenomona explained.

By the time a patient reaches the psychiatrist he will have had pain for months, if not years. To assist in pain control it is often important to give some rapid symptom relief. Tricyclic antidepressants should be prescribed in slowly increasing doses, at night to avoid side-effects. It must be explained to patients that the drugs have 'analgesic-like' actions which have a direct effect on the painful blood vessels and muscles as well as a central analgesic action. The fact that tricyclic antidepressants are used to treat migraine, arthritis, post-herpetic neuralgia, terminal pain and other chronic pains should be stressed.

The initial psychiatric consultation should help to educate the patient, interpret his anxieties and clarify his thoughts. The psychiatrist must listen, show empathy and appraise the patient's capacity to understand the problem (Redlich 1970). Successful coping with stress must meet the following conditions (Pasnau 1982).

1. Sufficient hope and self-esteem so that the task does not appear overwhelming.
2. Some control, which is within the patient's power, to affect change.
3. Sufficient information upon which to act.

The patients may find the initial consultation distressing as many may have not seen psychiatrists previously and the psychological aspects of their pain are unlikely to have been explored. Some time must be taken to allow recovery. The following case history illustrates the importance of the initial interview.

Case 3
A 64-year-old woman was referred to the oral surgery department with a 4-year history of pain and burning in her tongue and an inability to tolerate her dentures. Her pain developed shortly after the death of both parents, at the same time as her

younger son's marriage had broken up. Neither the patient nor her husband were in good health: she had recently had a hysterectomy and her husband had bilateral cataracts. She was extremely depressed and said she would be unable to face life if she were not able to wear her dentures. The patient also complained of a pruritus, spastic colon and tension headache.

Her personal and marital history was unremarkable. She said however that at the age of 34 she had a complete dental clearance because she felt dental appointments might have interfered with bringing up two young sons. It is possible she was depressed at this time.

She was extremely depressed at the initial interview because during her 4 years of pain she had seen a number of specialists, including psychiatrists, all of whom had told her that they could not understand her symptoms and that she would have to live with them. She regarded further psychiatric referral as confirmation of the fact that she was beyond help. The association between the stressful life events and pain development was explained to her, and the fact her attention was focused on her mouth was attributed to her dental clearance 30 years earlier.

A diagnosis of oral dysaesthesia was made. The patient was treated with a tricyclic antidepressant and reviewed at 3-weekly intervals and began to improve after 6 weeks. However, she did not gain complete relief until a small dose of phenothiazine was added. Six years later she is free from any discomfort but continues to take a small amount of medication and is reviewed at 3 monthly intervals.

Subsequent sessions

The patients should initially be reviewed at 3- or 4-weekly intervals to achieve compliance with treatment and improve symptom control. The patients must be made aware that any improvement in pain will be gradual although relief may be achieved much more rapidly than relief of depression. The therapist must be prepared continually to repeat the explanation of the relationship between emotions and somatic symptoms. Kellner (1982) comments that patients with somatic pre-occupation do not respond well to traditional insight-orientated psychotherapy, whereas explanation alone appears to be effective in a large proportion of patients. Kellner suggests that explanatory therapy should *always* be included in any psychotherapy.

According to the severity of the patient's symptoms follow-up interviews can last from 15 minutes to 1 hour. Many patients gain immediate benefit from reassurance and short courses of drug therapy, while others, particularly those who are psychiatrically disturbed, require longer and more frequent follow-up. The patients should be told that they will be seen for up to 6 months regardless of the presence or absence of symptoms, and a brief physical examination carried out when new symptoms appear. Repeated examination, minimal investigation, unqualified assurance about the benign nature of the symptoms and simple explanation reduces anxiety and promotes recovery.

Recognition of the association between stressful events and onset of pain also helps achieve pain control. Once pain control is achieved patients may return for a 3-monthly review. As many patients feel rejected by previous physicians, who may have been frustrated by their frequent demands for attention, it is essential that patients remain in follow-up, however infrequent.

Facial pain and headache relapse and remit and may return in association with stressful life events and patients must be aware that any return of their symptoms is not catastrophic but can be eased by short courses of antidepressants and/or counselling. However, some patients respond to advice and are much simpler to treat. The following two case histories illustrate how reassurance, medication and counselling can help control symptoms.

Case 4

A 31-year-old man had an 8-month history of a dull ache in his right temporomandibular joint, accompanied by clicking and grinding noises. He had had no previous dental treatment. He was neither depressed nor anxious but had been under considerable stress; his only sister had emigrated 3 years earlier leaving him to care for his elderly parents; he held a high-pressure job and he had recently broken off a long-standing affair. He was not very happily married and had two children. There was no past medical or psychiatric history.

A diagnosis of facial arthromyalgia was made, and he accepted the association between stress in his life and his pain.

He was treated with a tricyclic antidepressant and was given support and advice about changing his job and also attended marital therapy. After 6 weeks he was symptom-free. He stopped all medication at 3 months, was reviewed at 3-monthly intervals for a year and was pain-free at a 4-year follow-up.

This patient's uncomplicated case illustrates the management that could be carried out by a dental practitioner. Psychiatric referral in such cases is probably unnecessary.

Case 5

A 55-year-old American man had an 18-month history of an electric shock type pain in the left upper quadrant. Eating or facial movement precipitated the pain, which had not been relieved by carbamazepine (Tegretol), replacement of fillings or root canal treatment. No dental or neurological cause was found. There was no mental state abnormality and no significant past medical or psychiatric history.

The patient's brother, a Christian scientist, had died 1 year prior to the development of the pain, of an untreated cerebral tumour which had extravasated the skull. Shortly after this the patient had left his children in the United States to come and work in Great Britain with his wife. A diagnosis of atypical facial pain was made, the patient was treated with a tricyclic antidepressant and his pain began to resolve within 3 weeks. Six months later the patient was pain-free and returned to the United States.

This case illustrates how rapid symptom relief can be gained with appropriate diagnosis and medication.

DURATION OF TREATMENT

All patients should remain on medication for at least 3 months and in some cases up to a year, to prevent relapse. Reviewing the long-term prognosis of pain, Feinmann & Harris (1984) found that between 60% and 70% of patients are free of pain at 4-year follow-up, about 50% of patients experienced short-term return of symptoms in association with stress. Forty per cent of the patients had to be maintained on medication for 1 year to prevent relapse and 20% were still taking medication at 4 years. Freedom from pain at 12 months was associated with an adverse life event, such as bereavement, prior to pain development, implying that counselling of such problems may be beneficial. An early response to drug treatment was a strong predictor of freedom from pain after a year. Where there was no improvement after 2 months' therapy the pain was unchanged at 12 months. Patients who remained in pain were characterised by a long history of ill health as well as previous unsuccessful dental and surgical treatment for pain.

As some patients had to be maintained on medication for at least a year to prevent relapse, psychogenic facial pain and headache should be considered to be a chronic recurrent disturbance such as migraine or trigeminal neuralgia and treated with a comparable, continuous medical regime. The principal difficulty in the management of these patients is convincing them that they require medication as opposed to surgery, which tends to render their condition refractory to treatment.

The following case history illustrates how in some cases long-term treatment is essential.

Case 6
A 34-year-old woman presented with a dull ache in the left-hand side of her face. No dental cause was found and she improved when prescribed a small dose of a tricyclic antidepressant by a dental registrar. She took her medication haphazardly and returned 2 months later saying she was unable to cope. She gave a history of a herpes infection in her left eye 11 months prior to the onset of her pain to which she related both her son developing temporal Lobe epilepsy and her own complaint. She also said her face had changed beyond recognition, her eyes were shrivelled and the whole of her face hurt. She felt extremely depressed and felt that life was not worth living.

She was the third of five children in a Greek Cypriot family. Her childhood was very unhappy and she had had an arranged marriage at the age of 17, by which she had one son. The marriage lasted only 2 years, and for 10 years the patient brought up her son on her own. Just prior to the onset of pain, a 5-year relationship broke up. A diagnosis of facial arthromyalgia and dysmorphophobia was made and the symptoms explained to the patient.

She was treated with a tricyclic antidepressant and seen at weekly intervals for supportive psychotherapy. She gradually improved and while she still believe that her face had altered, as long as she took her medication it no longer distressed her. At 5 years she remains in monthly follow-up, she is attending a college course and coping well. She does have occasional pain, and at times requests plastic surgery for her face. She also gains support from a therapist at college.

Further Treatment

The group of patients who do not respond to straightforward reassurance, minimal dental intervention and antidepressant medication should be re-

assessed and referred for further treatment. Insight-orientated psychotherapy or cognitive therapy should be considered. It is possible, however, that
20% of patients will remain intractable to all forms of treatment and therapeutic strategies should be restricted in these patients.

Pinsky (1978) noted that patients learn to accept the previously unacceptable role as psychotherapy patients when one of their psychotherapists also
functions as a physician or a psychiatrist with a working knowledge of general
medicine. He recommended group therapy for chronic intractable benign pain
syndromes.

PROFESSIONAL ISSUES

Who should treat the patients? These patients represent a substantial service
problem. Because of the risk of overlooking serious physical illness, a physician must be involved in the initial assessment and in subsequent re-assess-
ment. There is no contra-indication to the provision of both psychological
management and physical care by the same person. Patients may, however,
require the attention of different specialists. Counselling and reassurance are
effective treatments which can be conducted by any concerned therapist. Drug
therapy, clearly, must always be carried out under medical supervision.

Problems may arise in relationships with other professionals who are
unfamiliar with the facial pain symptom complexes and unused to the
demands made by patients experiencing somatic symptoms. Ideally therapy
should be restricted to one individual, although a small group of patients gain
a great deal of support from a number of different therapists. As long as
communication is maintained between the specialists, problems should not
arise.

Diagnosis should not be considered as an either/or problem, in which
patients either fulfil criteria for an organic syndrome or fail the test and
become burdensome to their physicians, surgeons and dentists.

Interplay with other Professionals

Other professionals must be kept informed of all aspects of a patient's treatment. The general practitioner, physician or surgeon should all be involved,
and often joint appointments are necessary to clarify diagnostic difficulties and
therapeutic goals. Patients with unexplained somatic symptoms frequently
approach other paramedical specialists such as hypnotherapists, and
acupuncturists and communication channels should be kept open between all
therapists. The various facial pain symptoms are often not recognised by other
specialists so that some time must be devoted to education.

Interplay with the Patient's Family

Patient's relatives should be involved in treatment when appropriate. Patients are often secretive and it is inadvisable to approach relatives without their consent. It is very important however to explain to relatives why a patient is seeing a psychiatrist and why drugs are used. It is essential that the family and the patient believe that the pain is real and the problem is being taken seriously.

SUMMARY

The psychological management of facial pain and headache requires that clinicians recognise the association between external stress and pain. It also requires changes in clinical practice so that patients can reveal emotional problems without fear of rejection. Clinicians must have the training, time and privacy to evaluate emotional factors before they will have the confidence to restrict excessive investigations and provide appropriate reassurance and treatment.

The concept of 'cure' must also be re-evaluated. Patients with headache and facial pain suffer from a relapsing and recurring disorder which can be alleviated by treatment but which will probably not disappear. The disorders are common and long-term management has enormous service implications. Psychiatrists may alert other physicians and surgeons to the existence of emotional problems but only a small proportion of patients need formal psychiatric care and the majority can be effectively treated by dentist and physician alike.

REFERENCES

Ayer W 1983 Report of the president's conference on the examination, diagnosis and management of tempormandicular disorders. Journal of the American Dental Association 108: 75–77

Banks F R, Keller M D 1971 Symptom experience and health action. Medical Care 9: 498–502

Beecher H K 1959 Measurement of subjective response. New York University Press, New York

Berry D C 1978 Mandibular dysfunction and chronic minor illness. British Dental Journal 127: 170–179

Blumer D, Heilbrom M 1982 Chronic pain as a variant of depressive disease. Journal of Nervous and Mental Disease 170: 381–394

Bridges K W, Goldberg D P 1985 Somatic presentation of DSM III psychiatric disorders in primary care. Journal of sychosomatic Research 29: 563–569

British Dental Journal Leader 1984 Management of psychogenic facial pain. 156:250

Brooke R 1980 Atypical odontalgia. Oral Surgery 49: 196–199

Brown G W, Harris T 1982 Disease, distress and depression. Journal of Affective Disorders 4: 11–18

Costa P T, Mccrae R R 1985 Hypochondriasis, neuroticism and aging. American Psychologist 40: 19–28

Engel G L 1959 Psychogenic pain and the pain-prone patient. American Journal of Medicine 196: 129–136

Feinmann C 1985 Pain relief by Antidepressants: possible modes of action. Pain 23: 1–8

Feinmann C, Harris M, Cawley R 1984 Psychogenic facial pain: presentation and management. British Medical Journal 228: 436–438

Fine E W 1971 Psychological factors associated with non-organic temporomandibular joint dysfunction syndrome. British Dental Journal 131: 402–407

Gershman J A, Burrows G D, Reade P C 1977 Orofacial pain. Australian Family Physician 6: 1219–1225

Gessel A H 1975 Electro-myographic biofeedback and tricyclic antidepressants in myofacial pain-dysfunction syndrome: psychological prediction of outcome. Journal of the American Dental Association 91: 1048–1052

Gold S, Lipton J, Marbach J et al 1975 Sites of psychophysiological complaints in MPD patients. Areas remote from the facial region. Journal of Dental Research 54: 165

Goldberg D 1972 The detection of psychiatric illness by questionnaire. Oxford University Press, Oxford

Greene C S, Laskin D H 1972 Splint therapy for myofascial pain dysfunction syndrome. A comparative study. Journal of the American Dental Association 84: 624–628

Greene C S, Laskin D M 1983 Long Term evaluation of treatment for myofascial pain dysfunction. Journal of the American Dental Association 107: 235–276

Gross A, Gale E 1983 A prevalence study of the clinical signs associated with mandibular dysfunction. Journal of the American Dental Association 107: 932–936

Harris M 1975 Psychosomatic Disorders of the mouth and face. Practitioner 214: 372–379

Harris M 1981 Psychogenic facial pain. International Journal of Oral Surgery 1: 183–186

Helkimo M 1976 Epidemiological surveys of dysfunction in the masticatory system. Oral Science Review 7: 54–69

Heloe B, Heloe L A 1978 Characteristics of a group of patients with TMJ disorders. Community Dentistry and Oral Epidemiology 3: 72–75

Heloe B, Heloe L A, Heiberg A 1977 Relationship between socio-medical and TMJ symptoms in Norwegians with myofascial pain dysfunction syndrome. Community Dentistry and Oral Epidemiology 5: 207–219

Holmes T H, Rahe R H 1967 The social readjustment rating scale. Journal of Psychosomatic Research 11: 213–218

Kellner R 1982 Psychotherapeutic strategies in hypochondriasis: a clinical study. American Journal of Psychotherapy 36: 146–157

Kendell R E 1975 The classification of depressive illness. Maudsley Monograph no. 18. Oxford University Press, London

Kent G 1985 Prevalence vs incidence of the mandibular pain dysfunction syndrome; implications for epidemiological research. Community Dentistry and Oral Epidemiology 13: 113–116

Kydd W L 1959 Psychosomatic aspects of temporo mandibular joint dysfunction. Journal of the American Dental Association 59: 31–44

Lascelles R 1966 Atypical facial pain and depression. British Journal of Psychiatry 112: 651–659

Laskin D M 1969 Aetiology of the pain dysfunction syndrome. Journal of the American Dental Association 85: 892–895

Lee R, Spencer P S J 1977 Antidepressants and pain: a review of the pharmacological data supporting the use of certain tricyclics in chronic pain. Journal of Medical Research 5: 146–156

Lesse S 1956 Atypical facial pain of psychogenic origin. Journal of Nervous and Mental Diseases 124: 346–351

Lipton J A, Marbach J J 1981 Sex differences in reported reponses to clinical facial pain (Abstract.) Pain 76: 64

Merskey M 1979 The role of the psychiatrist in the investigation and treatment of pain. Bonica J J (ed) Association for Research in Nervous and Mental Disease. Raven Press, New York

Merskey M 1982 Pain and emotion: their correlation in headache. Advances in Neurology 33: 135–143

Merskey M 1985 Psychological profile of headache patients. Pain 23: 323–328

Miller H 1968 Pain in the face. British Medical Journal 2: 577–580

Moodey P M, Kemper J T, Okeson J P et al 1982 Recent life changes and myofascial pain dysfunction. Journal of Prosthetic Dentistry 48: 328–330

Moulton R 1955 Psychiatric considerations in maxillofacial pain. Journal of the American Dental Association 51: 408–414

Nabarro J 1984 How common is psychiatric illness in medical inpatients? British Medical Journal 289: 635

Nigl A J 1984 Biofeedback and behavioural strategies in pain treatment. MTP Press, Lancaster

Pasnau R O 1982 Consultation liaison psychiatry current concepts. Up John Company, Kalamazoo, Michigan

Philips C 1978 Tension headache: theoretical problems. Behaviour Research and Therapy 16: 249–261

Philips C, Hunter M 1981 The treatment of tension headache. EMG 'normality' and relaxation. Behaviour Research and Therapy 19: 499–507

Pinkham R 1984 Cranio-mandibular disorders. Dental Practise 2: 16–18

Pinsky J J 1978 Chronic intractable, benign pain: a syndrome and its treatment with intensive short term group psychotherapy. Journal of Human Stress 45: 17–21

Redlich F C 1970 The doctor and his patient: explaining illness. International Journal of Psychiatry and Medicine 1: 171–185

Salimen J K, Lentinen V, Jokinen K et al 1980 Psychosomatic disorder: a treatment problem more difficult than neurosis. Acta Psychiatrica Scandinavica 62: 1–12

Schwartz L L 1959 Disorders of the temporomandibular joint. W B Saunders, Philadelphia

Speculand B, Hughes A O, Gross A N 1984 Role of stressful life experiences in the onset of TMJ pain dysfunction. Community Dentistry and Oral Epidemiology 12: 197–202

Thomson H 1971 Mandibular dysfunction syndrome. British Dental Journal 130: 187–193

Turner J A, Chapman C R 1982 Psychological interventions for chronic pain: a critical review. Part 1 Relaxation, training and biofeedback. Part II Operant condition, hypnosis and cognitive behaviour therapy. Pain 2: 1–46

Waters W E, O'Connor P J 1971 Epidemiology of headache and migraine in women. Journal of Neurology, Neurosurgery and Psychiatry 34: 148–153

Watson J P 1985 Frame of reference and the detection of individual and systemic problems. Journal of Psychosomatic Research 29: 571–577

Weddington W W, Blazer D 1979 Atypical facial pain and trigeminal neuralgia: a comparison study. Psychosomatics 20: 348–356

Williams P, Tarnopolsky A, Hand D 1980 Case definition and case identification in psychiatric epidemiology: Review and assessment. Psychological Medicine 10: 101–114

Wilson D C 1932 Atypical facial neuralgia. Journal of the American Medical Association 19: 813–816

Wolff H G 1963 Headache and other head pain. Oxford University Press, New York

Chronic pain

INTRODUCTION

Pain is a symptom that all of us will experience to varying degrees on numerous occasions during our lives. Fortunately these pains are usually caused by minor traumas or illness and respond to simple interventions and are therefore only short-lived. Sometimes pain may be more severe and longer lasting, but investigations usually reveal an underlying pathology that accounts for it, and treatment, though more complicated and protracted, again will produce relief. There are however a small number of people who present to the medical services with pains which have not responded to the usual therapies and have been present for considerable periods of time; such people fall into the category of the chronic pain patient.

This book is designed to outline the psychological aspects of management of certain chronic conditions and this chapter will restrict itself to the management of pain. Although there has been much written about the nature of pain, its physiology and biochemistry, these interesting areas will not be covered except where they impinge on management. Information on these aspects of pain are available elsewhere (Melzack 1973, Wall & Melzack 1984). The ideas discussed in this chapter are only one person's view on pain management and cannot profess to be either necessarily the only or even the best approach to pain from a psychiatric viewpoint. Chronic pain is such a complicated and multifaceted problem that there can be no single correct management procedure and other therapists may have different but equally valid approaches.

The chapter is about *management*, not cure. To remove the sensation of pain from a chronic pain patient, who has probably already failed to respond to numerous other interventions, is rather uncommon. The goal of treatment has to be set at something other than just pain removal, and it is essential that both therapist and patient are agreed on the goals of management or both are likely to feel great disappointment and loss of morale if expectations are inappropriate and unachievable.

It may be asked why a liaison psychiatrist is involved in the management

Table 4.1 Duration of pain in 100 consecutive referrals

Duration	No. of referrals
Less than 3 months	4
3–12 months	12
1–3 years	21
3–10 years	39
Over 10 years	24

of pain. I was forced into developing an interest in this area, which I had not expected when I first started a liaison service, because of the high number of pain patients referred.

A study in Leicester (Thomas 1983) showed that approximately one-third of the referrals to a liaison service were for patients with psychogenic disorders, i.e. where there was no obvious or sufficient organic pathology to account for all the symptoms. Of these psychogenic patients, the symptom in over 85% was pain. Over the years the number of such pain referrals has increased and now the liaison psychiatry department sees on average two new patients with pain each week. These figures indicate that the management of such patients is perceived as being very difficult by the general hospital staff who make the referrals. Most of the patients referred have pain of considerable duration. Table 4.1 shows the duration of symptoms in 100 consecutive referrals.

It is obvious that the patients referred to a psychiatrist will usually be thought of by the referring agent as having a psychological problem that plays a relevant part in the pain syndrome and it will be these patients whose management will be discussed. There are patients with chronic pain who have definite physical pathology and psychological factors are less relevant. In recent years a number of new pharmacological and surgical interventions have been devised for these patients and there are a number of physically-based pain clinics in the country, often run by anaesthetists who specialise in nerve blocks, pharmacological analgesia, acupuncture and other procedures, with great success (Budd 1979, Miles 1983). I would suggest that if a hospital wishes to offer a comprehensive service for chronic pain sufferers, it is imperative that specialists from both the physical and psychological point of view are involved and that they often work closely together.

WHAT IS PAIN?

Pain is hard to define and even harder to measure. Many older concepts of pain restricted themselves to trying to define the sensory aspect, which alone may not be sufficient. Melzack (1973) has produced a better definition of pain for our purpose: 'Pain . . . has a unique, distinctly unpleasant, affective quality that . . . demands immediate attention and disrupts ongoing behaviour and thought. It motivates or drives the organism into activity aimed at stopping the pain as quickly as possible'. This definition implies four separate areas associated with pain.

1. The sensory aspect of pain — the usual descriptive labels that we attach to pain: 'a stabbing pain', 'an ache', 'a throbbing feeling'.
2. The affective aspect of pain — defines how the pain makes us feel: 'a worrying pain', 'a draining pain', 'the pain gets me down'.
3. The behavioural aspect of pain — defines how the pain makes us react when it is present: 'a pain that stops me working', 'a pain that interferes with sex', 'a pain that requires rest'.
4. The cognitive aspect of pain — how the pain makes us think about ourselves: 'I cannot cope with pain', 'makes me feel like an invalid', 'I can see no way out with this pain'.

When we come to treat pain it is important to consider the management of all four aspects of the experience. If the sensation can be removed (as is usually the case with acute pain) then the other three components usually correspondingly improve. With chronic pain, where pain sensation may not be much lowered, management should be directed as much towards the other aspects which are, perhaps, more amenable to intervention.

There have been various methods described to try to measure the amount of pain a person is suffering (Melzack 1983). None of these methods is entirely satisfactory, though most have some potential (Chapman 1976). Questionnaires have been used to try to give a pain score, most commonly the McGill Pain Questionnaire (Melzack 1975). Linear analogue scales have been used (Huskisson 1974) offering the advantage of simplicity and speed. Both questionnaires and analogue scales are of little use for comparing pain between individuals, but may be helpful in monitoring one person's pain and its change over time. There have been attempts to assess pain amongst different people by applying a similar increasing painful stimulus and noting when the person first reports the sensation of pain (threshold) and then the level at which it cannot be further increased because of its severity (tolerance) (Wolff 1977). These techniques do allow comparison of thresholds and tolerance between individuals, but cannot with certainty say that one person feels, or is in, more pain than another. An interesting approach has been described by Sternbach et al (1974) who tried to compare the patient's verbal reports of pain with their measured tolerance level. They were able to show that some patients complained of extreme or unbearable pain when there was evidence to suggest that their levels of tolerance had nowhere near been reached, and thus they were perhaps exaggerating their symptoms.

Whatever measurement is made, the problem still remains of not being able to determine how much pain any individual is suffering, and from a clinical point of view this may not be necessary. Too much effort is often made by clinicians in trying to decide whether a patient's pain is as much as they claim. If pain thresholds and tolerance have very wide variations, (as is probable) then many patients will report different levels of pain from the same stimulus and any opinion of medical staff about the degree of a patient's pain becomes a personal value judgement, usually based on their own (often grossly overestimated) pain tolerance.

If pain is viewed from the four aspects mentioned above, we can make better clinical decisions about the pain a patient has than if we only consider sensation. In particular, behaviour associated with pain is an important area to assess. Even if we imagine that the patient does not feel much pain, does he behave as though he is in much pain? I would suggest that in chronic pain management, it is the pain behaviour we should most concentrate on in our assessment. If the patient complains of pain, but is carrying on a normal life, with full occupational, social and domestic capabilities, then little intervention is probably needed. On the other hand, if a patient is spending most of the day in bed with family or friends carrying out all responsibilities for them, then whether the sensation of pain is mild or severe, the behaviour is incapacitating and requires attention.

Case 1
Miss A. L., a 52-year-old ex-secretary, claimed to have injured her back in a road traffic accident 26 years previously. Although no apparent injuries were received at the time, she complained of lower back pain a few days after the accident and this has been present ever since. It had gradually increased in severity over the years. She had been seen in the past by numerous orthopaedic surgeons, rheumatologists and neurosurgeons, none of whom had been able to demonstrate any physical lesion to account for her pain. Many of the doctors who had seen her had diagnosed her pain as hysterical and although she had been offered a variety of physical treatments none of these had been successful. She was surviving only by taking large quantities of analgesics to keep her pain at bay. The eventual advice to her general practitioner was that he should stop all her analgesic treatment as there was no possibility she could be in pain after such a long period of time with no lesion being demonstrated.

She had had to give up work because of her symptoms at the age of 44 years. She lived with her mother who had to do all the housework and undertake other responsibilities. The patient had spent most of the day either in bed or resting on the sofa for the preceding 6 years. She had not left home other than for hospital visits for 5 years. She was referred to me after her mother's death when she had been left to fend for herself.

Conclusion

Although it was debatable how much pain sensation she was experiencing there was no doubt that her pain behaviour was extreme.

WHO IS THE CHRONIC PAIN PATIENT?

The simplest answer to this question is that it is any person who suffers pain over a long time. Usually, however, the term 'chronic pain patients' is used when doctors are unable to detect a clear physical pathology that accounts for the symptoms. Patients who are thought to have an uncomplicated physical disorder are referred to as 'chronic arthritics' 'cancer patients' etc., where it is the disease that is seen as long-standing, not the symptom. Mostly when doctors use the term 'chronic pain patient' they are implying that they believe psychological factors are playing a part in the production of the symptom and that the physical disease is either non-existent or not sufficient to produce the level of pain.

The referrals made to the Liaison Psychiatry Department in Leicester for opinions therefore fall into two main groups (as perceived by the referring agent).

1. Patients whose pain appears out of proportion to the actual physical pathology (30%).
2. Patients whose pain appears to be due purely to psychogenic factors with no physical pathology (60%).

In the past, attempts have been made to define the 'typical chronic pain sufferer'. Engel (1959) has written with great authority on what he describes as the 'pain prone patient', and others have tried to outline characteristic personality or social factors to be found in chronic pain sufferers (e.g. Leavitt 1985, Katon et al 1985, Sternbach et al 1973, Woodford & Merskey 1972). It has been suggested that the symptoms in chronic pain patients with largely psychological causes are different from those in 'organic' pain patients, for example psychological pain does not cause insomnia, is not associated with physical signs, has obvious rewards and is described in more bizarre language, with dramatic overlay.

All of these factors may occur but it is dangerous to rely excessively on such descriptions as they are by no means invariable. They promote dualistic thinking — is this pain physical or psychogenic? — and such a division is unhelpful. We should be trying to determine in each patient how much of their pain is physical and how much is psychological, remembering that both may be playing important parts, and both need appropriate treatment. There may be factors other than the physical and psychological which influence pain manifestation. Social, cultural and personality aspects often need to be borne in mind when pain behaviour is examined (Elton et al 1983).

Case 2
Mr L. S., a 54-year-old salesman, 3 years previously had had surgical removal of cancer of the rectum with colostomy. For 1 year he had been complaining of severe perineal pain. He had been seen by the surgeons and oncologists and there was no obvious spread of malignancy. After his surgery he had experienced major marital problems which he himself blamed on the colostomy which his wife was unable to tolerate. At the same time as his pain had developed he had experienced a gradual onset of a depression which had become more severe and culminated in a suicide attempt which initiated his referral to the Liaison Psychiatry Department. There

was a history of previous 'hypochondriacal' behaviour since childhood and he had in fact seen his general practitioner and other hospital specialists at times in the past with various pains for which no physical pathology had been found. His mother had had severe arthritis during his childhood and had required much hospitalisation and care.

Initial conclusion

It was initially felt by the medical staff and by myself that his pain could well be an aspect of his personality and family history and that his pain had become accentuated through a depression largely brought about by the colostomy and marital disharmony.

He was initially treated with a combination of antidepressants and marital therapy, but his severe pain continued and after a few weeks it became apparent that his pain was increasing and he also started to lose weight. At that stage further investigations were carried out and a bone scan revealed that he had recurrent malignant disease in the pelvis.

Final conclusion

Pain due to organic pathology, but accentuated by personality and psychological factors.

There is one further type of pain referral made to the Liaison Psychiatry Department, which is less common and not necessarily associated with chronicity:

3. Patients whose pain is due to physical factors but who have developed psychological problems as a result of it (10%).

In all three types of referral psychiatrists are usually asked for help when the patient appears to suffer from those aspects of pain other than the pure pain sensation, in other words when the patient is either handicapped by the affective component or seeming to behave in pain excessively. It is in these two areas that perhaps the psychiatrist has most to offer.

THE MISSED ORGANIC PAIN

Whilst the chronic pain patient usually falls into one of the three categories described above, the psychiatrist needs to bear in mind that a physical factor may have been overlooked. If an organic process has been overlooked the pain is likely to continue and will not be greatly helped by psychological treatments alone. Obviously, great reliance has to be placed on medical colleagues to exclude all organic factors as it would be inappropriate to repeat numerous investigations or treatment that had already been carried out. Nevertheless when a chronic pain patient is seen for the first time by a psychiatrist it is essential that a proper history is taken and that the medical notes are fully reviewed to ensure nothing has been omitted. An early, influential study demonstrated that a number of patients whose physical symptoms were diagnosed initially as 'hysterical' eventually turned out to have underlying undiagnosed processes (Slater 1965). While there may be a natural reluctance to carry out further investigation on patients diagnosed as having psychogenic pain, if new physical symptoms or signs develop then they *must not* be ignored or automatically regarded as hysterical also. Certain conditions, traditionally thought of as hysterical, have been shown by recent research to have a probable organic basis (for example atypical facial pain, cluster headaches, abdominal migraine, causalgia and certain dystonias).

There is one situation, 'the histrionic cycle', that may lead to an organic process being missed by the medical staff. The cycle begins if the physical cause of pain is not found initially. This leads to an escalating process, with the patient continually behaving more and more in pain to convince the staff. The staff become more and more rigid in their conviction that histrionic behaviour *must* imply a psychogenic cause for the pain and this leads them to become 'blind' to its real cause. For these reasons it is particularly helpful to liaise closely with the clinicians who run the physical pain clinic. I frequently ask them to see patients referred to me where I am unsure that all physical factors have been excluded before embarking on psychological management alone.

PSYCHIATRIC CAUSES OF PAIN

If psychological factors are suspected as playing a major part in the cause of chronic pain, it is important to determine whether the patient has any psychiatric illness which warrants treatment. Psychogenic pain can be divided into two broad groups: firstly where pain is one symptom of a generalised psychiatric condition and secondly where pain is the only symptom of a psychiatric disorder.

Pain as one symptom of a psychiatric condition

The psychiatric illnesses where pain may occur are listed below; in all of the conditions a diagnosis is usually obvious because the patient will show many other symptoms of that illness.

Dementia
Schizophrenia
Depressive illness
Anxiety states

Very occasionally dementing patients have low tolerance and present with physical pains. The sudden onset of hypochondriacal complaints of any nature in people over 60 years of age when they have not shown such behaviour previously must always lead to a high degree of suspicion of an organic cerebral process, which is usually confirmed by the other mental changes of dementia. Schizophrenics may also complain of pain and this is rarely due to an actual delusion of pain or hallucination of the sensation of pain (Watson et al 1981). In these cases the description of pain is usually bizarre and associated with a secondary delusional elaboration and other symptoms of schizophrenia are present.

In depressive illness the complaint of pain is common. It has been claimed that nearly 60% of depressed patients report pain as part of their disorder (Merskey & Spear 1967). The pains are often in the head, face, chest or abdomen. They are frequently described as a sensation of weight or pressure. Pain in depressed patients may be due to a variety of factors. The pain threshold is lowered in depression (Sternbach 1970), therefore pain messages are registered that would not normally reach conscious awareness. The high frequency of pain in depressive disorders may be associated with the altered endorphin levels in the brain (Feinmann 1985).

Such patients nearly always have other symptoms of a depressive disorder and may show some of the classic biological disturbance of a severe affective illness. Sometimes the depression is viewed as an understandable emotional reaction to the physical pain and the primary nature of the depression is missed. If depression appears to be a major factor in a pain patient it is always worth giving the patient a therapeutic trial of *adequate* antidepressant treatment. If depression is causing the pain then there is usually a good response to such treatment and both the depression and symptoms of pain are greatly relieved promptly. Tricyclic antidepressants can have a direct analgesic as well as an antidepressant action (Feinmann 1985).

Pain is also a frequent symptom in patients suffering from anxiety states. The basis of pain in these patients is often muscular tension and is usually experienced as headaches, chest pain, back pain and occasionally limb pains. Some anxious patients develop abdominal pains that are associated with gastrointestinal disorders such as the irritable bowel syndrome. As with depression these tension pains are just one symptom of a psychiatric illness and the diagnosis is made from the presence of other classic symptoms suggestive of autonomic overactivity and the associated mood state of anxiety.

These anxiety pains often become chronic and this may be because the stress that has initiated the anxiety is chronic itself. It is not infrequent however that the original stress may have passed but the symptoms continue. In such cases, the concern now becomes the symptoms of anxiety itself, particularly the worry due to abnormal cognitions about the nature of the pain. Often the pain is misinterpreted, not as tension, but as a serious physical disorder and the worry about this produces further pain (Fig. 4.1).

If the anxiety state and autonomic overactivity can be reduced then there will be a reduction in the pain. Because of the problems associated with long-term anxiolytic use, the best method of dealing with such tension-based pain is through behavioural and cognitive anxiety management tech-

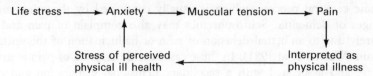

Fig. 4.1 Anxiety and pain

niques. These techniques will rely on explanation of the origin of pain, reassurance over its benign nature, mental distraction techniques, cognitive restructuring of abnormal thoughts, relaxation and occasionally biofeedback. The belief that the pain is based in physical illness can be very strong in some patients and they have great difficulty in accepting the correct interpretation of their symptoms which may make cognitive and behavioural interventions very difficult. On these occasions it may be of great use to prove to the patient that anxiety is the cause of their pain by prescribing a course of a benzodiazepine for a few days only. This should be presented to the patient as a diagnostic test that will be followed by non-pharmacological interventions.

Case 3
Mr A. P., a 28-year-old policeman, had a 1-year history of increasingly severe chest pains and palpitations. These were associated with sweating, breathlessness and paraesthesia in the fingers. The symptoms had first occurred after he had been promoted at work (which he recognised as a stressful situation) but had then continued long after he felt he had settled into his new position. He was convinced that he was having recurrent heart attacks and whenever his symptoms occurred he became extremely panicky and would often seek medical aid. He had been admitted to hospital on three occasions because of his symptoms and once had been on the intensive care unit. He had been fully investigated by cardiologists who were unable to demonstrate any cardiac abnormalities and he was referred to the Liaison Psychiatry Department with a provisional diagnosis of an anxiety state.

On his initial assessment he was asked to hyperventilate and this reproduced a number of the symptoms he experienced during his attacks. The diagnosis of anxiety with hyperventilation syndrome was confirmed and he was offered an anxiety management package. This consisted of a lengthy explanation of the nature of anxiety and production of his symptomatology. He was also taught some cognitive strategies to use when the attacks occurred, particularly in over-riding the negative ideas about heart disease with more correct cognitive interpretations of his symptoms. He was also encouraged to use both mental and physical diversion activities when attacks occurred so that his thoughts were diverted away from thinking about his body. He was taught rebreathing techniques and given some simple breathing exercises to slow and deepen his breathing during attacks. He was encouraged to participate in regular exercise and was provided with a relaxation tape to teach him general muscular relaxation.

He was also offered a short course of benzodiazepines, but he felt that as he now understood the nature of his symptoms he did not require medication to prove to him that it was anxiety. He made a very good response to the anxiety management package and was seen only on two subsequent occasions for further cognitive work. On reassessment 6 months later his symptoms had largely disappeared and on the few occasions that they had occurred at times of stress he had been able to bring them under his own control very rapidly.

Conclusion

Severe anxiety state and hyperventilation with autonomic overactivity.

Pain as the only symptom of a psychiatric condition

The majority of patients with chronic pain referred to the Liaison Psychiatry Department at Leicester do not have symptoms that allow a primary diagnosis of anxiety or depression (although many will have some mood disturbance as a consequence of their chronic pain). These patients' only symptom is the pain itself. If physical contributions to the pain do not appear to be major then a variety of labels may be used to describe the patient's disorder — hysteria, functional pain, malingering, hypochondriasis, abnormal illness behaviour and psychogenic pain being some of the commoner terms.

Ascertaining real differences between these labels is difficult, and as they are usually based in the value judgement of the observer, rather than the psychopathology of the patient, they are probably of little use. I prefer to use just the label 'chronic pain patient' as a descriptive diagnosis. Once physical disorder has been ruled out as a significant factor it is necessary to look at different psychological factors that might have initiated or maintain the pain.

Some, but by no means all, of these chronic pain patients may show certain background features that include large sibships, family history of pain, and previous episodes of undiagnosed pain (Elton et al 1983). It is often assumed that such patients have learned at some stage during their development that pain carried advantage — usually by deriving attention from other people. Other chronic pain patients may be shown to have experienced the onset of their symptoms at the time of a major life event. Again it is often suspected that the pain is in some ways conveying an advantage to the patient in dealing with or even avoiding the consequences of the stress. One of the commonest stresses prior to the onset of chronic pain is a genuine physical disorder that produces acute pain. While the patient is unwell they become aware of the advantage of the sick role and then continue to complain of the pain after the acute lesion has healed.

These hypotheses about chronic pain all contain the notion that the symptom has an advantage to the patient — the classic secondary gain. Unfortunately, this again has to be a value judgement of the observer, as there is no way to prove that pain definitely is conveying advantages, especially when the patient can give much evidence of the considerable disadvantages their chronic pain places them under.

Once pain has been present for more than a few months it is likely that any original precipitants will no longer be particularly relevant. In the majority of chronic pain patients seen by psychiatrists it is perhaps more important to look for factors that maintain the pain. These factors may be habitual patterns of behaviour that the patient has acquired or ongoing reinforcements from the patient's environment that encourage him to remain in pain.

The management of these chronic pain patients may be very difficult. It is important to try to work with, rather than against, the patients. If they correctly or incorrectly perceive the psychiatrist as being interested only in trying to find an emotional cause for their pain or uncover any advantages from their suffering, then co-operation is likely to be minimal and they will usually withdraw from any therapeutic relationship. The most essential aspect of the management is to show the patient that any investigation and treatment is ultimately directed only at helping them with their pain.

In Leicester the most severe of the chronic pain patients are offered treatment as either an inpatient or day-patient on a pain programme. The rest of this chapter will be devoted to describing this programme. The less severe chronic pain patient may well be offered some but not all the components of the programme on an outpatient basis, but the principles of management are the same as for the most severe cases.

THE PAIN PROGRAMME

The aims of the pain programme are listed below. It is possible that in certain patients one aim may be of more importance than others and more emphasis will be placed upon it.

To reduce all aspects of pain — sensory, affective, behavioural, cognitive
To rationalise analgesic procedures
To look for and remove any causes of pain — physical, emotional and social
To remove any reinforcements of pain
To re-establish non-pain patterns of living

Acceptance into the programme has of course to be voluntary. Explanation about the aims is of central importance before a patient makes the decision to enter the programme. It is extremely important that they understand and agree to these aims or there will always be a discrepancy between what the patient and the staff expect. As all the patients will have been very thoroughly physically investigated, emphasis needs to be placed on the fact that the programme will largely be devoted to the affective and particularly the behavioural and cognitive aspects of the pain experience. While it is necessary that the physical aspects are always kept in mind and new signs investigated if they develop, patients should realise that this is unlikely to happen. While they are on the programme they will not have further tests or treatment of a purely physical nature that have been carried out fruitlessly in the past. It is sometimes worthwhile to put both patients' and staffs' minds at rest for the physical aspects of the pain to be jointly reviewed before admission to the pain programme. Close liaison with the physically orientated pain clinic can be of great advantage here.

Hopefully, therefore, patients on the programme know that whereas the sensory aspects of pain are not ignored they are not as important as the others. To emphasise this point the patients are told that at the end of the programme the sensation of pain may not be altered, but perhaps it will not affect them so much and they will be less restricted by it. Before patients can really decide on whether to enter the programme they need to be provided with information about the sorts of interventions that are likely to be used to achieve the aims specified above. Patients are informed that the treatment approach is both multidisciplinary and multifaceted, they will be undergoing the different treatments as part of a combined package, as the results often seem better when treatments are carried out simultaneously rather than trying one after another until a successful therapy is found.

The first week of the programme is spent on making observations of the pain, particularly from a behavioural view point. During this initial period no treatment is carried out and the patients continue to receive analgesics as frequently and at the same dose as prior to admission. In this first week the patient is seen by the medical, nursing, psychology, occupational therapy and physiotherapy members of the team. Also during this week one of the ward nurses who has been trained in counselling techniques will see the patient to try to establish the need for any psychotherapeutic input. After the first week the staff meet to decide what therapeutic interventions will be used and the patient then has the programme explained again in detail with those particular strategies outlined. A degree of flexibility is allowed so that if they feel strongly, patients can decline certain interventions. If however (as sometimes happens) they argue about many suggested therapies it is pointed out that there is little point continuing until they are ready to try the programme and discharge is advised until that time. This situation usually occurs when the patient is still convinced that they really need only physical treatments. It does not matter if the patient still remains certain of a physical aetiology, providing they have accepted that there is no new physical intervention that will effect a cure. All that we can ask is for the patient to be reasonably motivated to try the therapeutic possibilities.

The interventions that are used to achieve the aims of the pain programme are shown below. Many of the interventions shown will be directed at more than one aim.

Rational use of analgesic drugs
Behavioural management of pain
Exercise
Physiotherapy

Relaxation, yoga and biofeedback
Hypnosis
Occupational therapy — specific and diversional
Cognitive therapy
Psychotherapy — individual, marital, family
Psychotropic drugs
Transcutaneous nerve stimulation (TNS)
Acupuncture

To allow these procedures a reasonable chance of success a lengthy period of therapy is required. The patients are told that they may need to stay in the programme for up to 12 weeks and occasionally even longer.

Use of analgesic drugs

Most patients at the time of entry to the programme are taking large quantities of strong analgesics, sometimes even on opiates for many years. They usually agree that the analgesics are not stopping their pain, but are very scared that the pain will worsen if they do not continue with them. It is usually agreed with the patient prior to admission that the use of analgesics will be reviewed whilst on the programme, and there will be a very serious attempt to get patients on to non-narcotic agents taken in the lowest dose possible. Analgesics are obviously reduced slowly, sometimes over several weeks.

When patients take analgesics they claim that this is an attempt to reduce their pain sensation (open reason). There are however a number of hidden reasons for continuation of drugs that patients may not be consciously aware of. These hidden reasons include the addictive nature of the drug, in that it may produce an affective response after consumption and also withdrawal symptoms if not taken. Another powerful hidden reason for taking pain killers are that they are a symbolisation of the pain to other people and also a legitimisation of the pain, particularly if they are prescribed by doctors. The message to the pain patient's family and friends is 'can you not see how much pain I must be in if I have to take so many of these tablets that my doctor has precribed'. Taking analgesics may therefore be an attempt by the patient to underline their being in the 'sick role' (Parsons 1957). These hidden reasons will reinforce the continued use of high dose analgesics in the future (Fig. 4.2).

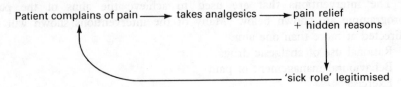

Fig. 4.2 Traditional analgesic use

In the pain programme there is an attempt to try to break this reinforcement not only by reducing the quantity, but also by giving the analgesics at set times, not when the patient complains of pain. Hopefully therefore the drugs are contingent on time and not in having or complaining of pain, thus reducing the pain behaviour (Fordyce 1974).

Behavioural management of pain

As with analgesic use there are other aspects of pain behaviour that may be open to modification through behavioural approaches (Fordyce et al 1985). One of the most important to concentrate on is the verbalisation of pain by the patient. Most chronic pain patients spend much of their time telling other people about their symptoms. The attention they receive from this will reinforce their 'complaining' behaviour and encourage them to continue with it. This continual discussion of their symptoms is the aspect that most families find hardest to tolerate. The patients, however, will continue to air their distress to reinforce their position as being sick and not being able to undertake certain responsibilities. If patients do continually talk about pain, it also keeps the pain foremost in their thoughts and never allows them the opportunity to try to forget or push the pain as far back into their minds as possible.

On the programme patients are told that everyone knows they have pain so there is no need to talk continuously about it. They are given one opportunity a week to meet with a doctor or nurse to discuss their pain in detail so that any changes or improvements can be related. At other times the staff ignore 'pain talk' as far as possible and will often walk away if a patient tries to engage them in it. If the patient wishes to talk of other, non-pain matters, then the staff actively listen and encourage, hoping that this will reinforce these more normal and socially acceptable verbal behaviours. All patients in the programme are given full occupational therapy activities to give them as little time as possible to talk about pain.

Other, non-verbal pain behaviour can be approached in the same way by inattention and reinforcement of normal non-pain behaviour. Groaning, sighing and body posturing may all need to be included. One of the most important to examine is resting because of pain. A number of patients have total or extensive bed rest prior to entry to the programme. When they complain of pain and are allowed to rest then there will again be reinforcement of pain. On the programme the patients are allowed rest at set times, not because of pain. If possible rest is given following a normal activity such as a period in occupational therapy or after exercise, hopefully the rest will then reinforce these normal behaviours and gradually to earn the rest the patient has to spend more time in such activity.

Exercise

Most chronic pain patients assume that their symptoms will prevent any exercise and have stopped doing any strenuous activity at all. It is important to show them that even though they are in pain, they can actually do much more than they believe. Patients are given gently graded exercise programmes so that they are not frightened by what seem to be unattainable goals. For the first week a bed-bound patient may be asked to walk only 5 yards, three or four times a day and then this is increased in small steps every few days. It is very important that when each exercise goal has been attained that the patient is given considerable praise from the staff and if possible their families and other patients. Staff should not convey to the patients an attitude of knowing they could do it because there was nothing the matter in the first place — this will only increase the patient's desire to show how bad they are by refusing to do more.

Physiotherapy

Many of the patients with musculoskeletal pain will have undergone previous physiotherapy without great success. Nevertheless it is worth considering more physiotherapy as part of the treatment package, particularly when it can be given on an individual basis by one physiotherapist who is part of the multidisciplinary team and who is aware of the great need to reinforce any small improvements made by the patient. As well as specific physiotherapy exercises for certain body parts, the physiotherapists can also advise on aspects such as bad posture and poor gait that have often developed over the years patients have been in pain.

Relaxation, yoga and biofeedback

Nearly all patients are encouraged to practise relaxation. This is carried out both in relaxation groups once a week and by providing a relaxation tape for patients to listen to on their own once or twice daily in their rooms. Many pains are increased by specific muscular tension around the painful part or by a generalised anxiety over the nature of the pain; if the patient can obtain a reasonable degree of muscular and then mental relaxation his pain sensation may decrease. Even if the sensation is not altered, a relaxed state of mind will undoubtedly reduce the affective aspect of the pain experience and make it easier to tolerate.

There are different approaches to relaxation and all may offer certain advantages. In the Leicester programme we were at one stage able to offer yoga through a therapist who was part of the OT department. Pain patients seem to benefit particularly from this, perhaps because it combines both relaxation with gradually increasing passive exercise. It may also have been popular because it was seen very much as a non-medical intervention which many chronic pain patients are keen on exploring.

Occasionally a specific pain may be associated with considerable localised muscular tension. In these cases biofeedback, designed to teach the patient to relax the particular muscle, may be of benefit.

Hypnosis

If a pain patient is both susceptible and agreeable then hypnosis may be a part of their programme, but it is not used for the majority. The hypnosis can be used for a variety of purposes. It is occasionally possible to suggest that the pain sensation is reduced or perhaps more successfully that the pain can be better tolerated and impose fewer restrictions on the patient. Under hypnosis the patient's cognitions of being a pain sufferer may be challenged to try to induce a more positive attitude to their abilities and their future. Sometimes under hypnosis possible antecedents or factors that maintain the pain behaviour can be uncovered, that can be later worked on in psychotherapy. Rarely the patient may have an abreactive experience under hypnosis and actually be considerably better when the procedure is ended. Our experience in Leicester that hypnosis does not often produce lasting responses may be due to our lack of experience with this intervention. Other workers do seem to seem to obtain better results (Finer 1974, Fadel 1984).

Occupational therapy

This forms an important part of the management of patients. Firstly there is often a need for specific OT activities to help in the rehabilitation to a non-pain life style. Sessions in the OT department are planned that will explore abilities to perform both previous and new work skills, eventually aiming to get some of the patients back into employment or into increasing work rehabilitation situations. Even if employment cannot be considered, the patients will often require OT guidance into resuming normal activities such as cooking, shopping, household activities or development of hobbies and useful leisure pursuits.

The second use of OT is to engage the patients whilst they are on the programme in as many diversional activities as possible when they are not undertaking any specific therapeutic interventions. This is aimed at trying to allow them to participate in normal activities rather than allowing them to continue pain behaviours when not in therapy. The more diverted the patients can be from thinking and acting in pain the better. Thus this form of OT is useful in keeping the pain as far back in the patient's mind as possible. It can be quite revealing to the patients themselves, when they have been active in the OT department doing something they enjoyed, to see how well they coped. They may have for a short period actually been unaware of their pain.

Cognitive therapy

Nearly all the patients think of themselves as being in chronic pain and have developed very negative cognitions about their situation and their abilities. It is possible that these cognitions can be challenged and shown not to be based in reality. If the patient thinks he is in pain and cannot perform an activity his behaviour is likely to correspond to his thoughts. A few patients seem to respond well to a cognitive approach when these thoughts are examined and alternative ones postulated. To change their thinking from 'I have chronic pain and therefore cannot walk' to 'I am in pain whatever I do and walking 10 yards will not make any difference' may help some patients considerably. This form of therapy however does not seem acceptable to most patients who are in the pain programme, their cognitions often seem too well entrenched for any real change until the pain has been altered in other ways first.

Other forms of cognitive approach are also occasionally useful (Jaremko 1978). These include distraction techniques, where the patient performs mental tasks when in pain to divert themselves from the sensation: use of fantasies that would be incongruous to the experience of pain and cognitively changing the labels they use for their sensation, avoiding the word pain. These techniques may be helpful in acute situations, but are perhaps of less value when the pain has been present for some time, although distraction techniques do seem to help a number of patients with chronic pain. For most of the chronic pain patients distraction in practice through activity is probably better than distraction in mind.

Psychotherapy

All the patients are offered sessions with one of the nurse counsellors on the ward. The nurse is encouraged to try to establish good rapport with the patient to enable the development of both a supportive and, if necessary, an exploratory role. During these sessions the patient may wish to talk about pain, but the therapist tries not to allow this to develop into just a recital of symptoms. The feeling that the pain produces and the meaning of the pain for the patient is discussed and explored. During the sessions the therapist also tries to look at possible dynamic factors that may be of relevance in understanding either the cause of the pain or the continuation of it. Unfortunately, although the patients might benefit from regular psychotherapy, many of them are very reluctant to be involved, often seeing it as an attempt to persuade them that the pain is all in the mind. This problem may be overcome by initially building the relationship through telling patients that if they have pain then they do not want other family, social or occupational stresses as well, and that discussing these areas in therapy may help relieve them of any extra burdens they have.

It is usually important to try to include spouses and family members in psychotherapy where possible. In nearly all chronic pain, the family play a large part in reinforcing the behaviour one way or another and they will need considerable guidance and support in helping them break these patterns. They will need to be told and preferably observe how the patients are not treated as permanent invalids by the hospital team. They will then be shown how they can adopt similar, but nevertheless caring, responses to the patient that do not allow him to slip back into chronic pain behaviours.

In family sessions the dynamics behind pain may also be explored and worked upon. The relatives themselves may need to be supported with their own feelings. They will often have been living with the pain for many years and their attitudes and feelings to the patient may be both negative and hardened. It is essential that their problems and grievances are listened to, and opportunities given for them to have some therapy time. It needs to be explained to them that the benefits that accrue from the programme should be of advantage to them as well as to the patient.

Psychotropic drugs

If the pain is associated with a significant degree of depression then an antidepressant is worth considering. Unless depression is the primary cause of the pain (see above) it is unlikely that the pain sensation will be completely removed; nevertheless once depression is added to the pain it makes it a much greater stress and antidepressants may well change an unbearable pain to a bearable one. The antidepressants, particularly tricyclics, do seem to have specific analgesic effects as well as their anti-depressant action (Feinmann 1985). The analgesic effect of tricyclics can sometimes be increased by the addition of a small dose of a phenothiazine (Kocher 1976, Merskey & Hester 1972). Very occasionally if tricyclics have not helped a monoamine oxidase inhibitor may be considered.

If there is considerable secondary anxiety to the pain, it is probably best to avoid the use of benzodiazepines because of the risk of dependence. If non-pharmacological methods of anxiety reduction are not sufficient and tranquillisers must be used then a phenothiazine is probably preferable.

Transcutaneous nerve stimulation and acupuncture

There is not sufficient space to give a detailed account of the theory or practice of these two therapeutic interventions. There are good reviews to be found elsewhere (Elton et al 1983, Vincent & Richardson 1986). It is possible that both procedures may reduce pain by increasing endorphin levels in the brain and TNS may also play its part by closing the postulated pain gate in the dorsal horn of the spinal cord (Elton et al 1983). Whatever their actions they both seem to have great value in a pain programme and chronic pain patients often derive considerable benefit. It is possible that some of this may be a placebo effect as patients often place great faith in these interventions. Patients on the pain programme are offered TNS once or twice daily for 30–60 minute periods. If they find they have much relief then some are allowed to keep the TNS going for considerable periods of time, even whilst carrying out other procedures such as exercise, physiotherapy or OT. They are also allowed to borrow a machine to continue the TNS at home whilst on leave or after discharge. If TNS is to be used it is important to move the electrodes around as sometimes better relief is obtained from different sitings.

Acupuncture is carried out once or twice a week during the programme. Many of the patients have tried acupuncture before with no relief. It is worth trying it again whilst on the pain programme as benefit is possible when it is combined with the rest of the treatment package. If the acupuncture is felt by the patient to have been an important aspect in improvement in pain then it can be carried out at less frequent intervals after discharge.

OUTCOME OF PAIN PROGRAMMES

Most of the patients who leave the Leicester pain programme still complain of their symptoms. However, a number of them seem to bear the pain better and are less restricted by it following their weeks of therapy. Unfortunately, it is not unusual for good results in the hospital situation to lessen when the patient leaves the programme. This is presumably due to the patient and perhaps their families slipping back into previous patterns of reinforcing pain behaviour. It is necessary to remember however that one is dealing with chronic patients who may have been in pain for many years. To enable a small percentage of these patients to gain improvement is both rewarding and probably cost effective as they use considerable amounts of medical time and money if not helped.

Case 4
Mrs I.D., a 42-year-old housewife had a 6-year history of abdominal and pelvic pain that occurred intermittently but quite frequently. She had been investigated by physicians, who had found that she was suffering from minor diverticular disease, but they did not feel this was sufficient to cause the severity of her symptoms. Prior to admission to the pain programme she had been bed-bound for 9 months and her general practitioner was visiting about three times each week to administer injectable opiates.

On admission to the pain programme she was encouraged to spend time out of bed and to start taking exercise, although this had to be started very gradually. She was given regular relaxation sessions and also used a TNS machine twice daily. After the first 4 weeks she was able to spend increasing periods in the occupational therapy department with diversional activities. She attended yoga sessions which she found of great help.

During the first week of her admission she was seen by one of the nurse therapists and considerable problems in the marital relationship were uncovered. It was decided that the nurse therapist should see the patient and her husband together.

They were seen for three sessions attempting to help them explore their relationship and in particular the role the husband took in dealing with his wife's pain. He treated his wife mainly as an invalid and took over most of her responsibilities while becoming extremely angry at her apparent inability to perform her normal duties The therapist also attempted to help them explore the long-standing problems there had been in the marital relationship. These particularly seemed to affect the perceptions they each had of various responsibilities within the marriage. There were also major sexual problems, but the couple did not wish to discuss these at all.

During the three sessions with the therapist it became apparent that whereas the wife was quite happy to discuss differences the husband clammed up and refused to talk about anything other than how to deal with his wife's pain. Although they were able to make some changes in how to deal with the pain both the patient and her husband remained firmly convinced that the pain was due to an underlying physical problem that had not been detected and little headway could be made in their long-standing relationship difficulties.

This patient stayed on the pain programme for 12 weeks and at discharge she was walking and did not require prolonged bed rest though she still enjoyed a nap midday for an hour. On returning home she started cooking and some of the cleaning activities which she had not carried out for some months previously. She and her husband started to socialise and as her pain behaviour diminished their marital relationship improved, although there were still some difficulties. On review 6 months after discharge she felt her pain was considerably less, though still present, but her restriction of the pain and her ability to cope with it were markedly improved.

PROBLEMS OF A PAIN PROGRAMME

A whole chapter itself could be devoted to the problems associated with managing chronic pain programmes. The programme looks very straight-forward when written down, but in practice it is far from simple and the pain patients produce more difficulties for the Liaison Psychiatry Department at Leicester than any other referrals. The patients are often very antimedical from experiences they have had in the past and even more antipsychiatric. Unfortunately, the programme has to be carried out on a psychiatric ward as there are no other beds available and this may not go down well with the patients or their families for obvious reasons. The treatment needs to be multidisciplinary, but with the current difficulties in the NHS it is becoming increasingly hard to find psychologists, physiothera-pists and occupational therapists with time to devote to such demanding patients and lengthy therapy. It can even be difficult to get sufficient nursing staff.

Finally, if anyone is considering establishing a similar service they need to be wary of the potentially litiginous patient. A few pain patients have created major problems by making serious complaints about the nature of the treatment which they claim was either not explained and/or has made them worse. It is for this reason that much time must be devoted to explaining the programme and making a verbal contract with the patient.

The patient who is referred and who complains about every treatment they have received in the past, saying they are worse because of treatments, should probably not be taken on for further therapy which is likely to produce a similar response.

CONCLUSIONS

Any psychiatrist who professes an interest in the management of pain is likely to receive a number of referrals from the general hospital of patients with chronic pain. If he is going to offer any effective interventions with this very difficult group he will need to be able to call upon a variety of different diagnostic and therapeutic skills in either himself or his para-psychiatric colleagues. He will also need to accept that there is more than the pure sensory component and much of his effort should be directed to the other aspects of the experience of chronic pain.

REFERENCES

Budd K 1979 The concept of chronic pain relief. Health Trends 11: 69–71
Chapman C R 1976 Measurement of pain: problems and issues. Advances in Pain Research and Therapy 1: 345–353
Elton D, Stanley G, Burrows G 1983 Psychological control of pain. Grune and Stratton, Australia
Engel G L 1959 Psychogenic pain and the pain prone patient. American Journal of Medicine 26: 899–918
Fadel K 1984 Psychogenic pain — the role of hypnosis. Psychiatry in Practice 2: 27–30
Feinmann C 1985 Pain relief by antidepressants. Pain 23: 1–8
Finer B 1974 Clinical use of hypnosis in pain management. Advances in Neurology 4. Raven Press, New York, pp 573–579
Fordyce W E 1974 Treating chronic pain by contingency management. Advances in Neurology 4. Raven Press, New York: pp. 583–589
Fordyce W E, Roberts A H, Sternbach R A 1985 The behavioural management of chronic pain: a response to critics. Pain 22: 113–125
Huskisson E C 1974 Measurement of pain. Lancet: 1127–1131
Jaremko M E 1978 Cognitive strategies in the control of pain tolerance. Behavioural Therapy and Experimental Psychiatry 9: 239–244
Katon W, Egan K, Miller D 1985 Chronic pain: life time psychiatric diagnosis and family history. American Journal of Psychiatry 142: 1156–1160
Kocher R 1976 The use of psychotropic drugs in the treatment of chronic, severe pains. European Neurology 14: 458–464
Leavitt F 1985 The value of the MMPI conversion V in the assessment of psychogenic pain. Journal of Psychosomatic Research 29: 125–131
Melzack R 1973 The puzzle of pain. Penguin, Harmondsworth, Middlesex
Melzack R 1975 The McGill Pain Questionnaire: major properties and scoring methods. Pain 1: 277–299
Melzack R (ed) 1983 Pain measurement and assessment. Raven Press, New York
Merskey H, Hester R A 1972 The treatment of chronic pain with psychotropic drugs. Post Graduate Medical Journal 48: 594–598
Merskey H, Spear F 1967 Psychological and psychiatric aspects of pain. Tindall and Cassell, London
Miles J 1983 Neurological advances in the relief of pain. British Journal of Hospital Medicine 11: 348–353
Parsons C M 1957 The social system. Free Press, New York

Slater E 1965 Diagnosis of hysteria. British Medical Journal 1: 1395–1399

Sternback R A 1970 Strategies and tactics in the treatment of patients with pain. In: Grune B L (ed) Pain and suffering: selected aspects. C. C. Thomas, Springfield, Illinois

Sternbach R A 1973 Traits of pain patients: the low back loser. Psychosomatics 14: 226–229

Sternbach R A, Murphy R W, Timmermans G, Greenhoot J H, Akeson W H 1974 Measuring the severity of clinical pain. Advances in Neurology 4:

Thomas C J 1983 Referrals to a British liaison service. Health Trends 15: 61–64

Vincent C A, Richardson P H 1986 The evaluation of therapeutic acupuncture: concepts and methods. Pain 24: 1–13

Wall P D, Melzack R 1984 Textbook of pain. Churchill Livingstone, Edinburgh

Watson G D, Chandarana P C, Merskey H 1981 Relationships between pain and schizophrenia. British Journal of Psychiatry 138: 33–36

Wolff B B 1977 The role of laboratory pain induction methods in the systematic study of human pain. Acupuncture and Electro Therapy Research International Journal 2: 271–305

Woodford J M, Merskey H 1972 Personality traits of patients with chronic pain. Journal of Psychosomatic Research 16: 167–172

5
Andrew Steptoe

Relaxation and stress management techniques for the treatment of hypertension

INTRODUCTION

Hypertension is a serious and widespread problem. Data from the 1976–80 National Health and Nutrition Examination Survey in the USA found that 32.6% of white and 37.9% of black males aged 18–74 years had blood pressure (BP) above 140/90 mmHg, with 25.3% and 38.6% being the corresponding figures for women (Roccella 1985). Although the majority of these people have BP in the mild hypertensive range (diastolic BP 90–104 mmHg), it is clear that elevated BP is ubiquitous. Substantial levels of hypertension have also been found in the United Kingdom, with large regional variations in prevalence (Shaper et al 1981). The prevention and control of hypertension represent major problems for medicine in the present day.

Physicians differ among themselves in the way in which they manage hypertension. Two areas of disagreement are what level of BP warrants treatment, and what form the treatment should take. When BP elevations are moderate to severe, with sustained diastolic BP of 110 mmHg or above, there is little argument that pharmacological treatment should be initiated promptly. Pharmacotherapy takes a number of forms, including β-adrenoceptor blockade, diuretics, vasodilators, centrally acting drugs such as methyl dopa, α-adrenoceptor blockers, angiotensin-converting enzyme inhibitors and calcium antagonists. More difficulties arise in the management of mild hypertension. These have been reinforced by the Medical Research Council trial of treatment of mild hypertension (1985) which found no differences in the incidence of coronary heart disease between drug and placebo groups over the 5-year prospective period. Stroke incidence was reduced, but it was estimated that 850 persons would need to be treated to prevent one stroke per year. Moreover, pharmacological treatment is not without adverse effects, including deterioration in mood, cognitive performance, sexual function and other indices of health and well-being in some patients (Rosen & Kostis 1985, Croog et al 1986). Recent international guidelines for the treatment of mild hypertension suggest that diastolic BP sustained over 100 mmHg should be treated pharmacologically, but pressures in the range 90–100 mmHg should be managed with behavioural methods (Strasser 1986).

A number of behavioural interventions have been studied for hypertension, including salt restriction, weight reduction, and to a lesser extent reduction of alcohol intake. These methods have recently been reviewed by Johnston (1987). Techniques based on relaxation and stress management can also be extremely beneficial. They have been subjected to well controlled clinical trials in several research centres, and considerable evidence for their effectiveness is now available. Given the enormous numbers of hypertensives in the western world, it can be argued that every effort should be made to manage the problem with behavioural methods, rather than initiate chronic pharmacotherapy in millions of people. This chapter outlines the relaxation and stress management techniques that have proven useful for hypertension, and the way in which they might be integrated into existing therapeutic practice. Before this, however, the involvement of psychological factors in the development of hypertension should be considered.

PSYCHOLOGICAL FACTORS IN HYPERTENSION

There is a large literature concerning the role of psychological factors in the aetiology and maintenance of hypertension, and only a brief summary will be given here (see Steptoe (1981, 1986) for fuller reviews). Interest in psychological aspects stemmed from the psychosomatic movement in the middle of the century, and progressed into the examination of personality factors in hypertension. In general, this approach has not been fruitful, since no special personality characteristics have consistently been identified in hypertensive patients. Many studies suffer from methodological defects such as confining assessments to patients identified through conventional medical channels. It has been found with screening studies that hypertensives who are known to the medical services are not representative of the hypertensive population at large, since they tend to have higher neuroticism, depression and symptom scores than the remainder (Cochrane 1973, Berglund et al 1975, Goldberg et al 1980). Whether these features predispose people to seek help, or arise as a result of labelling and treatment of hypertension, remains uncertain (Monk 1981). It is clear however that this pattern makes it difficult to draw firm conclusions about the role of psychological processes from studies of known, diagnosed hypertensives.

A more useful approach has been to consider BP responses to different forms of psychological stress and environmental stimulation. In the laboratory, it is well established that pressor responses occur to a variety of stimuli, including mentally demanding tasks and interviews of a personal nature (Krantz & Manuck 1984). Hypertensives show greater BP and heart rate responses than normotensives, particularly when confronted with situations that challenge the individual to cope actively with the environment

(Steptoe et al 1984). The haemodynamic changes underlying these acute responses parallel the patterns observed early in the disease process itself, with increases in levels of circulating catecholamines and raised cardiac output (Goldstein 1983). The general hypothesis to emerge is that autonomically mediated responses to psychosocial challenges may initiate the progression towards sustained hypertension in susceptible individuals. Studies with animal models and investigations of normotensives at genetic risk for hypertension are consistent with this notion.

Additional data support this perspective from an epidemiological standpoint, in showing relationships between BP, psychological coping responses and the external environment. For example, Harburg et al (1979) suggested that particular styles of coping with emotion under stressful conditions were associated with high BP. People living in stressful urban environments who responded to provocative situations resentfully, feeling anger or frustration without expressing it, had the highest incidence of hypertension. More recently, Cottington et al (1986) showed that job stress variables were related to prevalence of hypertension in white-collar factory workers, but only in the presence of suppressed anger. The effect persisted after controlling for body mass, smoking, alcohol, age and family history. Similar interactions between environmental stress, low expression of emotion and BP have been reported elsewhere (Gentry 1985, Julius et al 1986).

RATIONALE FOR STRESS MANAGEMENT

The data relating psychological factors with hypertension provide a rationale for using relaxation and other stress-coping skills in treatment. Blood pressure is sensitive to environmental stimulation and the way in which people cope with it. If exaggerated cardiovascular reaction patterns are repeatedly elicited in the patient's ordinary life, they may lead to a sustained elevation of autonomic and neuro-endocrine activity, which may in turn promote hypertension. The replacement of these inappropriate responses with relaxation and other positive coping skills may reverse this state of affairs, leading to better control of BP and the promotion of health.

Although this rationale underlies the use of stress management in hypertension, direct evidence concerning the mechanisms involved is sparse (Johnston 1986). A number of investigators have failed to show alterations in catecholamine or pressor responses to experimental stressors following therapy, despite positive effects on tonic BP level (Jacob & Chesney 1986). This suggests that other components of therapy, such as the acquisition of cognitive coping skills or changes in habitual behaviour, may be as significant as modifications in autonomic function *per se*.

An additional comment on the rationale for stress management is also in order. Despite the postulated relationship between pressor responses and environmental stress, it has not been found necessary to select patients for treatment on the basis of inadequate emotional coping skills or the experience of a stressful life style. It has been shown that BP responses to behavioural stimulation do not necessarily coincide with feelings of distress or negative affect, but may on the contrary occur when people are excited or exhilarated. Thus patients may be offered this treatment even if they do not show overt signs of behavioural stress.

More than 20 controlled trials have been published concerning the use of relaxation and stress management in hypertension (Johnston 1987). Relaxation and meditation, sometimes in combination with biofeedback, have produced greater BP reductions than attention/placebo conditions that control for non-specific effects (Bali 1979, Irvine et al 1986). Reductions in BP have been recorded not only in the clinic but at the worksite (Chesney et al 1987), and in ambulatory measures taken over the working day (Agras et al 1983). Follow-up studies have shown lower BP is maintained as long as 4 years after treatment (Patel et al 1985). Systematic evidence is not yet available demonstrating that these effects lead to reduced coronary morbidity, although suggestive results have been presented (Patel et al 1981, 1985).

ASSESSMENT OF PATIENTS WITH HYPERTENSION

The first problem with assessing patients for therapy is to establish their average BP, and how it varies with events and activities in their everyday lives. Systolic and diastolic BP may vary considerably over a normal day, typically with fluctuations of more than 50% within individuals. One of the commonest situations in which BP is high is when recordings are made by doctors. Floras et al (1981) showed that 54% of a series of untreated hypertensives produced diastolic BP that was 10 mmHg or more higher when measured by the doctor than when recorded automatically over a working day. This effect is not due to the discomfort or unfamiliarity of the measurement itself, but seems to result from the psychological stress of the situation (Mancia et al 1983, Parati et al 1985).

It follows that when patients are referred for behavioural treatment, it is sometimes uncertain what their tonic BP really is. Repeated measurements in a quiet, reassuring setting are helpful, as is self-monitoring on the part of patients. Self-monitoring of BP is now recommended by many authorities as a means of establishing genuine levels (Kleinert et al 1984), and there is evidence to suggest that such measures predict the complications of hypertension more accurately than do clinic values (Perloff et al 1983). It sometimes happens that after self-monitoring, the patient cannot even be classified as hypertensive any more. This pattern is particularly noticeable when people have previously had their BP measured under threatening conditions, for example in a health check at work where hypertension might mean loss of a job.

A 29-year-old woman (V.M.) was referred by her general practitioner with mild hypertension. It was suggested that behavioural treatment might be appropriate in order to avoid the need for chronic antihypertensive medication in such a young person. However, detailed evaluation indicated that the problem was artefactual. Eight months earlier, she had had her BP measured routinely at the family planning clinic. The physician had mentioned that her BP was a little high, and that if it stayed at this level she would have to stop taking the contraceptive pill. V.M was worried about this, since she did not find other forms of contraception acceptable. She went to her next family planning clinic in a state of some anxiety, and her BP was recorded as 160/95 mmHg. The clinic referred V.M. to her general practitioner, and when she visited her doctor 2 weeks later her BP remained above 150/90 mmHg.

The author measured V.M.'s BP after a quiet discussion of 30 minutes in which the nature of hypertension and possible non-pharmacological treatments were outlined. Readings of 125/70 mmHg were obtained, indicating a considerable discrepancy from the clinic values. V.M. was therefore taught to measure her own BP and was loaned a sphygmomanometer for 2 weeks. She was given a 'diary' in which to record BP values taken between 8.00 and 9.00 a.m. and 6.00 and 7.00 p.m. each day. When she returned a fortnight later, her BP was again low, and the values in the diary never exceeded 135/80 mmHg. She was therefore referred back to her general practitioner with a note suggesting that her hypertensive problem had probably arisen from anxiety about threats to her contraception practices, and that repeated measurements had failed to show sustained hypertension.

Patients can readily be trained to monitor their own BP with a sphygmomanometer and cuff, or with an inexpensive electronic sphygmomanometer. Care must be taken to ensure that readings are made under stable conditions, to avoid fluctuations due to recent physical exertion and other factors. Blood pressure can conveniently be measured in the morning and evening, but in developing behavioural techniques it is helpful to have readings from the day as well. Values should be registered on a daily diary sheet by the patient. In addition, it is useful to include an indication of what activities have preceded the BP reading, together with rating of stress and mood. Such information is valuable in the orientation phase of treatment described below. It is recommended that patients are asked to monitor their BP for several weeks before treatment, so that a stable pattern can be established.

The other issue that needs to be resolved in the assessment phase is whether the patient is suitable for relaxation and stress management. It is assumed that patients will have been investigated medically to ensure that hypertension is primary or 'essential' rather than secondary to some disorder such as phaeochromocytoma. The effectiveness of psychological therapies in patients with concomitant psychiatric disturbances is unknown. Cottier et al (1984) found that the hypertensives who responded best to progressive muscle relaxation had higher sympathetic nervous tone and anxiety ratings, but other research groups have failed to identify specific psychological or neurohumoral predictors. However, one important aspect of suitability concerns a patient's view of his or her own disorder, and willingness to be involved actively with treatment. Psychological approaches involve commitment and practice on the part of the patients, so are unlikely to be effective in people who take a passive view, wanting their health to be improved by the doctor with no personal effort. Of course, the patient's orientation may be altered when the rationale for treatment is presented, but informal assessment of this aspect is important if later attrition from treatment is to be avoided. One test of patients' interest in this approach is whether or not they carry out BP self-monitoring reliably. If a patient fails to measure BP in a satisfactory way before treatment, it is unlikely that he or she will practise the stress management exercises either.

A 54-year-old-man (M.T.) with well documented hypertension was referred for behavioural treatment since he had found a number of antihypertensive medications unsatisfactory because of adverse side effects. On interview, M.T. was unenthusiastic about the stress management approach. He accepted that behavioural and emotional factors might be relevant in some cases, but not in his own. He was convinced that his problem was physical and should be treated physically. He was prepared to go ahead because his physician had advised it, but was not enthusiastic. He was given three sessions of relaxation training at weekly intervals, but failed to practise the exercises between sessions — he claimed that he had no time. He continually requested that something 'real' should be done for him. After 3 weeks, M.T. made excuses for failing to keep an appointment, and subsequently the treatment was discontinued.

ORIENTATION TO STRESS MANAGEMENT

The next phase of treatment involves orientating patients towards the stress management approach. Prior to their referral, patients will generally have considered their BP to be an automatic function that is outside their control. Orientation involves showing the patient that BP is responsive to their acts and emotions, that they can control this pattern, and that it can be harnessed therapeutically to improve their clinical condition. The rationale for stress management must be presented, and this often involves educating patients in the role of the brain in regulating high BP. Extracts from educational films about stress or diagrammatic booklets can be helpful in this context.

The strong influence that emotion and behaviour have over BP can be brought home very strikingly by measuring BP during simple stress tests such as mental arithmetic. Hypertensives generally show large pressor responses in this situation, with immediate increases of more than 20 mmHg. In addition, BP diaries can be used to illustrate the relationship between fluctuations in BP and events or feelings during everyday life. It is possible to scan the diaries to discover instances where unusually high or low BP were associated with particular activities. The identification of such patterns is also helpful in discovering what types of event tend to raise the BP of the patient, since the cognitive management of such situations may be important in therapy.

THE ACQUISITION OF COPING SKILLS

The training phase of stress management will commence after the collection of adequate baselines and orientation of patients. Training may be carried out in groups as well as individually, since relatively standardised techniques have proved successful. Medicated subjects should be discouraged from making any alterations in antihypertensive regimes in the early stages of training, so as not to confuse the pattern of response.

It is difficult to make any general recommendations based on systematic data concerning which stress management technique should be used, as few comparative studies have been conducted. Different aspects of training may need to be emphasised for different patients. However, the most useful strategy is probably to teach patients to relax in the clinic, and then to train them to use relaxation as a coping skill when confronted with stressors in their everyday life. As far as relaxation is concerned, abbreviated versions of progressive muscle relaxation carried out over six to ten sessions of 30–60 minutes have produced reliable decreases in BP in several experiments (Southam et al 1982, Agras et al 1987). Very positive effects have also been generated with the technique developed by Patel (Patel et al 1981, Irvine et al 1986). This involves eight 1-hour sessions in which passive relaxation instructions are given in conjunction with meditative imagery and a 'mantra' or calming word. This is accompanied by auditory biofeedback of sweat gland activity which provides an index of autonomic arousal and degree of relaxation. Two vignettes illustrate the progress of these therapies.

It was decided when training a 56-year-old man (H.A.) in relaxation to use an adaptation of the progressive relaxation training method (Bernstein & Borkovec 1973). During the first session, H.A. was trained to relax 16 major muscle groups in turn, starting with the right hand and forearm, going through the entire body and neck and ending with the left foot. Tension–relaxation cycles were used, so each muscle group was tensed for a few seconds followed by relaxation. The aim of this procedure was to help H.A. discriminate states of tension from relaxation, and to acquire greater control over his muscles. The procedure was carried out twice during the session, and the session ended with a period of quiet relaxation. In Session 2, the procedure was repeated, this time more rapidly, and subsequently the body was divided into four larger muscle groups (muscles of the left and right arms, muscles of the face and neck, muscles of the chest, shoulders and back, and finally muscles of the legs and feet). After four sessions, whole-body relaxation was practised, and peaceful mental imagery was incorporated.

A 52-year-old male patient, C.R., began in the same fashion as H.A., but found the relaxation phase of each tension–relaxation cycle difficult to achieve. It was decided that brief voluntary tensing might be having an adverse effect, so training was switched to passive relaxation, in which different parts of the body were relaxed in turn without any tensing. At the same time, attention was paid to maintaining a steady pattern of breathing. In both cases, the patients were encouraged to become aware of tension in their bodies, 'monitoring' their limbs, torso, neck and head for minute signs of muscle contraction which were then to be 'smoothed away' with relaxation.

In trying to identify the procedures that appear most effective a number of factors emerge that seem important. The first is that the training procedures should not be too complicated, with attempts to engender change in several different areas (such as physical tension, social competence and the control of emotion) at once. Studies that have combined diverse 'effective' elements from a number of previous investigations have sometimes led to confusion among patients about what is required of them. Secondly, patients must be encouraged to practise relaxation or stress-coping skills at home, as well as attend training sessions in the clinic. Thirdly, explicit efforts must be made to transfer effects into everyday situations. Methods of achieving this generalisation are discussed below.

THE GENERALISATION OF COPING SKILLS

Effective behavioural treatment of hypertension involves teaching patients to use the skills they have learned in therapy in their everyday lives. Studies in which supposedly beneficial relaxation training has been confined to clinic sessions have not been successful in generating lasting BP responses. Generalisation can be achieved through encouraging home practice, and through discussion of situations in which patients should mobilise their stress-coping skills. A major element in therapy is helping patients identify sources of stress in their lives, and sensations of bodily tension. These can then serve as cues for brief relaxation, or attempts to reappraise a situation cognitively.

A hypertensive office worker, G.H., stated that she frequently felt stressed when given an additional piece of work late in the day by her supervisor. Although she usually accepted this without objection, she felt resentful and 'put upon', and conflicted about whether or not to stay late in order to complete the job. She had been trained to recognise the sensations of stress and to counter them by a short period of relaxation. She was therefore advised to go through a regular brief episode of relaxation late in the working day which would prepare her to cope with the supervisor's action. She was also encouraged to think about the situation differently, to recall that the supervisor was not being malicious in presenting work late in the day but was simply following routine, to remember that the same thing happened to her colleagues, so she was not being picked on, and to recognise that the world will not end if the job was not finished that day. These strategies proved successful, and this stressful period of the day (often anticipated uncomfortably for many hours), became less aversive. An alternative approach would have been to discuss different responses that G.H. might make in the situation, so that instead of passively accepting the extra work, she would tell her supervisor politely but firmly that the task was impossible to finish within the time allotted and would have to wait until the morning. It would have been possible to take G.H. through the scenario of the conversation with role-play and modelling, so that she felt confident about the responses she might make. However, this method was not thought appropriate in the present case, since it was apparent that the supervisor was not being vindictive but was following conventional procedures, and that a confrontation would not have been productive.

Some standard cues can also be used for relaxation. Patel (1981) advises placing red stickers on the patient's watch and telephone, and using the red traffic light as a signal for the person to carry out the brief survey of his or her body, becoming aware of tension and then relaxing if necessary. Other investigations have combined relaxation with cognitive stress management more formally, with training in coping using rehearsal, modelling and homework assignments (Crowther 1983).

It is important to monitor the progress of therapy with regular BP recordings both in the clinic and during everyday life. Clinic recordings are best taken at the beginning of sessions before training is conducted, otherwise the BP levels may reflect acute responses to the therapy rather than long-term effects. No definite schedule of medication reduction in patients who react well to treatment can be given, since this varies with the regime and the individual concerned.

INTEGRATION INTO CONVENTIONAL TREATMENT

If behavioural techniques are to make a lasting impact on the prevention and treatment of hypertension, they must be integrated into the routine care of patients. Relaxation and stress management should not be presented in opposition to drug treatment, challenging the conventional basis of therapeutics. Rather, they should be seen as supplementary to existing techniques. They are particularly relevant to two groups of hypertensives.

Patients who are newly identified as hypertensive but whose BP is severely elevated are in need of rapidly effective treatment. Behavioural methods often take longer to work than drugs, so will not be favoured under these circumstances. In patients with mild to moderate hypertension, immediate treatment responses are less essential, so relaxation and stress management can be considered as a first step, in conjunction with other behavioural techniques designed to modify diet, alcohol intake and exercise patterns. If these are effective, they may allow the patient to avoid the need for chronic antihypertensive medication.

The second group of hypertensives who may benefit are those already treated pharmacologically, who tolerate drugs poorly or whose BP is not well controlled, and who wish to have greater influence over their own health. In comparison with 20 years ago, lower and lower BP levels are being considered suitable for treatment. This means that large numbers of patients aged 30–50 years face a future of chronic medication. Any help that the medical profession can give such individuals so that they are able to treat their own problem must be welcomed as a positive development in health care. The use of relaxation and stress management in conjunction with advice on other aspects of behavioural change is a positive step towards this goal.

REFERENCES

Agras W S, Southam M A, Taylor C B 1983 Long-term persistence of relaxation-induced blood pressure lowering during the working day. Behavior Therapy 15: 792–794

Agras W S, Taylor C B, Kraemer H C, Southam M A, Schneider J A 1987 Relaxation training for essential hypertension at the worksite. II: The poorly-controlled hypertensive. Psychosomatic Medicine 49: 264–273

Bali L R 1979 Long-term effect of relaxation on blood pressure and anxiety levels in essential hypertensive males: a controlled study. Psychosomatic Medicine 41: 637–646

Berglund G, Ander S, Lindstrom B, Tibblin G 1975 Personality and reporting of symptoms in normotensive and hypertensive 50-year-old males. Journal of Psychosomatic Research 19: 139–145

Bernstein D A, Borkovec T D 1973 Progressive relaxation training: a manual for the helping professions. Research Press, Champaign, Illinois

Chesney M A, Black G W, Swan G E, Ward M M 1987 Relaxation training for essential hypertension at the worksite. I: The untreated hypertensive. Psychosomatic Medicine 49: 250–263

Cochrane R 1973 Hostility and neuroticism among unselected essential hypertensives. Journal of Psychosomatic Research 17: 215–218

Cottier C, Shapiro K, Julius S 1984 Treatment of mild hypertension with progressive muscular relaxation: predictive value of indexes of sympathetic tone. Archives of Internal Medicine 144: 1954–1958

Cottington E M, Matthews K A, Talbott E, Kuller L H 1986 Occupational stress, suppressed anger, and hypertension. Psychosomatic Medicine 48: 249–260

Croog S H, Levine S, Testa M A et al 1986 The effects of antihypertensive therapy on the quality of life. New England Journal of Medicine 314: 1657–1664

Crowther J H 1983 Stress management training and relaxation imagery in the treatment of essential hypertension. Journal of Behavioral Medicine 6: 169–187

Floras J S, Jones J V, Hassan M O, Osikowska B, Sever B S, Sleight P 1981 Cuff and ambulatory blood pressure in subjects with essential hypertension. Lancet 2: 107–109

Gentry W D 1985 Relationship of anger-coping styles and blood pressure among black Americans. In: Chesney M A, Rosenman R (eds) Anger and hostility in cardiovascular and behavioral disorders. Hemisphere, Washington

Goldberg E L, Comstock G W, Graves C G 1980 Psychosocial factors and blood pressure. Psychological Medicine 10: 243–255

Goldstein D S 1983 Plasma catecholamines and essential hypertension. An analytical review. Hypertension 5: 86–89

Harburg E, Blakelock E H, Roper P J 1979 Resentful and reflective coping with arbitrary authority and blood pressure: Detroit. Psychosomatic Medicine 41: 189–202

Irvine M J, Johnston D W, Jenner D A, Marie G V 1986 Relaxation and stress management in the treatment of essential hypertension. Journal of Psychosomatic Research 30: 437–450

Jacob R G, Chesney M A 1986 Psychological and behavioral methods to reduce cardiovascular reactivity. In: Matthews K A, Weiss S M, Detre T et al (eds) Handbook of stress, reactivity and cardiovascular disease. Wiley, New York

Johnston D W 1986 How does relaxation training reduce blood pressure in primary hypertension? In: Dembroski T M, Schmidt T H, Blumchen C (eds) Biobehavioral factors in coronary heart disease. Karger, Basel

Johnston D W 1987 The behavioral control of high blood pressure. Current Psychological Research and Reviews 6: 99–114

Julius N, Harburg E, Cottington E N, Johnson E H 1986 Anger-coping types, blood

pressure, and all-cause mortality: a follow-up in Tecumseh, Michigan (1971–1983).
American Journal of Epidemiology 124: 220–233

Kleinert H D, Harshfield G A, Pickering T G et al 1984 What is the value of home blood
pressure measurement in patients with mild hypertension? Hypertension 6: 574–578

Krantz D S, Manuck S B 1984 Acute psychophysiologic reactivity and risk of
cardiovascular disease: a review and critique. Psychological Bulletin 96: 435–464

Mancia G, Bertinieri G, Grassi G et al 1983 Effects of blood pressure measurement by the
doctor on patient's blood pressure and heart rate. Lancet 2: 695–698

Medical Research Council Working Party 1985 MRC trial of treatment of mild
hypertension: principal results. British Medical Journal 291: 97–104

Monk M 1981 Blood pressure awareness and psychological well-being in the Health
Nutrition Examination Survey. Clinical and Investigative Medicine 4: 183–190

Parati G, Pomidossi G, Casadei R, Mancia G 1985 Lack of alerting reactions to intermittent
cuff inflations during non-invasive blood pressure monitoring. Hypertension 7: 597–601

Patel C, Marmot M G, Terry D J 1981 Controlled trial of biofeedback-aided behavioural
methods in reducing mild hypertension. British Medical Journal 282: 2005–2008

Patel C, Marmot M G, Terry D J, Carruthers M, Hunt B, Patel M 1985 Trial of relaxation
in reducing coronary risk: four-year follow-up. British Medical Journal 290: 1103–1106

Perloff D, Sokolow M, Cowan R 1983 The prognostic value of ambulatory blood pressures.
Journal of the American Medical Association 249: 2792–2798

Roccella E J 1985 Hypertension prevalence and the status of awareness, treatment, and
control in the US. Hypertension 7: 457–468

Rosen R C, Kostis J B 1985 Biobehavioral sequelae associated with adrenergic-inhibiting
antihypertensive agents: a critical review. Health Psychology 4: 579–604

Shaper A G, Pocock S J, Walker M, Cohen N N, Wale C J, Thompson A G 1981 British
Regional Heart Study. Cardiovascular risk factors in middle-aged men in 24 towns.
British Medical Journal 283: 179–186

Southam M A, Agras W S, Taylor C B, Kraemer H C 1982 Relaxation training: blood
pressure during the working day. Archives of General Psychiatry 39: 7I5–717

Steptoe A 1981 Psychological factors in cardiovascular disorders. Academic Press, London

Steptoe A 1986 Psychophysiological contributions to the understanding and management of
essential hypertension. In: Christie M J, Mellett P G (eds) The psychosomatic approach:
contemporary practice of whole-person care. Wiley, Chichester

Steptoe A, Melville D, Ross A 1984 Behavioral response demands, cardiovascular reactivity
and essential hypertension. Psychosomatic Medicine 45: 33–48

Strasser T 1986 Guidelines for the treatment of mild hypertension: memorandum from a
WHO/ISH meeting. Journal of Hypertension 4: 383–386

Cardiac rehabilitation

INTRODUCTION

It is widely accepted that rehabilitation should be a part of the routine care of patients with heart disease. However, its practice is haphazard and rehabilitation is usually only available for a minority following infarction or surgery. In the United States where 800 000 people a year survive infarction and 150 000 undergo coronary artery bypass graft (CABG), fewer than 15% take part in any form of group rehabilitation programme. It must be assumed that most of the remainder receive little more than simple advice from their own doctors (Wenger 1982).

There are several major problems in cardiac rehabilitation and its aims and methods have received remarkably little critical attention. It is often unclear whether its main aim is to restore patients to their normal patterns of everyday life (rehabilitation proper), or to improve of physical fitness or change in risk factors for ischaemic heart disease (secondary prevention).

1. *Rehabilitation proper*
   a. Minimise immediate distress to patient and family
   b. Enable rapid return to normal everyday life:
      work
      leisure
      social
      family
      sex
   c. Continuing help for the physically impaired and those needing continuing medical care
2. *Secondary prevention*
   a. Encourage physical fitness
   b. Promote healthy lifestyle: diet, not smoking
   c. Reduce stress

There has been little evaluative research or interest in providing services to help the elderly or those with chronic symptoms such as angina and cardiac failure.

Cardiac rehabilitation is made up of a variety of components, which should supplement physical treatment in an organised and consistent programme of care, and have substantial benefits for morale and a full everyday life. This chapter concentrates on the psychological aspects of rehabilitation and particularly the management of the minority of patients who have special difficulties. Although the general principles are applicable to many forms of cardiac disorder, discussion will be limited to ischaemic heart disease, and mainly to recovery from myocardial infarction.

BACKGROUND

There has been considerable research on the psychological consequences of myocardial infarction, although this has often been based on unrepresentative patient groups. There has also been increasing recent interest in coronary artery surgery, but little has been written about patients with chronic cardiac disorders such as angina, cardiac failure and dysrhythmias.

Myocardial infarction

Modern active medical management has greatly improved psychosocial outcome, so that many patients are back to full activity within 4–6 weeks, which 20 years ago was the usual length of hospital stay. Even so, most patients and their families report emotional distress and practical difficulties in the early weeks. These are usually transient but at least a quarter describe persistent 'medically unnecessary' psychological and social difficulties, difficulties which most accounts oversimplify in terms of work, sex and depression (Mayou et al 1978).

Patterns of longer-term outcome are very varied and not closely related to cardiac impairment. A few patients describe improvements in their lives, especially family relationships, but between 20% and 30% of patients suffer persistent psychosocial problems. These are not only clinically important in themselves, but limit compliance with medical care and may even affect mortality (Ruberman et al 1984). However, not all such problems during convalescence should be attributed to the infarct — some are of long standing.

The main determinants of quality of life after infarction are: (1) cardiac status, (2) psychological coping abilities and (3) previous social adjustment.

Some patients who are at risk of long-term psychological and social difficulties can be recognised during their initial hospital admission, but it is more accurate and clinically simpler to concentrate on early detection in early convalescence (Mayou 1984). This can be summarised as:

1. Factors in the history
   a. Previous difficulty in dealing with stress (e.g. history of psychiatric consultation)
   b. Long-standing social problems (work, leisure, family)

2. Early signs of problems
   a. Anxiety or depression
   b. Overcautious expectations
   c. Slowness and difficulty in returning to activities (work, leisure and social activities, sex)
   d. Overprotective family
3. Symptomatic cardiac complications

Angina

Angina can be a severely limiting and distressing symptom but there is little association between measures of impairment of cardiac function, mental state and social handicaps. Some patients are able to lead full lives despite limited exercise capacity, whilst others are overcautious and avoid physical activity (Mayou 1973, 1986). The many trials of medical treatment demonstrate that it can be highly effective.

When medical treatment fails, CABG is increasingly seen as the answer. Despite the impressive clinical benefits for the relief of angina, figures for return to work are disappointing, and a small percentage suffer permanent neurological impairment (Shaw et al 1986, Mayou 1986). Even so, the majority of subjects have an excellent overall outcome, feeling less anxious and depressed, leading normal lives without restriction and often substantially increasing their leisure activities (Mayou 1986). In contrast, a third of patients have an unsatisfactory social outcome, not closely related to physical outcome. The social difficulties are very varied and associated with emotional distress and apparently hypochondriacal complaints such as atypical chest pain, breathlessness and physical restriction.

Poor outcome is particularly likely in those who before operation describe symptoms of anxiety or depression, a 'passive attitude' to physical activity or poor social adjustment. As with infarction, progress in early convalescence is a good guide to longer-term quality of life.

A preliminary report of coronary angioplasty, as an alternative to surgery for selected patients, suggests that social functioning at 6 and 15 months is better than after coronary artery surgery (Raft et al 1985).

Congestive cardiac failure

Occasionally ischaemic heart disease presents with right- or left-sided heart failure. More commonly failure follows infarction or other ischaemic symptoms. The psychosocial impact has received little special notice but our own current research supports clinical experience that depression and frustration are common and that they contribute substantially to the characteristic symptoms of fatigue and breathlessness. These psychological problems are not closely associated with any measure of impaired cardiac function or physical capacity. Severe uncontrolled failure can be extremely debilitating and frightening.

Secondary prevention in ischaemic heart disease

Returning to a full life after an infarct or surgery often means a return to habits which are risk factors for further cardiac morbidity: smoking, poor diet, lack of exercise and stress. Enthusiasm for secondary prevention programmes has overshadowed considerable evidence that many other patients, who have received no more than simple advice, make major changes in their lives. We find that after an infarct, half the smokers stop completely, more than half of those advised to modify their diet do so, and others increase physical activity and reduce stress. Similarly impressive changes are seen in the control groups for trials of β-blockers, exercise training and other forms of intervention.

Conclusions

Temporary distress following infarction and cardiac surgery is usual for most patients and most families. Most make excellent recoveries, even without planned rehabilitation, but a minority suffer persistent 'medically unnecessary' handicaps. Such handicaps are especially likely and for those with histories of previous psychological problems, poor coping with stress and social problems. Similar 'unnecessary' psychosocial and social handicaps are probably at least as common in chronic disorders such as angina or heart failure. These difficulties indicate two main tasks for rehabilitation.

1. Routine help for *all* patients and their *families* to enable them to cope with distress and practical problems.
2. Early detection and treatment of the varied and persistent 'medically unnecessary' effects on 'quality of life' described by 25–30% of patients.

In addition there is a need for rehabilitation to contribute to a 'preventive programme that is without great hazard, expense or inconvenience' (Kannel 1984) for those with ischaemic heart disease. This means stopping smoking, exercise training, stress reduction and weight loss alongside the medical components of multiple risk factor reduction such as the control of hypertension, β-blockers and control of lipid levels.

THERAPEUTIC APPROACHES: PHYSICAL TREATMENT

Myocardial infarction

Patients normally present with severe pain and are best managed by rapid admission to a coronary care unit, where disturbances such as dysrhythmias, shock and cardiac failure can be quickly detected and treated.

About half the survivors have suffered 'uncomplicated' infarction with relatively 'low risk' of early complications or subsequent morbidity. Such patients can be discharged from hospital within a few days, with an encouraging prognosis and advice to increase their activities back to normal. In contrast, patients with 'complicated' infarction (dysrhythmias, failure, large infarct) require pharmacological (or occasionally surgical) treatment in hospital, need a longer stay, and are often discharged taking drugs for failure, angina or rhythm abnormalities. They have a much poorer prognosis.

There is increasing interest in systematic 'risk stratification' before discharge so that 'complicated' and 'uncomplicated' infarcts can be distinguished and appropriate follow-up rehabilitation and medical care planned. Advice about not smoking and diet is routine but there is controversy about the role of long-term drug treatment in secondary prevention. There is evidence that β-blockers do confer a significant advantage but the advantage is small and side effects are common.

Angina

Angina is both a common presenting symptom of ischaemic heart disease and a common sequel of myocardial infarction. Patients with mild angina are able to live a normal or nearly normal life. For more severe symptoms modern medical treatment combined with adjustment of lifestyle is often highly effective.

The principal drug treatments are nitrates, β-blockers and calcium antagonists. The most useful drug is glyceryl trinitrate sublingually to prevent attacks or to stop them. Long-acting nitrates, such as isosorbide, are also useful but often cause headache, although this diminishes with continued use. β-blockers are now given routinely to all but the most mild cases of angina. They can, however, worsen cardiac failure and may cause a variety of irritating side effects such as fatigue, unpleasant dreams and depression. Calcium antagonists (verapamil, diltiazem, nifedipine) are usually regarded as most effective when they are used in association with β-blockers but can also be used alone.

Coronary artery surgery has become very popular as it offers a cure for angina for 80% of patients. The principal aim is to improve the quality of life but there are significant advantages in terms of expectation of life for small subgroups (occluded left main coronary artery, triple-vessel disease). There is a small mortality (1–3%) and angina may eventually recur because of progression of the disease. Coronary angioplasty is an alternative, especially for patients with small discrete lesions. Between 2% and 5% of such patients suffer infarction or require emergency coronary artery surgery.

Congestive cardiac failure

This is treated by diuretics and by digoxin. Although the use of the latter is traditional, its role remains somewhat controversial. In more serious heart failure which is not fully responsive to these drugs, vasodilator drugs (isosorbide, captopril) are helpful

In a very small number of patients with cardiac failure cardiac transplant may be considered. The results for prolongation of life are now encouraging and it is clear that the quality of life is very substantially better than in the period preceding surgery (Mai et al 1986).

THERAPEUTIC APPROACHES: PSYCHOLOGICAL

The main aims of rehabilitation are to achieve optimum physical and social function and to minimise psychological distress for the patient and the family (see above). The methods of rehabilitation are usually taken to cover all non-medical and surgical measures. Management of major psychological problems cannot be understood or successfully achieved without a full understanding of routine medical care.

Some cardiac units, provide impressive, flexible and comprehensive postinfarction care (Wenger & Hellerstein 1984) beginning as soon as the patient is admitted to hospital. It is more usual for programmes to have a rigid format, often separate from any continuing cardiological care (Oldridge 1986), which concentrates on exercise to improve the physical fitness and morale of 'low-risk' patients, rather than on treatments to reduce the handicaps of 'high-risk' populations. Such programmes take little account of the wide range of patients' individual problems and needs.

Enthusiasm is considerably more conspicuous than self-criticism, but there have been recent signs of more open-minded approaches (Staniloff 1984): awareness that improved quality of life may be a more appropriate aim than secondary prevention, less concentration on return to work as a measure of outcome and greater concern with those who are poor attenders, the elderly and those with cardiac complications (Oldridge 1986).

Although those who run rehabilitation programmes are usually highly enthusiastic and have a strong impression of benefits' (Gloag 1985) there have been very few adequate evaluations (Razin 1981, Garrity 1981, Oldridge 1986). Far too often it is assumed that apparently common-sense treatments, such as exercise or advice, are effective, even though this is not supported by the evidence on cardiac rehabilitation or on the management of other disabling illnesses.

Most published accounts of the benefits of rehabilitation are based on clinical experience with articulate volunteers and there have been only a handful of controlled trials, few of which come near to the standards we require in the evaluation of postinfarct medical and surgical care (Mitchell 1982). There have been few attempts to study representative patient groups, or to use standardised measures of outcome for quality of life, as well as for cardiac morbidity or mortality. Virtually all the evidence relates to myocardial infarction.

Exercise

Exercise has been by far the most popular component of both early and late rehabilitation and it is claimed to improve physical fitness and have wider benefits. *Early* exercise after myocardial infarction has modest training benefits. Although very popular with many patients and therapists it has disappointingly little effect on mental state or any measure of quality of life (Mayou et al 1981). It seems that well motivated patients enjoy training but do not need it, whilst those who are most at risk of problems either fail to attend or do not find standard programmes helpful. A well planned research programme with low-risk patients has shown that supervised exercise is more effective than home-based exercise and has little advantage over prescription, based on a single exercise test. It is clear that most low-risk patients do not require more systematic advice and more than exercise prescription, although individual extra help is required by a minority with special problems (De Busk et al 1986).

All major controlled trials of *late* long-term exercise training have reported high dropout rates and increased physical activity by many control subjects. All report reduction of mortality and morbidity in the exercise group, but none was large enough to provide statistically significant conclusions. However, analysis of the pooled results *is* significant, and it is reasonable to conclude that exercise is valuable as secondary prevention for enthusiastic subjects. It is also widely stated that exercise has considerable psychological benefits which by themselves justify its use. However, the only trial to have included measures of psychological outcome found no overall differences between exercise and control groups (Stern & Cleary 1982).

These disappointing findings about outcome and poor compliance have led to argument that the major priority for better rehabilitation is to improve compliance with exercise training. It is more reasonable to conclude 'until better evidence is produced demonstrating substantial and persisting benefits of exercise programmes potential and actual participants should decide for themselves' (Haynes 1984).

It is unfortunate that most early and long-term exercise programmes exclude both the elderly and those with chronic cardiac impairments. These large groups have particular difficulty in knowing how much exertion is possible or appropriate and it is probable that careful exercise testing and supervised exercise programmes would be important components of management.

Education

The need for information and advice is obvious, but it is not clear what are the best methods. Trials have shown no more than modest benefits for predischarge and outpatient education programmes in terms of rather varied criteria. There are major problems, problems which have been examined more thoroughly in other major illnesses, such as diabetes (Assal et al 1985), cancer and preparation for surgery (Mathews & Ridgeway 1984). Education is too often a didactic presentation of what doctors believe is important, rather than a discussion which takes account of patients' particular interests and needs (Tuckett et al 1985), families are ignored and written information is badly presented and overly complex. There is insufficient recognition of the established principles of effective communication: repetition and consistency, discussion with patients and families, clear written information, an emphasis on general principles of 'coping' with a gradual increase in activities during convalescence, rather than didactic and inflexible instructions, and close co-ordination with medical care. Wenger et al (1986) have recently pointed out that new technologies offer considerable scope for better and much more flexible education.

Psychological interventions

Apart from basic techniques of support, encouragement and reassurance, many specific psychological interventions have been used. It is probable that they have common features, such as education, encouraging physical activity, anxiety management and support. Their benefits after myocardial infarction are 'at best modest and there seems little reason to offer such help routinely' (Johnston 1985), although each may be effective with carefully chosen subgroups.

Group treatments

Group treatments are most satisfactory when they combine discussion and education. They are often not very popular with patients and have not been shown to be any more effective than other psychological interventions. A minority of motivated patients appear to enjoy groups and benefit (Kolman 1983). Group discussion can sometimes increase anxiety and uncertainty.

Counselling

The results of studies of hospital and postdischarge counselling parallel those of other methods of rehabilitation, with modest benefits and some suggestion that the majority have little need of extra help (Mayou et al 1981, Johnston 1985). Sexual counselling is helpful to some, although not all those thought to have 'problems' are dissatisfied or want help.

Behavioural

Anxiety (stress) management and cognitive techniques are now widely used in medicine and psychiatry and could have a larger role for overcautious anxiety patients and the common problems of atypical chest pain and hyperventilation. There have been no systematic trials.

There are also promising reports that a very intensive programme combining education, behavioural advice and group discussion can modify behaviour and reduce cardiac morbidity (Friedman et al 1984). We need to know whether these findings can be replicated using methods that would be feasible in ordinary clinical practice.

Psychotropic medication

Benzodiazepines are useful for short periods of stress but should not be used for more than a few weeks.

A small minority benefit from antidepressant therapy, although these must be used with care following infarction and in those with abnormalities of rhythm.

The organisation of care

Review of rehabilitation methods shows that a variety of treatment methods, of which exercise is the most popular, reduce early distress, increase satisfaction and encourage a rapid return to normal activities after infarction. These are important benefits, but it is disappointing that the very few controlled trials have found that such methods have few *longer-term* physiological and other benefits. None of the widely used methods have been shown to be effective or popular with the 25–30% who are most 'at risk' of persistent problems.

There is now consistent evidence that standard and apparently common-sense programmes are unnecessary for the majority of patients and too rigid for the important minority who do need help. It is probable that many of these 'problem' patients could be helped by more flexible rehabilitation using individually planned combinations of methods. Even so, we may have to accept that a small number, specially those with long-standing psychosocial problems, will be unable to make successful use of any form of rehabilitation.

If cardiac clinics are to provide flexible selective care for all new patients, they need a clear system in which everyone receives good simple routine care and those who need more than this are offered individually planned extra help:

Organisation of care:
1. Routine care
   a. Hospital:
      Identify special problems
      Information and advice (oral and written)
      Opportunity for discussion (patient and family)
   b. Follow-up:
      Review of progress
      Repetition of advice

Exercise testing and prescription
Answer questions
2. Selective rehabilitation
Counselling
Exercise training (individual unsupervised or group)
Practical help (work, accommodation etc.)
Behavioural advice (anxiety management)
Antidepressants for severe depression
Day or inpatient rehabilitation
Specialist sex therapy
3. Selective secondary prevention
Exercise programmes (individual unsupervised or group)
Smoking clinics
Weight and diet groups
Stress reduction programmes

The ways in which this is done will depend on local resources and systems of health care. Few cardiac units have resources to provide elaborate care for the very large numbers of cardiac patients, but much can be achieved by well organised care which ensures simple, clear, consistent advice and makes the maximum use of inexpensive aids.

1. Routine care

Well written booklets and audiovisual methods are useful, but every family should also have the opportunity for *discussion* of individual advice. Information required by patient and family before discharge from hospital includes the following.

1. Nature of heart attack: causes, treatment and outcome
2. Precise advice about physical exertion on return home
3. Information about common problems: atypical pains, depression and anxiety and associated tiredness, poor concentration, irritability, frustration
4. Discussion of plans for gradual return to normal activities: work, leisure and social activities, sex, driving, holidays
5. Medical advice: medication and how to use it, warning signs (e.g. chest pain), follow-up arrangements (hospital and GP)
6. Secondary prevention: not smoking, diet, exercise, stress
7. What the family can do
   a. Encouragement rather than overprotection
   b. Joint activities
   c. Discussion of long-term plans

The patient, relatives and all those involved need copies of the agreed plans. Discussion of these plans can often be informal. For instance, many patients who are reluctant to raise their worries with doctors during formal consultations are able to talk to nurses or physiotherapists during exercise or education classes. Indeed, it may be one of the main advantages of exercise classes that they allow the opportunity for patients and families to talk to one another and to therapists in a relatively relaxed setting.

New technology offers enormous scope for improving record keeping and assessment as well as for education (Wenger et al 1986). Early exercise testing is useful after myocardial infarction and in other cardiac conditions, both to boost confidence and allow detailed prescription of everyday physical activity.

Case example A 42-year-old assembly-line worker, who was noted to be anxious during his stay in hospital following an infarction, attended for a follow-up appointment and a routine exercise test. He complained of fatigue and breathlessness but was found to be physically fit. He was apprehensive about his exercise test, but with explanation of the medical safeguards and with encouragement he was able to manage without distress. Both he and his wife found it very reassuring that he was able to do a great deal more than he would have considered doing at home. The doctor who supervised the test discussed specific advice about walking and other exercises at home and suggested that he would be able to return to his job involving light manual work. The results were sent to the general practitioner together with the suggestion of an early return to work. At a later appointment, both the patient and his family reported that they had found the exercise test a very considerable relief and encouragement.

Patients disabled by angina or heart failure may also require considerable practical help and support.

Case example A 75-year-old retired greengrocer suffered a second infarction complicated by moderately severe cardiac failure. He lived alone in a large house and was very worried as to how he could manage everyday life. He was reluctant to accept that social-work help would be useful but his physician and social worker were able to see him jointly and to discuss the domiciliary services which could be provided and adaptations that could be made to his house. Later the social worker encouraged him to move to much smaller accommodation. The patient subsequently suffered from increasingly severe congestive failure which progressively limited his activities. His social worker and general practitioner were able to co-ordinate a variety of services which enabled him to live independently and also continue several social activities.

2. Selective rehabilitation

This requires the same combination of detailed assessment and individual treatment as cardiological management (De Busk et al 1986). Successful identification requires systematic review and we find that this is best done by seeing husbands and wives together. In large cardiac clinics, some time could be saved by using self-report questionnaires in the waiting-room, but there is no substitute for clinical assessment that covers all the important areas:

Review at follow-up
Cardiological assessment

Atypical chest pains and somatic symptoms
Physical and social activities: progressive increase?
Compliance with medical advice: medication, diet, smoking, activity
Work: plans and difficulties
Sex
Family: attitudes to convalescence
Driving
Any problems?

Enquiry about these areas need not be time consuming. Questions can be asked informally whilst examining the patient and will be particularly straightforward if the medical notes contain clear and brief summaries of premorbid adjustment and activities and of any subsequent problems or uncertainties. It is, of course, necessary to spend some extra initial time dealing with difficulties that are identified. It is all too common for difficulties to be noted during follow-up appointments but in no way be dealt with. The result is often continuing unnecessary distress and as well as persistent inappropriate use of medical resources. Many cardiologists find that with some re-organisation and a little extra help, they can provide better care even within the busiest clinics.

We have seen that standard all-purpose programmes of rehabilitation are not very effective and satisfactory individual care requires access to the whole range of rehabilitation procedures. It is, however, possible to outline some general principles.

(a) Since many of the 'problem' patients also have cardiac complications, medical and rehabilitation care should be co-ordinated.

(b) Advice should follow general *behavioural* principles. It should be clear, discussed and agreed with patients and have realistic short-term and long-term goals. This includes detailed exercise prescription, step-by-step and long-term aims and sometimes keeping a daily diary of progress and problems.

(c) Exercise testing and training are valuable but should be used as part of an overall rehabilitation plan. Home-based exercise may be more effective than standard hospital programmes.

(d) Relatives should be involved, both so that they can provide support and motivation also to relieve the anxieties and prevent overprotection.

Some kinds of specialist treatment that need to be available after infarction were listed above under 'Organisation of Care'. Anxiety and depression usually improve with counselling, encouragement and explanation, but 2–5% of patients need antidepressant medication and 5–10% need specialist anxiety treatment. Most sexual problems respond to simple discussion and advice, and only a few couples require specialist treatment. A very few patients require day-patient or inpatient rehabilitation.

Rehabilitation concentrates on the problems associated with the heart disease but we have seen that some of the difficulties attributed to heart disease are unrelated and of long standing. We cannot expect to be as successful with such problems but the crisis of a serious illness can be particularly good opportunity for change, since many patients review their lives and ambitions and become more appreciative of family life. The sensitive doctor will encourage them to turn good intentions into constructive changes.

3. Secondary prevention

Advice about secondary prevention should begin early after infarction and progress should be reviewed during convalescence. If the resources are available, extra help should be available for those who can be encouraged to make use of it. Rehabilitation programmes can make a useful contribution to multiple risk factor reduction in promoting stopping smoking, stress reduction and regular exercise. The precise role of long-term exercise training remains uncertain, but it may have considerable physical and psychological advantages for a subgroup of enthusiastic subjects.

SPECIAL PROBLEMS

Coronary care unit

Although denial is one of the most prominent features psychological reaction to a heart attack, anxiety, delirium and behavioural disturbance are all frequent clinical problems. In the early days of intensive care, patients normally spent several days in a rather intimidating special unit, psychiatric referrals were common and it was often believed that there was a need for regular visits by a liaison psychiatrist. Coronary care units have now been made more friendly and comfortable places for patients and their families and length of stay has been much reduced, and as a result psychological problems appear to be fewer.

Pain should be adequately treated and organic mental states recognised and treated if distressing or disturbing. Medical and nursing staff are able to provide reassurance, information and advice as a part of routine care. Since staff take a very considerable responsibility and often act quickly and decisively to treat medical problems, it is essential that they have plenty of support from their seniors. Normally they require no more than occasional assistance from a psychiatrist.

It is often said that the use of mild tranquillisers should be routine but it is more sensible to reserve small doses of benzodiazepines for night-time sedation and for the management of more anxious patients. It is, of course, essential that any such prescription should be reviewed regularly, since it is all too easy for patients to be given medication for an early transient problem but for the prescription to be then continued even after discharge. Haloperidol is useful for the management of disturbed behaviour.

Depression

Depression and associated symptoms such as insomnia, poor concentration, irritability and fatigue are very common in the early days and weeks after infarction. Patients need to be warned about such symptoms, so that they do not become overconcerned or misinterpret them as medical problems.

Early depression usually improves but is more persistent in perhaps 10% or 15% of patients. In most cases advice and counselling is all that is required, but more severe depression (hopelessness, crying, insomnia, social withdrawal etc.) requires psychiatric assessment. We find that between 2% and 5% of patients require an antidepressant medication in the year after infarction or coronary artery surgery. The cardiological side effects of antidepressants mean that they are relatively contra-indicated immediately after infarction and in those with disturbances of rhythm. It is usually unnecessary to delay treatment if there are clear symptoms of a major and distressing depressive disorder.

It is often believed that newer tetracyclic antidepressants are the most suitable, but this may be because there is, as yet, too little clinical experience to be certain about their possible cardiac side effects. The decision should be based upon current opinion and it may be helpful to talk to a psychiatrist and cardiologist about this.

Case example A 56-year-old university administrator had a history of major depressive illnesses in early adult life and 1 year prior to the onset of having angina. The second illness had been satisfactorily treated with amitriptyline, although he continued to suffer from mild long-standing phobic anxiety symptoms. Four months after coronary artery surgery he became depressed, being unable to sleep, tearful and unwilling to be left alone. After discussion with the cardiologist, he was treated with a full dose of a tetracyclic antidepressant with rapid improvement of his depressive symptoms. However, he remained fearful of going out and his chronic phobias apparently being made worse by anxiety about his heart. He was assessed by a clinical psychologist.

Behavioural analysis indicated that the patient became tense and panicky when left alone and when walking or travelling by himself. He described increasing worry about his heart accompanied by breathlessness and panic. He was given a relaxation tape and also practised relaxation exercises under supervision. He was taught breathing exercises to control his hyperventilation and discussed ways in which he could distract and occupy himself when alone at home. He found these techniques helpful and began a self-monitored programme of increasing periods of time alone and going out by himself locally for walks and in his car. There was substantial improvement, but he remained, as he had always been, a rather anxious man inclined to minor worries.

Anxiety

Anxiety very frequently accompanies depression and is a common feature of recovery from infarction. It may also occur as a disabling complication. Worries about the heart and dying and pre-occupation with atypical chest pains and other hypochondriacal physical pains are very common. Full assessment and authoritative reassurance is essential and is often effective. Patients who are not reassured need specialist assessment. Some respond to antidepressants but usually behavioural treatment is necessary.

Anxiety management depends upon detailed behavioural analysis of: (1) the situations in which symptoms occur, (2) the nature and progression of symptoms and (3) the response of the patients and others. Hyperventilation is common and systematic enquiry should be made about breathlessness and associated symptoms. It is always useful to encourage patients to begin diaries of their somatic and anxiety symptoms and to discuss these with them regularly throughout treatment. Many patients respond to simple breathing exercises and to techniques such as relaxation and distraction. Relaxation tapes are helpful but it is also useful to discuss the general principles and any problems directly with the patient and perhaps with a relative.

Case example A 60-year-old man with angina and moderately severe heart failure underwent coronary artery surgery. Following this he remained severely disabled by a variety of physical complaints, became highly agitated and depressed, gave up his social activities and made repeated dramatic demands on emergency medical services. His cardiologist found that he no longer had angina and that his cardiac failure was moderately well controlled, and concluded that the symptoms were predominantly those of anxiety together with somatic complaints attributable to autonomic arousal and hyperventilation. Psychiatric assessment concluded that the depressive symptoms were minor and that the patient was suffering from an anxiety state. A behavioural analysis was made and he was treated with a combination of anxiety management, breathing exercises and a graded progressive increase in activities. The patient and family reported a slow improvement in mental state and increasing physical activities. He resumed an active part in family life and was able to take up his hobbies of rose-growing and judging at rose shows. He remained restricted by symptoms of cardiac failure but these did not prevent him leading an enjoyable and active life.

Work

The proportion of patients returning to work after an infarction varies from country to country. In Britain most patients have managed until recently to return without undue difficulty, excepting those with major cardiac complications, those in specific restricted occupations (e.g. driver of heavy goods vehicle, airline pilot) and some of those with very manual occupations. In the last year or so, at a time of increasing unemployment, many patients have found considerable difficulties at returning to work, difficulties which are greatest for those who are at an age when retirement is seen as an alternative and for those in heavy manual jobs.

Return to work after coronary artery surgery is disappointing. The main reasons for not returning appear to be related to employers' and patients' attitudes, and the nature of the job rather than any cardiac factor. More could be done to discuss problems and to promote realistic attitudes both before surgery and in early convalescence.

It is often extremely helpful if a doctor or a member of the rehabilitation team has direct contact with a patient's employers to discuss the patient's medical state and the demands of the work. Far too often misunderstandings arise between those involved.

Case example A 55-year-old man worked in large factory in a semiskilled post for 35 years. Following coronary artery surgery he was declared fit and returned to work, where he was given a new and more strenuous job working on the assembly line. He was unable to manage this for more than a few days and had to take further sick leave. He became anxious and increasingly upset as his cardiologist continued to declare him fit for work whilst his employers refused to offer him either an alternative job or the opportunity for a gradual return to full hours. He was diagnosed as suffering from depression with marked anxiety features and his mood improved following treatment with a full dosage of an antidepressant. However, he remained anxious and worried about his employment. The psychiatrist initiated discussion between all those involved it was agreed that the patient should apply for early retirement on medical grounds since he was unfit to resume work on his employer's excessively demanding terms. Once he retired with a pension he was able to use his considerable skills as a carpenter in a variety of voluntary activities which he felt enjoyable and worthwhile.

Sex

Sexual difficulties amongst cardiac patients have attracted considerable medical attention. They are undoubtedly common but it is often not realised that many of them are frequently not related to the heart disease and that very often they reflect waning interest in later middle life by one or both partners. The majority of those are classified as having some form of sexual problem are not dissatisfied and have little interest in any special help. Others are worried and keen to resume a normal sexual relationship. They need reassurance, advice and sometimes a specialist sex therapy.

Case example A 54-year-old man suffered an uncomplicated myocardial infarction. He was told that he could resume normal sexual intercourse, but 3 months later reported to his general practitioner that he had not done so, both because he felt uncertain himself, and because his wife believed it would be unsafe. They had enjoyed regular sexual relations before the infarct. He wished to resume but had not discussed this with his wife. The general practitioner reassured the patient that sexual intercourse is not physically unsafe after an infarct and makes rather mild physical demands. He arranged to see the couple together during the next follow-up appointment. During this, the general practitioner enquired generally of the progress and suggested that sexual relations could now be resumed. It was possible to discuss this without embarrassment as part of the general review of convalescence. The wife was able to discuss her fears and worries and was reassured. There were no further problems.

Family problems

Concern about a serious illness, of anxiety and depression and the practical burden may all cause considerable distress and difficulties for relatives. Relationships may suffer and disagreements about the appropriate response to illness are common. Relatives need to be involved in rehabilitation so that they can be reassured, misunderstandings can be resolved and they can learn how best to encourage and support the patient. It cannot be expected that long-term marital and family difficulties can be resolved although occasionally the occurrence of life-threatening illness has dramatic benefits for family relationships.

PROFESSIONAL ISSUES

Cardiac rehabilitation should offer routine and selective treatment for large numbers of patients. Good organisation is fundamental and methods will depend upon the system of health care and resources. Ideally it will be a flexible system with access to therapists of a variety of skills. More realistically most patients will continue to rely on much simpler care provided by their own cardiologist or family doctor.

Case example A 49-year-old man suffered an infarct complicated by an episode of cardiac failure and abnormalities of rhythm. He was discharged to his general practitioner's care. On follow-up the patient was concerned about physical activity and resuming his active life as a salesman travelling around a large area. His wife accompanied him and was obviously anxious and very protective. The family were well known to the general practitioner and he felt he should continue to supervise rehabilitation. However, he was uncertain of the patient's physical capabilities and therefore asked for exercise testing at the local hospital. The results of this were encouraging and the general practitioner was able to advise the patient to resume his former work. He was also able to speak to the employers and reassure them. Nine months later, the patient developed angina and was referred back to the cardiologist for reassessment. Coronary artery surgery was recommended. The general practitioner discussed the operation with the patient and his family beforehand, spoke to the employers and also took on the principal responsibility for follow-up care.

Few rehabilitation services have close liaison with psychologists and psychiatrists and this may account for an overemphasis on standardised physical therapies and relative neglect of treatable psychological problems. As the number of cardiac patients is large it is inevitable that the main responsibility for rehabilitation will continue to lie with cardiologists and physicians aided by nurses and physiotherapists. Heart clubs and self-help groups can be very helpful to those who do need close cardiological supervision. Psychiatrists can best contribute by an involvement in training and research and by being available to see the small proportion with major psychological difficulties and offering them appropriate standard psychiatric treatments. Liaison psychiatrists must understand the principles and practice of modern cardiology.

Case example A 55-year-old woman was referred by her cardiologist to a psychiatrist for assessment of depression following coronary artery surgery. She complained of continuing chest pain, of breathlessness and of feeling more limited than before operation. She was tearful and pessimistic. The psychiatrist reviewed the medical notes which indicated an excellent surgical outcome and he confirmed this in an informal lunchtime talk with the cardiologist. He was then able to discuss with the patient and her family the extent to which the atypical chest pain was due to the surgical wound and the influence of anxiety and depression. There was a good and early response to an adequate dose of an antidepressant.

Any substantial increase in the availability of cardiac rehabilitation must depend on making the maximum use of simple and cheap methods. Much can be done by good organisation, the use of written information and co-operation with self-help groups; it is probable that even with limited resources selective care can be highly cost effective in reducing morbidity and continuing use of medical services. There is little prospect that such improved rehabilitation in hospitals or health centres will diminish the importance of care by the patient's own physicians. The evidence reviewed suggests that if they are well informed they will be able to do much to rehabilitate and promote healthier living. However, they need access to specialist assessment and treatment services for a proportion of patients.

CONCLUSION

At present cardiac rehabilitation is haphazard and we need to clarify aims and methods so as to make care available to all who need it. This must entail making cardiac rehabilitation available for patients with chronic problems and with disorders other than those with ischaemic heart disease.

Psychological care cannot be separated more than other aspects of management. It should not be seen as a specialist responsibility, even though a proportion of patients will require assessment for treatment by psychiatrists and psychologists. It is hoped that psychiatric interest in rehabilitation will lead other members of the rehabilitation team to take on increasing responsibility for psychological components of treatment.

REFERENCES

Assal J P, Muhlhauser I, Pernet A et al 1985 Patient education as the basis for diabetes care in clinical practice and research. Diabetologia 28: 602–613
De Busk R, Blomqvist G, Kouchoukos N T et al 1986 Identification and treatment of low-risk patients after acute myocardial infarction and coronary artery bypass graft surgery. The New England Medical Journal 314: 161–166
Friedman M, Thorenson C E, Gill J J et al 1984 Alteration of Type A behaviour and reduction in cardiac recurrences in post myocardial infarction patients. American Heart Journal 108: 237–248

Garrity T F 1981 Behavioural adjustment after myocardial infarction: a selective review of recent descriptive, correlational, and intervention in research. In: Weiss S M, Hard J A, Fox B H (eds) Perspectives on behavioural medicine. Academic Press, New York

Gloag D 1985 Rehabilitation of patients with cardiac conditions. British Medical Journal 290: 617–620

Haynes R B 1984 Compliance with health advice: an overview with special reference to exercise programs. Journal of Cardiac Rehabilitation 4: 120–123

Kannel W B 1984 Potential for prevention of myocardial reinfarction and cardiac health. In: Wenger N K, Hellerstein H K (eds) Rehabilitation of the coronary patient, 2nd edn. Wiley, New York

Kolman P B R 1983 The value of group psychotherapy after myocardial infarction: a critical review. Journal of Cardiac Rehabilitation 3: 360–366

Johnston D 1985 Psychological interventions in cardiovascular disease. Journal of Psychosomatic Research 29: 447–456

Mai F, McKenzie F N, Kostuk W 1986 Psychiatric aspects of heart transplantation: preoperative evaluation and postoperative sequelae. British Medical Journal 292: 311–313

Mathews A, Ridgeway V 1984 Psychological preparation for surgery. In: Steptoe A, Matthews A (eds) Health care and human behaviour. Academic Press, London

Mayou R A 1973 The patient with angina. Symptoms and disability. Postgraduate Medical Journal 49: 250–254

Mayou R A 1984 Prediction of emotional and social outcome after a heart attack. Journal of Psychosomatic Research 28: 17–25

Mayou R A 1986 The psychiatric and social consequences of coronary artery surgery. Journal of Psychosomatic Research 30: 255–271

Mayou R A, Foster A, Williamson B 1978 Psychosocial adjustment in patients one year after myocardial infarction. Journal of Psychosomatic Research 22: 447–453

Mayou R A, MacMahon D, Sleight P, Florencio M J 1981 Early rehabilitation after myocardial infarction. Lancet 1: 1399–1404

Mitchell J R A 1982 'But will it help my patients with myocardial infarction?' The implications of recent trials for everyday country folk. British Medical Journal 285: 1140–1148

Oldridge N B 1986. Cardiac rehabilitation, self-responsibility, and quality of life. Journal of Cardiopulmonary Rehabilitation 6: 153–156

Raft D, McKee D, Popio K, Haggerty J 1985 Life adaptation after percutaneous transluminal coronary angioplasty and coronary artery bypass grafting. American Journal of Cardiology 56: 395–397

Razin A M 1981 Psychosocial intervention in coronary artery disease: a review. Psychosomatic Medicine 44: 363–387

Ruberman W, Weinblatt E, Goldberg J D, Chaudhary B S 1984 Psychosocial influences on mortality after myocardial infarction. New England Journal of Medicine 311: 552–559

Shaw P, Bates D, Cartlidge N et al 1986 Neurological complications of coronary artery bypass graft surgery: six month follow-up study. British Medical Journal 293: 165–168

Staniloff H 1984 Current concepts in cardiac rehabilitation. American Journal of Surgery 147: 719–724

Stern M J, Cleary P 1982 The national exercise and heart disease project: long-term psychosocial outcome. Archives of Internal Medicine 142: 193–297

Tuckett D, Boulton M, Olson C, Williams A 1985 Meetings between experts. Tavistock Publications, London

Wenger N 1982 Physician practice in the management of patients with uncomplicated myocardial infarction: changes in the past decade. Circulation 65: 421–427

Wenger N, Hellerstein H K 1984 Rehabilitation of the coronary patient, 2nd end. Wiley, New York

Wenger N, Cleeman J, Herd A, McIntosh H 1986 Education of the patient with cardiac disease in the twenty-first century: an overview. American Journal of Cardiology 57: 1187–1189

Management of psychological food intolerance

BACKGROUND

In recent years food allergy has attracted attention in both the medical and the lay press. Publicity has been given to the claim that food allergy is becoming more common and that the medical profession in not sufficiently well informed to deal with it. The view is also expressed that food processing and additives exacerbate the problem. The subject has become mixed in the public mind with the vexed concept of health diets.

It is clear that specific immune reactions following food ingestion are present in only a minority of patients who report an unpleasant reaction to food and request medical help with it. Just as there is little scientific evidence to support the hypothesis that specific immune reactions underpin food intolerance, there is similarly little evidence to support the oft-expressed clinical opinion that psychological factors are important in both the aetiology and maintenance of these disorders. In fact, the clinician who attempts to be impartial will soon find that there are few like him: claim tends to be followed by counterclaim, bias and uncontrolled report are the order of the day, and opinions seem to be based more on faith, masquerading as clinical judgement, than on scientific methods.

From our review we have formed the opinion that the clinician who treats patients with food intolerance will find much of interest in the research literature but little to indicate a management protocol of obvious and over-whelming superiority. In this situation, we believe that the principles of most utility are those of a clinical classification and a pragmatic management strategy which we detail below.

CLASSIFICATION

The following classification (Table 7.1) is based closely on the report of the Royal College of Physicians and the British Nutrition Foundation (Royal College of Physicians 1984).

Table 7.1 Food intolerance and food aversion

	Complaint of adverse reaction	Reproducible adverse reaction when		Abnormal immunological reaction
		Aware of food	Unaware of food	
Food avoidance	Maybe	No	No	No
Psychological intolerance	Yes	Yes	No	No
Food intolerance	Yes	Yes	Yes	No
Food allergy	Yes	Yes	Yes	Yes

Food allergy

Food allergy is a specific form of food intolerance in which there is evidence of an abnormal immunological reaction to food. The relevant immunological mechanisms are not fully understood but may include induction of IgE antibodies, mucosal T-cell mediated reactions and systemic immune reactions involving serum antibodies of different classes forming large antigen–antibody complexes (Ferguson 1976). Whilst food allergy does cause protean symptoms, it must be distinguished from other clinical conditions which are related to diet. Two main conditions have been identified: physical food tolerance and food aversion.

Physical food intolerance

Food intolerance is a reproducible adverse reaction to a specific food or food ingredient which is not psychologically based nor a specific allergic reaction. It occurs even when the affected person cannot identify the types of food which he is given, for example if they are disguised or given by nasogastric tube. It may be caused by enzyme defects, e.g. in people who cannot tolerate cow's milk because they cannot digest lactose; it may follow a direct pharmacological effect, e.g. caffeine toxicity after strong coffee; or it may follow direct irritant or toxic effects, e.g. following an overspiced curry.

Food aversion

Food aversion comprises both psychological intolerance, in which unpleasant bodily reactions are produced by food when given in identifiable form but not when given in concealed form, and food avoidance, in which the subject avoids certain foods for psychological reasons. The degree of food aversion necessary to cause requests for help varies widely. The distinction between a phobic avoidance without specific symptomatic responses to food and the psychosomatic conversion responses in psychological intolerance is important for management.

PREVALENCE

As might be expected in view of the range of problems, there are essentially no definite figures available indicating the prevalence of these problems. There are some figures for definite allergies, e.g. EEC figure of 0.03–0.15% for allergic intolerance of food additives (EEC 1981). An updated, 1983 EEC report, while noting the impossibility of giving a single convincing figure for overall prevalence, nevertheless noted that the problem was 'common'. It is difficult to improve on this summary!

PSYCHOLOGICAL FOOD INTOLERANCE

As we have suggested, psychological food intolerance is the manifestation of an adverse physical or acute psychological reaction caused not by the food itself but by the associations with that food and its ingestion. Such a reaction may be quite indistinguishable from those of a physical food intolerance or allergy, but the diagnosis is made by the failure to reproduce the adverse reaction when the patient is unaware that the food is being ingested. This is typically achieved by the use of a nasogastric tube.

The trigger food may be a single commodity, a related group of foodstuffs, or a collection of chemically unrelated foods. The symptoms are usually vague and fluctuating and affect different bodily systems but, as with many psychosomatic illnesses, in any particular patient one bodily system is usually particularly affected. Most commonly, apart from feeling unwell, the patient complains of: gastrointestinal symptoms such as abdominal swelling, discomfort, pain, nausea or diarrhoea; cardiovascular and respiratory symptoms such as palpitations or chest pain and breathlessness; and, less commonly, neurological symptoms such as dizziness, or migraine. Hyperventilation may be an unrecognised feature exacerbating other symptoms. Psychological symptoms are usually depression, irritability and sleep disturbance but may be described either as a direct effect of the food or secondary to the worry about the 'food allergy'.

In one study of 23 patients whose bowel symptoms were thought to be due to food intolerance, objective evidence of physical hypersensitivity was sought by the use of exclusion diets and provocation tests (Pearson et al 1983). A direct relationship of food was confirmed in only four cases. A high prevalence of psychiatric disorder was found in the remaining 19. The severity was well within the range seen in new psychiatric referrals. A controlled study of 50 patients with the similar problem of the 'irritable bowel syndrome' (IBS), showed significantly greater improvement when psychotherapy was part of the treatment (Svedlund et al 1983).

These particular careful studies confirm a view held by many clinicians working in this area, that psychological food intolerance can be understood and managed in general psychiatric terms. We will return to this topic in the discussion of the clinical management.

FOOD INTOLERANCE BY PROXY

In rare cases, so far only reported in children, the intolerance lies not so much in the patient as in one or more other members of the family. The family are unable to accept that the 'patient's' behaviour or 'symptoms' are other than the result of physical illness. The suggestion, often of medical origin, that the problem could be 'allergic' is seized upon to avoid upsetting an often precarious family equilibrium. The patient gives the impression of being a passive or acquiescent pawn in a game played by the others. A recent study of 17 healthy children presenting in an allergy clinic (Warner & Hathaway 1984), showed that the mothers had imposed severe dietary restrictions on the children in the mistaken belief that a food allergy was the cause of a variety of vague and unsubstantiated symptoms. The mothers' beliefs had, in many cases, been reinforced by contact with organisations purporting to be able to diagnose food allergy by the use of dubious techniques. The characteristics of the maternal involvement have led to the suggestion that, through the proxy of their parents, these children manifest a variant of Munchausen's syndrome (Meadow 1982).

Case history. Two sisters, aged 8 and 7 years, were reported by the school authorities for persistently poor attendance. The children were questioned and revealed that each evening their mother carefully wrapped them in toilet paper and silver foil and put them to sleep in the back of an upturned wardrobe. They were not given blankets because their mother was concerned to exclude dust to which, she believed, they were allergic. She also believed they were allergic to many foodstuffs and had placed them on a restriction diet. The mother refused psychiatric interview even after the children had been taken into care. However, the children's paediatrician considered that the mother did not show formal psychotic symptoms, but that her beliefs were extensions of overvalued ideas. When she was confronted with evidence that her children did not have a food allergy she 'created havoc in the waiting room' (Warner 1988).

These cases, clumsily referred to as 'food allergy by proxy' are characterised by a positive family history of asthma or food allergy and, in several members of the nuclear family, an unusual level of interest in food, food preparation or body weight prior to the onset of the 'disorder' in the family member who is presented for (or protected from, as above) treatment.

In the absence of conventional help from medical sources such families often seek unorthodox methods of treatment and the whole behaviour pattern becomes entrenched. Such large sums of money may be spent that the family becomes almost literally 'invested' in their belief in an allergic mechanism.

Case history. One family, treated by the second author, ran itself heavily into debt building a 'completely allergen-free house'. The mother clearly had a covert and chronic eating disorder and, recognising that her adolescent daughter's own developing anorexia might reveal the mother's problem, developed the idea that the daughter had a food allergy. The father became completely involved emotionally and financially in the idea to the extent that he could not accept the diagnosis of anorexia in the daughter: to do so would have meant questioning his wife, his marriage and the entire family harmony.

Treatment with family therapy resulted in the daughter gaining some weight and her physical symptoms remitting somewhat, at which point the family terminated therapy saying that 'everything is fine now'.

These cases where the family is clearly in a pathological state of organisation need to be distinguished from the rarer cases where the parents of a child with an identifiable disease, such as schizophrenia, have read of the possible role of diet in mental illness and initiate an amateur trial elimination diet.

THE 'TOTAL ALLERGY SYNDROME'

This term, as currently used, applies to patients who are claimed to show severe symptoms affecting multiple bodily systems. It does not describe those unfortunate atopic individuals who have specific reactions to a very wide variety of allergens. Medical responses to the syndrome have been sceptical, perhaps because, taken literally, the condition would be incompatible with life!

The symptoms of the condition are vague and variable. Weakness, lethargy, convulsions, faintness, fits, wheezing, migraine, gastrointestinal and urinary symptoms, aches and cutaneous hypersensitivity have been described. Some critics of the allergy theory have suggested that these symptoms more closely resemble those of hypocarbia following hyperventilation than those of an allergy (Nixon 1982, Lum 1982).

The aetiology, if it is not allergic, is unclear because few detailed reports have been published. Some descriptions suggest that the patients are avoiding food (Kinnell 1982), others that psychological intolerance is at the root of the problem. The general impression is that the condition might be a bizarre example of the abstaining form of anorexia nervosa occurring in a hysterical personality, or that it is a personality disorder in its own right, characterised by a severe conversion reaction to conflict (Cotterill 1982). There are a number of similarities with anorexia: both groups of patients (a) declare a fear of food; (b) insist on preparing their own food and tend to eat alone; (c) have a deep-rooted interest in food and food preparation; (d) place themselves on exclusion diets even at low body weight; (e) claim lethargy but show intermittent periods of hyperactivity; (f) display a plethora of bodily symptoms and have signs in common, such as low body weight and amenorrhoea. Whether or not this link is important, and whatever the status of the 'total allergy syndrome' as a diagnostic entity, it is clear that a significant number of patients who have been claimed to have the disorder can be diagnosed as having a psychiatric illness. To this may be added problems of nutritional disturbance which, in patients treated with an elemental 'diet', may include well defined biochemical abnormalities (Mike & Asquith 1983).

THE IRRITABLE BOWEL SYNDROME

The irritable bowel syndrome is discussed here because it complicates the understanding of food intolerance but may also provide the one encouraging indication of the possibility of successful psychological contributions to management. The irritable bowel syndrome is, very roughly, the presence of significant gastrointestinal symptoms related to the large bowel and not apparently explicable on the basis of any well recognised physical disease process. It may occur in as many as 33% of young people and there can be difficulties in distinguishing it from food intolerance or a complication of food intolerance. The problem is that the investigation and management of food intolerance, whether amateur or professional, may well involve complicated dietary manipulations and call for obsessional devotion (a high percentage of parents of children with proven allergic skin reactions to food fail to maintain demanding exclusion diets despite evidence of deterioration on deviation from the diet). During the investigation of intolerance the demand for obsessional thoroughness is linked with the demand for self-observation. It is probable that the diet alone can produce problems in susceptible subjects and the role of a personality parameter of 'introspection' as a mediator of requests for treatment in young adults has been shown by Mechanic (1983, 1986). We believe that a person with a high level of introspective concern is particularly likely to present requesting investigation of a possible food allergy and that within the group where no response to blind challenge can be found, the investigation itself may easily potentiate the introspection, producing a final pattern of symptoms distinguishable from those in IBS.

ANOREXIA NERVOSA

Two psychiatric conditions are of particular importance in the differential diagnosis of food intolerance. These are anorexia and bulimia nervosa. Essentially anorexia nervosa may be regarded as the most malignant form of food avoidance possible. Despite the name, loss of appetite is not a feature, so expression of hunger in the context of food aversion does not exclude this diagnosis. While most clinicians would agree with Thoma (1967) when he says that the 'most obvious hallmark of anorexia is a psychologically determined refusal of food', it is the fear of normal adolescent body weight which is the psychological basis of the condition (Crisp 1967). Diagnostic criteria have been developed (Russell 1970, Crisp 1977, American Psychiatric Association 1980, 1987) and the reader is referred elsewhere for a comprehensive discussion of the area (e.g. Garfinkel & Garner 1982, Crisp 1980). Although the disorder may manifest itself prepubertally or in the twenties or later, the peak prevalence is in early adolescence and the crucial process is a phobic avoidance of the psychological and physical consequences of adult sexuality. This concept of a phobic stance, i.e. an avoidance motivated by abnormal fear or anxiety, is crucial not only for diagnosis but also for treatment.

BULIMIA NERVOSA

Bulimia was first described in detail by Russell (1979). It is a disorder characterised by powerful and intractable urges to overeat, particularly carbohydrate foods. The fatness that would ordinarily result from such binge-eating is prevented by self-induced vomiting, purgation, exercise or inter-mittent periods of starvation so that the patient (usually a woman) remains within a normal range of weight. The bulimic episodes are associated with disgust and anger such that the behaviour may remain secret. Diagnostic criteria have been established (American Psychiatric Association 1980, 1987) and clinical details published (e.g. Lacey 1984). Symptoms associated with the disorder are common and a prevalence of about 3% has been reported.

On examination, and following binge-eating and vomiting, the patient appears sweaty and tremulous. The teeth may be eroded and the salivary glands swollen but painless. The abdomen is distended, often with marked borborygmi. Menstrual irregularities are common, although the patient is at normal body weight. Electrolyte disturbances can occur, particularly if the patient combines vomiting with the use of laxatives or diuretics.

A number of features are common to bulimia nervosa and food intoler-ance: (a) an unusual pre-occupation with food and food presentation which usually precedes the onset of the disorder; (b) food fads in childhood and adolescence; (c) gastrointestinal symptoms and marked fluctuations in weight; (d) episodes of sweating unrelated to exercise; (e) abdominal disten-sion; (f) bouts of tachycardia; (g) a tendency when the diagnosis is first suggested to react with hostility, a reaction which stems from guilt and shame. Despite these similarities, which clearly place bulimia on the differ-ential diagnosis list, there should usually be little problem in distinguishing the two provided that non-judgemental enquiry is made about binge-eating.

CONVERSION AND PSYCHOSOMATIC ILLNESS

The concept of a phobic stance or process has been discussed above. The other crucial psychological process to an understanding of psychosomatic illness is that of conversion. A conversion process is one in which feelings are expressed not directly in speech or action, but are converted, often with symbolic significance, into a physical disturbance. The classical examples are of course those of the hysterical paralyses where the accompanying dissociation from fear or depression is often blatantly apparent in a 'belle indifférence'. However, less dramatic conversion processes may underlie a variety of psychosomatic symptoms. In order to detect a conversion process it is necessary to be able to formulate clearly the evidence that there is an emotion that the person is not expressing directly, and that it is has some temporal and perhaps symbolic connection with the physical symptom. In this context the practical importance of eating and the central position of feeding and being fed within parent–child relationships and, often, husband–wife roles, may make gastrointestinal symptoms and food intolerances particular signifiers. Conversion is almost invariably associated with a denial of the underlying problems or feelings and a determination not to relinquish an explanation for the disturbance in physical terms. Whilst denial of problems may also occur in phobic conditions, the importance of a physical explanation to the patient with a conversion element to their illness is not a feature of a phobic stance.

CLINICAL MANAGEMENT

Assessment and diagnosis

As with any other condition, the essential first step for management is a good assessment! This involves physical and psychological assessment of all patients and both components must start at the first contact with the medical services. The physical investigation begins with a full physical examination and investigations to exclude other major physical illness and then the specific investigations to classify any food intolerance. Small-bowel biopsy may be indicated to exclude coeliac disease or to find changes similar to those in childhood intolerance of cow's milk, soya, fish or chicken. It may also be useful in eliminating giardiasis, sucrose-isomaltase deficiency and in revealing the chronic changes which may follow gastroenteritis.

Diagnosis of specific food allergies, as is already clear, demands a skilled blend of clinical pragmatism and laboratory science. The crucial diagnostic investigation is a sequence of elimination diets and testing for precipitation of symptoms by blind challenge with the incriminated foodstuffs. Elimination will take at least 3 weeks; the diagnosis is made on recurrence of the original symptoms on blind challenge. Although this is the simple diagnostic result, the possibilities of complex interplays of multiple antigens, permeability effects, separate immunological systems and possible immunological regulatory processes, guarantee that one can always postulate a mechanism of hypersensitivity compatible with any given result of any combination of elimination and challenge.

In view of this vulnerability to interpretation, tests of reactivity other than such clinical empiricism have considerable appeal. There has been a wide variety of tests for subclinical evidence of response on challenge, including measuring histamine levels, RAST (radio-allergosorbent tests), skin-prick testing for cutaneous hypersensitivity, intestinal release of prostaglandins, increased liability to develop asthma on inhalation of histamine, etc. Some of these are now largely discredited; others are under very active development. There appears to be a wide variety of expert opinion in the field. At present none of these tests has true diagnostic status. As for the interpretation of mixed responses to blind challenge, the skill comes in wielding Occam's razor to shave cleanly!

As with the assessment of the physical state of the patient, the psychiatric assessment should exclude other major pathology, particularly an extremely rare delusional psychosis, either schizophrenia or a monosymptomatic hypochondriacal psychosis, or the more common and more hopeful cases where hypochondriacal preoccupations complicate what is basically a depressive illness. Apart from these exclusion issues there is the crucial classificatory issue of uncovering either a phobic or a conversion process.

The psychiatric investigation of the patient is a systematic appraisal of the history for psychological determinants. These include: a family history of psychiatric illness, in particular any family history of weight disorder or unusual eating habits or alcoholism; a family history of physical illness, particularly any allergic or gastrointestinal illness; and any illness, such as illness of the parent during the patient's childhood, which may have had particular developmental significance. It is also important to explore, at least briefly, the pattern of 'sick role' adopted within the family, i.e. whether illness has removed a member from normal obligations for any extended period or in a way that markedly affected family structure. In the personal history the dietary history will be explored both for its physical and psychiatric importance, the effects of early food faddism, intolerance or avoidance of the family and the extent to which eating was equated with health and good mood can be a pointer to a psychological focus on food. Evidence of particular difficulties negotiating the transition from child to adult may include school avoidance and truancy, forensic problems, adolescent drug abuse, a school record markedly inferior to the evident ability at the interview, failure to progress to a personally satisfying sexuality, and poor occupational history. These may all point to underlying conflicts and adaptational difficulties which may be exonerated by a 'sick role' or 'abnormal illness behaviour' (Pilowsky 1969, 1978). There may be evidence of a pattern of recurrent mood swings or a consistent pattern of disturbed interpersonal relations suggestive of a personality disorder. Particular attention should be paid to discussion of the patient's view of his own weight and shape. Whilst it is common for women to want to be somewhat under the normal weight for their height and age, just as it is common for men to wish to be taller and stronger than the norm, this attitude must be distinguished from the intense fear underlying a phobic avoidance of a normal body weight (avoidance which may or may not be successful). Binge-eating should be enquired after in a direct but non-judgemental fashion. Again, occasional binges are common in both sexes but a recurrent pattern of bingeing associated with a powerful experience of loss of control is virtually pathognomonic of bulimia nervosa. Examination of the mental state may occasionally reveal that ideas about food are held at a delusional level not attributable to culture or family, and overvalued ideas are more common. Very occasionally delusions about food may be part of a schizophrenic illness which may be revealed by direct questioning about voices, thought interference or passivity ('I would just like to check out some routine questions. Do you ever hear voices when there is no-one visible near you? Do you ever feel that your thoughts are being interfered with?) Biological features of depression including sleep disturbance and a diurnal mood variation may be present. The facies may reveal anxiety, depression or a degree of histrionic masking of feelings.

Differential diagnosis

The differential diagnosis should be fairly clear at this stage! It includes physical conditions of which the most important are coeliac disease, itself a form of physical intolerance, insulinoma and carcinoid syndrome, and psychiatric conditions — schizophrenia, monosymptomatic hypochondriacal psychosis, depression and anorexia and bulimia nervosa.

Treatment

There are no clear guides to treatment in the literature so this account is, necessarily, personal. The crucial issue is to move the focus of distress from the symptoms and the postulated physical explanation. Ideally this should be associated with the provision of alternative expression of distress and the learning of new coping mechanisms.

The basic requirement is to be able to engage the patient in treatment while aiming to remove the phobic or conversion process. This is not an easy undertaking, as the following case histories illustrate. The first history shows a conversion process and simultaneous obvious psychiatric pathology.

Case history. This 18-year-old boy was referred with a variety of behavioural problems that his mother attributed to a food allergy. He had been using cannabis heavily, had become dependent on an alcohol intake of half a bottle of spirits a day and was sniffing glue and exhibiting a number of other self-harmful activities, such as cutting and burning his forearms and prostituting himself. Unsurprisingly this pattern had led to his expulsion from a series of private schools.

His alcohol consumption had started at 13 and he had not gone a day without alcohol for 2 years and experienced withdrawal tremors in the mornings by the time of referral. He described a pattern of mood swings associated with the self-destructive behaviours and recognised that he started drinking heavily to feel happier. He experienced periods of severe depersonalisation and had had one period of hyperactivity at the age of 8 which was not clinically investigated in any detail.

There was a considerable family history of psychiatric and physical illness. Psychotic illness with paranoid and depressive features was present in the uncle, and maternal grandmother and greatgrandmother. The parents, both aged 42, had no formal psychiatric history, neither had the two younger siblings. The patient had had no serious medical illnesses and the only previous psychiatric treatment had been a period on tricyclics from the private doctor who had placed him on an exclusion diet 8 months prior to referral.

The patient was born prematurely at a low weight but showed normal developmental milestones. He was described as 'difficult' and was particularly noted to have been 'difficult to feed' and 'hyperactive'. His schooling had been affected by the family's moves around the world necessitated by the father's job and the patient's mother had suffered from a tropical infection resulting in a prolonged period of hospitalisation and convalescence in this country while the patient remained with his father in the tropics at the age of 2 years. He had been sent to boarding school in the UK at the age of 8.

The premorbid personality, judged from the patient's own evaluation and from other sources, was an introverted, shy child who had become markedly more withdrawn over the 2 years prior to referral.

The mother described the patient as quieter and happier when he kept to his strict diet which excluded all dairy and wheat products. The patient also thought he was better when able to keep to the diet but also commented that it was a difficult diet to keep to and that he didn't really understand 'what it was all about'. It was difficult to disentangle any obvious causal sequence to his mood swings, varying alcohol consumption and varying compliance with the diet. Examination of mental state revealed mild depressive features; physical examination revealed an enlarged liver and superficial scarring of the forearms but little else of note.

The initial diagnosis was of alcohol dependence and drug abuse in the context of a probable personality disturbance. He was admitted to the inpatient unit for withdrawal from drugs and alcohol and for assessment of mood, personality and behaviour after the period of detoxification. The admission lasted a month and although initially he did abstain from drug abuse and drinking and started to make some relationship with staff and other patients, this pattern appeared to change markedly when the father returned to the country to reinforce the mother's increasingly desperate complaints that the hospital staff were 'poisoning' him with the normal hospital diet. He was discharged after a month.

Detailed immunological investigation at another unit without blind challenge revealed a mixed pattern of abnormalities, including a generally elevated IgE level and specific reactions to common household allergens, but no reactions to the foodstuffs postulated to cause his symptoms. After a period at that unit he was admitted to another psychiatric unit, where he remained for 5 months, successfully abstained, eventually, from drugs and alcohol and appeared to undergo a marked improvement in personality.

This case illustrates the common finding that a psychological treatment may have to develop throughout a period in which the family or patient seeks other treatments, usually physical. In this case the end result appeared to be a successful psychological treatment at another unit. It is obviously preferable to keep the treatment under one team and often much of the work in managing these cases may be in developing a rapport that will ensure a return to the one team and liaison work to dissuade other carers, physicians or psychiatrists, from assuming a central role. The active collaboration of the patient's general practitioner is almost a *sine qua non* in these negotiations. The second case illustrates very clearly a conversion process.

Case history. Mrs D. was a 35-year-old divorcee working as a hospital laboratory technician and living on virtually an elemental diet of biscuits and vitamin tablets. She had seen a series of eminent physicians, had had many investigations and treatments, including indomethacin and plasmapheresis, before her referral to the psychiatric outpatient clinic. She had been adopted at the age of 2 months and all that is known about her genetic family is that she was the illegitimate child of an Irish mother and Polish father. She had had a number of illnesses as a child, including scarlet fever and recurrent otitis media and partial deafness. She also had her tonsils and adenoids removed at the age of 5 years and still has recurrent sinusitis. She developed migraine in late childhood. Her problems of diarrhoea and vomiting started in infancy and fluctuated throughout childhood but tended to follow a pattern of about six attacks a year. At the time of referral her symptoms were of right-sided abdominal pain and bloating and episodes of watery diarrhoea and rectal bleeding (although sigmoidoscopy on the morning of a reported attack revealed no blood and normally formed stool in the rectum). She was missing time from her work and this was reaching a crisis. She agreed, on prompting, that her symptoms also ruined her life more generally and prevented her having any form of social life.

Her adoptive parents had been experienced as cool and distant. The father had died a year before the assessment. He was described as distant and placid, sometimes sad, but a strict disciplinarian. The mother was still alive and was described as domineering, bitter and rather obsessional — 'I have a concern for her but I don't love her. I don't like her as a person.' They had adopted one other child 2 years younger than the patient and the two had previously been on good terms but had argued shortly after the death of the father and had not spoken since.

The patient remembered an unhappy childhood dominated by illness and by a feeling that her abandonment by her natural parents (of which she was told at a young age) was being matched by an emotional abandonment by her adoptive parents. She was happier at school than at home and did respectably well at her '11 +' and 'A' levels, but getting into great trouble with her parents after 'making a mess' of her 'O' levels. She described being a generally quiet and compliant pupil. She had a relatively early menarche and gained weight rapidly at 13 years old to 10 stones. She denied dieting but reduced her weight to 8 stones by the age of 18. Her abdominal symptoms worsened and rectal bleeding had started by the age of 22, shortly following the discovery that she was pregnant by a casual boyfriend, a discovery that was followed by an operative abortion and the collapse of the relationship. She was married at 23 but soon discovered that her husband had, or had developed, a drink problem and the marriage started to deteriorate rapidly, although they were not divorced until she was 29. During this period her symptoms escalated and she started a sequence of consultations which culminated in plasmapheresis. Intensive investigation found no evidence of laxative abuse nor any gastrointestinal abnormality. Immunological investigations, including immunoglobulin levels, were abnormal on a number of occasions although not markedly so. No specific reactivity to foods was found on in-vitro tests and the only response to blind food challenge via a nasogastric tube was a subjective response of abdominal pain following egg protein. Her physician noted a history of improvements following any major change in the medical regime, usually sustained for about 3 months. Relapse occurred before change in the regime except in the case of plasmapheresis which was used for a period but discontinued by the team who had carried it out.

Examination of her mental state revealed no specific psychiatric abnormalities. The history clearly revealed that exacerbations followed a period of months after major life difficulties, particularly difficulties with relationships with men, including a further pregnancy which had led to a spontaneous abortion. The patient was adamant that, although these historical sequences were correctly noted, they were not causal and she was noted to be extremely angry with the referring team who, she felt, were preventing her from receiving regular plasmapheresis, which she saw as the appropriate treatment for her condition. She was well aware of the extent to which her symptoms cramped her life, preventing social contact with men or the development of any new relationships. She also noted that she was unsure whether she could cope with the pain of any more relationships within which she was abandoned. She volunteered that the collapse of her marriage had a been a miserable experience which she had only 'survived' through per pre-occupation at the time with the investigation of her then very severe symptoms. She listened politely to discussion of the possibility that a period of psychotherapy might alleviate these psychological pains, possibly independent of her symptoms or possibly in a way that might reduce those symptoms, but she remained adamant that she wished to pursue a medical cure. However, on receipt of the psychiatric formulation of the case, her physician managed to reach an agreement with her that they would not discuss treatment for the next 6 months and that during that period she should not consult any medical person about her now familiar symptoms, so that she would have an opportunity to re-assess her position without distractions. At a follow-up meeting at the end of that period her symptoms had abated considerably, she had gained weight and held onto her job and, though still a very unhappy woman, was no longer determined to seek plasmapheresis or another physical treatment.

Here again the patient did not engage in treatment; however, it appears that the psychiatric assessment enabled the physician to put into action a management plan which was at least partially successful in improving the patient's condition.

Our psychological treatment strategy is that the psychiatrist or other clinician must identify what is being avoided (phobic stance) or transmuted (conversion process) and that he must, by a non-judgmental stance and thorough evaluation, engage the patient. The strategy must then be to reduce or remove any physical treatments and treatment teams and to aim to broach discussion of the underlying issues. This is best achieved within an eclectic treatment programme in which any avoidance of food is directly prevented. The programme should emphasise the importance of stress in reducing bodily efficiency and producing debilitation and alternative coping strategies to deal with such 'stress' should been encouraged using behavioural or cognitive techniques. It is often best if the nature of the 'stress' is not addressed too directly in the first instance. Occupational therapists often have a particularly potent role in this educational component of the treatment using communication and social skills training, art, movement, or other relatively non-verbal therapies and highly practical sessions, such as planning cooking for a meal not restricted by excluding certain foods. The final stage of treatment should probably enable the patient and therapist, often the therapist who conducted the earlier components, to address directly the issues underlying the illness.

CONCLUSIONS

Food aversion and psychological food intolerance are common and can come in various forms. Among those claiming to have allergic disorders there are significant numbers who can be diagnosed as being psychiatrically ill and who may respond to psychiatric treatment. Much systematic research into the aetiology, pathogenesis and clinical features is needed.

REFERENCES

American Psychiatric Association 1980. Diagnostic and Statistical Manual of Mental Disorders, 3rd edn. APA, Washington DC

American Psychiatric Association 1987 Diagnostic and statistical manual of mental disorders, 3rd edn (revised). APA Washington, DC

Cotterill J W 1982 Total allergy syndrome. Lancet i: 628

Crisp A H 1967 Anorexia nervosa. Hospital Medicine 1: 713–718

Crisp A H 1977 The differential diagnosis of anorexia nervosa. Proceedings of the Royal Society of Medicine 70: 686–690

Crisp A H 1980 Anorexia nervosa: let me be. Academic Press, London

EEC, Commission of the European Communities 1981 Report of a working group on adverse reactions to ingested additives, III, 556–81-EN. Brussels, Commission of the European Communities

Ferguson A 1976 Coeliac disease and gastrointestinal food allergy. In Ferguson A, McSween RNM (eds) Immunological aspects of the liver and gastrointestinal tract. MTP Press, Lancaster: pp. 153–202

Garfinkel P E, Garner D M (eds) 1982 Anorexia nervosa: a multi-dimensional perspective. Brunner Mazell, New York

Kinnell H G 1982 Total allergy syndrome. Lancet i: 628–629

Lacey J H 1984 The bulimic syndrome. In: Ferguson A (ed) Advanced medicine 20. Royal College of Physicians/Pitman Publishing, London, pp 253–263

Lum L C 1982 'Total allergy syndrome' or fluctuating hypocarbia. Lancet i: 316

Meadow R 1982 Munchausen's syndrome by proxy. Archives of Diseases in Childhood 57: 92–98

Mechanic D 1983 Adolescent health and illness behavior: review of the literature and a new hypothesis for the study of stress. Journal of Human Stress 9: 4–13

Mechanic D 1986 The concept of illness behaviour: culture, situation and personal predisposition. Psychological Medicine 16: 1–7

Mike N, Asquith P 1983 Total allergy syndrome: what evidence can be established? In: Second Fisons' food allergy workshop. Medical Publishing Foundation, Oxford: pp. 79–83.

Nixon, P G F 1982 'Total allergy syndrome' of fluctuating hypocarbia. Lancet ii: 404

Pearson D J, Rix K J B, Bentley S J 1983 Food allergy. 'How much in the mind?' Lancet i: 1259–1261

Pilowsky I 1969 Abnormal illness behaviour. British Journal of Medical Psychology 42: 347–351

Pilowsky I 1978 A general classification of abnormal illness behaviours. British Journal of Medical Psychology 51: 131–137

Royal College of Physicians and British Nutrition Foundation 1984 Food intolerance and food aversion. Royal College of Physicians, London

Russell G F M 1970 Anorexia nervosa — its identity as an illness and its treatment. In: Price J M (ed) Modern trends in psychological medicine, vol 2, Butterworth, London, pp 131–164

Russell G F M 1979 Bulimia nervosa: an ominous variant of anorexia nervosa. Psychological Medicine 9: 429–448

Svedlund J, Sjodin I, Ottosson J O, Dotevall G 1983 Controlled trial of psychotherapy in irritable bowel syndrome. Lancet ii: 589–592

Thoma H 1967 Anorexia nervosa (trans. Brydone G). International Universities Press, New York

Warner J O 1988 Personal communication

Warner J O, Hathaway M J 1984 Allergic form of Meadow's syndrome (Munchausen by proxy). Archives of Disease in Childhood 59: 151–156

8

Jan Svedlund, Ingemar Sjödin

Irritable bowel syndrome

THEORETICAL BACKGROUND

Biomedical aspects

Irritable bowel syndrome (IBS) is characterised clinically by bowel dysfunction and abdominal pain in the absence of detectable organic disease. It is by far the commonest of all gastrointestinal disorders, accounting for a large proportion of new outpatient referrals to gastro-enterological clinics (Harvey et al 1983), and about 15% of apparently healthy people have complaints of IBS-type (Thompson & Heaton 1980).

Besides the cardinal symptoms used to define IBS, patients with IBS frequently have both upper gastrointestinal and a wide range of other gastrointestinal symptoms (Svedlund et al 1985) and minor medical afflictions. Furthermore, an increased prevalence of psychoneurotic disorders have been established and according to some studies there is a close association with depressive illness (Hislop 1971, Liss et al 1973, Young et al 1976, Latimer et al 1981). A specific abnormality in the colonic myo-electrical rhythm has been suggested (Snape et al 1976, 1977, Taylor et al 1978a) as an underlying biologically determined predisposing factor, and there is now good evidence that IBS is a disorder of intestinal motility that may affect any level of the gastrointestinal tract.

However, this evidence indicating a constitutionally determined predisposition has as yet no clinical significance. The colonic myo-electrical disturbance found in IBS patients seems to be trait rather than state-dependent and therefore unrelated to symptoms (Taylor et al 1978b). It does not explain the clinical features of IBS, which still has to be diagnosed on the basis of the symptoms and by the exclusion of organic disorders. Recent findings indicating that the abnormalities of gut function are intermittent and that IBS is a paroxysmal motor disorder which may be detected in the small bowel (Kumar & Wingate 1985) hopefully will result in future tests for confirming a positive diagnosis of IBS.

129

Behavioural aspects

The reported high prevalence of psychopathology among the patient population with IBS may be due to behavioural patterns that lead to seeking health care. Why then, do some people with long-standing symptoms perceive them as serious enough to require medical attention while others do not? Is it that their symptoms are more severe or are they less able to cope with them? If this is not the case, what other factors lead to the visits? It may be that many of these patients recognise that they have psychological problems, but find it more acceptable socially to be identified as having a medical problem. It makes clinical sense to determine, therefore, whether the patient has underlying concerns, or has recently experienced a life-stress with which he or she is unable to cope and because of which is seeking support from the health care system. To pay attention to these factors instead of overemphasising just the bowel motility aspects of the disorder may be the key to more successful management of patients with IBS.

In a telephone survey (Whitehead et al 1982) of randomly selected adults, people with symptoms of IBS were more likely than people with peptic ulcer (and also more likely than the general population) to have multiple somatic complaints. They viewed their colds and flus as more serious than those of other people, and consulted a physician more often for minor illnesses. People who recalled being given gifts or special foods when they had a cold or flu as a child were also more likely to have IBS. These data indicate that chronic illness behaviour defined by frequent visits to physicians, multiple somatic complaints, and disability disproportionate to physical findings is more likely to be exhibited in IBS than peptic ulcer. It appears to be due to early learning experiences suggesting that a history of social rewards for illness contributes to the aetiology of IBS but not peptic ulcer.

In another survey of apparently healthy subjects (Sandler et al 1984) it was found that a majority of those affected with symptoms compatible with the IBS had never seen a doctor for these complaints. Those who consulted physicians for bowel symptoms also reported more non-gastrointestinal symptoms and were also more likely to see physicians for these other symptoms. They were also more likely to report an association of symptoms to psychosocial stress. These data suggest that seeking health care is not only related to symptom severity but other influences must also be considered.

In studies involving clinical samples of IBS, females are more commonly affected than males with a ratio of about 2:1 but in the general population there is no such difference, suggesting that women seek medical attention more readily. Furthermore, female patients with IBS present a higher mental symptom profile than males.

These observations concerning illness behaviour and the seeking of health care suggest that effective treatment of IBS patients requires a thorough understanding of the behavioural component (Latimer 1983a). They also suggest that the significance of the symptoms from a psychodynamic point of view should concentrate on benefits of being ill (secondary gains), such as special concern, increased sympathy and tolerance from those around the patient, and interplay with relations in family and social life where they can act as communications.

Psychopathological aspects

Irritable bowel syndrome seems to vary in the population in a dimensional rather than categorical way with continuity between the normal state and extreme severity of the disorder. In some studies concerning the patient population with IBS, more than 90% have been assigned a psychiatric diagnosis (Hislop 1971, Liss et al 1973, Latimer et al 1981). On the other hand there is a clinical impression that among these patients there is a wide range of personality types and many are psychologically robust and normal. Selection issues must therefore be considered in evaluation of these studies involving psychiatric assessment. On average, IBS patients have been found to be more anxious and depressed than the general population (Whitehead et al 1980) as well as patients suffering from other medical conditions (Young et al 1976). Their psychological problems are greater than those found in patients with more severe and disabling gastrointestinal diseases (Esler & Goulston 1973), and therefore unlikely to be solely a reaction to the digestive symptoms. The high prevalence of non-gastrointestinal symptoms, such as headaches, backaches and infections, found in IBS patients is also unlikely to arise secondarily to the digestive symptoms.

As regards personality characteristics, IBS patients are described as compulsive, overconscientious, dependent, sensitive, guilt-ridden and unassertive, but little evidence exists that IBS patients have a distinct personality profile (Latimer 1983b). They have been found to be significantly more neurotic and less extroverted than the normal population on the Eysenck Personality Inventory. In studies concerning alexithymic and neurotic features in digestive diseases, IBS patients were found to be the most neurotic, whereas those with chronic pancreatitis, ulcerative colitis and peptic ulcer disease presented more prominent alexithymic characteristics (Nakagawa et al 1979). 'Alexithymia' alludes to difficulties in expressing emotions verbally as conscious feelings, which instead manifest as bodily sensations in situations provoking emotional arousals. Alexithymia is also a characteristic thought to be inversely related to neuroticism in a dimensional manner. It is considered to predispose to the development of psychosomatic disorders rather than psychoneurosis in individuals under emotional stress.

Indecisiveness resulting in increasing inner tension followed by the onset of gastrointestinal symptoms has been described by Paulley (1984). He considered that the provocative life situation most common during episodes of IBS is indecision and 'sitting on the fence'. Life situations demanding important decisions, such as moving, marriage, having a baby, starting a new job etc. were judged the determinant factors. He found that identification of the actual situation and empathetic encouragement for the patient to resolve it was a most valuable short cut in management.

THERAPEUTIC APPROACHES

Physical treatments

Irritable bowel syndrome often becomes a chronic relapsing condition and it is generally agreed that the treatment of IBS represents a major clinical problem. No specific physical treatment has been shown to affect its clinical course significantly. Medical treatment involving different dietary regimes and drugs has had only limited success and the term 'wrestling' has been used to refer to the difficulties met in the management of these patients (Almy 1978). Dietary counselling intended to increase the amount of fibre in the food, bulk-forming agents and the drugs commonly used (for example anticholinergics and minor tranquillisers or antidepressants) are of some value and may have additive effects (Dotevall 1985). There are conflicting reports of the usefulness of medication, however, and follow-up studies designed to answer questions about either the course of the disorder when medication is discontinued or the effects of long-term maintenance medication have yet to be published.

Psychological aspects of treatment

Although the close association of IBS with psychological factors has been frequently alluded to, this has had little impact on the treatment and there has been continued reluctance to make use of findings of psychosocial significance in the handling of IBS patients and to record the role of psychotherapy in the treatment.

Against this background, it seemed important to investigate whether treatment could be improved by a more systematic consideration of the psychological aspects and a clinical trial in collaboration with the Division of Medical Gastro-enterology at our hospital was therefore undertaken.

A controlled study of psychological intervention in IBS

One hundred and nineteen consecutive IBS outpatients from the division of Medical Gastro-enterology IBS, aged 16–60 years, with complaints for at least 1 year and no other somatic or mental disorder were studied. Eighteen patients declined participation. The remaining 101 patients were randomly allocated to two treatment groups. Further details of the study are given by Svedlund et al (1983).

Treatments. The control group received routine medical treatment from members of the gastrointestinal team with bulk-forming agents, supplemented, when appropriate, by anticholinergic drugs, antacids and minor tranquillisers. The treatment also included advice about diet, smoking and drinking habits, plus reassurance about worries over cancer and other serious illnesses and information on possible causes of the symptoms.

The psychotherapy group received the same medical treatment plus individual, dynamically oriented, short-term psychotherapy. This was provided in weekly 1-hour sessions spread over 3 months and limited to ten sessions. Our aims were to work on conscious problems selecting treatment goals which could be achieved within the time-limit. We focused on the patients' means of coping with stress and emotional problems. Our approach was mainly supportive, occasionally more demanding with those patients with the resources for insight and anxiety-provoking therapy. The therapeutic strategy therefore varied from pointing out connections between symptoms and stressors (a more educational approach) to the handling of more specific conflicts of great importance to the patient (a more psycho-dynamic approach). For the patients given supportive psychotherapy the therapeutic style could naturally include insight-promoting elements on circumscribed areas and vice versa for the patients given anxiety-provoking therapy where the insight-promoting style did not exclude support. Flexibility was the hallmark.

Assessments. Outcome was assessed by independent raters, and by self-ratings at admission to the study, after 3 months (at the termination of psychotherapy) and at 15 months from the start of the study. Changes in the severity of symptoms and social adjustment were the main criteria of outcome.

Results. Both groups improved somatically during treatment but after 3 months there was a significantly greater improvement in favour of the psychotherapy group. The difference became more pronounced a year later, with the psychotherapy group showing further improvement, while the control group showed some deterioration. There was also a greater improvement in mental symptoms and in social adjustment in the psychotherapy group, but the difference was not as obvious as that in somatic symptoms. The course of illness was similar in the groups at intake to the study but during the follow-up year the psychotherapy group had a more episodic course with fewer symptomatic weeks, implying a change to a more benign course. Self-confidence and ability to cope with problems of everyday life had also improved significantly more among these patients. Patients' self-ratings accorded well with the independent assessments. No significant confounding factors were found.

Conclusion. Our conclusion is that by combining medical treatment with brief psychotherapy, the outcome can be substantially improved, not only in the short term but also in the long run. Perhaps the most striking finding, indicating a specific effect of psychotherapy, was the continued somatic improvement, which, given the chronic or recurrent nature of IBS, would not otherwise have been expected. The patients in our control group received more attention than is usual in the conventional management of IBS, thus balancing to some extent the placebo effect of attention inherent in psychotherapy. The improvement after completion of the psychotherapy, was probably due to the acquisition of more effective ways of coping with emotional problems. A new security based on a better understanding and feeling of control of the abdominal disorder may also have contributed to the more favourable outcome in the psychotherapy group.

Discussion. There are few controlled studies of psychotherapy in the treatment of IBS and more research needs to be done before we can draw definite conclusions about guidelines for the selection of patients suitable for different types of treatment.

In a controlled trial of hypnotherapy in the treatment of severe refractory IBS, Whorwell et al (1984) reported impressive results. The hypnotherapy consisted of seven $\frac{1}{2}$-hour sessions over a 3-month period. In addition, the patients were given a tape for daily autohypnosis. Hypnotherapy was solely directed at general relaxation and control of intestinal motility, and no attempt was made at exploration using hypno-analysis. It was concluded that the mechanism by which hypnotherapy acts is uncertain, but a direct action on gut motility was favoured by the observation that although well-being improved with hypnosis, emphasising general relaxation, IBS symptoms did not improve until control of intestinal function was introduced.

In another recent controlled study (Berndt & Maercker 1985) beneficial effects were reported from autogenic group training once a week for 14 weeks and after that every third month during a 1-year treatment period. Besides the autogenic training, the patients were given individual psychotherapy which could be either symptom or conflict oriented. Psychotherapy was found to be very useful only in those patients with a neurosis and it was concluded that if a neurosis is diagnosed in IBS patients, individual psychotherapy is indicated, with autogenic training as basis therapy. These encouraging results from different forms of psychotherapy in IBS will hopefully lead to further studies to elucidate the extent to which psychotherapy can serve as an effective primary or adjunct treatment in the management of IBS.

Patients with IBS are often severely restricted by their symptoms with limitations imposed on their everyday life. In our study 22% of the patients had to give up important plans and goals because of onset of illness and about 90% had at least some degree of impairment during the acute phase of their illness. The patients' perspective of their disorder needs to be emphasised since IBS disrupts roles and activities in a manner out of proportion with clinical seriousness. Failure by the physician to recognise emotional factors and to deal with these problems might set a trap by which symptoms become fixed and the resistance to face underlying emotional difficulties reinforced.

The advantage of a more flexible and holistic approach lies in its capacity not only to produce improvements in symptomatic aspects, but also in its ability to improve the patient's coping mechanisms, which may alter the course of the disorder in the long run to an extent where the management of IBS become less of the wrestling match described by Almy. A psychosomatic approach to treatment is also more likely to deal successfully with the patients' psychological needs and expectations from treatment, which was indicated in our study by the fact that significantly more patients in the control group than in the psychotherapy group were of the opinion that neither talks with the doctors nor the medical treatment had been of any benefit.

The way our study has been conducted means that the results can be generalised to IBS patients interested in exploring the role of social and emotional stressors in their condition. In our experience, this characteristic applies to a large proportion of IBS outpatients. We do not, however, suggest referral of all these patients to a psychiatrist for dynamic short-term psychotherapy. There are not the resources to provide such an intervention for all patients. Instead, we would emphasise the need for a flexible therapeutic and individually tailored approach because of the heterogeneity of the IBS patients. Undoubtedly, many patients benefit from reassurance and support from a good, sympathetic physician and treatment by the usual medical means. An attempt should be made to explain the cause of the symptoms and specifically cover concerns about cancer and other serious illnesses and to avoid the use of psycho-active drugs in the first lines of treatment. Clearly, anxiolytic or antidepressant drugs may be used on rare occasions if the patient has more serious symptoms of anxiety which cannot be managed otherwise, or primary depression. The value of frequent follow-ups has been shown in a study of the prognosis in IBS by Waller & Misiewicz (1969), and the efficacy of only a few interviews, conducted without special psychological training, aimed to understand and express the patient's subconscious distress, was demonstrated in an open follow-up study by Hislop (1980). These requirements correspond to already well established aspects of conventional management and the majority of patients are helped by this traditional approach. If, however, these measures prove insufficient there must be a willingness to extend the therapy to involve a more profound penetration of and systematic work with the patient's emotional problems. In most cases the psychotherapeutic management should be developed through the phases of (1) symptom orientation, (2) reassurance and (3) support, before deeper emotional problems and conflicts can be focused upon.

The traditional psychodynamic approach must therefore be modified to suit these patients. Motivation for psychotherapy must also be developed during the preparatory phase of the psychotherapy, since most patients initially present their problems in terms of medical illness. In our study, the character of therapy promoted insight in about half of the patients and the goals of therapy were reached in a majority of these patients within the time limit set. For the remaining patients a more didactic strategy to draw attention to associations between stressful life events and abdominal symptoms was found to be useful. The following example illustrates our way of working.

Case history

History. This 25-year-old woman had been working as a secretary after leaving school with good marks. She had been living with her boyfriend for 2 years, and had no children. Before the onset of the present abdominal disorder she had been healthy, both physically and mentally. She drank little alcohol and did not smoke. Her abdominal disorder started 3 years earlier, after her return from a holiday in Morocco. At that time, because of her complaints, she was examined at the department of medicine and referred to the infectious diseases clinic as a typhoid gastro-enteritis was suspected. There were no signs of any organic causes to her gastrointestinal complaints. From that time onwards she had had almost permanent complaints except for short asymptomatic periods.

During the last year her complaints had been continuous and at times so severe that she was unable to work. She had dull pains during most of the day and bouts of colicky pains several times a week. She complained of alternating hard and loose stools, abdominal distension, fullness and nausea. She reported increased fatigue and sleeping difficulties, which she thought to be due to her abdominal symptoms. She had a fear of the dark since childhood and still slept with the light on. Previous treatment had involved prescription of bulk-forming agents, diet counselling and advice to excercise. She thought this had temporarily alleviated her suffering, but otherwise had not led to any improvement at all.

Setting for treatment and initial consultation. She was referred to a psychiatrist. She accepted the referral after having been informed that it was to discuss the possible influence of psychosocial factors on her disorder. The first interview was devoted to clarifying mutual expectations. She was offered investigations at the department of medicine and psychiatry and in addition a maximum of ten weekly 1-hour sessions with the psychiatrist for further talks about her situation. The time limit was therefore clear from the very beginning. Initially she was encouraged to talk about herself and her opinion of the nature of her disorder. In this case the patient believed that there had to be some organic cause, something physically wrong with her gut, and rejected the idea that psychological factors might contribute to her illness.

Course of therapy. When her history was obtained at the second session, however, she described how her complaint had started 2 hours after her arrival home from a journey she had undertaken with her boyfriend against the wishes of her parents, especially that of her mother. She recalled being very tense on returning, having to face her mother's reaction. They were on openly bad terms with each other after the journey. The relationship had worsened since that time and contact between them was now restricted to a couple of telephone calls every month.

The next session was almost immediately focused on the inter-relations in her family. She described how her relationship with her mother had been deteriorating since she was 15 years old and beginning to leave home to meet friends. The situation at home became successively more strained such that she considered moving out at 17 years of age. She remembered that her mother strongly criticised her in an insulting way and among other things repeatedly called her a 'whore'. When talking about these events she was upset and began to cry. Already it was clear to the therapist to focus on the relationship with the mother as a theme for the following sessions.

At the fourth session it became evident that the patient had not realised until some years previously that her father was not her biological father. She only had realised several years after that a funeral she attended at 9 years of age was that of her biological father. About a year previously she had made contact with her grandparents, having obtained the information at the registrar's office. Her mother had reacted in a very negative way to the patient's contact with the grandparents and tried to prevent the patient's younger sister, who obviously was her half-sister, being informed.

The forthcoming six sessions were aimed at working through these problems presented by the patient in order to make her more successful in dealing with her difficulties with her mother. The advantages and disadvantages of different ways of approaching the mother were discussed, thus helping her discover her freedom of choice in their relationship. She was encouraged to test herself in contact with her mother. She thereby had the opportunity to articulate and thus structure her emotional experiences.

Comments on therapy. The abdominal complaints almost vanished after the second session and the patient was then pre-occupied with the cause of her symptoms. In this case the successful course of therapy was probably because she discovered early in the treatment, with the therapist's help, a crucial, emotionally loaded focus. This created favourable conditions for further development, where the therapist (1) facilitated emotional outlet by a permissive, empathetic attitude aiming at reducing her inner tension and (2) promoted insight by helping the patient to structure the problem more cognitively.

Here the doctor could advance into the role of the psychotherapist quite easily. In most other cases the doctor–patient relationship must be developed through a longer preparatory phase before a psychodynamic stage of therapy can be reached. The doctor makes use of the physician's role in obtaining the history and paying attention to the impact of the patient's symptoms on family and daily life. After establishing this it is possible in most cases for the doctor to shift to the role of the teacher aiming at elucidating psychosomatic mechanisms and their applications to patients and their specific situations. By systematically making use of these two working alliances most patients are able to reformulate their problems from terms of just a medical illness to a condition where the symptoms are seen in a broader context, with the possibility that the patient can gain some control by his own actions.

This patient described her mother as a very rigorous, exacting and authoritarian person, inclined to provoke feelings of guilt in her. She experienced strong fears of confrontations with her mother, which she explained as emerging from fears that 'anything might happen' to her mother, which she was not able to define more clearly. These fears, which were probably founded in unconscious feelings of aggression, prevented her from going further with the problems. Instead she chose to live with them, but now with a new awareness and perspective of her part in the relationship with her mother. Her personality had discernible traits of unassertiveness, high demands on herself, easily evoked feelings of guilt and difficulties in handling aggressive impulses. In part the therapist utilised findings about her personality to increase her awareness of its significance in her way of handling the problems focused on in the therapy. This helped the patient to be more conscious of her coping style and thus to improve her adaptation to her problems, especially those concerning the relationship with her mother.

The work in this case was distinguished by looking at the significance of conscious psychological problems in collaboration with the patient and by the support given to her own efforts to overcome her difficulties. Thus the therapist focused on conscious problems and tried to work these through within the time limit set and refrained from interpreting unconscious conflicts such as feelings of love for her stepfather which her mother might have felt threatening. In this working alliance the therapist also emphasised the patient's involvement and responsibility for the success of the treatment and gave her encouragement to grapple with the problems on her own. At follow-up 12 months later the patient had remained practically symptom-free.

She considered that the talks with the therapist had been of crucial importance for her improvement and she still considered the disturbed relationship with her mother as the cause of her abdominal disorder. This relationship with her mother was essentially unchanged in a practical sense but she thought there had been a significant change in how she experienced and managed the problem. She felt more free in the contact and had achieved an increased independence in relation to her mother and was no longer so distressed by their relationship.

The termination of psychotherapy requires special attention as it often evokes strong feelings. Many proponents of short-term psychotherapy have emphasised that the time limit itself is a significant constituent of the therapy, as it increases the demands on both the therapist and the patient to attain reasonable results. In our work the patients were frequently reminded of the time limit from the start of the therapy which probably eased the final separation at the termination. The therapist either chose to focus on the separation if the patient had good anxiety tolerance or else offered to keep one or two sessions for the future to avoid provoking too much anxiety if this could not be managed. The termination of the therapy thereby became more supportive as the initial agreement on the time limit was changed. Many patients accepted this offer and felt secure with the opportunity to make further contact, although very few did.

Summary and conclusions

To summarise our approach to psychotherapeutic management of IBS patients the following three phases can be distinguished.

1. Examination: the careful history-taking and recording of symptoms to obtain relevant information from medical, behavioural and psychodynamic perspectives for correct diagnosis and a plausible psychodynamic hypothesis.

2. Explanation: the development of a psychosomatic perspective by means of a pedagogic approach, where the concept of pure organic illness gradually can be reformulated and experienced as a psychosomatic condition.

3. Elaboration: the working through of central themes to relieve inner tension and enhance coping mechanisms, thus achieving improved adaptation to the problems and conflicts focussed on in therapy.

It seems reasonable to believe that our mode of treatment applied to IBS patients might also be useful in other functional bowel disorders and can serve as a model for treatment even beyond this sphere as far as psychosomatic conditions are concerned.

PROFESSIONAL ISSUES

The short-term character and relative simplicity of the type of psychotherapy given in our study, enable it to be used by interested general physicians and general practitioners, who meet these patients in their daily practice. The primary physician makes an accurate psychiatric assessment in only a minority of his patients and are often completely unaware of the presence of psychiatric illness (Young et al 1976). An increased awareness of the patient's psychiatric illness and an accurate psychiatric diagnosis is necessary for the physician to provide effective pharmacotherapy, as for primary depression, and to spare the patient needless medication and investigations, where they would be better off with psychotherapy. Physicians who are interested in working this way may therefore profit from guidance by psychiatrists trained in psychotherapy.

In many cases short-term psychotherapy will prove insufficient. Our choice of time limit was dictated by the study design. For some patients even shorter therapies might be sufficient, whilst for others longer therapies might be indicated. The time limit of therapy should be a matter of clinical judgement and be determined during the preparatory phases of therapy, depending on the patient's resources and the goals formulated. Referral to other forms of psychotherapy may also be indicated. In these cases other professionals with training in psychotherapy may provide the psychological management in collaboration with the physician who is responsible for the physical care. However, one should be aware that patients who are prematurely referred for psychotherapy may view such a referral as ignoring their somatic complaints and feel insulted. This can result in their seeking other doctors for second opinions. We believe that the physician should deal with this problem at the start to prevent disappointed patients circulating from one doctor to another. The patient must be fully convinced that the diagnosis is correct and that no further tests are needed. To promote this the doctor should teach the patient the basic anatomy and physiology of the gastrointestinal tract, including the significance of the brain–gut connection. Thorough information about expectation of normal findings on clinical examination and diagnostic tests, aimed at excluding organic disorders, may also contribute to establish that kind of confident and enduring working alliance which is indispensable for success in treating psychosomatic patients.

The best person to conduct the psychotherapeutic management in the first preparatory phase is the physician. Detailed comprehensive history-taking at the beginning of this phase also enables the physician to make a more accurate medical diagnosis and thereby increase his diagnostic confidence and reduce the amount of investigation and unnecessary referrals.

Later on in this preparatory phase the major goal is to define the patient's complaints in terms of a psychosomatic disorder rather than just a medical illness and to provide an understanding of the psychological factors involved. This stage of treatment is an important prerequisite to the establishment of any effective psychotherapy alliance and should not be bypassed. Once the IBS patient becomes accessible for a more psychodynamic approach, treatment is in no way different from that of other mildly neurotic patients.

REFERENCES

Almy T P 1978 Wrestling with the irritable colon. Medical Clinics of North America 62: 203–210

Berndt H, Maercker W 1985 Zur Psychotherapie beim Reizkolon. Zeitschrift für die Gesamte Inner Medizin und Ihre Grenzgebiete 40: 107–110

Dotevall G 1985 Irritable bowel syndrome. In: Stress and common gastrointestinal disorders. A comprehensive approach. Praeger Publishers, New York, ch. 7, pp. 97–144

Esler M D, Goulston K J 1973 Levels of anxiety in colonic disorders. New England Journal of Medicine 228: 16–20

Harvey R F, Salih S Y, Read A E 1983 Organic and functional disorders in 2000 gastroenterology outpatients. Lancet 1: 632–634

Hislop I G 1971 Psychological significance of the irritable colon syndrome. Gut 12: 452–457

Hislop I G 1980 Effect of very brief psychotherapy on the irritable bowel syndrome. Medical Journal of Australia 2: 620–623

Kumar D, Wingate D L 1985 The irritable bowel syndrome: a paroxysmal motor disorder. Lancet 2: 973–977

Latimer P R 1983a Functional gastrointestinal disorders. A behavioral medicine approach. Springer Publishing Company, New York

Latimer P R 1983b Irritable bowel syndrome. Psychosomatic illness review: no 7. Psychosomatics 24: 205–218

Latimer P R, Sarna S K, Campbell D, Latimer M R, Waterfall W E, Daniel E E 1981 Colonic motor and myoelectrical activity: a comparative study of normal subjects, psychoneurotic patients and patients with irritable bowel syndrome. Gastroenterology 80: 893–901

Liss J L, Alpers D, Woodruff R A 1973 The irritable colon syndrome and psychiatric illness. Diseases of the Nervous System 34: 151–157

Nakagawa T, Sugita M, Nakai Y, Ikemi Y 1979 Alexithymic features in digestive diseases. Psychotherapy and Psychosomatics 32: 191–203

Paulley J W 1984 The psychological management of irritable colon. Hepato-Gastroenterology 30: 53–54

Sandler R S, Drossman D A, Nathan H P, McKee D C 1984 Symptom complaints and health care seeking behavior in subjects with bowel dysfunction. Gastroenterology 87: 314–318

Snape W J, Carlsson G M, Cohen S 1976 Colonic myoelectric activity in the irritable bowel syndrome. Gastroenterology 70: 326–330

Snape W J, Carlsson G M, Matarazzo S A, Cohen S 1977 Evidence that abnormal myoelectric activity produces colonic motor dysfunction in the irritable bowel syndrome. Gastroenterology 72: 383–387

Svedlund J, Sjödin I, Ottosson J O, Dotevall G 1983 Controlled study of psychotherapy in irritable bowel syndrome. Lancet 2: 589–592

Svedlund J, Sjödin I, Dotevall G, Gillberg R 1985 Upper gastrointestinal and mental symptoms in the irritable bowel syndrome. Scandinavian Journal of Gastroenterology 20: 595–601

Taylor T, Darby C, Hammond P, Basu P 1978a Is there a myoelectrical abnormality in the irritable colon syndrome? Gut 19: 391–395

Taylor T, Darby C, Hammond P 1978b Comparison of rectosigmoid myoelectrical activity in the irritable colon syndrome during relapses and remissions. Gut 19: 923–929

Thompson W G, Heaton K W 1980 Functional bowel disorders in apparently healthy people. Gastroenterology 79: 283–288

Waller S L, Misiewicz J J 1969 Prognosis in the irritable bowel syndrome. Lancet 2: 753–756

Whitehead W E, Engel B T, Schuster M M 1980 Irritable bowel syndrome. Physiological and psychological differences between diarrhea-predominant and constipation-predominant patients. Digestive Diseases and Sciences 25: 404–413

Whitehead W E, Winget C, Fedoravicius A S, Wooley S, Blackwell B 1982 Learned illness behavior in patients with irritable bowel syndrome and peptic ulcer. Digestive Diseases and Sciences 27: 202–208

Whorwell P J, Prior A, Faragher E B 1984 Controlled trial of hypnotherapy in the treatment of severe refractory irritable bowel syndrome. Lancet 2: 1232–1234

Young S J, Alpers D H, Norland C C, Woodruff R A 1976 Psychiatric illness and the irritable bowel syndrome. Gastroenterology 70: 162–166

Disorders of Micturition

INTRODUCTION

This chapter is concerned with the treatment of the chronic urinary symptoms of frequency, urgency, urge incontinence and nocturia. For anatomical reasons these symptoms are much commoner in women and this chapter is written with particular reference to them.

Incidence

Urgency and frequency are troublesome lower urinary tract symptoms which are found in 20% of women aged between 20 and 65 years (Bungay et al 1980). In a survey of over 4000 nurses Wolin (1969) found that 16% leaked urine once or more each day. Neither survey distinguished clearly between urge incontinence and simple leaking of urine without urgency, due to sphincter weakness. They do, however, suggest that a substantial morbidity exists.

At the case level, Jeffcoate & Francis (1966) estimated that at least two out of three patients attending their clinic with complaints of incontinence had, in fact, urge-type leakage. In the older population, they considered that incontinence was nearly always due to an unstable bladder, contrary to the commonly held belief that sphincter incompetence was likely to be the cause. Frewan (1972) noted that 80% of patients presenting as gynaecological outpatients with symptoms of urge incontinence had detrusor instability.

Diagnostic categories

Chronic urinary symptoms may be the result of a number of conditions, the most important of which are:

1. Genuine stress incontinence (GSI)
2. Detrusor instability (DI)
3. Sensory urgency (SU)

142

A survey of 211 patients attending a urodynamic clinic showed that 31% had GSI and 40% had DI or SU (Macaulay et al 1987).

Genuine stress incontinence is caused by incompetence of the sphincter at the bladder neck. Incontinence occurs during momentary rise of intra-abdominal pressure, for example during coughing. This condition is usually regarded as a mechanical problem in which the bladder neck cannot be kept closed.

Detrusor instability and *sensory urgency* both produce symptoms of frequency, urgency, urge incontinence and nocturia. The two conditions are clinically indistinguishable and the diagnosis is made on cystometry (see below). The most common form of DI is idiopathic, non-neuropathic detrusor instability. However, it can be congenital or secondary to some other disease process such as multiple sclerosis or arteriosclerosis. SU is diagnosed in the presence of some or all of the symptoms of frequency, urgency, incontinence and nocturia, when cystometry is normal.

Investigation procedure

Where facilities exist, patients with chronic urinary symptoms may be referred to a urodynamic clinic which specialises in the investigation and treatment of disorders of the female lower urinary tract.

Following routine history and examination there are special investigations to measure the function of the bladder and urethra. Cystometry is an invasive procedure in which a narrow catheter and pressure transducer are introduced into the bladder via the urethra. The bladder is slowly filled with normal saline. A pressure transducer is also introduced into the rectum to record the intra-abdominal pressure. It is then possible to calculate the detrusor pressure by subtracting the intra-abdominal pressure from the intravesical pressure.

During normal filling the bladder volume increases without any significant rise in pressure. A diagnosis of DI is made if there are any involuntary detrusor contractions, either spontaneous or on provocation (such as coughing or the sound of water running from a tap). SU is diagnosed in a patient with urinary symptoms and normal cystometry.

Patients with GSI may be investigated by means of videocysto-urethrography (VCU). In this procedure the bladder is filled with a radio-opaque dye. The patient coughs and then urinates under X-ray screening. The results are recorded on video tape. This enables the action of the bladder neck to be scrutinised.

REVIEW OF LITERATURE

Emotions and bladder function

There has been little published research on the relationship between the psyche and this particular area of the soma. Mosso & Pellicani (1882) were the first to investigate bladder function, using cystometry in female dogs. They found that strong emotion or the sound of running water led to detrusor contraction. They later confirmed their findings in humans.

Menninger (1941) suggested that from a psychodynamic standpoint urination had many conscious and unconscious meanings, such as the erotic and aggressive components. He also referred to self-destructive and self-punitive elements. He presented a number of case histories to support his hypothesis. One in particular illustrated the erotic aspect and also the dangers of treatment. A 64-year-old woman with a life-time history of frequency was treated with gradual dilatation of the bladder. No sooner had this been achieved than the patient became restless, anxious and attempted suicide. The urinary hyperactivity was a means of sexual gratification, which required that the erotic significance remain unconscious. Menninger continues, 'Her physician quite unwittingly took from her the only outlet for erotic gratification, and as we know, the blocking of all erotic outlets usually results in anxiety, which may, as in this case, be unendurable'.

This earlier work concentrated on the possible relationship between intrapsychic stress and bladder function. An alternative approach is to measure aspects of personality and neurotic symptomatology.

Jeffcoate & Francis (1966) gained a clinical impression that patients with urgency incontinence were anxious and introspective. In a study of 15 patients with urgency and urge incontinence and 42 patients with other urological diagnoses, Crisp & Sutherst (1983) found that those with DI and SU were significantly more anxious and neurotic.

Two studies (Rees & Farhoumand 1977, Stone & Judd 1978) have shown a relationship between detrusor instability and hysterical personality traits. This is not a consistent finding: Freeman et al (1985) did not find increased hysterical personality traits in their study of DI.

Frewen (1972, 1978, 1980, 1982a,b) maintained that DI is a psychosomatic condition. In his view, DI was caused by the patient's abnormal urinary symptom. This suggests that patients with SU go on to develop DI if the symptoms persist. His evidence rested, first, in the ability to elicit a history of emotional trauma antedating the onset of the symptom. Secondly, the efficacy of psychological treatment was thought to support a significant psychogenic component in the genesis of DI and SU. Frewen's treatment included bladder retraining and education about supposed anatomical and psychological mechanisms. The fact that patients with emotional or social problems had a poor response to his treatment provided him with further support for his views on aetiology. However, factors that may be therapeutic need not imply any causality.

In a recent study by Pierson et al (1985) 23 patients with DI were compared with 23 matched patients with GSI. Those with DI had significantly higher scores on the Rahe & Holmes life stress measure, as well as being more depressed. This is the only study so far to report on the possible contribution of life events to urinary symptoms.

In a clinic survey of 211 patients Macaulay et al (1987) found that urodynamic patients were more anxious and depressed than an age-matched normal population. Patients with GSI were as anxious as general medical inpatients whilst patients with SU were significantly more anxious. Patients with DI were as anxious as those with SU and in addition had higher scores on ratings of hysteria and obsessionality. Twenty-five per cent of patients, including members of all three diagnostic groups, claimed their urinary symptoms rendered life intolerable. These patients were as anxious, depressed and phobic as psychiatric inpatients, emphasising the serious psychological morbidity experienced by patients with urinary symptoms.

Thus, there have been positive findings suggesting that emotional factors are important in the causation and maintenance of urinary symptoms. Two themes emerge: first, there are characteristic personality traits related to DI and SU; secondly, there is a suggestion that such patients use characteristic intrapsychic mechanisms.

Treatment

Genuine stress incontinence is conventionally treated by pelvic floor exercises or bladder neck surgery. There is, however, no generally accepted approach to the treatment of DI and SU. Over the years a number of empirical treatments have been advocated including surgery, cystodistension, drugs and psychological methods. Turner-Warwick & Whiteside (1979) summarised the clinical situation by concluding that no surgical, pharmacological or neurosurgical procedure will effectively convert an unstable detrusor mechanism to a stable one with any degree of reliability. Drug treatment, usually with an anticholinergic such as propantheline, is perhaps the only conventional treatment which is widely used. However, the results are disappointing and symptoms usually return when the medication is stopped (Cardozo 1979).

Bladder training

Jeffcoate & Francis (1966) are credited as being the first to describe bladder training as a treatment for urge incontinence, quoting a symptomatic cure rate of 55%.

Frewen (1978) reported a study on 40 patients. Bladder training was explained to the patient who then kept a urinary diary. The author referred to the additional use of supportive therapy, anxiolytic and anticholinergic drugs, though this was not quantified, nor was any attempt made to evaluate the relative contributions of the pharmacotherapy. Frewen reported an objective cure rate of 82.5% at 3 months. Of the seven failures, five had chronically ill husbands. Frewen considered that their 'environmental obligations' made it impossible for them to be amenable to any form of treatment. Further psychological analysis of this cohort would have been interesting.

Inpatient bladder drill cured or improved the majority of patients in studies reported by Jarvis & Millar (1980), Elder & Stephenson (1980) and Jarvis (1981).

These treatment studies were carried out by surgeons or research nursing staff who had no formal training in behavioural techniques. None of the studies controlled for any possible non-specific factors such as informal giving of advice or counselling. The purpose of admission to hospital, or the use of additional techniques such as anxiolytic medication, was rarely defined. However, such criticism cannot be applied to Pengelly & Booth (1980). In their outpatient treatment study, patients with DI were provided with a micturition chart and measuring jug. In addition, the therapist explained the possibility of an emotional aetiology. These two aspects, the documentation of symptoms and explanation of the rationale of treatment, form the basis of bladder training. Thus, the authors appeared to have a good grasp of the necessary elements of bladder training as understood today. Nineteen out of 25 patients were cured or improved symptomatically and 11 out of 25 cured or improved on cystometry. These results probably represent the most realistic cure rate for DI patients treated with outpatient bladder training.

Recently, there have been two reviews of the longer-term effects of bladder training. Frewen (1982b, 1984) presented the results of outpatient bladder training, a procedure that he has developed over a number of years, and quotes a subjective cure rate of 86% at 6 years. Holmes et al (1983) reviewed 56 patients 1–5 years after inpatient bladder training. Those with SU responded well to bladder drill: 94% improved and of these only 6% relapsed. In the group of patients with DI the results were less good: for those with idiopathic DI, the response rate was 90% and the relapse rate 44%; there was a 55% response rate in patients with congenital or arterio-sclerotic DI but all relapsed.

Hypnosis

Hypnotherapy has been used with success by Freeman & Baxby (1982). In this trial 50 patients with DI underwent 12 sessions of hypnosis. The treatment consisted of induction of the hypnotic state, relaxation, ego strengthening and suggestions regarding symptom removal. Patients were instructed to practise daily at home using a prerecorded tape.

At the end of the trial 29 patients were symptom-free, 14 improved and 7 were unchanged. This study also showed that hypnosis improved bladder function: 3 months after the end of treatment 44 patients underwent cystometry and the objective measures obtained then correlated positively with the reported symptomatic improvements. In addition to the hypnotic techniques described, Freeman (1985) found that the patients also used the sessions to discuss personal stresses and worries.

Biofeedback

Treatment with biofeedback was reported by Cardozo et al (1978a,b). This study recruited 27 patients with DI who had failed to respond to other therapy such as medication or outpatient bladder training. The patients were given an auditory signal which altered in tone in response to changes in bladder pressure as recorded by a bladder pressure catheter. Over a period of an hour the bladder was slowly filled and emptied, usually three times. Patients were asked to keep the tone low by whatever means possible. This varied from patient to patient, some preferred to talk, others found that tightening certain muscle groups was helpful. Most patients attended for six to eight sessions. Using objective and subjective methods of assessment 81% of the patients improved. These were good results but the procedure was time consuming of staff and equipment.

Psychotherapy

Hafner et al (1977) reported a study of 26 patients with frequency, urgency and urge incontinence. They were divided into two groups on the basis of their neuroticism score on the Eysenck Personality Inventory (EPI) and Middlesex Hospital Questionnaire. Most patients were treated with four to six sessions of autogenic training (a type of relaxation treatment). Seven patients refused treatment. Patients in the most neurotic group reported either a great or moderate improvement in urinary symptoms whilst the majority in the least neurotic group showed slight or no benefit. The authors suggested that this latter group of patients were denying or disclaiming their symptoms, citing as evidence the patients' biographical and medical histories. Unfortunately, there was no record of the measures of improvement, so it is difficult to draw any firm conclusions from this study.

A recent randomised trial (Macaulay et al 1987) of 50 patients compared bladder training, brief psychotherapy and propantheline. Patients were assessed by bladder diaries, psychological questionnaires and cystometry before and after 3 months of treatment. The psychotherapy group experienced significant improvement in urgency, incontinence and nocturia. There was no major change in psychoneurotic profile, but there was an improvement in symptoms relating to the physical correlates of anxiety. Bladder training was an effective treatment for frequency and the patients became less anxious and depressed. There was only a modest improvement in frequency in the propantheline group. These results suggest that bladder training is effective for frequency whilst patients with urgency, urge incontinence and nocturia would derive more benefit from psychotherapy.

Summary

Urodynamic patients appear more anxious and depressed than normal, although in patients with GSI the changes are no more than in inpatients with other medical conditions. Abnormalities in psychoneurotic profile have more often been reported in DI and SU. Not all studies agree on the type of profile although several studies have linked neuroticism and hysterical traits to DI. No study has satisfactorily resolved the question of causation; Frewen (1982b) maintains that psychological abnormalities can generate bladder dysfunction. Conversely, chronic urinary symptoms are an undoubted source of stress and worry.

Pelvic floor exercises and surgery are well established treatments for GSI. In contrast, the optimal treatment for DI and SU is controversial. There is little evidence that conventional treatments such as surgery or drug therapy are effective. They have complications or troublesome side effects and their use is difficult to justify in a chronic condition which is not life-threatening. Trials of psychological treatments seem promising, even if the mechanisms that might have brought about any improvement are not understood or poorly quantified. Most work has been reported on bladder training, with the overall conclusion that patients with SU or idiopathic DI respond reasonably well. For SU patients at least, this improvement is sustained. There is a suggestion that patients with frequency predominating might benefit most from bladder drill, while urgency and nocturia may respond better to psychotherapy. A number of trials suggest that, regardless of the treatment offered, patients with gross psychological disturbances respond poorly.

I believe that a combination of outpatient bladder training and psychotherapy represents the best approach for most patients with DI or SU.

CLINICAL MANAGEMENT

Introduction

Patients with DI or SU can be effectively treated by the interested general practitioner, continence nurse or practice counsellor. Seeing patients with micturition disorders infrequently, they may feel inexperienced and, as a result, lack confidence in their own therapeutic abilities. However, the following suggestions and guidelines should provide a framework to enable the treatment of such patients without necessarily referring them to a gynaecological department or specialist urodynamic unit (which may have a waiting list of many months for non-life-threatening conditions). 'Warmth, genuineness and empathy' (Truax et al 1966) are important non-specific components of any treatment regime. It is often this aspect of treatment which is most valued by the patients and which can be effectively applied in primary care.

Different considerations apply in a hospital department. Treatment for chronic urinary symptoms is difficult to administer in the setting of a busy outpatient clinic. However, the larger number of patients allows the therapist to develop a greater depth of understanding. There is also the possibility to organise treatment in a group setting. As well as expediency, there are distinct therapeutic advantages to group therapy for patients with micturition disorders, which are discussed later. In contrast to routine outpatients, where appointments may be booked in at 10-minute intervals, psychological treatments require time — the initial interview needs an hour for a full assessment. There is no short cut. A recognition of this fact is a prerequisite for the organisation of a clinical service for such patients. Nevertheless, in a cost–benefit analysis of micturition disorders McDonnall (1982) considered that 'if psychiatric treatment is able to cure or relieve symptoms of urgency, urge incontinence or frequency there may be vast non-pecuniary benefits to be reaped from its introduction' and finally concluded that 'once established, psychological treatment is less expensive than conventional methods of treatment'.

The consultation

The undergraduate is taught first to take a detailed history. I recall being told by one of my teachers that after taking the history you should have a pretty good idea of what the problem is and the physical examination should merely be an opportunity to confirm your diagnosis. This advice is particularly true in the diagnosis of micturition disorders.

The intention of this chapter is to discuss the treatment of DI and SU. However, patients present with symptoms, not diagnoses. Important conditions to consider in the differential diagnosis are: urinary tract infection, genuine stress incontinence and systemic disease first presenting with micturition symptoms (such as multiple sclerosis). A physical examination reveals no abnormality in patients with DI or SU. Diagnosis by exclusion requires that the clinician retains an open mind and is willing to review the situation if progress is not satisfactory.

Special investigations should always include a midstream urine specimen and possibly culture for chlamydia and acid fast bacilli if the history is suggestive of non-specific urethritis or tuberculosis. Cystometry or cystoscopy may be required: on rare occasions frequency may be the only presenting symptom of functionally reduced bladder capacity caused by a pelvic mass or bladder tumour. The timing of cystoscopy is a matter for careful judgement. Invasive investigation is unlikely to be required in a young, timid woman who is constitutionally anxious and about to start a new job or move away from home. However, further investigation is appropriate in a woman in her sixties presenting with frequency who has never needed to attend her general practitioner and does not appear to be under any emotional stress. The reality of long waiting lists means that treatment becomes an investigative procedure. The reader is referred to standard gynaecological textbooks for further advice on the subject.

Idiopathic DI and SU are clinically indistinguishable. The relationship between the two is a matter for conjecture (Frewen 1982). However, the diagnosis does not affect the treatment offered, although long-term follow-up studies suggest that patients with SU have a better prognosis.

Symptomatology

There are four main complaints: frequency, urgency, incontinence and nocturia. The balance of symptoms may have therapeutic implications (Macaulay et al 1987). Thus, in the history it is worthwhile attempting to assess the relative contributions of each symptom to the presenting complaint.

Frequency is a symptom when the patient is voiding more than seven times during the waking day. However, the patient may not see it that way. They may accept frequency as perfectly normal behaviour. The following case illustrates this point as well as throwing some light on its possible origins.

V. B. was a single girl in her mid-twenties who only presented for treatment when she changed jobs to work in a bank where they took exception to her frequent absences from the counter to void. Prior to this, it had not occurred to her that there was anything abnormal in her behaviour. In discussion she was certain that this had started in childhood when her mother would always send her to the lavatory before they were to go out anywhere 'just in case'. Thus, regardless of the need, she had learnt, as a habit, always to void when there was an opportunity.

The symptoms of urgency and urge incontinence can cause considerable distress, resulting in social embarrassment and the need to change clothes. Urgency is defined as a strong desire to void which allows little time for delay. Incontinence associated with urgency needs to be distinguished from stress incontinence — in this context the word stress refers to an anatomical and physiological disorder, rather than stress at a psychological level. It is usually possible to distinguish the two conditions on the history. GSI (often simply referred to as stress incontinence) can follow childbirth for example. Typically, small amounts of urine are voided following coughing or bending. In stress incontinence there is no abnormal detrusor muscle activity. This is in contrast to urge incontinence in which the symptom is generated from the detrusor muscle contracting at the 'wrong' time. That is, the patient does not wish to void but is unable consciously to inhibit the detrusor contraction. Depending on the strength of the contraction and other anatomical factors incontinence may or may not occur.

Nocturia is defined as the arousal from sleep twice or more every night to void. It is important to distinguish this from another frequent occurrence: the patient wakes at night and then voids before attempting to go back to sleep. As it happens, it is likely that both behaviours have their origins at a psychological level, but the latter is more appropriately considered a sleep disorder. Nocturia without any additional daytime symptoms is an uncommon presentation of DI or SU.

The timing of urinary symptoms may be important. Obviously urge incontinence occurring at work or away from home will be more distressing. In addition, the timing may have some symbolic significance.

Symptoms occurring at the weekend but not during time at work suggest difficulties at home — despite claims by the patient that all is well. The therapeutic aim would be to help her openly acknowledge the problems, frequently marital, and, perhaps with your guidance, resolve the conflict, either in individual sessions or by seeing the couple together. The following case illustrates some of these points.

F. S. was 31 years old and had been married for a number of years. Her main complaint was urgency and incontinence. It was particularly bad when waiting for the train to go into work in the mornings. Sometimes, she would have to go home to change because she was so wet. After two or three psychotherapy sessions the symptoms worsened, so much so that she was unable to go in to work for 2 weeks.

She had supported her husband through university by taking an office job and was now very keen to have a baby, but her husband was not earning enough money to enable her to stop working. Initially, she had denied that there was anything amiss with the marriage but as therapy progressed difficulties became apparent. The suppressed hostility and anger towards her husband had initially found expression when waiting to go to work — work she disliked. As the symbolic meaning of the symptom became clear she was able to express in words how she felt let down by him. When the problems had come out into the open in therapy she was able to discuss them with her husband and shortly afterwards her symptoms subsided. By the end of therapy they had made arrangements to sell their flat and move to a town outside London. He found a better paid job and F. S. was trying to get pregnant.

This patient's symptom may be explained in a number of ways. A psychoanalytic interpretation would attach symbolic significance to the nature of the symptom — related to the lower urinary tract and therefore of possible sexual significance. The timing of the symptom might perhaps be governed by the stress generated by the marital discord, the suppressed hostility towards her husband gaining outlet in the urinary symptoms. When the stress was relieved the symptoms subsided.

In addition to an account of the presenting symptoms, a detailed personal, family and developmental history is required to make a formulation. This is a summary of the important aspects of the case including a statement about the underlying difficulties, suggested lines of treatment and possible response. Psychiatrists often use a formulation to answer the question 'why has this patient become ill now?' and this approach has value in the treatment of patient with DI and SU.

Treatment

Treatment has already begun by taking a history and demonstrating a willingness to understand the problem. More so than in surgery or the prescription of medication, psychological treatments require the trust and readiness of the patient to accept your interpretation and explanation of the symptoms. Even if you are right in your assessment, if the patient rejects your suggestions or fails to return for further sessions she is unlikely to have been helped.

After the first consultation you may wish to arrange special investigations. At this stage it is helpful to have, at least in your mind, a plan of action. Patients get anxious awaiting investigations so it is best to arrange them all as a batch. An appointment sent for a second test will lead the patient to wonder what has been revealed by the first. Investigations should not be used as a way of buying time — it is not good medical practice to leave difficult patients for your successor to solve! In general practice this can lead to frustration on the part of the patient and possibily difficulties in future with the doctor–patient relationship.

The next stage is arguably the most important. You will need to explain to the patient what you think is going on and how you propose it should be treated. Most patients' understanding of biology is minimal. Some will fear they have cancer whilst others might think the incontinence means they are 'going senile'. It is only too easy to speak to patients as though they know only a little less than you whereas the reality is usually very different. Time spent at this stage pays dividends.

You will also need to raise the idea that anxieties and worries might be important in the causation of the urinary symptoms. A characteristic feature of many patients with 'psychosomatic' disorders is their particular ability to deny or disclaim that they have problems that upset and worry them. The very nature of the defence mechanism of denial means that it is not amenable to confrontation. Sometimes it is helpful to use examples that they may be able to relate to — such as anxiety prior to an exam causing urinary frequency. In spite of your best efforts you may still get the response 'that's all very well doctor, but I don't think it applies to me'. At this stage it is probably best not to push the point any more but to talk about the psychological treatments, emphasising the 'training' aspects. There is little point in boxing the patient into a psychological corner.

Although the patient may consciously want treatment for the urinary symptoms, there will, as in any maladaptive behaviour, be consequences of the return to normality, such as less attention from the spouse. It is worth asking yourself 'How will losing the symptoms change this patient's life?'

Available evidence shows bladder training to be an effective psychological treatment. I would recommend it particularly in a patient whose predominating urinary symptom is frequency, or who seems unlikely to benefit from a psychodynamic approach. The first stage is to document the pattern of micturition using a bladder diary for 1 week. This can be a preprinted form or something made up by the patient. It should record the following:

1. The time she urinates and if possible the amount passed. You will need

a supply of plastic measuring jugs! Urination at night should be marked in a different colour. It is then easy to work out a daily mean.

2. She should mark the form with a tick any time she experiences urgency. I would suggest you rate the symptom on a four-point 'symptom severity' scale such as: 0 = no complaint; 1 = urgency less than twice a day; 2 = not on every occasion but on more than two occasions during the day; 3 = occurring on every occasion or more prior to micturition.

3. Any incontinence and the amount lost. In practice most women with urinary symptoms are content to accept the loss of a few drops up to seven times a week as a 'minor symptom' whereas soaked pants or emptied bladder even once a week is rated as a 'significant symptom'.

Such detailed symptom documentation may strain the compliance of some patients but is justified as it formalises the approach for the patient and provides an accurate pretreatment baseline. Retrospective accounts of the exact severity of urinary symptoms are notoriously unreliable.

The essence of bladder training is to get the woman to urinate at pre-determined times, regardless of bladder cues. For Week 1 this should be the shortest time between voidings on the bladder diary. This gives the patient confidence in you and the approach — after all, you are asking her to do something she can achieve. The difference in this week is that voiding is at a predetermined time, suggested by you. The time between urinations is gradually increased until voiding takes place at bladder fullness, usually at 3–4-hourly intervals. The patient should be seen weekly. During these sessions she should be taught pelvic floor exercises as well as being generally supported and encouraged. In this way she should gain confidence and develop anatomical and psychological control of her symptoms. Treatment should continue for 3 months, with bladder diaries in the middle and at the end of treatment to document progress.

If the complaint has been mainly frequency and you consider the symptom to be a habit disorder, without any significant secondary gain operating, this approach alone is likely to be successful. The patient may be back to a normal pattern of voiding within 2–3 months.

An alternative approach is to take the view that it might be helpful to 'talk about the things that are worrying you'. This might apply to patients with predominantly urgency and nocturia, or where diagnostic interview suggests psychological conflict and distress, or in a woman who, for what-ever the reason, failed to benefit from the more behavioural approach of bladder training. The first task is to link, in the patient's mind, the urinary symptoms and the psychological difficulties, related either in a causal manner or now working powerfully to maintain the symptom. There are three areas worthy of enquiry: difficulties at work, at home and intrapsychic difficulties. The first two can often be seen as being based on frustration or loss of control of a situation, whilst the third tends to revolve around problems of sexuality or existential difficulties — who am I and where am I going in life?

Most patients have their own substantial personality resources. Your task is to facilitate and maximise their use. In this context, it can be very therapeutic to give patients a chance to talk through their worries. The task of psychotherapy is both to help people change in ways that they would like and/or be more comfortable with themselves as they are.

There are a few basic ground rules for psychotherapy, although none of them are absolute. The first is the most important — do not overcommit yourself, as there are only so many hours in the day. As a group, doctors are not good at organising time or setting limits. Talking to patients is work. You, and others such as your secretary or colleagues, need to remember this! This difficult task will be made even more so if the telephone is demanding your attention or your bleep is summoning you elsewhere. The task needs your exclusive attention if it is to succeed! Why make it harder for yourself?

The following framework is a guide when seeing a patient for 'brief psychotherapy' for treatment of urinary symptoms. The sessions should be at the same time, in the same place, each week, lasting 40 or 50 minutes and agreed in advance with the patient. The sessions must start and finish on time and should be seen as a firm commitment on both sides, so do not make a promise you cannot keep. Eight sessions is a good number, although it does depend on personal style and the nature of the patient's difficulties. Finally, let the patient do the talking!

The following is an account from a session with a 30-year-old married woman with three children. She presented with symptoms of frequency, some urgency and occasional nocturia. In many ways she is a typical patient.

At the beginning of the second session I usually ask patients what they had thought about the first assessment interview.

Patient: I thought about it quite a lot . . . you know, what set it [the urinary symptoms] off. . . . Most of the things we talked about were worries . . . recent worries, more so — you're thinking it's worries that cause this . . . . It's been going on for longer than most of some of the things we were talking about last week. So I don't know if what I said was relevant quite honestly. That's basically what I think.

Therapist: So it's something you've been thinking about quite a lot during the week?

Patient: Yes, it's funny, you know it's like when you give somebody a licence to speak you don't really think about what you've been saying until afterwards . . . .

Therapist: Would you say you had much opportunity to talk in the way that we talked last time?

Patient: . . . Yes . . . (hestitatingly). Yes I do. I'm not the type to bottle up things, I talk to friends or my husband . . . . I'm not the type to keep things inside . . . .

Therapist: (*sotto voce*) Um . . . .
(long pause)

Patient: You keep going 'um'! (giggles.) Something I noticed last week . . . there was sort of deadly silences at times, I don't know if you, what you expect from me, if you expect me to carry on talking, if you're just observing me or what, I'm not sure . . . .

Therapist: (pause) Well, our task is to try and look at your urinary problems from a rather different perspective, try and see whether there is an emotional side to it in terms of everyday stresses or strains that are related to it (pauses) . . . or perhaps going back a bit further . . . (patient listening) or having a more subtle cause . . . .

Patient: Er, um, yes.

Therapist: Does that make sense?

Patient: Yes, yes it does (sounds convinced).

In this section the patient demonstrated her interest in the sessions and has noticed for herself that the psychotherapeutic relationship was not like everyday relationships with friends and family. The last couple of paragraphs showed that she was sensitive to the therapist's comments and was willing to look at the urinary symptoms in a novel way.

She said that she was not the type to bottle things up and denied having any trouble talking to people. This may have been true at a superficial level but perhaps there was more to the matter than she was expressing. This possibility was confirmed later.

Patient: I mean, I find it difficult to find, not so necessarily to express myself, but to find the right words to express what I think . . . . I have one of these problems, erm, I call it a dyslexic mouth. It's probably nothing to do with that but I find sometimes to say words, erm . . . I get like a mental block I can't think of the word I want to say; if I wasn't thinking about it I could probably say it.

Therapist: I was wondering whether, when you were very little, given that you couldn't express yourself with words very much.

Patient: Yes . . . .

Therapist: Whether, in fact, you did express yourself in other ways? You said that you were able to express emotions by crying and showing people how you felt.

Patient: Yes.

Therapist: I wonder whether it was at that early stage that you learnt to use the urinary symptoms?

Patient: (impatient to speak) Something I've just thought of actually.

Therapist Yes? (encourages)

Patient: You were saying at school, when I was nine, maybe younger than that, I had a kidney infection.

Therapist Yes.

Patient: and erm, I was off school six weeks and of course when I went back to school I had a note to say that you know, that if I ever wanted to go to the toilet, could I go, and I must admit I used to use it as an excuse.

Therapist: Ah um. (*sotto voce*)

Patient: Even when I got into senior school I tended to. I'm a fidget, I can't sit still, I've never been able to. If I got bored I used to use it as an excuse,

        to go for a walk; I didn't necessarily go to the toilet but I used to maybe
        go for a walk or go to the cloakroom and look out the window for five
        minutes!

Therapist: Yes.

Patient: Because I used to get bored . . . but er, I've just thought of that
        actually (slightly surprised tone of voice) just thinking about school.

Here, the therapist's suggestion triggered a repressed memory that turned
out to be relevant to the urinary symptoms. It also shows how the symptom
can lead to a secondary gain for the patient. The theme of expressing
emotion was touched on once more in one of the sessions towards the end
of therapy.

Patient: Unless you have an opportunity like this, and I suppose talking like this
        [referring to therapy] has made me start thinking, apart from here, you
        know, different things that could be causing . . . . You know, has made
        me think about it more, whereas before I never even thought about
        it maybe being an emotional problem. I assumed it was something
        physical . . . .

Here, the patient expresses a view held by the overwhelming majority of
the patients — a genuine surprise to find that the urinary symptoms have
an emotional component.

(Patient   I suppose coming here has made you think about things inside of you
continues) more . . . and why you do things. It's funny my husband and I, I mean
        we've always been able to talk to each other, but erm, not like this. It
        was last week sometime we had a big, erm, what's the word for it? —
        'discussion' I suppose, about his football and his possessiveness [giggles
        — a note of triumph and confidence in it] it's something we haven't
        done for years, is to sort of sit and talk about how *I* felt and about he felt
        about things.

She then went on to relate how she had been able to discuss with her
husband how resentful she felt about him playing football so much.
Although this suggests that the therapy had influenced her thinking and
behaviour it was also clear that serious difficulties in the marriage had now
been exposed. Later, she was able to talk about how in the early days of
the marriage she had considered divorce. The uncovering of suppressed
hostility is a recurring theme in such patients. By the end of therapy she
had become symptom-free and was able to tell her husband about her feelings and thought that it was a more secure relationship.

    Although I have discussed bladder training and psychotherapy separately
they can advantageously proceed hand-in-hand. In bladder training, attention to detail and anticipating difficulties is important. For example, do you
want the patient to take the measuring jug with her when she goes out
shopping? Do not expect any 'talking therapy' to go smoothly! Any behavioural programme tests motivation and ambivalence — are the symptoms
troublesome enough to warrant the effort involved? Patients incorporate the

symptoms in their way of life. For example, one couple bought a motor-caravan with a built-in toilet as a result of the wife's urinary symptoms. In such a case you would need to know her husband's views before deciding whether she could 'afford' to get better. In psychiatry, this is called understanding the 'psychodynamics' of the case. When treatment does not appear to be working, reassessing such factors (and sometimes seeing the spouse) may clarify why she is not getting better.

Sometimes you will need to resort to 'trickery' to give her psychological room to manoeuvre. An obvious example of this is admission to hospital. 'Going into hospital' is powerful magic which legitimises symptoms and impresses friends and family. It will also give you a chance to observe the patient and have the symptoms charted by an independent witness. Any procedure stands a good chance of success under such circumstances (for a short time at least), providing you say and do it with enough conviction. It is probably just this 'magical' mechanism which explains the widely differing results of some of the treatment trials referred to in the earlier part of the chapter. On the other hand, however appropriate, admission to a psychiatric ward will confirm to the patient, relatives and friends that the psychological factors are central in causation. It may as a result have a catastrophic effect on the dynamics of any relationship. If she and her spouse can then sort out the difficulties which have been exposed then a lasting cure becomes likely.

Whether as psychotherapy or bladder training, treatment can be organised as a group activity. This has some advantages, in addition to economies of time for the therapist. A 'positive group ethos' needs to be cultivated. This means that staff should be seen to have the attitude and expectation that this is the best treatment for the patient's condition, rather than a last ditch desperate measure! Patients will pick up this message and approach the group in the appropriate frame of mind.

In this setting I think the best results are obtained when the group is led by somebody who is prepared to be active and extrovert. Patients join the group as and when they are referred and leave when they are better. In this way the culture of the group carries on although the original members may have left some time ago. New members are subjected to peer group pressure to get better as well as gaining support and encouragement from older hands. Each patient keeps a weekly bladder diary and the results are 'made public' at the beginning of the group. Success is praised and the patient is congratulated, including a round of applause if the group leader can 'spontaneously' lead it. Reasons for failure are discussed. I have observed that patients tend to be more blunt and confronting than most group leaders, and yet because the comment does not come from an 'expert' the patients are often more able to accept it. The general supportive aspects of the group should be encouraged. For example, the provision of tea and biscuits before the group starts can help to set the right caring attitude. Clearly, this differs from an analytic psychotherapy group but it does not mean that intrapsychic and relationship matters are neglected. They can be discussed as and when appropriate and the patient feels it is safe to do so.

This chapter has attempted to cover in some detail bladder training and psychotherapy for patients with DI and SU. However, other techniques do have a place for some patients. Hypnosis is an obvious example. In general drugs are disappointing; they may help in the short term but the symptoms return when the medication is stopped. Antidepressants are of value only if the patient has depressive symptoms thought likely to respond to drugs; they should not be used for any supposed anticholinergic action on the bladder. Anxiolytics may help is the short term but are probably best avoided in patients who are temperamentally anxious, as it is just such patients who become 'addicted' to medication as a way of avoiding solving life's difficulties.

Conclusion

The second part of this chapter has suggested some possible approaches to the treatment of DI and SU. It may be that you are already intuitively working along similar lines. If this is so, hopefully this chapter will have increased your confidence in treating such patients who, at times, can be very taxing.

The philosophy which underpins this approach to the 'psychosomatic' patient is:

1. Education and explanation
2. Time with a 'therapist'
3. An opportunity to learn to be different in the future.

REFERENCES

Bungay G T, Vessey M P, Mcpherson C K 1980 Study of symptoms in middle life with special reference to the menopause. British Medical Journal 281: 181–183
Cardozo L D 1979 The investigation and treatment of detrusor instability in women. MD thesis, University of Liverpool
Cardozo L D, Stanton S L, Hafner J, Allan V 1978 Biofeedback in the treatment of detrusor instability. British Journal of Urology 50: 250–254
Cardozo L D, Abrams P D, Stanton S L, Feneley R C L 1978 Idiopathic bladder instability treated by biofeedback. British Journal of Urology 50: 521–523
Crisp A, Sutherst J 1983 Psychological factors in women with urinary incontinence. Proceedings of the ICS/UDS 1: 174–176
Elder D D, Stephenson T P 1980 An assessment of the Frewen regime in the treatment of detrusor dysfunction in females. British Journal of Urology 52: 467–471
Freeman R M, Baxby K 1982 Hypnotherapy for incontinence caused by the unstable detrusor. British Medical Journal 284: 1831–1834
Freeman R M, McPherson F M, Baxby K 1985 Psychological features of women with idiopathic detrusor instability. Urology Internationalis 40: 257–259
Freeman R M 1985 Personal communication
Frewen W K 1972 Urgency incontinence. Review of 100 Cases. Journal of Obstetrics and Gynaecology of the British Commonwealth 79: 77–79
Frewen W K 1978 An objective assessment of the unstable bladder of psychosomatic origin. British Journal of Urology 50: 246–249

Frewen W K 1980 The management of urgency and frequency of micturition. British Journal of Urology 52: 367–369

Frewen W K 1982a A reassessment of bladder training in detrusor dysfunction in the female. British Journal of Urology 54: 372–373

Frewen W K 1982b Bladder training in general practice. Practitioner 226: 1847–1849

Frewen W K 1984 The significance of the psychosomatic factor in urge incontinence. British Journal of Urology 56: 330

Hafner R J, Stanton S L, Guy J 1977 A psychiatric study of women with urgency and urgency incontinence. British Journal of Urology 49: 211–214

Holmes D M, Stone A R, Bary P R, Richards C J, Stephenson T P 1983 Bladder training — 3 years on. British Journal of Urology 55: 660–664

Jarvis G J 1981 A controlled trial of bladder drill and drug therapy in the management of detrusor instability. British Journal of Urology 53: 565–566

Jarvis G J, Millar D R 1980 Controlled trial of bladder drill for detrusor instability. British Medical Journal 281: 1322–1323

Jeffcoate T N A, Francis W J A 1966 Urgency incontinence in the female. American Journal of Obstetrics and Gynecology 94: 604–618

Macaulay A J, Stanton S L, Stern R S, Holmes D M 1987 Micturition and the mind: psychological factors in the aetiology and treatment of urinary disorders in women. British Medical Journal 294: 540–543

McDonnell R J A 1982 Feasibility study of costing the treatment of women with micturition disorders. MSc dissertation, University of York

Menninger K A 1941 Some observations on the psychological factors in urination and genito-urinary afflictions. Psychoanalytical Review 28: 117–129

Mosso A, Pellicani P 1882 Sur les fonctions de la vessie. Archives Italiennes de Biologie 1: 97–128

Pengelly A W, Booth C M 1980 A prospective trial of bladder training as treatment for detrusor instability. British Journal of Urology 52: 463–466

Pierson C A, Meyer C B, Ostergard D R 1985 Vesical instability: a stress related entity. Proceedings of the ICS 1: 176–177

Rahe R H, Holmes T H 1967 The social re-adjustment — rating scale. Journal of Psychosomatic Research 11: 213–218

Rees D L P, Farhoumand N 1977 Psychiatric aspects of recurrent cystitis in women. British Journal of Urology 49: 651–658

Stone C B, Judd G E 1978 Psychogenic aspects of urinary incontinence in women. Clinics in Obstetrics and Gynaecology 21: 807–815

Truax C B, Wargo D G, Frank J D, Imber S D, Battle C C, Hoehn-Saric R, Nash E, Stone A 1966 Therapist empathy, genuineness and warmth and patient therapeutic outcome. Journal of Consulting Psychology 30: 395–401

Turner-Warwick R, Whiteside C G (eds) 1979 Urologic clinics of North America: symposium on clinical urodynamics. Saunders, New York, Vol 6(1), p 213

Wolin L H 1969 Stress incontinence in young, healthy, nulliparous female subjects. Journal of Urology 101: 545–549

SUGGESTED READING

The following books are useful introductions to psychotherapy. They are all small and easy to read.

1. An introduction to the psychotherapies 2nd edn. Block S (ed) Oxford Medical Publications, Oxford

2. The art of psychotherapy. Storr A. Secker and Warburg, London

3. Introduction to psychotherapy. Pedder and Brown. Tavistock Publications, London

Clinical gynecologic urology 1984 Stanton S L (ed) Mosby, St Louis, is an authoritative and up-to-date reference book for workers in urodynamics.

Menstrual disorders

INTRODUCTION

The higher rates of both physical and mental illness consistently reported in women have traditionally been attributed to a biological vulnerability, imposed by the female reproductive system. In addition, psychological symptoms and behavioural changes have long been recognised as common accompaniments of the menstrual cycle. The prevalence of these symptoms is such that many regard them as 'normal' accompaniments of the physiological changes. The specific question of what relationship, if any, exists between mood and the menstrual cycle has been the subject of intense investigation in recent years, both from the biological and psychosocial perspectives. A recent review of the evidence for a physiological basis to mood disturbances associated with premenstrual syndrome, dysmenorrhoea and the climacteric syndrome stressed that, despite increasing evidence, there has been considerable reluctance to accept such mood changes as having a biological basis — particularly when personality disturbance and social stresses are present and appear to influence the clinical picture (Bell & Katona 1988).

This chapter will review the role of psychological and social factors in the premenstrual syndrome, dysmenorrhoea, menorrhagia and the climacteric syndrome, emphasising the varying degree to which such factors are relevant in individual cases. This in turn determines the nature and degree of psychological intervention appropriate in any particular individual. We have found a re-educative and cognitive approach, which allows a woman to reframe issues raised by these conditions, a useful way of dealing with these problems. It is essential to avoid dealing with a woman's symptoms as *either* physical *or* psychological. The importance of undertaking a detailed history, a thorough physical examination and, where indicated, appropriate investigations and specialist referral cannot be overemphasised. This complements and lays a firm foundation for psychological management from the outset.

In general, it is much easier to obtain a useful account of the patient's problems and to share the management of them with her if this is obtained in a relaxed and comfortable situation, and a great deal of attention needs to be paid to the setting in which the interview takes place. Interviews should take place sitting in chairs, face to face. Although a physical examination is often necessary, it is an inappropriate situation in which to take a history and establish rapport. We have found that women may be understandably concerned about discussing the relationship of interpersonal stresses to specific gynaecological symptoms with a male doctor. It may be helpful to acknowledge this early on in the initial interview. Frequently this results in better communication, although it may occasionally be appropriate to arrange for the patient to be seen by a female doctor.

1. THE PREMENSTRUAL SYNDROME

The premenstrual syndrome (PMS) can be defined as 'distressing physical and psychological symptoms, not caused by organic disease, which regularly recur during the luteal phase of each menstrual cycle, and which significantly regress or disappear at or soon after the onset of menstruation'. A cyclical pattern of symptoms is clearly necessary for a diagnosis of PMS, although there is considerable disagreement over the nature and duration of symptoms in the premenstrual and menstrual phases and over their relationship to any symptoms persisting after menstruation (Bell & Katona 1988). In addition to the variety of both physical and psychological symptoms seen, a number of behavioural changes such as aggressive behaviour and accidents have also been reported, although most studies have produced inconclusive results. The reported relationship of PMS to criminal behaviour has received considerable publicity in recent years (d'Orban & Dalton 1980), although a clear link between PMS and criminal behaviour remains to be established. Estimates of the prevalence of PMS vary widely and are dependent upon the nature of the studies (retrospective versus prospective), as well as on different definitions and methods of subject selection. Retrospective studies have reported cyclical changes occurring in women to vary from 29% to 97%, although severe premenstrual symptoms are limited to approximately 2–3% of women. Cross-cultural studies have shown no difference in prevalence in varying groups of women, although substantial differences in symptom presentation has been noted (Janiger et al 1972).

Numerous psychosocial and biochemical hypotheses have been advanced as possible explanations for PMS. The relationship between PMS and psychiatric illness has received considerable attention. A large number of studies, reviewed by Clare (1983), have looked at a variety of psychiatric disorders, including affective disorders, neurotic illness, personality disorder and suicide and parasuicide. There is increasing evidence for an association between subtypes of PMS and subtypes of affective illness (Endicott et al 1981). Clare (1983) has suggested that the severity of psychological, but not physical, symptoms in PMS sufferers can be used to discriminate between patients with and without psychiatric histories.

Among biological hypotheses, circulating levels of gonadal steroids, prolactin, and aldosterone have received most attention. The clear relationship between mood, physical symptoms and hormonal phases of the menstrual cycle provides strong support for a hormonal basis for PMS (Sanders et al 1983), yet studies examining gonadal hormones have produced either inconclusive or contradictory findings (Rubinow & Roy-Byrne 1984). Other variables which have been putatively linked with PMS, but in which investigations have generated negative results, are pyridoxine, serotonin uptake, prostaglandins, and androgens.

Presentation

A woman may present at any time after menarche through to the menopause, although more severe cases tend to be in women in their thirties. Commonly reported psychological symptoms are depression, anxiety, tension, irritability, impaired concentration and sleep disturbance, whilst the most frequently encountered physical symptoms are breast swelling and tenderness, abdominal swelling, peripheral oedema, weight gain and headaches (Magos & Studd 1984). If a woman presents primarily with psychological symptoms, she may not herself have recognised the relationship of such symptoms to her menstrual cycle. While it is important to consider and exclude other physical and psychological disorders, it would appear that PMS has been underdiagnosed in the past and is still doubted by some to be a true clinical entity. A history of PMS over a number of years is commonly elicited, with a period of well-being during pregnancy often followed by postnatal depression and a worsening of premenstrual symptoms thereafter. It is unclear whether this represents a worsening of symptoms with age or is related more to the increasing demands and stresses of family life.

Management

The first stage in the management of patients with premenstrual complaints is the daily monitoring of symptoms over two or three menstrual cycles, as a clear pattern of cyclical symptoms is necessary to establish the diagnosis. A number of daily rating scales have been devised for this purpose. We have found the one developed by Sanders (1981) to be useful. It consists of core physical and psychological symptoms, and is scored on a visual analogue scale (Fig. 10.1). The importance of seeing patients every 2–3 weeks to monitor their recording and provide reassurance and general support during this assessment period cannot be overemphasised. We explain that the completion of these daily rating scales, which takes only a few minutes at the end of each day, will assist us in reaching a diagnosis and planning treatment. By involving patients in their own management at

Menstrual period   0 _____ 10
(leave blank if not bleeding)

MOODS
Cheerful and happy   0 _____ 10
Irritable   0 _____ 10
Energetic and active   0 _____ 10
Depressed and unhappy   0 _____ 10
Fatigued and tired   0 _____ 10
Tense and anxious   0 _____ 10
_____   0 _____ 10

PHYSICAL STATE
Breast tenderness   0 _____ 10
Body swelling   0 _____ 10
Period-type pain   0 _____ 10
_____   0 _____ 10
_____   0 _____ 10

Note any significant events which occurred _____

Note any physical changes or symptoms (other than those mentioned above)
_____
_____

Note any drugs or medication _____

Fig. 10.1 Daily rating scale for PMS (after Sanders 1981)

this early stage, they are usually prepared to put up with what are often quite distressing and disabling symptoms a little longer.

Drug treatments advocated in PMS are many. Because of the cyclical nature of symptoms, the main treatment modality has been hormonal. Progesterone has been widely used and has recently been shown to be superior to placebo. The synthetic progestogen dydrogesterone (Duphaston) has also shown encouraging results (Haspels 1981). Suppression of cyclical ovarian activity by either a gonadotropin-releasing hormone (GnRH) analogue and or subcutaneous oestradiol implants has produced more encouraging results (Muse et al 1984). Other treatments used in PMS are bromocriptine, diuretics, lithium, pyridoxine and mefenamic acid. Choice of treatment is determined both by patient preference as well as the nature and severity of symptoms.

A woman presenting with premenstrual complaints needs the opportunity to express any concerns or anxiety she has about her symptoms and the effect these have on her life. Simple education and reassurance together with advice about diet, exercise and relaxation may be all that is required. A woman's attitude to medication, as well as her willingness to discuss present or past stresses in her life, will be important determinants of treatment. This, in turn, will largely dictate the form of psychological support provided by the practitioner, as the following case history demonstrates.

Case History

Miss R.K., a 36-year-old high-school teacher, saw a new partner to the practice for a routine repeat prescription. She was currently taking pyridoxine, the oral contraceptive pill, a diuretic and progesterone pessaries for moderately severe premenstrual symptoms, from which she had suffered for a long time. She had been on the present medication for the last 3–4 years. The general practitioner expressed his concern about the 'cocktail' of medication she was taking and said that he would like to see her again in a month's time to review the matter in more detail.

They met on four subsequent occasions. Initially the general practitioner took time to explain that PMS was a complex clinical entity, and that whilst not devaluing its biological basis, stressed the important role emotional factors and life stresses played in effecting the severity of symptoms. Miss R.K. agreed to stopping both the oral contraceptive pill and the diuretic. She subsequently found herself more willing to look at current emotional problems without feeling that her physical symptoms were being dismissed or devalued. She was about to take on a new and more challenging post, but was concerned about the close relationship that was beginning to develop between her and her prospective boss. She had not had a close relationship with anyone since university days and was worried about the risks involved in embarking upon such a relationship, particularly with someone responsible for her work. She then spoke of a very traumatic relationship at university and how she feared repeating the experience. She also revealed that she had suffered from anorexia nervosa for a period as a teenager, but was never ill enough to require hospitalisation. At university she experimented with drugs and described the whole experience as a very destructive one. Miss R.K. felt quite relieved to have the opportunity to express some of her fears and to discuss old unresolved issues and thanked the general practitioner for confronting her. At this point she agreed to try and manage without progesterone pessaries.

Two months later she came to say goodbye as she was moving to the new job in another county. She expressed gratitude for being confronted with both present and past difficulties and felt more able to recognise the significant effect that psychological factors were playing in her life. She said that she had spoken to her new boss about their relationship and told him that they must take things slowly while she was adjusting to the new post. She felt greatly relieved that she had been able to set firm limits on this relationship and was surprised at how understanding he was. She had virtually stopped using progesterone pessaries and found pyridoxine provided adequate symptom relief.

In the above cases, Miss R.K. was initially reluctant to accept the general practitioner's suggestion of a link between her physical symptoms and emotional life. Initial education and explanation of the nature of PMS allowed the patient then to identify a link between the severity of her physical symptoms and current emotional difficulties in her life. Although most women presenting with premenstrual symptoms will not have a past psychiatric history as such, many may have concurrent interpersonal and social difficulties which will exacerbate symptoms experienced, and in turn effect coping strategies. These difficulties need to be explored in a sensitive manner, helping the woman to see the effect of one upon the other, care being taken not to imply that the basis of such symptoms is purely psychological.

2. DYSMENORRHOEA

Dysmenorrhoea is defined as 'painful menstruation' and can be classified as primary (idiopathic) or secondary to organic pathology such as uterine fibroids, endometriosis or pelvic inflammatory disease. Typically, the patient experiences cramping lower abdominal pain, radiating into the back and lower limbs, and usually worst at the onset of menstruation. Other symptoms which commonly occur are nausea, vomiting, diarrhoea, headaches and urinary frequency. In dysmenorrhoea, unlike PMS, there appears to be little evidence for a direct connection between the physiological symptoms and neurotic disturbance although the psychological distress experienced as a result of the physical symptoms can nevertheless be of a severe and disabling nature. The prevalence of primary dysmenorrhoea, which most commonly affects teenage girls and diminishes with increasing parity but not with advancing age alone, has been estimated to occur with sufficient severity to require time off work or studies in 7% and 39%, depending on the definition used and the population studied. A recent prospective study of the prevalence and severity of dysmenorrhoea in a representative sample of 19-year-old women found the overall prevalence of dysmenorrhoea to be 72%, while that of severe dysmenorrhoea was 15% (Andersch & Milsom 1982).

The interaction of psychological and physical factors are important in understanding the severity of any painful condition. It is inevitable that personality and social learning will influence the way symptoms, particularly pain, are perceived by an individual and will modify behaviour (Pilowsky 1984), although no particular relationship between dysmenorrhoea and specific personality traits has been identified. In contrast, biological factors appear to play an important part in the aetiology of dysmenorrhoea. An elucidation of the role of prostaglandins (PGs), particularly PGF_2, and the finding that PG synthetase inhibitors are capable of relieving menstrual pain suggest that uterine ischaemia is the most likely explanation for dysmenorrhoea (Lumsden 1985). Dysmenorrhoea can be regarded as a function of a complex interaction of PGs, gonadal hormones, vasopressin and pain perception and it may be postulated that the biological abnormalities act as a stress on the background of a psychological diathesis.

Management

As with PMS, the importance of an adequate history and a thorough physical examination cannot be overemphasised. Evaluation of the severity of pain should be made prospectively over at least two cycles, graded on a four-point scale together with an assessment of the effect of symptoms on daily activity, as well as the presence of any systemic symptoms and analgesic requirements (Fig. 10.2).

Once a proper assessment of the severity of symptoms has been made and

	Not at all	Mild	Moderate	Severe
Please rate how painful your menstrual period was today				
Specify any other symptoms and rate each one as above				
To what degree have the above symptoms interfered with your daily				
Please specify				

Have you taken any analgesics today?   Yes/No
If so, how many and which? _____

Fig. 10.2 Daily rating scale for dysmenorrhoea

the diagnosis established, appropriate treatment should be commenced immediately. PG synthetase inhibitors have an analgesic effect in addition to inhibiting the synthesis of prostaglandins, while the oral contraceptive pill exerts its effect by inhibiting ovulation and thereby eliminating the luteal phase rise in endometrial PG concentration. Symptom relief is often dramatic, with complete resolution of psychological as well as physical symptoms. The choice of treatment is usually determined by the contraceptive needs of the patient, although if one treatment is unsuccessful the other is usually tried. If both treatments fail, calcium antagonists (nifedipine) are sometimes successful in low doses (15–30 mg/day) during menstruation. The distressing and often misunderstood nature of dysmenorrhoea means that supportive psychotherapy often forms an essential part of the overall management. In our experience, it is a disservice to deal with the problem as primarily psychological and to ignore its physiological basis.

Case History

Miss L.S., a 17-year-old student preparing for 'A' levels, presented to her general practitioner with a 6-month history of increasingly painful periods. At first, simple analgesics were sufficient to give good relief; however, over the last two cycles the pain had been so severe that she had missed a couple of days of classes and was taking excessive amounts of analgesics. She was very distressed about the time lost from her schoolwork and was anxious that the pain might be psychological in origin, as her mother had suggested that it was almost certainly related to worry over her forthcoming examinations. She was an otherwise pleasant and well adjusted girl who had coped perfectly well with examinations and other pressures in the past, but felt that she was now becoming 'neurotic' and was anxiously anticipating how bad her next period would be.

Her general practitioner found it difficult to convince her that the problem was primarily a physical one and not a 'neurotic' reaction to examination stress. He asked her to return in a couple of days with her mother. Mrs S. admitted that she had only experienced mild symptoms of dysmenorrhoea as a teenager and said it was commonly regarded as something one 'just put up with'. She had always kept in good health and from the general practitioner's experience, tended to be somewhat intolerant of illness in other family members. Despite this, she seemed willing to accept the general practitioner's explanation of the physical basis for painful periods. Miss L.S. appeared to be greatly reassured by her mother's acceptance of this explanation, making it easier for her also to accept the general practitioner's explanation for herself.

The general practitioner prescribed a PG synthetase inhibitor and arranged to see Miss L.S. shortly after her next menstrual period. The improvement was dramatic, although she did admit to anticipatory anxiety just prior to the onset of menses. She felt quite confident that it would not be there next time.

The time spent educating both mother and daughter was necessary to ensure not only compliance with the treatment prescribed but also to ensure that the patient's symptoms did not become 'psychologised'. It forms an essential part of management in disorders where pain is the central symptom and where it has been previously attributed to psychological mechanisms.

3. MENORRHAGIA

Menorrhagia is an abnormal increase in menstrual blood loss. There are a number of causes of menorrhagia: it may signify uterine pathology, such as fibroids, carcinoma, or endometriosis; it can also be caused by general disorders, such as severe anaemia or bleeding diatheses. Where there is no physical cause, it is known as dysfunctional uterine bleeding (Dewhurst 1972). In these latter cases it is frequently associated with psychosocial stress (Jeffcoate 1975). The prevalence of menorrhagia has been estimated at about 10% in normal populations (Hallberg et al 1966). Dysfunctional uterine bleeding accounts for 10% of all new women referred to gynaecology outpatient departments, and almost 25% of all gynaecological surgery. Menorrhagia affects no particular age group, although the dysfunctional group are generally younger (Jeffcoate 1975).

A study by Greenberg (1983) demonstrated that nearly two-thirds of women referred to a gynaecological outpatient clinic with menorrhagia had a psychological disorder. Those with psychological disturbance are more likely to have a mother with gynaecological disorders and a past history of gynaecological surgery themselves.

Presentation

The presence of menorrhagia is usually established by obtaining an account of increased menstrual blood loss from the patient, which is generally followed by the confirmation or exclusion of significant gynaecological pathology both by clinical examination and performance of a dilatation and curettage. Although there are objective measures of menstrual blood loss, either direct (by eluting red blood cells from tampons) or indirect (by measuring blood haemoglobin), these are rarely used, and the assessment is usually a clinical one.

The way in which a woman will present for treatment varies with the cause of her menorrhagia. When this is local uterine pathology she will generally give a clear account of a prolonged change in her menstrual pattern. She is likely to complain of more 'clots', an increased use of tampons and sanitary towels, 'blood running down my legs', etc. Furthermore, she is likely to proffer this information spontaneously, and not to need prompting by direct questions. She may also give a clear account of abnormal menstrual bleeding if it is due to some general disorder such as cardiac failure or hypothyroidism. However, in such cases she is also likely to give an account of preceding ill health.

When menorrhagia is severe, prolonged, uncontrollable and unpredictable, a woman is likely to become miserable as a result of the distress and discomfort caused. This is often exacerbated by a developing anaemia and by the bulky and uncomfortable fibroids that are the frequent cause of the menorrhagia. An understandable anxiety about a possible underlying cancer may also aggravate her unhappiness. In these circumstances a woman is likely to attribute any deterioration in her mood to the change in her periods, and she will describe how, and over what period of time, this has developed.

It is not uncommon for a woman to describe an increase in her menstruation after a stressful experience. In such circumstances the period seems to be brought on earlier than usual and is described as heavier than usual, but without the same dramatic quality described above. The change also tends to affect only one or two periods before a return to normal. In such cases the complaint of menorrhagia can be best understood as an expression, rather than as a consequence, of a psychosocial disorder. It is unlikely to reflect a significant increase in menstrual blood loss, but it validates the attention a woman seeks from a medical carer. It is certainly easier to talk about menorrhagia to a doctor than a more complicated issue, like marital difficulties and stress at home, which are not treatable in the same sense. The woman can easily assume a 'sick role' because she is vulnerable, because her social group perceives her 'illness' as an acceptable explanation for her problems, and because it is convenient for both her and her doctor to negotiate around a physical complaint. All of these factors contribute to the development of what is called 'illness behaviour'. When such women are referred to a gynaecologist they will describe only a minor change in their menstrual pattern, a minor increase affecting one or two periods, which are easily attributable to some obvious factor like a stressful event or the onset of menopausal change. Although these women are referred to gynaecologists for assessment, and do describe increased menstrual blood loss when this is addressed directly, if asked non-directive questions like 'what is your problem?' they are likely to talk about things other than their periods. Sometimes if the situation is conducive to further discussion, they will talk about their emotional problems spontaneously.

Although many GPs recognise that the predominant problem with these women is psychosocial, they do not state this in their referral, and concentrate on the menorrhagia. As a result most gynaecologists pursue this aspect of the problem, even though they frequently recognise the underlying psychosocial problems (Munro 1969). As a result, these women often enter into a cycle of treatment which progresses from dilatation and curettage to hormonal therapy, and which frequently results in hysterectomy. It may be that the GP is concerned that his patient's gynaecological symptoms will not be taken seriously if he describes psychosocial factors in his referral. However, we have found that the management of these women is improved if a more comprehensive account is presented, and if the practitioner makes clear why he has sought a consultant's opinion.

Management

It is clear, therefore, that the effective psychological management of women who complain of menorrhagia depends upon its aetiology, and this can generally be ascertained by a careful history of the blood loss, a physical examination and, when appropriate, special investigations. In practice a low blood haemoglobin will reflect significant menorrhagia; however, in doubtful cases it will be necessary to collect tampons and measure the blood loss directly.

Although a detailed physical evaluation is essential, it should not be assumed that the only, or major, pathology is confined to the woman's gynaecological system, and an assessment of her general health, including her mental state and her social situation, should be made at the same time. As a result the doctor will have a clear view of the severity of the menstrual blood loss and its relationships with any physical, psychological or social disturbance.

This information is best obtained by clarifying the details of her complaint without the use of direct questions, since the menorrhagia is more likely to be severe if this is described spontaneously. It is self-evident that a woman will find it easier to discuss any psychosocial problems if her doctor is sympathetic and available, and this can be facilitated by the clinical setting. For example, a woman is much more likely to provide a comprehensive history if she is relaxed and, in turn, this is far likelier if she is dressed and facing the doctor, than if she is undressed and in the lithotomy position.

Although the specific management of each woman will need to be related to her personal circumstances, in most cases the psychological management takes the form of re-education. The doctor encourages her to recognise that social problems, and the stresses they generate, are valid causes of distress: a physical symptom is one means of expressing distress and improvement is more likely when the underlying problems are tackled. Some women will recognise the usefulness of this approach and respond to it quite quickly. Others, however, may appear less 'psychologically minded'. In these cases it will be necessary to address directly any social problems, which may appear overwhelming. A small group of women will require a more detailed psychological assessment in order to discover whether they are likely to respond to more intensive psychotherapy.

Case history

Miss G.F., a 34-year-old personal assistant to a publisher, presented to her GP with a history of increased menstrual blood loss during her last two periods. She described clearly an increase in length of her periods from 3 to 5 days, an increase in actual blood loss requiring more tampons and the additional use of towels, and a qualitative change, with 'far more clots'.

G.F's general health was very good and she had no significant medical history, apart from a similar episode which had lasted 3 months, 2 years previously. This had followed the ending of a 3-year relationship and she had been referred to a hospital gynaecologist, who had performed a dilatation and curettage, after which her periods had returned to normal. On direct questioning she said that an affair had ended 2 months previously.

She was a healthy-looking woman, with no signs of anaemia, and a normal pelvic examination. She was an attractive, well made up, rather mournful-looking lady dressed in black. She gave a clear, coherent account of her symptoms and admitted that she been a little sad after her last relationship had ended, and that she had found it difficult to fall asleep. However, she said that she 'was over this now'. When the GP suggested that the stress might have caused her menorrhagia, and that it might be helpful to talk about this, she replied that she could 'see that this might be true, but would like to see a gynaecologist anyway'.

In his letter of referral to the consultant gynaecologist, the GP described the woman's complaint, her psychosocial circumstances, and asked for a specialist assessment. He explained that he had arranged to see her again, in order to discuss any emotional problems.

Two months later G.F. returned to her GP. Her periods had returned to normal before the arranged appointment with the gynaecologist, which she therefore cancelled. She had not returned to see her GP until now, because she had felt better, but the situation had deteriorated suddenly 3 weeks ago. She had begun to feel increasingly miserable, was crying at the slightest provocation and had increasing difficulty falling asleep. On this occasion she looked far more miserable and seemed close to tears. She occasionally found herself wondering 'what's the point of it all?', but always felt that 'things will sort themselves out'. She had never reached a stage of feeling that life was not worth living, but when she stated this, tears welled up in her eyes. Although she was obviously depressed, her GP was able to reassure himself that she was coping pretty well by confirming that she was continuing to work effectively, and that she was still maintaining contact with her friends. He arranged to see her again for a longer session, when he was able to take a more detailed history, and several important features of her background emerged.

She was the only child of professional parents, and had always felt emotionally neglected, particularly by her mother. The only time she had ever felt her mother was concerned about her was when she was physically unwell, and at these times she gained considerable attention. Her mother had had a hysterectomy when she was 40 years old, for 'heavy periods due to fibroids'. She remembered that at that time her mother was very preoccupied with her work, and that following surgery her career seemed to blossom. G.F. had been put under a lot of pressure to achieve academic success, and had therefore concentrated on her studies at the expense of a social life.

She had done well at university, and was highly thought of in her present job. She had had several boyfriends, but the relationships always ended when they began to expect more commitment from her. She said that she did get upset when these affairs ended, but usually recovered rapidly. The last two relationships had ended more painfully than usual, when she felt that she was being made to choose between her career and the possibility of a family life.

After she had given this account, the GP said that it might be a new experience for her to realise that she did not need to be physically ill in order to elicit concern. She then became much more relaxed and said that it was the first time she had revealed herself in this way, and that it felt 'such a relief to have said all this'. They met on three further occasions, when the GP encouraged G.F. to talk more openly about her feelings. It became increasingly clear that she desperately needed to succeed in order to do better than her mother, whom she always wanted to impress. The more she talked about her relationship with her mother, and the way it influenced her, the more relaxed she became. Several months later she returned to the GP to have a pregnancy test, which proved to be positive. She was living with her previous boyfriend and the pregnancy was planned. She said that she was enjoying her work, but would not decide whether to return to work until after the delivery.

4. THE CLIMACTERIC SYNDROME

The climacteric is that phase in the ageing process of women marking the transition from the reproductive to the non-reproductive stage of life, while the menopause indicates the final menstrual period and occurs during the climacteric. The term 'climacteric syndrome' is used to describe specific symptomatology associated with the climacteric, namely hot flushes, perspiration and atrophic vaginitis (generally attributed to a decline in ovarian activity with subsequent hormonal deficiency), as well as psychological symptoms (Van Keep et al 1976). The clinical picture will vary from woman to woman and is the result of an interaction between physical, social and psychological factors peculiar to each individual.

Whether oestrogen deficiency is directly related to the increase in other symptoms, both physical and psychological, reported around the time of the menopause still remains to be established. The main psychological symptoms reported by menopausal women in one study (Bungay et al 1980) were difficulty in making decisions, loss of confidence, anxiety, forgetfulness, difficulty in concentration and feelings of worthlessness. These peaked (although less impressively than vasomotor symptoms) just prior to the menopause. Greene (1984) suggests a vulnerability model to explain the increase in psychological symptoms reported during the climacteric, in which the physiological instability resulting from a decline in ovarian function, together with predisposing socio-economic stresses and life events, results in the precipitation or exacerbation of psychological symptoms.

An increase in neurotic disorders has long been attributed to physiological changes occurring in women at the climacteric, although a recent well designed study failed to identify the menopause as a precipitating factor for neurotic disorder (Hallstrom & Samuelsson 1985).

Presentation

Despite the wide variation in methods employed, studies have consistently reported an increase in vasomotor symptoms (hot flushes, night sweats) as being closely associated with the menopause, occurring in 61–75% of subjects. There has been little agreement however as to the prevalence of other symptoms and their relationship to the menopause. Although symptoms such as depression, anxiety, fatigue, poor concentration, lability, headaches and insomnia do increase significantly around the time of the menopause, the increase is not to the same degree as for vasomotor symptoms.

Management

Treatment approaches to climacteric symptoms need to consider: (1) the degree of distress suffered, (2) that the decline in gonadal function is itself normal and (3) the potential side effects of any therapy. The main approach to treatment, however, has been oestrogen replacement therapy, either orally, percutaneously, transvaginally or by subcutaneous implant. The majority of women gain significant relief of symptoms with oral oestrogens. A significant improvement in psychological symptoms with oestrogen therapy over placebo has been demonstrated in two large studies (Campbell & Whitehead 1977, Dennerstein et al 1978), although such improvement may have simply been due to the abolition of distressing physical symptoms. Whilst oestrogen therapy is of greatest benefit in relieving the vasomotor effects of the climacteric, it may also be of benefit in relieving psychological and sexual symptomatology, although the exact nature of the relationship between hormonal changes and mental symptoms remains unclear.

No easy prescription for the association management of women with distressing psychological symptoms occurring with the climacteric can be given. It is essential that a formal psychiatric disorder, in particular a depressive illness, be excluded and a detailed assessment made of the woman's present psychosocial circumstances. A considerable amount of time may be required for this, but is often cost effective in the long run, given the often lengthy duration of menopausal symptoms. It is important not to dismiss or minimise the effect that various changes in a woman's life around the time of the menopause can have on her psychological well-being. Children leave home and there is a need to establish a new way of relating to them. Husbands may take early retirement or become redundant, often with little warning. Re-education should aim at helping the woman not to give up in the face of such stresses and life changes and explain her distress away as being due to the menopause.

Case history

Mrs P.L., a 52-year-old housewife whose husband worked as the manager of a branch office of a firm of mortgage brokers, had been consulting her GP over the last 6–7 months because of troublesome menopausal symptoms. In addition to being bothered by hot flushes and dizzy spells, she found it increasingly more difficult to cope with household tasks and was starting to withdraw from social activities. She lived with her husband and the youngest of their three children, who was preparing for his 'O' levels. Both of the older children were now married and lived in other parts of the country and so visited the parental home only once every 2–3 months.

Her GP prescribed oestrogen replacement therapy and this quickly provided good relief from the vasomotor symptoms. She still found running the house very difficult and remained socially isolated. Further inquiry revealed that Mrs L.'s major worry at present concerned her husband. Mr C.L. was a devoted husband and father but had a poor work record. He had a lifelong tendency to procrastinate and to leave small but important aspects of clients' work unfinished. This had resulted in a number of disciplinary proceedings in the past, although he had always managed to salvage things and start afresh. Recently a number of major unfinished deals had resulted in clients loosing large sums of money and his employers had asked him to resign. He had become severely depressed at the prospect of turning 50 years old and being no longer employable. Mrs L. had always supported her husband through previous, less severe episodes of depression (always work related). She now found, however, that her own reserves were considerably limited and this made her feel worthless and guilty.

Her GP felt that he should see Mr and Mrs L. together and so suggested this to Mrs L. She expressed some reluctance, wondering whether her husband would agree, although she did admit that she was at the end of her tether. Mr L. was, to her surprise, keen on the idea and they attended their GP a few days later. Mr L. did admit that he had never been as depressed as this before, but added that the circumstances were more serious than ever before. His wife was surprised to hear him say that he had found her as supportive as ever, although he understood that she was in other ways not herself because of a bad menopause. She was greatly relieved by this and admitted that she had been reluctant to express her own concerns and worries for fear of upsetting her husband. They arranged to meet in 2 weeks' time and agreed to discuss each other's worries openly and to go out as a couple socially on at least three occasions in the meantime.

At the next appointment Mrs L. reported that she had enjoyed their evenings out, was starting to cope with household tasks better and had felt more able to support her husband through what remained a very difficult period for him. Mr L. for his part was pleased with the improvement in his wife over the last 2 weeks and found the extra support he had given to his wife quite therapeutic. They agreed that it had been helpful to agree on going out on a number of occasions and said they would continue this. A month later Mrs L. reported that she was seeing old friends again and was coping adequately with the housework. Her husband also felt less depressed and was starting to talk in a very realistic way about future plans.

In the above case the GP was quick to recognise the importance of seeing both husband and wife together. The clarification of misconceptions and challenging the validity of old underlying assumptions improved communication, as did the setting of very practical tasks for them to undertake both singly and as a couple.

CONCLUSION

Whilst all four cases demonstrate the central place of a re-educative and cognitive approach, allowing a woman to reframe issues raised by menstrual complaints, it is also clear that a flexible approach to their psychological management is imperative. Once the physical basis of such disorders is acknowledged, patients are usually prepared to look more closely at their present and past life circumstances and explore how these may be influencing their symptoms. Other psychological approaches — psychodynamic, family and marital and behavioural — are all relevant and can be utilised (often in varying combinations depending on the individual problem) by the general practitioner without the need of referral to specialist psychiatric services.

REFERENCES

Andersch B, Milsom I 1982 An epidemiologic study of young women with dysmenorrhoea. American Journal of Obstetrics and Gynaecology 144: 655–660

Bell G, Katona C 1988 Neurotic disorders associated with menstruation, pregnancy and the postpartum period. In: Prasad A (ed) Biological Basis and Therapy of Neuroses. Florida, CRC Press, chap. 9

Bungay G, Vessay M, McPherson C 1980 Study of symptoms in middle life with special reference to the menopause. British Medical Journal 281: 181–183

Campbell S, Whitehead M I 1977 Oestrogen therapy and the menopausal syndrome. Clinics in Obstetrics and Gynaecology 4: 31–47

Clare A W 1983 Psychiatric and social aspects of premenstrual complaint. Psychological Medicine, Monograph Supplement 4

Dennerstein L, Burrows G D, Hyman G, Wood C 1978 Menopausal hot flushes — double blind comparison of ethinyloestradiol and norgestal. British Journal of Obstetrics and Gynaecology 85: 852–856

Dewhurst C J 1981 Integrated Obstetrics and Gynaecology for Postgraduates. Blackwell, Oxford, pp. 565–591

d'Orban P T, Dalton J 1980 Violent crime and the menstrual cycle. Psychological Medicine 10(2): 353–359

Endicott J, Halbreich U, Schacht H T, Nee J 1981 Premenstrual changes and affective disorders. Psychosomatic Medicine 43: 519–529

Greenberg M 1983 The meaning of menorrhagia: an investigation into the association between the complaint of menorrhagia and depression. Journal of Psychosomatic Research 27: 209–214

Greene J G 1984 The Social and Psychological Origins of the Climacteric Syndrome. Gower Publishing Co, Aldershot

Hallberg L, Hogdall A M, Nillson L, Rybo G 1966 Menstrual blood loss — a population study. Acta Obstetrica et Gynaecologica Scandinavica 45: 320–351

Hallstrom T, Samuelsson S 1985 Mental Health in the Climacteric. Acta Obstetrica Gynaecologica Scandinavica, Supplement 130: 13–18

Haspels A A 1981 A double -blind, placebo-controlled, multicentre study of the efficacy of dydrogesterone (Duphaston). In: Van Keep P A, Utian W H (eds) The Premenstrual Syndrome. MTP Press, Lancaster, pp. 81–92

Janiger O, Riffenburgh R, Kersh R 1972 Crosscultural study of premenstrual symptoms. Psychosomatics 13: 226–235

Jeffcoate T N A 1975 Principles of Gynaecology. Butterworth, London, pp. 537–546

Lumsden M S 1985 Dysmenorrhoea. In: Studd J W W (ed) Progress in Obstetrics and Gynaecology, Vol. 5. Churchill Livingstone, Edinburgh, pp. 276–292

Magos A, Studd J 1984 The premenstrual syndrome. In: Studd J W W (ed) Progress in Obstetrics and Gynaecology, Vol. 4. Edinburgh, Churchill Livingstone, pp. 334–350

Munro A 1969 Psychiatric illness in gynaecological outpatients: a preliminary study. British Journal of Psychiatry 115: 807–809

Muse K N, Cetel N S, Futterman L A, Yen S S C 1984 The Premenstrual Syndrome — Effects of Medical Ovariectomy. New England Journal of Medicine 311(21): 1345–1349

Pilowsky I 1984 Pain and illness behaviour: assessment and management. In: Melzack R, Wall P D (eds) Pain. Churchill Livingstone, Edinburgh, pp. 767–775

Rubinow D R, Roy-Byrne P 1984 Premenstrual Syndromes: overview from a methodological perspective. American Journal of Psychiatry 141(2): 163–172

Sanders D 1981 Hormones and Behaviour during the Menstrual Cycle. PhD. Thesis, University of Edinburgh

Sanders D, Warner P, Backstrom T, Bancroft J 1983 Mood, sexuality, hormones and the menstrual cycle: 1. changes in mood and physical state: description of subjects and method. Psychosomatic Medicine 45: 487–501

Van Keep P A, Greenblatt R B, Albeaux-Fernet M 1976 Consensus on Menopause Research. MTP Press, Lancaster, pp. 1–5

Infertility

INTRODUCTION

Infertility is not an illness. It is not life-threatening nor often associated with bodily discomfort; indeed it is fully compatible with perfect health. Why then should it appear in a handbook on the psychological management of the physically ill? A possible justification is that several of the disorders featured in this book can properly be regarded as psychosomatic. Reproductive failure, be it an inability to conceive or carry to term, or stillbirth, has strong claims to be brought within a psychosomatic framework. Moreover it is deeply distressing to the individuals concerned, who are usually partners in a marriage. Awareness of the possible value of psychological approaches cannot but contribute to improve the management of the problem, regardless of whether or not a successful outcome is achieved. Even where there is a clear-cut physical cause, such as premature hysterectomy, disease of the fallopian tubes or absence of sperm, the importance of psychological aspects is in no way diminished. Those who *know* they cannot hope to become parents in the normal manner may indeed suffer more than most.

Since the publication of the Warnock Report (1984) more prominence has been given to the various techniques of 'assisted reproduction', including artificial insemination by donor (AID) and in-vitro fertilisation (IVF). These call for particularly astute psychological management, which may or may not be provided. Later in the chapter we shall be drawing on our experience of counselling couples in hope of AID, which at St George's Hospital (though not at all other infertility clinics) is viewed as an essential preliminary to treatment. There are fewer centres offering the far more demanding procedure of IVF, but the emotional challenge faced by such couples is not to be underestimated. Adoption and fostering may be seen by many couples as a less acceptable route to parental experience, especially now that the supply of unblemished infants has dwindled almost to vanishing point. However, some consideration will need to be given to this form of surrogate parenthood for those who are unable to reproduce.

INCIDENCE

Census data indicate that about 20% of the population are childless at any one time, but the hard core of permanently childless couples is no more than half this figure. It can be estimated that in England and Wales between 30 000 and 50 000 infertile marriages will be contracted annually. This does not allow us to infer the number of *involuntarily* childless couples in the general population, which might well reach a million (Humphrey 1984). Here we are handicapped by uncertainty as to what proportion of infertile marriages remain so from choice. Veevers (1972, 1979) has calculated that it could be at least half, based on the unusually low rate of permanently childless couples to be found for example in rural Quebec with its strong Catholic ethos. Yet we do not really know the true situation, and there is less variation in the incidence of childlessness among European countries than might be predicted on this argument. A further difficulty is that for statistical purposes it would be unsafe to polarise all childless marriages under the headings of 'voluntary' or 'involuntary'. Some couples may fluctuate in their wish for a child, engaging in a 'month-on month-off' policy of contraception; others may be swayed by a change of circumstance following a period of effort to conceive, as when ill health or financial crisis supervenes. How far can such couples be described as childless from choice? It can be just as awkward to determine whether an individual pregnancy was 'planned' or 'unplanned'.

A careful study by Hull et al (1985) in the west of England appears to confirm the often quoted estimate that one couple in six (17%) are sufficiently concerned about their infertility to be referred for specialist advice. However, when those seeking a second or subsequent child are excluded the figure is 12%. If we assume, as in an earlier study by Humphrey & Mackenzie (1967), that up to half of the group with primary infertility will eventually produce at least one child, then only 6% of the population will remain childless despite specialist help. The remaining 4% or so must therefore comprise those who either do not consult a doctor or do not get beyond the GP, as well as those opting out of parenthood. It would be hard to obtain reliable information about the relative proportions of these three categories.

AETIOLOGY

Investigation of the infertile couple tends to follow a set pattern. It has to be established that both partners are anatomically normal and in good health. It must be shown that the male partner is capable of delivering sperm in adequate quantity and quality, whilst a regular menstrual cycle is a hopeful sign (although no guarantee) of fertility in the female. It is believed that even mature women are prone to the occasional anovular cycle, but when this occurs persistently it is clearly a negative factor. Antibodies in the sperm can be detected in up to 10% of cases with a male element, and these react with antibodies in the cervical mucus (Hendry et al 1977). Recent evidence suggests that gross anatomical or physiological disorders can be found in at least 60% of couples attending infertility clinics (Hull et al 1985). In this particular study sperm defects or dysfunction were diagnosed in 24%, ovulation failure (amenorrhoea or oligomenorrhoea) in 21% and tubal damage in 14% of cases. Given adequate co-operation it is easy to perform a semen analysis, and laparoscopy has proved its value in screening for tubal and ovarian factors.

Prolonged investigation of a couple may fail to disclose any abnormality whatsoever. The incidence of unexplained infertility in the population at large is unknown, and estimates of its frequency in clinical populations have varied a good deal. Templeton & Penney (1982), in their review of 17 studies conducted over the past 40 years, found a range of 6–58%, with a weighted mean of 15%. Their own series of 400 couples included 130, almost a third, who satisfied their criteria of unexplained infertility. Using life tables they estimated that more than a quarter of these inexplicable cases would remain infertile after 9 years. Couples with and without known causal factors were comparable in age, social class and reported coital frequency. One obvious reason for the variation in estimates is that not all clinicians are equally zealous in their pursuit of an explanation. For example, in one of the studies reviewed by Templeton and Penney the original figure of 10% unexplained, already lower than most, was reduced to 3.5% after various abnormalities had been revealed on laparoscopy (Drake et al 1977). However, whether all these abnormalities (which included mild endometriosis) had been interfering with conception remains open to debate.

The absence of anatomical or physiological findings is by no means tantamount to a psychological diagnosis. Much of the earlier literature on psychological aspects, reviewed by Noyes & Chapnick (1964), was anecdotal and unsystematic. Psychoanalysts have seldom been able to resist the temptation to speculate about their childless patients, and it is not hard to concoct a plausible story. A need to remain emotionally dependent on a husband or mother, or a severe conflict between motherhood and career, might in some cases help to explain why conception has failed to occur. Yet we need a more convincing mechanism than is usually offered, and certainly nothing as wildly speculative as the 'antimotherly orgasm' proposed by Deutsch (1945). Mai et al (1972), in a study of 50 consecutive couples referred to an infertility clinic in Adelaide, proposed strict criteria for the diagnosis of psychogenic infertility: (1) the couple must be having regular intercourse with the expressed intention of producing a child; (2) there must at the same time be unmistakable evidence of ambivalence towards parenthood in the female if not also the male partner, with interview data corroborated by developmental history; and (3) there must be a clear-cut mechanism whereby conception is prevented despite an avowed wish to conceive. Such criteria were met by only two couples, even if there was conspicuous psychopathology in some of the other 48. The mechanism was clearly discernible, i.e. failure to ejaculate in one case and a mysterious preference for intercourse during the menstrual period in the other. The authors conceded that some of the mechanisms put forward by psychosomatic enthusiasts would be hard to demonstrate by available techniques.

In the last 20 years a number of other investigators have looked at the question of whether infertile differ from fertile couples, or whether couples with unexplained infertility differ from those with adequately explained infertility, on a variety of psychological features. Many of these later studies have been more rigorous than the earlier ones reviewed by Noyes & Chapnick (1964), despite a wide range of methods, measures and patient characteristics. Edelmann & Connolly (1986) have published a useful summary of nine such studies, including the one by Mai et al already mentioned. After their statutory criticisms of research method they conclude that 'on the basis of the available evidence there appears little to support the suggestion that psychological factors play a part in the aetiology of childlessness . . . it seems likely that only by carefully conducted longitudinal studies will the relationship between infertility and psychopathology be satisfactorily investigated and disentangled'. The case for a prospective enquiry, here as in many other dark corners of psychosomatic medicine, is hard to refute. How else could one hope to discover whether psychological factors predispose certain couples to become infertile, or whether it is simply that infertility may lead to psychological problems?

Advances in neuro-endocrinology may promote our understanding of causal mechanisms without allowing us to predict which partnerships will be hampered in their reproductive performance. Nevertheless we can offer two general propositions without fear of rebuttal. The first is that couples with all manner of psychological disturbance become parents with regrettable ease — and there is nothing we can do about that! The second is that relief of anxiety by psychological means cannot be detrimental in carefully selected cases, whether or not it has anything to contribute to the relief of infertility. Psychological management assumes a particular importance in cases of unexplained infertility, which can be demoralising in its effects. For instance, Lenton et al (1977) found that some of their still infertile patients were greatly reassured by a follow-up interview, having been depressed by the earlier verdict that they were completely normal after full investigation at the clinic.

THERAPEUTIC APPROACHES

What proportion of successful pregnancies among couples complaining of infertility can be confidently attributed to medical intervention? Probably not as many as doctors would like to think. The non-specific effects of seeking help, once the problem has been acknowledged, may lead to rapid resolution for a minority of couples. Disorders of ovulation can be expected to respond well to hormonal treatment where other parameters are satisfactory. However, the prognosis for couples with other problems in the female partner, and more especially with problems in the male partner, is far from reassuring. It is doubtful whether the picture has changed significantly since Campbell (1958) argued that, in the absence of gross pathology, age and duration of infertility were the most reliable prognostic indicators. Or in other words, time is the great healer for an unexpectedly large number of couples. This would mean that the endless pursuit of further investigations and second (or third and fourth) opinions can all too easily become counterproductive.

Even if the value of medically unorthodox techniques such as relaxation training or hypnosis remains to be proved, they deserve to be considered before too much anguish has resulted from a relentlessly physical approach. We ourselves would be still more wary of specifically psychological methods such as cognitive therapy or analytical psychotherapy, which might nevertheless have something to offer in carefully selected cases. What we *are* prepared to advocate is close attention to the social and psychological repercussions of a couple's infertility from the moment they present for help. Here we are echoing the philosophy of the National Association for the Childless (NAC), who over the past 10 years have been campaigning for the provision of expert counselling at infertility clinics; this is what a representative sample of their membership responding to a postal questionnaire found most lacking (Owens & Read 1984).

In what follows we aim to illustrate the role of the psychologist in the management of the childless couple. This is not to dismiss secondary infertility as unworthy of psychological concern, although it is less common as well as less obviously heart-rending than the childless state. Some 10% of the couples we have been asked to see have a child of the current partnership, or sometimes more than one child from a previous partnership. Much more rarely have we been confronted by that most poignant situation of all, the couple who have been diagnosed as infertile after losing their only child (e.g. from leukaemia). But it seems appropriate to focus on the most frequently recurring case, of the couple who married with normal expectations of a family, yet are still childless after an average interval of 5–7 years, though sometimes much longer. For reasons that need not detain us here, we are most often consulted about couples who are interested in AID as a means of bypassing male infertility. This might be described as a psychological minefield, and certainly offers ample scope for counselling and other forms of psychological intervention. We shall also indicate a possible role for the psychologist where the male partner is presumed to be fertile but the female partner needs help in accepting her infertility as a prelude to fostering or adoption. The possibility of effective intervention in cases of unexplained infertility will be explored next. We then consider the couple who on preliminary assessment have raised doubts as to their fitness for parenthood, or are seen as premature in their request for help.

THE MANAGEMENT OF MALE INFERTILITY

In view of the poor response to hormonal treatment for oligospermia, and the irremediable nature of azoospermia (save in rare instances where obstruction of the vas can be treated surgically), resort to a sperm donor is effectively the only solution for couples whose problem has been traced to severe defects in the male partner. Little is known about the characteristics of those who can accommodate to the involvement of a third party as a means to a child, but the survey of NAC members indicated that not all childless couples find this psychologically acceptable (Owens 1983). On the other hand it was often those who were not themselves faced with this dilemma who felt inclined to hold out against it, and it may well be that doubts or moral scruples are more readily entertained by those who are under no psychological pressure. Even so, there is probably no shortage of infertile husbands who are capable of resisting the idea of donor insemination when it is put to them by a physician or by their partner.

Some years ago it was laid down by the St George's Hospital Ethical Committee that couples interested in pursuing the possibility of AID should receive counselling from an independent member of staff. The merits of psychological screening for donor parenthood have been debated elsewhere (Humphrey & Ainsworth-Smith 1988), but to provide information about the procedure whilst exploring the couple's own attitudes and feelings is surely a non-controversial aim. All the same, such counselling, which is intended to be essentially non-judgemental, is not universally on offer. Macnaughton (1984), a member of the Warnock Committee, queried whether it ought to be imposed as a condition of treatment; we suspect that, where it is left entirely to the couple's own initiative, it will more often than not be dismissed. Yet it could perhaps be argued that those who most strongly repudiate the need for counselling are also more likely to require it.

Over the past 8 years we have seen more than 170 couples for this purpose, and an analysis of the first 100 couples has been published (Humphrey & Humphrey 1987). Apart from one or two consulting privately, all had first attended the hospital fertility clinic where the husband was told of his infertility, if he had not already learnt of it elsewhere. Most couples had reached a firm decision and were no longer looking for guidance as to whether this was the right step for them. However, a fair number were in need of factual knowledge, to say nothing of moral support. Some were uncertain whether to confide in their closest relatives and friends, others had already done so but without intending to be open with any child thus conceived, so that we felt bound to make them aware of their self-imposed vulnerability to disclosure from an outside source. The selection of donors also merits discussion, and we have latterly been asked for reassurance about freedom from transmissible disease, especially since an Australian report of four cases of the AIDS virus transmitted through semen (Stewart et al 1985). There are many other possible sources of anxiety that may need to be looked at.

Unless there has been prior treatment in the private sector (usually without success) we expect every couple to come for a second interview 2–3 months later, mainly in order to guard against hasty decisions. Moreover, first impressions are notoriously unreliable, and we have more than once been seriously misled. Two couples decided to separate before the second meeting could take place, whilst several others have dropped out without explanation. Adjusting to the discovery of a man's inability to father a child is a stressful process for any couple, and it would be unwise to embark on a course of inseminations until the effect upon their relationship and his self-esteem has been carefully appraised. Indeed, it would be no exaggeration to construe male infertility as a marital crisis even where previously the marriage was not thought to be at risk (Humphrey 1986).

The first interview is spent taking a brief personal history from each partner before enquiring into the marriage. We are especially interested in the couple's passage to the infertility clinic and their individual responses to the investigations. Unlike Berger (1980) who found that a diagnosis of male infertility was apt to induce temporary impotence in the husband and aggressive dreams or fantasies in the wife, we have failed to elicit evidence of any marked sexual disturbance at the time of our initial interviews. But there may be a history of reduced spontaneity and loss of sexual satisfaction in response to the actual investigations, which can happen regardless of the diagnostic outcome (Elstein 1975). Whether or not we have elicited such a history we take the precaution of asking the couple to choose independently from a set of printed statements about the sexual aspect of their marriage. Where a specific problem comes to light (for example premature ejaculation in a man who was several years younger than his wife and without premarital experience) we tell them that skilled help is available and offer to refer them to the sexual dysfunction clinic. We see this as no barrier to donor insemination when the time is ripe, but hope to convince them that pregnancy is no substitute for sexual adjustment. However, we must emphasise that situations of this kind have been rare in our experience to date.

The decision to resort to a donor is less straightforward than might appear from some of the accounts we have received. Most of our informants had heard of AID before it was put to them as a possible solution (typically by a consultant), yet few had read about it. The brief guidebook by Snowden & Snowden (1984) was written expressly for couples in this predicament, but is not yet sufficiently well known to be widely recommended by doctors. These authors lay stress on the need for greater openness about male infertility and its consequences, making a useful distinction between confidentiality and privacy. A perceived need for secrecy is clearly a potential handicap for AID parents as the years go by, and greater public awareness of the meaning of infertility as distinct from impotence would help to create a more favourable climate for this form of assisted reproduction.

Meanwhile men will continue to vary in their individual reactions to what is still seen as an unflattering diagnosis. Unfortunately the link between sexuality and parenthood is stronger for men than for women (Humphrey 1977), but some will find it relatively easy to handle the threat to their self-esteem. Here we have been at some disadvantage owing to the retrospective nature of our material. At least two-thirds of our husbands had known for more than a year, and almost a quarter of them more than 5 years (one man for as long as 20 years). Where the verdict had been delivered within the past few months we have identified detachment, anger and pain as the commonest reactions from the husband. These may overshadow concern for the welfare of his partner, yet the emotional effect upon her is an equally important factor. Outright condemnation of a sterile mate is happily rare, but subtler forms of disparagement may lurk behind a façade of acceptance. The balance of power within the relationship may come to be a critical factor, yet this is hard to elucidate in the space of 3 months. We can but hope to detect a militant need for a child in some women, or an excessive drive to make amends in some men. These are properly regarded as warning signals but can easily be missed.

We have also seen couples who have adapted well to their childlessness until stirred by a chance event. The health visitor who was introduced to a living instance of AID in her practice, and went on to produce a healthy donor child of her own at the age of 37 years, is a dramatic illustration. We may note in passing that wives of fertile men can undergo a similar change of heart at this time of life, when the menopause has yet to cast its shadow but can possibly be glimpsed on the horizon.

To amplify our interview data we ask couples to complete two brief marital questionnaires (Locke & Wallace 1959, Ryle 1966), which they do independently in our presence to avoid collusion. Despite the well known limitations of self-report instruments, we have sometimes found these unexpectedly revealing. Ryle's Marital Patterns Test (MPT), which had proved its value in an earlier study of childless couples waiting to adopt (Humphrey 1975), appears to be the more useful measure of the two. At all events it has yielded a wide variety of scores for more than 200 respondents, with valuable evidence as to the degree of mutual corroboration. Whilst the temptation to 'fake good' might be anticipated in this context, one must bear in mind that some couples or individuals are sufficiently ambivalent about this form of parenthood to display their uneasiness in a series of negative test responses. The two affection scales, 'affection given' (AG) and 'affection received' (AR), are more sensitive to individual variation than the dominance scale, which not only contains fewer items (ten instead of 14) but may also be restricted by conventional assumptions of male ascendancy in any long-term partnership that deserves to survive — not that such assumptions are always borne out in reality! On average, however, our AID couples have reflected only a slight trend towards male dominance, with 40% laying claim to a reasonably egalitarian relationship.

Ryle's concept of affection is broader than in ordinary discourse. It reflects mutual support rather than the expression of loving sentiments, and is thus particularly apt to our purposes. A man with shattered self-esteem, or temporarily mortified by the knowledge that he cannot hope to gratify his wife's maternal needs, may look to her for emotional support. At this stage of the marriage she herself may be too upset to provide it, or he may be inordinate in his demands (sometimes both). Hence we are concerned with the ratio of his AR to her AG score. Less than 5% of our couples seemed to agree that he was receiving too little affection from her, and we think it more likely that the infertile husband goes through a phase of requiring enhanced proof of his wife's enduring love. Interestingly the AID wives as a group claim to give more affection than their husbands acknowledge, whereas in the earlier study of prospective adopters the scores were more evenly balanced; in the control group of ordinary parents the ratio was even reversed, with young mothers perhaps uneasily aware of their degree of emotional investment in the children (for details of the test findings see Humphrey & Humphrey 1987).

Whilst the final decision on treatment still rests with the consultant in charge of the clinic, we are now expected to express an opinion on a couple's personal suitability for the treatment programme. Where the two interviews have highlighted grossly adverse factors, such as marital conflict or current psychiatric illness (as in a few instances only), we scarcely need the supporting evidence of low affection scores on the MPT. Where the interview findings are acceptable though not strongly positive, we would hesitate to put too much weight on the questionnaire data in the absence of systematic follow-up enquiry. This is not only beyond our resources but ethically questionable, since the couples would feel on trial as well as being forcibly reminded of their incomplete parental status.

At least 40% of our couples have already become parents through AID, whereas fewer than 10% (clearly a self-selected group) have called on us to show off their child. The short-term outcome was glowingly successful in every case bar one.

A nanny had been married to a policeman for 6 years. Her need for motherhood had become almost obsessive, and with some hesitation he had agreed to the use of a donor. She conceived promptly, the pregnancy and delivery were uncomplicated, and a boy was born about 12 months after our second interview. At first the husband seemed able to share in his wife's delight at becoming a mother, and outwardly his behaviour was reported as like that of any other young father. Within 3 months he had become involved with a nurse who was separated from her husband, and 3 months later he told his wife that he was going to leave her.

Apparently his 'artificial family' (Snowden & Mitchell 1981) was an unacceptable commitment, serving merely to remind him of his own biological inadequacy.

In this case the marital questionnaire results were broadly acceptable, and the only tell-tale indicator from the interview material was the husband's comment (almost unheeded at the time) that if he had his time over again he would look for a woman who did not want children. Possibly he had found such a woman in the nurse who now shared his guilty secret. When we saw the couple, briefly, with their appealing infant they gave us to understand that there was no hope of a reconciliation. Fortunately the wife was of a robust personality and had already made plans to support herself and the child. She realised now, when it was too late, that with more self-restraint she might have given her husband time to adapt inwardly as well as outwardly to this deceptively simple solution to their problem. Be that as it may, there is a strong suspicion that he wanted to be mothered.

Even if there were more satisfactory evidence as to the quality of AID family life than can be gleaned from the limited follow-up study by Snowden et al (1983), we would remain sceptical of the 1% divorce rate proclaimed by some authors (see Joyce 1984). We look for 3 years of marriage and/or cohabitation as a minimum period of readiness for AID, though longer would be desirable. Under normal circumstances transition to parenthood is not an unduly stressful experience (Elliott et al 1985), but prolonged childlessness is hardly the best preparation unless it can strengthen the couple's sense of mutual commitment. Whilst the couple just quoted gave us no undue cause for concern after two meetings, there were others we viewed with considerably more suspicion. Yet when readiness for parenthood is put to the test it is human adaptability that counts. Two men may be equally dependent on their wives for emotional support, whereas one of them may be much better equipped to become self-reliant as a father, or one of the wives may be better able to sustain a dependent husband as well as a dependent child. This is what makes prediction so hazardous. Although in the absence of contrary evidence we would like to believe that couples requesting AID *are* well above average in their marital stability, for the time being this must be taken on trust.

We have dwelt at some length on the management of male infertility on the strength of our special interest and experience. We shall now turn more briefly to other situations encountered at the infertility clinic that are open to psychological management.

THE MANAGEMENT OF FEMALE INFERTILITY

The birth of the first 'test-tube baby' in 1978 saw the dawn of a new era in reproductive technology (Edwards 1980, Edwards & Steptoe 1980). Scientific interest in IVF and embryo transfer grew rapidly over the next few years (e.g. Edwards & Purdy 1982, Wood & Westmore 1983, Singer

& Wells 1984). This research, albeit still in its infancy, has already brought new hope to couples whose infertility can be relieved only by direct implantation of the fertilised ovum into the uterus. Ideally this calls for a fertile male partner, although there are indications that it may also provide a means of overcoming the problem of oligospermia (Mahadevan et al 1983, Cohen et al 1984, Hull & Glazener 1984). In the climate of growing enthusiasm for these developments, reinforced at every turn by the media, it is easy to overlook two major limiting factors.

The first is that up to now the technique has been worth considering in only a minority of cases, less than 20% according to Hull et al (1985). These would include some cases of unexplained infertility as well as oligospermia and tubal damage (the main category).

The second is the disappointingly low success rate — 8% for a single attempt, according to Lopata (1983), and variously estimated at 15–30% even with repeated attempts — of which practitioners are more soberly aware than their ever hopeful patients. In this respect IVF is much more of a gamble than AID, which with careful selection of patients and improved methods of pinpointing ovulation can be expected to succeed in up to 80% of cases. Thus the need for counselling of possible IVF candidates is even greater at those few centres which are in a position to offer a service, though at present we cannot write from personal experience.

Prior to the development of IVF the only effective help for the patient with tubal damage was surgery, which too has a relatively poor prognosis. A survey of the literature up to 1979 revealed an overall success rate of 25–30% (Chamberlain 1982), although with microsurgery this rose to nearly 60% (Winston 1980). Apart from being a major operation it also carries an increased risk of ectopic pregnancy, which IVF is more likely to avoid. At a time when it was much easier to adopt an infant (say 15–20 years ago), the woman with a tubal problem could guard against the disappointment of surgical failure by registering with an adoption agency. This is scarcely a viable option today, although a number of couples still willing to consider it have been referred for counselling over the past few years. Those with a sense of commitment towards children deprived of normal home life can still occasionally find fulfilment in this way, as the following case demonstrates.

Mrs A. was 30 years old when her second tubal operation was rated as technically unsatisfactory. She was referred to M.H. for counselling and help in coming to terms with her situation. She was tearful at first and plainly very distressed by her failure to conceive. Her early life was traumatic in that her father had committed suicide when she was 4 years old, and during periods when her harassed mother had been unable to cope with the three children they had been taken into care. She had met her husband when they were both 19 years old and married him 3 years later. He was a devout man who believed in prayer as the solution to most of life's problems, but could not offer her the strength and maturity that she craved.

During 9 years of childless marriage they had acted as foster parents to various handicapped and disturbed children for sometimes up to a year or more, and she had experienced the usual sense of loss when these children were returned to the local authority. Then an opportunity arose to adopt a 7-week-old girl from Bangladesh, and all went well with the adoption after some supportive psychotherapy during the probationary period. However, this more whole-hearted commitment to the maternal role for Mrs A. led her husband to withdraw into his religious pre-occupation, and an offer of brief marital therapy was accepted. Communication between the couple improved in the course of several sessions, with some benefit to their sexual life. They found it hard to decide on a second adoption, especially as they were not well off, but could not resist the offer of a white newborn baby when their older daughter was just turned 4 years old. At the last contact, a year later, the 4-year-old was said to have been plastering her face with talcum powder, which did not counteract the impression that a happy family life had been achieved. Two or three years earlier Mrs A. had taken herself off a waiting list for intensive psychotherapy as recommended for her deeper problems, but more recently she had attended a course of self-assertiveness training with the result that her husband would now wash up the supper dishes without waiting to be asked! She expressed immense gratitude for the help received earlier.

Adopting a child has always been a potentially stressful experience, and this is now aggravated by the long delays and greater uncertainties involved. It can be helpful to discuss these realistically with a couple before referring them to their local social services department if they so wish. Some authorities run group meetings for prospective foster parents, and now that the boundaries between adoption and fostering have become somewhat blurred following the 1975 Children Act (Rowe 1983), the bad image of foster parenthood is due for correction. Whilst 'tug-of-love' dramas can still occur when a child is reclaimed by the natural parent(s), some protection is afforded to foster parents who wish to adopt, in that after 5 years the child cannot be removed without a court order. And where there is reasonable evidence to suggest that the child's interests are best served by staying put, an order will not usually be granted. Thus the situation, so graphically portrayed by Rowe & Lambert (1973), in which a national survey of nearly 3000 children in care showed that 22% were regarded by their social workers as in need of a permanent substitute family, can now more readily be turned to the advantage of couples willing to accept an older child of the kind traditionally regarded as 'hard to place'. However, it is our conviction that only a minority of childless couples are well equipped to handle the emotional problems of long-term fostering with a view to adoption. For a sensitive account of these problems from a child psychiatrist, the reader is referred to Hersov (1985).

The relative improbability of overcoming stubborn infertility through the adoption process has been demonstrated in several studies (e.g. Humphrey 1969a,b, Arronet et al 1974, Lamb & Leurgans 1979). Evidence of an apparent psychosomatic relationship has been confined to individual case reports, such as Orr (1941) and Aronson & Glienke (1963).

Women with ovulatory disorders have not so far been referred for psychological help in view of their heartening response to a series of drug trials. Where hormonal therapy is not rapidly successful (and before adoption is considered) they might be seen as possible candidates for an anxiety management programme of the kind found promising in the context of hysterectomy (Young & Humphrey 1985). When ovulation is disturbed by the stress of failing to conceive from repeated donor inseminations (Vere & Joyce 1979) there might also be scope for such an approach. However, a small pilot study conducted as part of our AID project was inconclusive, perhaps partly because the infertility was long-established in all three cases.

THE MANAGEMENT OF UNEXPLAINED INFERTILITY

As already indicated, this far from rare predicament can cause untold distress, and when self-reproach alternates with hostility towards the partner the marriage may come under severe strain. So far only a few couples have been referred for psychological evaluation and possible management, but rapid resolution was achieved in the following case.

Mrs B. was 27 years old when first seen by M.H. and a female cotherapist. She had married at 18 with a '5-year plan' of preparation for motherhood, but within 2 years had begun to weaken and put pressure on her husband for a child. Thus she had been trying to conceive for about 7 years, and during the past 5 years the couple had been extensively investigated. The husband, who was 33, did not appear to be subfertile even if his sperm count had fluctuated over this time. Mrs B. herself was free of any obvious abnormality.

It soon emerged that Mr B., a cautious and rather melancholy man, was unenthusiastic about fatherhood. As an only child he was more than satisfied with his wife's undivided attention; she in contrast was a fraternal twin with an older sister and five younger siblings, of whom only the 13-year-old was still childless. A complicating factor was that parenthood had brought no visible joy to any of her siblings, whose marriages had almost without exception gone into decline. Moreover the twin, who had never wanted children, had suffered from postnatal depression and found it hard to relate to her 5-year-old. Thus Mr B. had plenty of ammunition in his campaign against adoption, and would not welcome AID even if the normal criteria were applicable. Essentially the couple had reached a stalemate. Her clerical job was no basis for a career, and although she expressed a sense of commitment to the marriage, he plainly felt that it was in jeopardy.

In the course of three sessions we gave the couple permission to feel anxious about the prospect of parenthood whilst stressing the value of their 9 childless years as evidence of a stable partnership. We tried to convey a profound faith in the future of their marriage, even if it was destined to remain childless, but pointed out that a woman of 27 had time on her side. Relaxation exercises were taught by the female counsellor, who had originally trained as a physiotherapist.

When last seen, 2 or 3 months later, the wife reported that her period was 6 days overdue (3 days longer than on any previous occasion) and a do-it-yourself pregnancy test had been positive. The husband's response was less than rhapsodic. Despite our scepticism the pregnancy was confirmed in a subsequent telephone call, when tribute was paid to our intervention.

Evidently the marital relationship was already much improved. Two years later a further telephone conversation established that the couple had a son of 15 months, and Mrs B. was in midpregnancy, having conceived within a few months of abandoning postnatal contraception. She now realised how 'uptight' she had been in earlier years, but especially at the time of our meetings. Her husband had been 'marvellous' as a father.

There can be no proof from a single case that the switch from a medical to a psychological approach had been instrumental in the success. Wisely the couple had been given a 6-month break from the clinic before seeing us, and luckily they were receptive. A similar history in a 32-year-old woman might have had a different outcome. Yet the information we elicited from leisurely conversations in a non-clinical setting was probably of some relevance. The effect of prolonged medical investigation had been unhelpful, and no attempt had been made to enquire into the meaning of parenthood for this particular couple.

READINESS FOR PARENTHOOD

Doctors are not slaves to their patients' every wish. For example, a request for abortion or sterilisation may be turned down unless convincing reasons are given in support of it. Yet help in achieving a pregnancy is not usually withheld, and indeed any doctor taking a magisterial stance might be accused of arrogance. Even in the special context of AID it has been argued that the couple know best, although surely thought should be spared for the donors, who are entitled to expect some discretion in the use of their services (Humphrey & Ainsworth-Smith 1988). But the occasional patient has been referred for an opinion on readiness (not fitness) for parenthood, either because of adverse social circumstances or for other reasons, as in the following case.

Ken and Patsy had been living together for only a few months when introduced to M.H. She was 27 years old, he a year or two younger, and each had been married briefly. They had started to notice one another whilst working side-by-side in a kitchen, but as he was still married at the time she had turned her attention to a man who had undergone vasectomy. Since she herself had been treated for endometriosis the outlook was unpromising, but they had attended the clinic to discuss whether the operation could be reversed. Before any steps could be taken the relationship floundered, and meanwhile Ken's wife had left him. Patsy could see the wisdom of waiting for a while before actively trying for a baby with her new partner, who ironically was found to have a low sperm count on preliminary testing. However, as she was convinced that her endometriosis (though virtually in abeyance now) would be a bar to conception anyway, she was not interested in birth control. They had a vigorous and rewarding sex life.

The couple planned to marry at the earliest opportunity. However, it was put to them that other goals should take priority over parenthood until it became more realistically urgent. They were intending to look for a new home after selling their respective properties, and Patsy was encouraged to have another go at the driving test. Meanwhile she agreed to advice on anxiety management. When last seen, 9 months after the initial visit and a few weeks after their marriage, they had sold her flat and moved into his house. She was now enjoying her leisure, without the same sense of panic about becoming pregnant. She had rehearsed the techniques acquired during her anxiety management sessions, and was about to resume driving lessons after practising on her husband's car.

A mere 7 months later it was learnt that she was expecting a baby in 3 months' time. Both partners were delighted.

PROFESSIONAL ISSUES

Throughout the past few years a link has been maintained with all members of the clinic team, including the nurse in charge of the donor insemination programme. Most of the patients seen for psychological evaluation and management have been referred by senior registrars, one of whom had experience of group therapy and the other of sex therapy. Contact with general practitioners and social workers has been minimal. As a university teacher holding an honorary clinical contract, the senior author has considerable freedom, subject to the usual rules of professional etiquette. There is scope for a great deal more counselling than has hitherto been undertaken, but the initial procedure of attending the clinic every week proved unsatisfactory for a variety of reasons. To remain on call during clinic hours seemed a better arrangement, but pressure on staff has made it hard to relay messages in time for action. Consequently only a small proportion of patients who might have gained from psychological appraisal have been referred.

Apart from counselling patients and providing factual information where needed, the psychologist can draw on specific skills in the realm of anxiety management and cognitive therapy (Beck 1976, Meichenbaum 1983). Men and women may need help in learning to counteract negative thoughts and feelings of helplessness and hopelessness. Those who must reconcile themselves to the probability of a childless future will be faced with a need to rethink their attitudes. To give a simple example, no longer must the recurrent menstrual period be treated as a symbol of personal failure. Whilst life crises of various kinds are commonplace, and are resolved by most people without a psychologist at their elbow, it remains true that infertility has a special poignancy all of its own. Human reproduction has been brought within voluntary control to the extent that inability to conceive at the appointed time is becoming almost intolerable. Medical advances towards the achievement of healthy pregnancy among those who seek help have been distinctly limited. Measures to relieve self-destructive emotions, and thereby in some cases to promote fertility, must have something to contribute in this area of psychosomatic medicine.

ACKNOWLEDGEMENTS

We thank Professor Geoffrey Chamberlain for his helpful comments on an earlier draft, and Bill Hendry, FRCS, for advice on the technical aspects of male infertility.

REFERENCES

Aronson H G, Glienke C F 1963 A study of the incidence of pregnancy following adoption. Fertility and Sterility 14: 547–553

Arronet G H, Berquist C A, Parekh M C 1974 The influence of adoption on subsequent pregnancy in infertile marriage. International Journal of Fertility 19: 159–162

Beck A T 1976 Cognitive therapy and emotional disorders. International Universities Press, New York

Berger D M 1980 Couples' reactions to male infertility and donor insemination. American Journal of Psychiatry 137: 1047–1049

Campbell H 1958 Infertility: its incidence and hope of cure. British Medical Journal i: 429–433

Chamberlain G V P 1982 The results of tubal surgery. In: Chamberlain G, Winston R (eds) Tubal infertility: diagnosis and treatment. Blackwell Scientific, Oxford

Cohen J, Fehilly C B, Fishel S et al 1984 Male infertility successfully treated by in-vitro fertilisation. Lancet i: 1239–1240

Deutsch H 1945 The psychology of women: a psychoanalytic interpretation. Motherhood, Vol 2. Grune and Stratton, New York

Drake T, Tredway D, Buchanan G, Takaki N, Daane T 1977 Unexplained infertility — a reappraisal. Obstetrics and Gynecology 50: 644–646

Edelmann R J, Connolly K J 1986 Psychological aspects of infertility. British Journal of Medical Psychology 59: 209–219

Edwards R G 1980 Conception in the human female. Academic Press, London

Edwards R, Purdy J 1982 Human conception in vitro. Academic Press, London

Edwards R, Steptoe P 1980 A matter of life. Hutchinson, London

Elliott S A, Watson J P, Brough D I 1985 Transition to parenthood by British couples. Journal of Reproductive and Infant Psychology 3: 28–39

Elstein M 1975 Effect of infertility on psychosexual function. British Medical Journal 3: 296–299

Hendry W F, Morgan H, Stedronska J 1977 The clinical significance of antisperm antibodies in male subfertility. British Journal of Urology 49: 757–762

Hersov, L 1985 Adoption and fostering. In: Child and adolescent psychiatry: modern approaches, 2nd edn. Blackwell Scientific, Oxford: pp. 101–117

Hull M G R, Glazener C M A 1984 Male infertillty and in-vitro fertilisation. Lancet 2: 231

Hull M G R, Glazener C M A, Kelly N J et al 1985 Population study of causes, treatment and outcome of infertility. British Medical Journal 291: 1693–1697

Humphrey M 1969a The hostage seekers: a study of childless and adopting couples. Longman, London

Humphrey M 1969b The adopted child as a fertility charm. Journal of Reproduction and Fertility 20: 354–356

Humphrey M 1975 The effect of children upon the marriage relationship. British Journal of Medical Psychology 48: 273–279

Humphrey M 1977 Sex differences in attitude to parenthood. Human Relations 30: 737–749

Humphrey M 1984 Infertility and alternative parenting. In: Broome A, Wallace L (eds) Psychology and gynaecological problems. Tavistock, London

Humphrey M 1986 Infertility as a marital crisis. Stress Medicine 2: 221–224

Humphrey M, Ainsworth-Smith I 1988 Screening couples for parenthood by donor insemination. Submitted to Bioethics

Humphrey M, Humphrey H 1987 Marital relationships in couples seeking donor insemination. Journal of Biosocial Science 19: 209–219

Humphrey M, Mackenzie K M 1967 Infertility and adoption: follow-up of 216 couples attending a hospital clinic. British Journal of Preventive and Social Medicine 21: 90–96

Joyce D N 1984 The implications of greater openness concerning AID. In: AID and after. British Agencies for Adoption and Fostering, London

Lamb E J, Leurgans S 1979 Does adoption effect subsequent fertility? American Journal of Obstetrics and Gynecology 134: 138–144

Lenton E A, Weston G A, Cooke I D 1977 Long-term follow-up of the apparently normal couple with a complaint of infertility. Fertility and Sterility 28: 913–919

Locke H J, Wallace K M 1959 Short marital-adjustment and prediction tests: their reliability and validity. Marriage and Family Living 21: 251

Lopata A 1983 Concepts in human in vitro fertility and embryo transfer. Fertility and Sterility 40: 289–301

Macnaughton M C 1984 Personal communication

Mahadevan M M, Trounson A O, Leeton J F 1983 The relationship of tubal blockage, infertility of unknown cause, suspected male infertility and endometriosis to success of in vitro fertilisation and embryo transfer. Fertility and Sterility 40: 755–762

Mai F M M, Munday R N, Rump E E 1972 Psychosomatic and behavioural mechanisms in psychogenic infertility. British Journal of Psychiatry 118: 22–28

Meichenbaum D 1983 Coping with stress. Century, New York

Noyes R W, Chapnick E M 1964 Literature on psychology and infertility. Fertility and Sterility 15: 543–558

Orr D W 1941 Pregnancy following the decision to adopt. Psychosomatic Medicine 3: 441–446

Owens D J, Read M W 1984 Patients' experience with and assessment of subfertility testing and treatment. Journal of Reproductive and Infant Psychology 2: 7–17

Rowe J 1983 Fostering in the eighties. British Agencies for Adoption and Fostering, London

Rowe J, Lambert L 1973 Children who wait. Association of British Adoption Agencies, London

Ryle A 1966 A marital patterns test for use in psychiatric research. British Journal of Psychiatry 112: 285–293

Singer P, Wells D 1984 The reproduction revolution: new ways of making babies. Oxford University Press, Melbourne

Snowden R, Mitchell G D 1981 The artificial family: a consideration of artificial insemination by donor. Allen and Unwin, London

Snowden R, Mitchell G D, Snowden E 1983 Artificial reproduction: a social investigation. Allen and Unwin, London

Snowden R, Snowden E 1984 The gift of a child. Allen and Unwin, London

Stewart G J, Cunningham A L, Driscoll G L et al 1985 Transmission of human T-cell lymphotropic virus type III (HTLV-III) by artificial insemination by donor. Lancet 2: 581–585

Templeton A A, Penney G L 1982 The incidence, characteristics and prognosis of patients whose infertility is unexplained. Fertility and Sterility 37: 175–182

Vere M F, Joyce D N 1979 Luteal function in patients seeking AID. British Medical Journal ii: 100

Veevers J E 1972 Factors in the incidence of childlessness in Canada: an analysis of census data. Social Biology 19: 266–274

Veevers J E 1979 Voluntary childlessness: a review of issues and evidence. Marriage and Family Review 2: 1–26

Warnock Committee 1984 Report of the Committee of Enquiry into Human Fertilisation and Embryology. HMSO, London

Winston R M L 1980 Microsurgery of the fallopian tube. Fertility and Sterility 34: 521–527

Wood C, Westmore A 1983 Test-tube conception. Hill of Content, Melbourne

Young L, Humphrey M 1985 Cognitive methods of preparing women for hysterectomy: does a booklet help? British Journal of Clinical Psychology 24: 303–304

Problems in women undergoing surgery for breast cancer

INTRODUCTION

Up to one in four women who undergo mastectomy for cancer of the breast develop a depressive illness and/or anxiety state within a year of surgery (Morris et al 1977, Maguire et al 1978, Hughson et al 1986, Dean 1987). A fifth of women develop persistent body image problems. These present as a heightened self-consciousness, loss of physical integrity, or a feeling of being less feminine and attractive (Maguire et al 1983). Up to a third of those women who had an active and enjoyable sex life with their partners before mastectomy develop sexual difficulties (Maguire et al 1980a). Contrary to expectation, women who undergo surgical procedures which conserve the breast because they have no strong treatment preference and then have radiotherapy seem no less immune to psychiatric morbidity (Fallowfield et al 1986).

Unfortunately, much of this psychological morbidity remains undisclosed, undetected and untreated. So, this chapter will discuss why this morbidity remains hidden and then suggest how the recognition and treatment of the psychological problems associated with surgery for breast cancer can be improved.

HIDDEN MORBIDITY

Poor recognition

Only 20–40% of those women who develop anxiety and/or depression after mastectomy are recognised and offered appropriate treatment by the surgeon or general practitioner (Maguire 1985). Women who develop sexual difficulties or body image problems are even less likely to receive help. This poor recognition is due to adopting strategies of communication (albeit unwittingly) which serve to keep them at a safe emotional distance from their patients. These strategies are called distancing techniques and need to be recognised and understood if they are to be relinquished.

Distancing strategies

These have been revealed by direct observation of consultations between patients with breast cancer, doctors and nurses. They include the following.

Restricted focus — the simplest distancing technique used by doctors and nurses is to restrict enquiry to physical aspects of care. Thus, a surgeon might begin by asking, for example, 'How's that pain in your arm been since I saw you last?' The focus of the consultation then continues to be her physical well-being. This makes it unlikely that she will volunteer any concurrent psychological problems. Such avoidance of psychological matters was evident in a study of the aftercare given by general practitioners to mastectomy patients. No woman was asked directly about her sexual relationship following mastectomy. Questions about how patients felt about losing a breast were almost as rare (Rosser & Maguire 1982), while those concerning changes in mood were uncommon. The practitioners justified this on the grounds that if there were any problems the women would have disclosed them.

Leading questions. It was found that doctors and nurses often started their consultations with leading questions which biased women's answers towards a favourable outcome. The bias was often so explicit that the women found it hard to counter, even though they had problems which they wanted to disclose.

Surgeon: Well, I am delighted to say I can't find anything on physical examination or on your X-rays — and you are looking pretty well, aren't you? — So I don't think I need to see you again for another 3 months. That's good news isn't it? You *are* doing well! I am very pleased.
Patient: (hesitatingly) I suppose so. All right, I'll see you in 3 months time.
Surgeon: Goodbye then.

While the surgeon's comments were reasonable, since the patient was free of cancer and looked well physically, he did not consider the possibility that she might have developed serious body image problems. Faced with the strong statement by the surgeon that 'it was good news', the patient found it impossible to indicate that she had psychological problems which needed attention.

Premature reassurance. Surgeons and nurses within the clinic often realise that patients are emotionally distressed. They may acknowledge this by saying 'I can see you are very upset' but then try to explain it away as being only natural and understandable. Hence they might say: 'We will have to get you in to take some of that lump out and look at it under a microscope to see if it is serious. So, you are bound to be worried, it's only natural, you're bound to be'. They may then add, in an attempt at reassurance: 'You are in good hands, you have come to the best place. We know what we are doing. We will soon sort you out. There is no need to worry'.

This reassurance is premature because no attempt has been made to find out why she is distressed. If the surgeon had said 'I can see you are upset.

Would you like to tell me why?', the patient would have disclosed that her sister had also had breast cancer but died 6 months after diagnosis despite being reassured that everything was going to be all right. He might then have been able to reassure her genuinely that her prognosis was better than her sister's but that he did not expect her to believe him since her sister's doctor was wrong.

In a bid to soften bad news, doctors and nurses are also tempted to provide *false reassurance* by saying 'I think everything will be alright' when they are aware that the prognosis is grave.

Normalisation. This tactic is used in the hope that it will help patients to realise that they are not alone in their predicament. So, the surgeon or nurse explains: 'Of course you are upset. Everybody is when they know they have to go in for surgery'. Instead of reassuring them, this is more likely to cause patients to feel that no one is interested in them as unique persons. However, if the surgeon or nurse first explored why the patient was distressed but then added that other people have also experienced such distress, this would have been perceived as helpful.

Switching the focus. When a doctor or nurse begins to talk to a patient he or she may be faced immediately with a difficult problem and deal with it by switching the topic as in the following example.

Surgeon: How are you feeling today?
Patient: I can't understand it. You said that I would be feeling better by now but
            I am beginning to think I'm not going to get better. Am I going to get
            better?
Surgeon: Has the pain in your ribs been any easier?

The surgeon was obviously discomforted by the direct question 'am I going to get better?' and switched his attention to her rib pain. Yet he did not realise that he had done this until he heard a tape-recording of the consultation.

Jollying along. Nurses especially tend to react to emotional distress by trying to jolly patients out of it. Thus, when a nurse was confronted with a postmastectomy patient who seemed low in mood she responded by saying 'Come on, there is no need to look so glum. You know that everything is clear now'. This nurse was responding genuinely because she was pleased to learn that this patient was considered to be clear of cancer but was having radiotherapy to further ensure this. So she thought that the woman had good reason to be cheerful, and encouraged her to look on the 'bright side'. Had she explored why the patient was looking glum she would have discovered that she had two major concerns. The patient had learned that breast cancer was already disseminated by the time of diagnosis and was worried about early recurrence. She also believed that having radiotherapy indicated a poor prognosis.

Selective attention to cues. If a doctor or nurse asks an appropriate 'open question' at the beginning of a consultation, for example 'How have you been getting on since I saw you last?', this permits a patient to disclose her key problems whether they be physical, psychological or social in nature. However, there is then a danger that the doctor or nurse will selectively attend to cues about physical matters and ignore those concerning psychological and social problems.

Surgeon: How have you been getting on since I saw you last?

Patient: My arm's been a lot better. I can almost raise it above my head now but it still swells from time to time. My wound has healed nicely. But I still can't help wondering about the future. I even get to thinking whether I have a future. It gets me down at times. I get very low.

Surgeon: Just as I expected. I am delighted your arm's better apart from the swelling and your wound has healed. I think you are going to continue to make good progress. Shall we say 2 months? I'll check to see if the swelling is any easier.

Thus, important cues about 'wondering about the future' and feeling 'down' and 'very low' were ignored. This led the patient to believe that it was not legitimate to mention psychological matters.

Premature advice. When patients mention their key concerns, doctors and nurses often assume that they know what patients mean and offer information and advice before they have fully understood the nature and extent of the problem. There is then a serious risk that any advice and information that they offer is inappropriate and remains unheeded.

Patient: The pain in my hip is getting worse. I can't bear to put weight on it. I am so slowed down. It is getting very frustrating and worrying.

Surgeon: In that case we'll do an X-ray to see what's going on. How bad is your pain?

Patient: It's terrible. I have so little relief now.

Surgeon: In that case I will up your pain killers, I'll come back to the ward again tomorrow and see you. Goodbye.

The surgeon assumed that the patient was primarily concerned about her hip and the associated pain. He thought that she would be relieved to hear that he was prepared to give her more analgesia and monitor her progress the next day. However, instead of being reassured she was distressed because she was given no opportunity to discuss other major fears. She had realised that her cancer had recurred, was spreading and causing the difficulty with her hip. She had also overheard two nurses saying that she was going to have a further course of chemotherapy. She dreaded this because she had suffered unpleasant adverse effects during the first course. The temptation to offer premature advice rather than check whether there are other concerns is also likely when the problem is a practical one.

Patient: I am fed up with this prosthesis. It's so heavy. It keeps moving around. I am terrified it's going to fall out.

Surgeon: Oh, that's OK. There's no need to worry. We have much lighter ones now. I'll ask our specialist nurse to come and sort that out.

This patient's worry about the prosthesis was only 'the tip of the iceberg'. She had serious body image problems and sexual difficulties which she had not disclosed. Once doctors and nurses move into this information and advice mode it is difficult for them to heed any contrary signals from their patients, as the following example illustrates.

Patient: I am worried about how my husband is going to react to me now that I have only got one breast.

Nurse: Haven't you talked to him about it yet?

Patient: No, I'm not sure how he will react.

Nurse: Well, I would advise you to tell him. I am sure it would help if you did so. I am sure you'll find that he will be understanding and that your fears are groundless.

Patient: But I have tried and I have not found it easy.

Nurse: I think it important that you heed my advice and tell him, otherwise you are not going to be able to sort the situation out. I really would advise you to go straight home and tell him that you are worried about his reaction. I am sure he'll understand.

Patient: (rather disconsolately) Oh, all right then.

In this consultation the nurse repeatedly advised the woman to talk to her husband without exploring why she had not been able to tell him. Had she done this, she would have found that there were pre-existing difficulties in their relationship. Her husband had been unsympathetic to her during previous crises during their married life. So, it was reasonable for her to predict that his reaction to her operation would not be helpful. Despite this, the woman followed the nurse's advice and told her husband about her concerns. This led to his rejecting her and leaving her. Consequently, she felt extremely bitter about the nurse's advice.

Although these distancing tactics are common, it should be emphasised that they are not usually used consciously. So, it can be hard for doctors and nurses to accept that they use them unless they are given video- or audio-tape feedback of their consultations. It is also important to stress that there are good reasons for their use, and that they are used because of concern about patients rather than a lack of it.

Reasons for distancing

Doctors and nurses fear that active enquiry about how patients are adjusting after surgery for breast cancer will unleash strong emotions like despair ('I'm sure the cancer is going to get me in the end') or anger ('Why me, what on earth have I done to deserve this?'). They worry that they will not be able to deal with these emotions and that attempting to do so will take up too much time during busy clinics. They also fear that if they explore how patients are reacting emotionally they will cause more harm than good and hinder patients' adaptation. Eliciting the reasons for any distress may reveal serious difficulties which the doctors and nurses do not know how to handle. They may also avoid probing because they have no-one to whom they can refer those patients who they discover are not coping. As one surgeon indicated, 'what's the point of finding out if a patient has become depressed after a mastectomy, if I can't get the psychologists and psychiatrists interested in doing something sensible about it'.

Doctors and nurses are also concerned that if they establish an effective dialogue this will prompt women to ask them difficult questions like 'How long have I got?', 'Do I really need more chemotherapy?', or 'Am I going to get better?' Such questions are difficult to handle even when they have enough time and knowledge about how to respond. If the doctor or nurse establishes how distressed a patient is he or she may then be confronted with serious questions about their own work or philosophy which are hard to bear and resolve.

Surgeon: How have you been feeling since I last saw you?
Patient: Terrible.
Surgeon: In what way terrible?
Patient: I have been feeling so miserable. I have got to feeling there's no point in my carrying on.
Surgeon: Why are you feeling so low?
Patient I just can't get used to how I look. When I look at myself in a mirror I feel revolted. I know I'll never feel like a woman again. I can't see how I can live with myself like this. I don't see any point.
Surgeon: Are you feeling that you shouldn't have had a mastectomy.
Patient: Yes I am very angry about it. I have found out that you can have other operations for breast cancer. So, I know that I didn't have to lose my breast in the first place. Why on earth didn't you mention that there were alternatives.
Surgeon: Because I believe a mastectomy is still the best bet.
Patient: In all cases? There is no way I would have agreed if I had known.

In another example, a patient questioned the value of chemotherapy.

Surgeon: How's it going?
Patient: Not too well.
Surgeon: Not too well?
Patient: You said I would only have a little sickness with the chemotherapy. But it has been horrible. All my hair has fallen out. I have felt so sick with each treatment. There is no way I would go through it all again. Do you realise how tough it is? I am not sure I can even finish this lot.
Surgeon: But you have only three treatments left. You must try to see it through.
Patient: You would not say that if you really knew what it is like — besides you also told me there were no guarantees that this would cure me. Wouldn't it have been kinder to let me alone?

The patient's contribution

It is important to recognise that patients are as responsible as doctors and nurses for non-disclosure. They are reluctant to disclose difficulties because they perceive doctors and nurses as too busy and do not wish to add to their burdens. They are not sure that it is legitimate to mention psychological problems since they are never asked directly about them and the focus is usually and exclusively on their physical well-being. They also worry that if they admit that they are not coping they will be judged inadequate, uncooperative and weak. Some withold their problems because they believe that they are inevitable and that nothing can be done about it.

If assessment is to be effective, these barriers to disclosure need to be allowed for and reduced by avoiding distancing and by asking appropriate questions on each occasion.

PSYCHOLOGICAL ASSESSMENT

First assessment

When a woman first presents with a probable breast cancer it is important to inform her that you are interested in her as a person as well as in her breast disease. This can best be achieved by asking directive questions about her responses to her disease and her perceptions of it.

Surgeon: What's the problem?
Patient: I've got this breast lump. It's been getting bigger.
Surgeon: When did you first notice it?
Patient: Five weeks ago.
Surgeon: How did you notice it?
Patient: I was having a bath, just soaping myself, felt it and thought I'd better see if it went away, but it didn't so after 3 weeks I went to my doctor. She examined me and said I better see you to make sure it wasn't serious.
Surgeon: How did you feel about that?
Patient: Very worried. She wouldn't have referred me so quickly if she wasn't concerned about it.
Surgeon: What did you think it was?
Patient: Cancer, I thought it could be cancer.
Surgeon: Any other reasons you have worried that it is cancer?
Patient: It wasn't painful and I am 55 years old, the peak age isn't it for breast cancer?
Surgeon: Yes it is, so it is a possibility I have to consider. But I'd like to ask you a few more questions about your lump and then I'll examine you.

Thus, it is already clear that the woman is aware she might have cancer and has good reason for thinking so. It is also evident she has been 'worried'. This cue needs to be picked up and clarified if the woman is to believe it is legitimate to mention psychological aspects.

Surgeon: You mentioned you have been worried. Can you tell me about it?
Patient: I can't stop thinking about my lump. I keep thinking it's cancer and that it is going to kill me.
Surgeon: Just how worried do you get?

Patient:　At times I think I will go mad with worry. It's on my mind all the time. I can't get rid of it.

The surgeon is now aware that her worry could be excessive and will check this (see section on distinguishing abnormal reactions).

Another way of eliciting reactions is to obtain a history of the woman's breast trouble and then ask a more general question: 'How has all this affected you in yourself?' If such a question fails to elicit any mood disturbance it is worth asking screening questions, including 'have you at any time since finding your breast lump felt especially worried, on edge, tense or unable to relax?' (anxious mood); 'Have you at any time felt low, miserable, or depressed?' (depressed mood).

Having established her reactions and perceptions to date it is useful to determine whether there are any factors which could increase the likelihood of the woman developing psychiatric morbidity. These include a history of previous psychiatric illness (have you ever had trouble with your nerves?), and perceived lack of support (have you talked to your partner about how you felt; how did he react; did you feel he understood?; what about other people?).

After diagnosis

Once the diagnosis has been established, by fine-needle aspiration, true-cut biopsy, or biopsy, there should be an opportunity to convey the diagnosis and discuss treatment options before embarking on definitive treatments. Taking patients' views into account even if this does not alter the ultimate decision about treatment will at least leave them feeling that they were heeded. Thus, the surgeon should first indicate his findings and treatment preference, for this will reassure the patient that the surgeon knows what he is doing.

Surgeon:　I have now had the results of your biopsy. I am afraid that it is more serious than I thought.

Patient:　More serious? You mean I have cancer?

Surgeon:　Yes, I am afraid so. But I'd like. . . .

Patient:　That's what I was afraid of?

Surgeon:　Why?

Patient:　I had this premonition, that something awful was going to happen, I knew the lump must be serious.

Surgeon:　Would you like me to tell you what I would like to do?

Patient:　Yes please.

Surgeon:　The good news is that your cancer is small and well contained. There is no, absolutely no, evidence of spread.
　　　　　　(Pauses to allow information to sink in)

Patient:　Do you mean you can remove it?

Surgeon:　Yes, I think I can. In fact I think that all I need to do is to take the cancer out and then give you a course of radiotherapy to mop up any remaining cells. Is that OK?

Patient: I would rather you took my breast away.
Surgeon: Why?
Patient: I want to be sure all the cancer has been removed.
Surgeon: But how will you feel about losing a breast?
Patient: Take them both if you like. I just want to be rid of my cancer. Whether or not I have radiotherapy.
Surgeon: I think in your case that I can achieve as good a result by conserving your breast.
Patient: Are you sure?
Surgeon: I'm pretty confident, yes. How do you feel about that option?
Patient: As long as you feel confident that you could get rid of the cancer I'll go along with your advice.

Sometimes, because of lack of access to suitable diagnostic facilities or other factors, diagnosis and treatment are conducted as a one-stage procedure (biopsy, frozen section, proceed?). Here it is important that the surgeon is prepared to warn the patient of the likely outcomes and promote discussion of treatment options. Otherwise the woman may be seriously misled about her condition and the surgeon's concern about her as a person.

Surgeon: I want to get you in for a biopsy, that is to take a bit of that lump out and look at it under a microscope. If I find any of the lump is cancerous I shall want to operate.
Patient: Operate? How do you mean?
Surgeon: I would need to remove your breast. Is that all right?
Patient: Is there no other option?
Surgeon: I don't think so. Your lump is too big, I think, to be dealt with by simple removal. On the other hand, I think that removing your breast and giving you a course of radiotherapy will do the trick. How do you feel about that?
Patient: Very upset. I hate the idea of losing my breast.
Surgeon: I honestly can't see any alternative.
Patient: I suppose that there is no alternative then?
Surgeon: I am afraid not.
Patient: Then I have no choice, do I?
Surgeon: Yes, you could just have the cancer out and radiotherapy, but I wouldn't be happy about it. I could arrange for a second opinion if you like.
Patient: No, there is no need for that. I'll do it your way.

Assessment after surgery

Once surgery has been carried out, the surgeon or nurse should reassess how the patient is adjusting psychologically while the patient is still on the ward. This will reinforce the patients' belief that they are interested in them as persons.

Surgeon: As I warned you the lump was cancerous so I had to remove your breast. How are you feeling about losing a breast?
Patient: It hasn't sunk in yet. I'm just relieved you have got the cancer. I

suppose it will hit me later. But I have never been a vain person so I'm not sure it will be a problem. Only time will tell.

Surgeon: When I see you after discharge I'll check on that. Do you anticipate any other problems?

Patient: No, no I don't think so apart from this arm. Its still very painful — will it recover?

Surgeon: I hope it will but it is important that you do your exercises. I'll check when I see you next. Anything else you would like to mention?

Patient: No, no thank you.

Asking 'anything else you would like to mention?' indicates a real interest in determining what problems the patient may be experiencing, regardless of their domain. Screening questions should also be asked, as at the initial assessment, about the possibility of anxious or depressed mood.

Follow-up

This is critical for it is often only when a woman returns home that she realises the seriousness of her predicament. So, assessments on the ward can be misleading. Hence, it is useful to begin with an open question and then acknowledge, clarify and organise any important cues.

Surgeon: How have you been since you left hospital?

Patient: Not so good, really.

Surgeon: Not so good?

Patient: I have felt OK physically. No problems with my wound or arm. I've recovered all right in that respect.

Surgeon: But in other respects?

Patient: I can't understand it — I can't get used to having only one breast. I feel such a freak. It's getting me down, I can't be bothered to do anything. I have just let things go. I can't bear my husband to come near me.

Surgeon: That's very helpful. You've mentioned several problems: feeling a freak, feeling down, letting things go, and not wanting your husband near you. I would like to ask you about these in a moment — but before I do is there anything else that has been troubling you?

Patient: No.

Surgeon: Good. Then which problem is bothering you most?

Patient: Feeling a freak.

Surgeon: Tell me about it.

If no problems are disclosed, the patient should be asked a series of directive questions to elicit how she is adjusting to her diagnosis and treatment. These questions should include: 'How do you see things working out?' (to get her view of her prognosis); 'How have you felt about losing a breast; how has it affected you; has it had any effect on your relationship with your partner, your social life; has your operation affected you in any other way; how have you been coping at work, at home; how has your mood been; have you been especially worried — or miserable at any time?

If the patient is being given radiotherapy or chemotherapy as an adjuvant it is important to establish the full nature and extent of any adverse effects and the patient's views of treatment ('Has the treatment caused any problems? Just how has it been affecting you? Give me an example. . . . How do you feel about continuing the treatment?'). Once a patient has been assessed in this way, she is likely to disclose any problems which arise later.

When psychological problems are evident the surgeon's task is to decide if they represent morbidity and require attention.

DISTINGUISHING ABNORMAL REACTIONS

Depressive illness

The patient reports that she has been feeling persistently low and miserable to an extent which represents a significant departure from her normal mood. She cannot distract herself out of this or be distracted by others. She has been experiencing other symptoms of depression including irritability, impaired concentration, forgetfulness, loss or increase in appetite, loss or increase in weight, loss of libido, loss of energy, repeated waking or early morning waking, agitation or retardations, feelings of hopelessness, feelings of guilt, worthlessness, feeling of being a burden, and suicidal ideas. Her depression may also be accompanied by marked social withdrawal and difficulty coping with her chores and work. She will usually recognise how different her mood is from normal and explain that she has not felt as bad as this before.

Anxiety states

Women who develop an anxiety state find themselves plagued by worry and cannot be distracted from it. They are unable to relax and feel constantly on edge and tense. They have difficulty getting to sleep, feel increasingly irritable and experience impairment of concentration and decision making. They also tend to suffer autonomic symptoms like palpitations, headaches, breathlessness, shakiness and tremor. As with depression they recognise that this is a distinct departure from their normal mood, both qualitatively and quantitatively.

The anxiety may present as a phobic anxiety state where the patient complains that she is afraid of going out of the house alone and fears she will collapse and die if she does so. Thus, she will avoid going out alone, shopping in supermarkets, and travelling on buses or trains. Alternatively, she may complain of fear of meeting people because she feels self-conscious and is worried that they will notice her behaviour. She may then begin to avoid going out socially and make excuses for this. When anxiety and depression are present to morbid degree it is important not to dismiss them as merely understandable reactions which will get better of their own accord.

Sexual problems

Patients who had an active and enjoyable sex life before surgery report that they now obtain much less enjoyment of sex, find it harder to achieve orgasm, and may avoid intercourse altogether.

Body image problems

The woman will complain that she has been unable to accept the loss of a breast despite the passage of time. She still feels self-conscious, more vulnerable psychologically, or less feminine and attractive and finds it hard to look at her chest wall without feeling distressed. Indeed, she may have avoided doing so. Alternatively she may be very dissatisfied with her external prothesis.

The effects of adjuvant chemotherapy

The use of cyclophosphamide, methotrexate and 5-fluorouracil (CMF) results in a greater psychiatric morbidity than can be accounted for by mastectomy alone (Maguire et al 1980b, Hughson et al 1986). The depressive illness may be due to the attrition of adverse effects like nausea and vomiting or be due to a direct effect on the brain. The anxiety state may be due to the adverse effects of treatment or the development of conditioned responses (Morrow & Morrell 1982) where any stimulus which reminds a patient of chemotherapy causes her to feel sick or to vomit. Combination chemotherapy, like CMF, reduces oestrogen levels and elevates follicular stimulating and lutenising hormones. So, premenopausal women undergo an artificial menopause and experience a profound loss of libido.

Other aetiological factors

When an anxiety state or depressive illness has been diagnosed other possible causes should be considered since these will influence management. Assessment before and after surgery should have elicited whether the mood disturbance is due to a fear of recurrence, an inability to adapt to the loss of a breast, or adverse effects of radiotherapy and chemotherapy, including conditioned responses. But the development of mood disturbance may also indicate that the disease has recurred, spread or caused metabolic changes like hypercalcaemia. Steroids also provoke psychiatric disorder. When sexual problems are found it is important to consider possible physical causes such as chemotherapy, diabetes, recurrent disease and multiple sclerosis, and psychological causes including anxiety, depression and body image problems.

TREATMENT

Depressive illness

A depressive illness should be treated promptly with the appropriate anti-depressant medication. Newer antidepressants such as mianserin or dothiepin cause fewer adverse effects than established tricyclic antidepressants such as amitriptyline and imipramine. They are to be preferred because compliance is greater and patients with cancer tend to attribute any side effects of the drugs to recurrence or spread of the disease. Whichever drug is chosen it should be given in an effective dosage and continued for 4–6 months to minimise the risk of relapse.

It is important to explain to the patient that her depression has developed because of the stress she has experienced in trying to come to terms with the diagnosis or treatment and that this has altered her body chemistry. Consequently the antidepressant is not a tranquilliser but a drug aimed at restoring her chemistry to normal. Key side effects should be explained (particularly sedation and anticholinergic effects) and the patient invited to get in touch if she is worried about any other effects. She should be warned that the medication will take up to 4 weeks to work, but told that it is likely to be effective in due course. As the depressive illness responds to treatment it will become clear whether fears of recurrence or problems in adapting to body image changes remain and need separate attention.

Anxiety state

If the anxiety state is impairing the patient's ability to function an anxiolytic drug (such as a benzodiazepine) should be used in the short term. When somatic symptoms of anxiety are predominant a β-blocker (such as propranolol) may be tried. If the anxiety is severe and disorganising a major tranquilliser (such as thioridazine or chlorpromazine) should be considered.

If benzodiazepines are used for more than a few weeks there is a risk of dependence, so it is helpful to teach patients how to manage their own anxiety as soon as possible. This can be done by referring them to a clinical psychologist or psychiatrist who will teach them progressive muscular relaxation. They are shown how to contract and relax major muscle groups systematically and encouraged to relax mentally (Janoun et al 1982). Instructional audio tapes can assist this. Once the woman has learned to relax she is asked to employ these techniques whenever she begins to feel anxious.

Women who develop agoraphobia or social phobias usually benefit from desensitisation. This involves constructing a hierachy of situations or thoughts which are least or most likely to provoke anxiety. The woman is then taught to relax and asked to imagine an item low on that hierarchy, for example, 'when I think of leaving the house'. If she can imagine this situation without becoming anxious, she moves to the next item. If the goal is not achieved, she is asked to relax again and to re-imagine the situation. Once she has managed an item in imagination, the patient is encouraged to test it out in real life.

Sexual problems

Most women respond well to the Masters and Johnson approach where the woman and her partner are helped together (Masters & Johnson 1970). This begins with a ban on sexual intercourse in order to reduce the couple's apprehension about it. The couple are then taught to find ways of pleasuring each other, other than by genital contact. Once they have become more confident they can proceed towards full intercourse. A major barrier to this approach can be a woman's refusal to accept her breast loss (see below).

Body image problems

The use of progressive muscular relaxation and desensitisation to looking at her chest wall, first in imagination and then in real life, can overcome body image problems. The therapist may then involve the husband or partner and encourage the woman to allow her partner to look after using relaxation and desensitisation. Despite such approaches, body image problems may remain. A cognitive approach may then be useful which involves challenging the woman's assumption that she is no longer attractive or of any use. It also requires her to consider potentially positive aspects of her situation, for example, the fact that her cancer was caught early (Tarrier et al 1983).

Psychological approaches may fail to make any impression on body image problems. It is then worth considering breast reconstruction. Women who want a reconstruction for themselves rather than because pressure is being put on them by someone else, who are aware that they will get a cleavage rather than a breast as good as the original, and who are realistic about the possible complications of plastic surgery, respond well. Women who dislike the external prosthesis because it slips around or reminds them of their cancer are also likely to benefit.

Conditioned responses

It is important to act promptly otherwise the patient may withdraw from treatment. Covering each major injection or infusion with an anxiolytic (such as lorazepam) or major tranquilliser (such as chlorpromazine) together with an anti-emetic may be sufficient. Teaching anxiety management techniques can be effective (Morrow & Morrell 1982). It is also important to treat any associated depression with antidepressant medication.

Cognitive therapy

When unreasonable fears of recurrence persist, it is worth considering cognitive therapy. This involves detailed examination of what is reasonable about a woman's fears and what is unreasonable, as well as exploring what triggers these fears off and their consequences (Tarrier et al 1983).

PROVIDING SUPPORT

When patients are experiencing problems it is worth asking whether they would like to talk to someone who has had similar experience but has overcome her problems. Such volunteers must be chosen carefully (Mantell 1983). They should be able to listen, be flexible in their approach, avoid imposing their own experiences on the patient, and help her explore options rather than advise solutions. Otherwise, they may cause more harm than good. They require careful selection, training and supervision.

Self-help groups are attractive to some patients because they reduce their sense of isolation and allow them to receive practical and emotional support. However, it is important that they are led by leaders who have a grasp of group dynamics and can help the group work at a level which is constructive without being too intrusive. Unfortunately, only a minority of women (about 10%) will avail themselves of such groups.

Back-up services

While the surgeon or practitioner may be willing to embark on the treatment of anxiety and depression using psychotropic medication in the short-term, some patients will still need to be referred to a clinical psychologist or psychiatrist. It is imperative therefore, that these professionals accept that they have an active role to play in helping the surgeon or practitioner manage women with breast disease and are prepared to give a prompt and effective opinion.

PREVENTION

The provision of counselling

It has been claimed that many of the problems that arise after surgery for breast cancer are related to the lack of adequate information and emotional support. So, the employment of specialist nurses to remedy these deficiencies should prevent morbidity. While there is some evidence that they do promote an earlier return to work, earlier restoration of social and leisure activities, and a better adaption to the external breast prosthesis (Maguire et al 1983) there is as yet no convincing evidence that they prevent psychiatric morbidity (Maguire et al 1980a, Watson 1983). However, these counselling studies were carried out at a time when the diagnostic procedure involved a biopsy followed by a frozen section and the decision to proceed was taken when the patient was anaesthetised. This left little opportunity for counselling to take place after a definitive diagnosis had been made; it is possible that counselling will be effective now that a two-stage diagnosis is often possible (biopsy by fine-needle aspiration or Truecut, then surgery later).

The employment of a nurse to counsel and then to monitor psychological adjustment through asking appropriate questions every 2 months led to a much earlier recognition and treatment of those with problems. Consequently there was a threefold reduction in psychiatric morbidity 1 year after mastectomy (Maguire et al 1980a). If the surgeon or non-specialist nurse does not have time or is not prepared to ask the appropriate questions it would be prudent to employ a specialist nurse to do so since this will markedly reduce the level of psychiatric morbidity.

Since specialist nurses are effective in this monitoring role it ought to be possible to teach non-specialists nurses to do it and a further study was carried out to assess this. It also sought to determine whether women could be trusted to report problems if they received only one detailed assessment after surgery instead of being monitored every 2 months by the specialist nurse. While this study showed that a nurse who limited her visits to one home visit after surgery could rely on patients to report any subsequent problems and that she was just as effective as when she monitored patients every 2 months, the women followed up by ward nurses and nurses in the community who had been trained in similar assessment skills fared much worse (Maguire et al 1987). While the ward nurses improved their ability to assess (Faulkner & Maguire 1984) the nurses in the community actually grew worse. They saw the additional role of counselling women after surgery for breast cancer as unreasonable and were not prepared to carry this out in addition to their duties of looking after the young and the elderly.

The study also showed important differences between two specialist nurses who had been trained identically in assessment, interviewing and counselling skills. While one nurse was able to maintain a high level of monitoring and recognise and refer all her patients who developed problems the other nurse increasingly distanced herself (as discussed earlier) and was less effective. This highlights the need to audit the performance of specialist nurses continuously if their effectiveness is to be maintained. It also emphasises how difficult they can find it at the sharp end and when dealing with problem patients all the time. The provision of support for the specialist nurses is therefore mandatory if they are to be effective.

Changing treatment policies

Adopting a two-stage diagnostic procedure whenever possible is to be preferred since it does allow an opportunity for the surgeon to discuss treatment and utilise a counseller if one is available. It also allows the surgeon to discuss clinical options if he has them, for example the relative merits of breast conservation versus mastectomy. If he has no option and has to go ahead with a mastectomy then if the woman anticipates body image problems he can consider offering her immediate or delayed breast reconstruction. If he is able to go with the woman's preference then she is likely to make a much better psychological adaption (Fallowfield 1988, Ashcroft et al 1985).

Several studies have found that continued pain and swelling of the arm affected by surgery is linked to later psychiatric morbidity, so when it is possible to minimise the extent of surgery within the axilla without compromising survival, this should be done. Chemotherapy has also been found to increase psychiatric morbidity, particularly when given for longer than 6 months (Hughson et al 1987) so, if combination chemotherapy (CMF) is to be given as an adjuvant, its toxicity and adverse effects must be monitored carefully and limited to a course of 6 months. The clinician should be particularly alert to the development of conditioned vomiting and nausea, phobic avoidance of treatment and depressive illness. Radiotherapy has also been linked to the development of depressive illness particularly when the patient receives over 15 fractions, so if radiotherapy is used adverse effects need to be monitored and the effect on mood checked (Lucas 1987).

While changes in policy may reduce psychiatric morbidity considerably, it is unlikely to do so altogether (Fallowfield et al 1986). There will, therefore, still be a need to counsel and monitor women undergoing surgery for breast cancer. If specialist nurses, social workers, surgeons and practitioners are to deal effectively with women after surgery for breast cancer they will have to know how to deal with certain difficult situations that commonly arise. Otherwise they will be tempted to revert to distancing tactics and the morbidity will remain hidden.

DEALING WITH DIFFICULT SITUATIONS

The angry patient

As soon as it becomes obvious that a patient is angry, the doctor or nurse should acknowledge that he has noticed this and invite her to explain why ('I can see that you are pretty angry, would you mind telling me why?'). Once the patient has explained the reasons, and it is important to tease out all the reasons ('Are there reasons other than you felt there was an undue delay?'), it is more important to let the patient ventilate her anger. For this will gradually defuse it and allow an effective dialogue to be developed. When the anger is reasonable because there has been some problem in her care, it is important to acknowledge this and apologise, as in the following example.

Patient: You said I had to have a mastectomy and that there was no other option. I have since found out from one of my friends that one of the other surgeons in this hospital is prepared to conserve the breast. If I had known that, I would not have gone ahead. I could strangle you!

Surgeon: Would you mind telling me why?

Patient: I am finding it extremely difficult to get used to having only one breast. I feel so self-conscious. I feel far less attractive. I feel if I had kept my breast everything would have been different.

Surgeon: I can understand then why you are so distressed about it. But I did a mastectomy in the belief that it was in your best interests. Would you like me to explain why?

Patient: Yes. Why was it?

Surgeon: Well, although your lump was well encapsulated, that is it hadn't spread anywhere, I thought it was too large, at 4 cm, to allow me to get away with conserving your breast, otherwise I would have considered it. You may not know that I am prepared to do this operation when it is appropriate. I am very sorry I was not able to do it in your case.
However, given that you seem to have considerable worries about losing your breast, maybe there is a way that we can help you.

Patient: What's that?

Surgeon: Well, we could reconstruct your breast if you wish.

The very distressed patient

Here again the doctor or nurse should immediately acknowledge that they have observed that the patient is distressed and explore all the reasons for the distress *before* attempting to provide any reassurance. The act of encouraging the patient to talk through her distress and explain it will help her contain it and also allow the doctor, nurse or social worker to understand the basis of it.

Nurse: You seem very upset?

Patient: Wouldn't you be if you had just heard you had cancer?

Nurse: Just how upset do you feel?

Patient: I feel devastated. It's the thing I have dreaded ever since my mother died of it. She only lived 4 years after surgery. I am convinced the same is going to happen to me.

Nurse: Is there any other reason why you feel so devastated?

Patient: I am afraid it is going to spread through my bones and to my brain because that happened to an aunt of mine.

Nurse: I can see why you are so upset then. Are there any other reasons?

Patient: No.

Nurse: Well can I take your worry about only living 4 years first?

Handling difficult questions

Once an effective dialogue has developed and strong emotions defused it is likely that the patient will trust the doctor or nurse with difficult questions like 'Are you going to be able to cure it?' It is important that this is dealt with by first asking why the patient has put the question since this will give a clue to the kind of answer the patient actually wants. The reassurance can then be pitched at an appropriate but genuine level.

Patient:	Has the cancer come back?
Surgeon:	I would be happy to answer your question in a minute or two but would you first like to tell me why you are asking me that today?
Patient:	Well, you know I had my breast off a year ago. Over the last 2 weeks I have had this pain in my ribs. It has been getting worse and there is nothing I seem to be able to do to ease it. I have been worried that the cancer has got to my bones. Has it?
Surgeon:	Clearly that could be a possibility but there could be other less serious reasons why your ribs are hurting. What we need to do is to do some X-rays and check it out and then I will talk with you. The period while you are waiting to find out what is going on is going to be worrying for you isn't it?
Patient:	Yes, very, but I'm glad you have levelled with me. Are you going to be able to do anything for me if it is cancer?
Surgeon:	Well I am hopeful there will be something we can do but obviously I can't say until we have had a good look at you. I will get on with that and see you as soon as possible.
Patient:	Thank you very much.

In contrast to this patient who indicated a clear awareness, some patients would indicate that they do not want any more information, as in the following example.

Patient:	Is it cancer?
Surgeon:	I would be happy to answer your question but would you like to tell me why you think it might be?
Patient:	Oh I am just being silly, it's just some information I got, you do what you think is best for me.
Surgeon:	Are there any questions you would like to ask me?
Patient:	No.

CONCLUSION

If professionals involved in caring for a woman with breast cancer are prepared to relinquish distancing tactics, ask the appropriate questions and adopt particular counselling strategies when faced with difficult situations, they will find it much easier to establish an effective dialogue, recognise serious problems early and initiate appropriate treatment. Alternatively, if they are prepared to utilise a specialist nurse or social worker who has the necessary time and skills, this will also do much to reduce the considerable psychiatric and social morbidity associated with cancer of the breast and its treatment.

REFERENCES

Ashcroft J J, Leinster S J, Slade P D 1985 Breast cancer — patient choice of treatment. Journal of the Royal Society of Medicine 78: 43–46

Dean C 1987 Psychiatric morbidity following mastectomy: preoperative predictors and types of illness. Journal of Psychosomatic Research 31: 385–392

Dean C, Chetty U, Forrest A P M 1983 Effects of immediate breast reconstruction on psychosocial morbidity after mastectomy. Lancet 1: 459–462

Fallowfield L J 1988 Personal communication

Fallowfield L J, Baum M, Maguire G P 1986 Effects of breast conservation on psychological morbidity associated with diagnosis and treatment of early breast cancer. British Medical Journal 293: 1351–1354

Faulkner A, Maguire G P 1984 Training ward nurses to monitor cancer patients. Clinical Oncology 9: 319–324

Hughson A M M, Cooper A F, McArdle C S, Smith D C 1987 Psychosocial effects of radiotherapy after mastectomy. British Medical Journal 294: 1515–1518

Hughson A V M, Cooper A F, McArdle C S, Smith D C 1986 Psychological impact of adjuvant chemotherapy in the first two years after mastectomy. British Medical Journal 293: 1268–1271

Janoun L, Oppenheimer C, Gelder M 1982 A self-help treatment programme for anxiety state patients. Behaviour Therapy 13: 103–111

Lucas D 1987 Personal communication

Maguire P 1985 Improving the detection of psychiatric problems in cancer patients. Social Science and Medicine 20: 819–823

Maguire G P, Lee E G, Bevington D J, Kuchemann C S, Crabtree R J, Cornell C E 1978 Psychiatric problems in the first year after mastectomy. British Medical Journal 279: 963–965

Maguire P, Tait A, Brooke M, Thomas C, Sellwood R 1980a The effect of counselling on the psychiatric morbidity associated with mastectomy. British Medical Journal 281: 1454–1456

Maguire G P, Tait A, Brooke M et al 1980b Psychiatric morbidity and physical toxicity associated with adjuvant chemotherapy after mastectomy. British Medical Journal 281: 1179–1180

Maguire P, Brooke M, Tait A, Thomas C, Sellwood R 1983 The effect of counselling on physical disability and social recovery after mastectomy. Clinical Oncology 9: 319–324

Maguire P, Wilkinson S, Tait A, Faulkner A, Sellwood R 1987 A comparison of three different methods of aftercare for mastectomy patients. Unpublished report to the Department of Health

Mantell J E, 1983 Cancer patient visitor programmes: a case for accountability. Journal of Psychosocial Oncology 1: 45–50

Masters W H, Johnson V E, 1970 Human sexual inadequacy. Churchill, London

Morris T, Greer S H, White P 1977 Psychological and social adjustment to mastectomy. Cancer 40: 2381–2387

Morrow G R, Morrell C 1982 Behavioural treatment for the anticipatory nausea and vomiting induced by cancer chemotherapy. New England Journal of Medicine 307: 1476–1480

Rosser J, Maguire P 1982 Dilemmas in general practice: the care of the cancer patient. Social Science and Medicine 16: 315–322

Tarrier N, Maguire P, Kincey J 1983 Locus of control and cognitive therapy in mastectomy patients. British Journal of Medical Psychology 56: 265–268

Watson M 1983 Psychosocial intervention with cancer patients: a selective review. Psychological Medicine 13: 839–846

13
H. E. Pelser, J. J. Groen

Diabetes mellitus

INTRODUCTION

The first challenge for the authors of this chapter is to describe their own personalities and behaviour towards their patients in general and those with diabetes in particular. Both of us have undergone standard medical studies in a western medical school. After training in anatomy, physiology and biochemistry, we were taught how to apply this biotechnical education to the diagnosis and treatment of diseases. We were 'indoctrinated' that medicine was based on exclusively natural scientific methods. Our teachers displayed how a doctor should keep his personal attitudes suppressed (except for an occasional show of humour!) under the 'equanimity' of his behaviour, and to regard personal exchanges with patients as a waste of time or even hazardous by distracting attention from their disease.

The majority of physicians and clinical scientists still persist in this, professionally prescribed, medical behaviour. A minority however, changed this attitude under the influence of what they learned from their practice and observations. Thus we now regard our medical task as an *integration* of our technical skill to diagnose and treat diseases, with the cooperation of our patients in coping with disease as part of their life situations. We regard the management, especially of chronic diseases, as a joint task, a partnership of a patient and his doctor. The result of this form of treatment, perhaps better designated as 'guidance', depends largely on the ways in which both the doctor and the patients are motivated and equipped for their technical and personal cooperation.

We will not elaborate here on the scientific requirement; we intend to describe what we have recently come to understand as the psychological aspects of our speciality.

THE DIABETOLOGIST'S PERSONALITY AND BEHAVIOUR

Living with diabetes means that a patient not only has to meet the challenge of his life in his family, work situation and society at large but also has to be aware constantly of the duties which his treatment requires, in particular the dangers and fears which confront him if, for a shorter or longer time, he neglects these rules. The difficulty for the diabetic patient at present is that while the effects of diet, drugs and exercise on the course of his disease are much better known (so that it is now possible to lead an almost 'healthy' life), in order to achieve this possibility a much more demanding selfcare routine is required. The lives of our diabetic patients may have become more normal physiologically but at the price of continuous selfcontrol and selfrestraint. They need knowledge of the disease and its treatment in the first place because they themselves have to implement it day by day, hour by hour. Experience shows that this task is impossible to discharge unsupported. Quite naturally, in addition to the normal support from their keyfigures the patient expects from the doctor not only technical instructions, but also human understanding and support.

As students, most doctors are taught to direct their patient's behaviour by prescription, and to expect 'compliance'. In their later practice most doctors find out that trying to influence their patients' way of life by prescription is often unsatisfactory: ordering diabetic patients to follow complicated daily instructions is rarely effective. Instead of authoritarian 'teaching', cooperative education is needed. Education involves mutual cooperation for a common aim, in which the doctor must adjust his own behaviour to the expectations and needs of the 'pupil'. It is also a long-term programme during which the attitude of the educator gradually develops into that of a co-worker, while his pupils develop more and more towards independence.

This widening of his own field of vision renders the diabetologist disposed to learn not only from his colleagues in the natural sciences, but also from educators and psychologists. Such an orientation is relatively new in internal medicine and although accepted and practiced by only a minority of present day specialists, it can be designated as a paradigm of psychosomatic or holistic medicine.

PSYCHOLOGICAL FACTORS AS CONTRIBUTING CAUSES OF DIABETES MELLITUS

The cause of diabetes mellitus is unknown. Extensive research into possible endocrinological and immunological mechanisms have not produced a *firm* theory about the aetiology of the disease. The possibility that psychological factors could play a role, is an idea that is so much in conflict with the generally accepted 20th century medical paradigm, that few investigators have tried to test the hypothesis that the disease started when the patient felt lonely and sad by not being understood by his key-figures.

In the case of young patients with insulin-dependent diabetes, this often occurred as an acute event; in the middle-aged diabetic loneliness and sadness had come on more gradually. The circumstances, acute or chronic, had produced in them a state of 'masked depression'. Our diabetic patients tried to live on, to continue their work as usual and yet felt so unhappy that in many of them thoughts of suicide occurred. In describing their feelings, they used expressions like: 'I will not kill myself, I have my duties and my work, but at times I feel that I wouldn't mind if something would happen to me', or 'I continue to live, to take care of my husband who needs me, but for myself I feel no need to continue', or 'My parents have no idea what goes on inside me, and I do not want to bother them. They only care about my diabetes. They never ask how I feel myself'. In several of our patients these feelings were so strong that they interfered with their motivation to check their blood sugar and regulate the disease: 'I did not regard my life as important enough to make so much effort'.

The possibility that emotional events of the types described often precede the onset of diabetes, is no more than a hypothesis based on clinical experience. In a monograph by one of the authors (Groen & de Loos 1973), several case histories are described and since then many more cases have been observed. Cases in girls of school age, where the diabetes started when they became aware that their fathers were unfaithful or when their parents divorced, are now so common as to merit investigation. In the elderly diabetics we more often found the situation of a 'stable' marriage in which the patient felt not understood by the partner, and tried to adapt to a situation of chronic deficiency of love and tenderness. Active quarrels did not occur, and these patients found no outlet for their disappointment in divorce or promiscuity. A common compensation, however, was excessive eating resulting in obesity. Indeed, many overeating obese non-diabetic patients live in a similar situation of subjective loneliness, of not being understood, in which overeating is a substitute for affection, which for them comprises more a source of tenderness than sexual gratification.

The above hypothesis about the role of an unfavourable, 'stressful' life situation as a possible cause of diabetes, is regarded by most diabetes experts with scepticism. On the other hand however, the unfavourable influence of certain stress situations on an already existing diabetic state occurs so often that the reality of such an effect is widely accepted. Blood sugar levels of diabetic patients measured regularly show that the degree of control varies continually. These variations in blood sugar level not only occur in 'brittle' diabetics (known to be irregular in their eating habits and insulin injections) but also in patients who keep their dietary and insulin regimes constant. The marked fluctuations in the diabetic state of these patients usually cannot be explained by purely 'somatic' influences, like infections or menstrual cycle variations. Monitoring the patients' life events, experiences and moods, one is impressed by the influence of psychological factors on their diabetic state (eg. Hinkle & Wolf 1949, 1950, 1951, 1952, and Baker & Barcai 1970).

Is clinical deterioration nonspecifically related to stress or are there certain emotions which show a specificity in their impact on diabetes?

Our clinical observations favour a specific relationship. Situations of overt fear for instance, in our experience do not increase the severity of the diabetic state. During the German occupation of the Netherlands, many Jewish diabetics were arrested in their homes, usually during the night, and transferred to transition camps from where they were later sent to the extermination camps in Auschwitz. Yet we do not know of a single patient who under these circumstances went into diabetic coma or required more insulin. One diabetic girl was ordered to appear before a German police-court next day. She was terribly frightened and reacted, like many others, with a severe diarrhoea. But her blood sugar was, if anything, lower than usual and she had to diminish her insulin dose for that day.

Another diabetic girl in the ward, who was very attached to one of us (JJG), whenever she had open rows with the nurses would have low blood sugar levels and sometimes attacks of hypoglycaemia. Once however, when she had a conflict with me, about which she felt very sad, she went into keto-acidosis. The same often happened to her when her mother, by whom she felt misunderstood, came to visit her.

Similarly diabetes was rarely aggravated by the stresses of combat in the Second World War. We believe rather that the diabetic combatant is not exposed to the specific type of stress mentioned above, and in particular there are rarely unexpressed depressive feelings of loneliness. Such situations occur more commonly in normal life of western civilised society. In assessing the degree of stress in a patient's life situation, it is not so much the 'objective' event, but its *meaning* for this specific person, and how he or she *experiences* it, which determines whether it would increase or decrease the severity of the diabetic state.

THE BEGINNING OF THE TREATMENT

The psychological approach to patients with diabetes begins at the moment when the disease has been discovered and the patient has to be informed. Most doctors know now by dire experience that it is no use starting immediately on a medical monologue about the symptoms of the disease, the diet and the prescription of tablets or insulin. Time should be allowed in this first interview for the patient to speak and the doctor to listen, and to find out whether the patient has any understanding at all of what 'diabetes' means.

After this first interview, in which in most cases only a few facts need be told, the patient should be asked to return for the next visit within a couple of days. In this interview the patient is given further opportunity to ask questions and receive answers which serve both his understanding of the technique of the treatment and to foster the feeling that the doctor will be his ally. The same approach is recommended for the first meeting with the dietitian. In our experience a new diabetic should not be transferred to the dietitian routinely, but should continue to see both of them.

With diabetic children, special time must be given to the education and support of the parents. In several textbooks the psychological management of the different types of parents of diabetic children is now dealt with. We find it valuable to have at least one interview with the parents alone. There is considerable variation in parents' attitudes and in fathers' and mothers' willingness to share the duties of educating their diabetic child. Often the father tends to leave this burden entirely to his wife. The interview with parents may provide indications of important parental problems which need addressing.

In our experience the main problems for parents of a diabetic child are:

1. To learn not to become overprotective or overpunitive as some degree of 'cheating' is almost universal and normal among diabetic children.
2. To balance the extra care which the diabetic child needs with the needs of other children in the family. In some cases under our guidance, the parents even adapted the diet of the whole family more or less to the diabetic requirements (which is not too difficult!) and thus diminished the risk that the child felt exceptional. A common error is to fail to ensure that there is more reward than punishment, more encouragement than discouragement, both for the patient and the other siblings.
3. To encourage the child's independence and to give him interest in and praise of his own management of the diabetes, eg. injecting himself, and conducting urine and blood sugar tests.
4. To avoid 'moral' terms with regard to the child's metabolic regulation, eg. referring to results of urine or blood sugar estimations in terms of 'good' or 'bad', but simply as too high or too low.
5. To trust the child when he denies cheating, and rather help him to look for an alternative explanation, particularly emotional events, for an elevated blood sugar level.
6. Not to burden the child with parental anxiety and worries concerning diabetes and its consequences for the future. Children easily attribute parental distress to their own wrongdoings, and such diabetic children tend to feel guilty about their diabetes because it makes their parents feel bad.

In addition to all this, the parents also need instruction in the elementary facts of nutrition, injection techniques, hypoglycaemia etc. in parallel with the child's training.

The doctor must resist the temptation to condemn the patient suspected of 'cheating'. Moralistic or punitive attitudes may produce guilt but this, as a rule, does not stop the cheating. We have found that telling patients off, preaching to them or punishing them did not help. Instead, we ask him or her to return more frequently for control and when on their return visit we find they have improved, give them praise and show appreciation. Young diabetics often cheat in the company of their peers because they do not want to be 'different'. They may go on a binge in protest over a conflict with one of their parents or a teacher. We try to listen and show understanding and often increase the frequency of visits during this period as they appear to need us 'as a person' in such situations.

This attitude may require more time and patience in cases of so-called 'brittle' diabetics where we feel it is not the pancreas, but the personality which is labile. These patients need a combination of diabetes management and 'psychotherapy'. It is our experience that they are best served if the diabetologist has sufficient experience in the psychotherapy of patients with chronic diseases in general so that he can fulfil this task himself. In Holmes' (1986) review of psychiatric referral, in a series of 108 diabetic patients more than 40% of them were referred for pessimistic or depressive attitudes, and several others because of conflicts with one or both parents. Very few were mentally ill. Obviously it is better if the diabetologist himself learns enough 'psychotherapy' to deal with the common psychological problems. The same holds for dietitians and nurses.

CONTINUING TREATMENT; THE DIABETIC LIFESTYLE AND CONFRONTATION WITH COMPLICATIONS

Living with diabetes differs from coping with most other chronic diseases. After the diagnosis is made and the first measures of treatment have been carried out, the illness does not produce disturbing symptoms and signs any more. Although in most cases this remains so during the next years, it nonetheless means that the patient has to assume a particular way of life without justification by an improvement of his condition. He is repeatedly reminded that, despite the absence of signs or symptoms, he must take great care to prevent the development of life-threatening complications. It is soon taken for granted by his relatives and the doctor that he will follow his doctor's advice for if he does not, he may develop such terrible complications as blindness, gangrene, heart or kidney disease. In other words, diabetic life means living under the constant threat of the complications, the avoidance of which by following strict rules however, is only rewarded in the distant future. There is no consistent prompt reward. Some react to this situation by denial: 'How can I be ill, when I do not feel ill?' Others react by more or less loosening their rules, so long as they do not notice that it does them any harm. Many of them feel the need of receiving at least some appreciation from key-figures and certainly from their doctors for virtuous behaviour. Possibly because so many patients are reluctant to express this need for appreciation, it has taken the diabetologists a long time to realise that even well-controlled diabetics suffer under this burden. Every patient when satisfactorily regulated, needs and deserves our support, appreciation and even praise if he succeeds in managing the disease. He also needs interest and understanding when he occasionally fails to do so. In no circumstances should a patient be punished or 'told off' by their 'support' figures.

We find it helpful to ask the patient, after discussing the technical arrangements of their metabolic situation, the simple question: 'And how are things at home?'. We listen and, if indicated, give additional time to the psychosocial aspect of their diabetic life. The answer to this question might result in our suggestion to invite mother or father or another key-figure to come and see us. Younger patients may find the burden of school examinations such that some go into ketotic subcoma. We always inquire after the school situation and make contact with their teachers. We ask the teacher to give a word of support — it's surprising how often it works!

Once complications manifest themselves, psychological attention is, if anything increased, supplemented by the care required by the various affected organ systems. Complications demand more time from all the patient's attendants. In general, patients with complications should be given more frequent appointments. This is often overlooked in a busy clinic because the patient does not dare to ask for the extra time which he wants, in particular the elderly, who may accept new problems as their 'fate'.

Hypoglycaemia

We used to consider hypoglycaemia as an unpleasant and undesirable side-effect of insulin administration, which once experienced, the diabetic patient would recognise and prevent. The patient was instructed to control it by immediately taking one or two lumps of sugar which he carried in his pocket at all times. As well as the unpleasant physical experiences of hypoglycaemia, patients may become ashamed of their behaviour after attacks in public and develop an intense fear, or even phobia, of a recurrence.

The frontal part of the limbic brain, responsible for tact, decorum, ethical behaviour and control is especially sensitive to a low blood sugar level.

We have known patients who purposely refused to adjust their blood sugar level to normal values for fear that they would occasionally go into hypoglycaemia again, and therefore kept their blood sugar consistently above 10 mmol/l. With the introduction of long-acting insulin, hypogly-caemic episodes became even more fearful to many patients because they were less easy to control. Some of our patients preferred taking insulin three or more times a day, rather than a long- or medium-acting preparation for this reason, and we accepted their initiative.

Our interest in the life situation of our diabetic patients also increased our understanding of the emotional events which apparently can induce hypoglycaemia, especially in well regulated patients. An unexpected disturbing telephone call at the time the patient used to take his insulin injection, for example, can make the patient forget that he had already done so and repeat the action. A similarly upsetting event might interfere with the patient's routine of taking his snack on time. Both 'mistakes' are likely to cause a hypoglycaemic attack which for the patient comes completely out of the blue. If the doctor who is called in to correct the hypoglycaemia, or who later is asked for his advice, fails to enquire after the circumstances which could have induced the episode, he might reduce the insulin dose for the days to follow, thereby upsetting the patient's metabolic regulation.

Repressing feelings of anger or aggression from a conflict with a keyfigure on whom they are dependent is another situation which seems to induce hypoglycaemia. The physiological mechanism may be extreme muscular tension causing enough energy expenditure to lower the blood sugar level equal to physical exercise. Patients, once they are aware of this relationship may be able to avoid the hypoglycaemia, either by expressing their anger or by relaxing consciously.

Hypoglycaemias may develop during social events such as parties or bridge club meetings, because patients are embarrassed to bring their snack with them and eat it in public. This would both draw attention to their diabetes and also possibly embarrass their hostess for not having provided for them. As a result, they may develop hypoglycaemia on their way home or cause embarrassment during the party. For some patients, a few of such experiences leads to withdrawal from such social events altogether leading to their feeling isolated and depressed.

Patients — usually youngsters or adolescents, but occasionally elderly patients may *intentionally* provoke a hypoglycaemic attack because of the anxiety, fear or panic it would produce in friends or relatives. Such patients, almost invariably characterised by unstable personality, immature behaviour and low self-esteem, are usually enmeshed in ambivalent relationships and denied responsibility for common personal decisions while materially very well looked after. Their parents were often over-protective (as if they were to blame personally for the diabetes of their child), expressing their feelings through protective care for 'the poor handicapped child'. We found a similar attitude occasionally being displayed by a husband. In such a situation of combined emotional entanglement and denial of interpersonal communication, the helpless and despairing patient might welcome or use a severe hypoglycaemic attack for many reasons simultaneously eg. temporarily escaping from the oppressive situation; hoping to be better understood by a doctor or nurse at the hospital; showing oneself that after all one is still capable of making a decision on one's own; obtaining revenge on the overprotective and yet uncomprehending parents or partner, etc. Such a process is, however, a dangerously inefficient communication.

Another reason why hypoglycaemias deserve serious attention is the experience of some of our patients that hypoglycaemia affects their memory. This can be confirmed objectively during the first hours or sometimes days after the attack, but when intelligent patients assure us that the disturbance can last longer, we should not dismiss their observations lightly.

EDUCATING THE EDUCATORS

Recent years have witnessed a great increase in interest in diabetes education. One of the achievements of Elliot Joslin was the emphasis on teaching diabetic patients about their disease in order to conduct their part of the treatment. Since then it has become increasingly recognised that the education of diabetic patients is an essential part of treatment. Doctors, however, may have too narrow an idea of what education means. It is more than the transmission of knowledge and skills. The educator puts his experience and knowledge at the service of the pupil, in order that he may achieve independence. It should end in mutual cooperation based on equality. *Both* partners are actively involved in mutual communication in a complementary way. When both fulfil their functions adequately, the learning process proceeds step by step towards results which meet their mutual expectations. Education involves both intellectual and emotional features. In order to achieve optimum results, the establishment of a reciprocal emotional relationship is needed. This is promoted by consistency, regularity and predictability in the relationship. A flexible approach to accommodate patient-doctor differences is obviously necessary.

In medicine the activities of education and treatment are so intermingled that they cannot be separated without harm. The diabetologist who does not succeed in *educating* his patient to help him acquire the necessary knowledge, skills and motivation to 'co-regulate' his metabolic equilibrium consistently, is partly failing in his task of proper medical treatment.

THE GROUP APPROACH

In our search for better forms of education in which both the cognitive and emotional consequences of having diabetes could be addressed we increasingly focussed on groups. A group (a limited number of people in close proximity, sharing one or more goals) provides a 'natural' setting for educational communication. Groups which use mainly verbal communication, are designated as 'discussion groups', some use role-play or psychodrama or other, more sophisticated psychotherapeutic techniques.

In 1974, in the framework of the Netherlands Diabetics Association, we started a pilot project of group discussions with diabetic patients. Altogether 35 patients (22 females and 13 males) participated for 15 to 18 months with a remarkably high attendance rate. Three groups were formed, two of which were conducted by a physician and an observer in weekly sessions; the third by two psychologists acting as co-therapists convening fortnightly. The details of the organisation and functioning of these groups have been published elsewhere (Pelser et al 1979, Groen & Pelser 1981).

Our main observations can be summarised as follows:

1. The subjects discussed 'spontaneously' in the three groups were remarkably similar and dealt equally with technical knowledge of diabetes, its complications and treatment, and with emotional problems of the participants (both connected with the disease and with life problems in general). Most of these problems had to do with ambivalent relationships

between the patients and their key-figures, including the treating phys-icians. In all three groups several members complained that their doctor mainly showed interest in their urine and blood sugar levels and had no time to listen and talk about the difficulties of having to live with diabetes. Some described how only after several visits to the doctor, had they realised that diabetes was an incurable disease, and that they had to follow the treatment for life. Almost all had gone through more periods of despair, depression, inner protest and episodes of cheating and non-cooperation than they had confessed to anybody, least of all to their physicians.

2. Several patients with juvenile diabetes suffered from not being under-stood by their mothers, with whom they could not talk about their emotional problems. In some this had resulted in different forms of protest behaviour, eg. going on sprees, running away from home or, more frequently, episodes of refusing to test their urine or stick to their diet. Others had felt lonely, depressed or desperate, when they some-times 'forgot' to eat after having injected insulin, developing hypogly-caemias. At other times they told themselves that they 'could not care less' and 'plunged themselves' into binge-eating to 'feel better.'

3. The fear of complications inevitably came up in the discussions, often when faced with the sequelae of retinopathy in some of the participants. The opinion of the medical discussion leader, that prevention of late complications depends upon consistent maintenance of a physiological glycaemia by a regular diet, adjusted use of insulin, exercise and emotional stability, repeatedly provoked heated and sometimes very emotional discussions. In the view of the younger group members especially this opinion would charge them with an impossible burden. It inflicted guilt feelings about complications which would occur anyhow, no matter how hard they tried. They even blamed the group leaders for lack of comprehension for their efforts to regulate themselves, and for their despair when they did not succeed in doing so.

4. Some patients feared hypoglycaemic attacks so much that they preferred to keep their blood sugar high. This fear sometimes provoked an attack of hyperventilation, misinterpreted as hypoglycaemia, resulting in intake of sweets and consequently even higher blood sugar. It was obvious after a number of sessions that as long as patients felt unhappy and inwardly hated their disease, they could not learn how to handle it effectively.

5. The group discussions with fellow patients gave the participants (most of them for the first time in their life) the opportunity to talk freely and express or act out their feelings, while at the same time deal with tech-nical problems of diabetic life, such as dietary variations, injection tech-nique, what to do during vacations etc. and above all, the nature and prevention of late complications. Discussing both the nature of, and anxiety around, these threatening complications within the safe support of the group, the patients could help each other to develop a more

rational attitude than when the complications and associated emotions had been either avoided or inadequately expressed in their previous consultations with their doctors. Patients also learned to talk more freely about emotions in general, including to physicians and spouses. In a number of cases this contributed to an improved relationship both in the family and with their physicians.

It seemed as if this group education, because it applied the *combined* discussion of the cognitive aspects with the emotional approach to the problems of the disease, and because the group members gave each other mutual understanding and support, also contributed to their *conscious acceptance* of the diabetes and the rules for keeping it under control.

At the end of the first phase of the project the participants in all three groups considered that they had gained both important technical information and skills and emotional support in their difficulties with having diabetes. They unanimously judged the group approach superior to any form of diabetes education they had experienced before and wished it were available to all diabetics.

Joint training of patients and doctors to become discussion group leaders

To guide group discussions with diabetic patients, both sufficient knowledge of diabetes and ability to conduct a group are required. This combination was only found among a minority of professionals. Encouraged by the group leaders, a number of the former group members opted for a training to enable themselves to function as group leaders and observers to discussion groups with fellow patients. They were joined by a number of family doctors and medical and psychology students who had become interested in this new approach to doctor-patient cooperation. A training programme was drafted by one of the authors, which was discussed, amended and finally agreed upon by all prospective participants.

In this second phase of the pilot project 17 diabetic patients (most of them former members of the 'primary' groups), 7 family doctors, 2 medical students and 3 psychology students cooperated with 3 trainers. Two of the trainers (JJG and HEP) had been functioning as group leaders in the primary phase; the third (H. van Dis), who has a combined psychological and medical training, had been a stand-in group leader for one of them during vacations. The aim of the second phase was a training '*to become discussion leaders and observers of discussion groups in which patients would have the opportunity to discuss among each other the problems associated with having diabetes mellitus and life problems in general*'.

Central components of the training were:

1. The main part would take the form of group discussions. Participants would learn both the basic principles of diabetes and its management,

and the technique of group discussions, while undergoing the 'confluent learning' experience of being group members themselves.
2. In each training group the number of participants should not exceed about ten, the majority of which should consist of group-experienced diabetic patients.
3. Each group would be led in turn by all three trainers to expose the trainees to both the similarities and differences of their approaches.
4. Each weekly training session would begin with an hour's group discussion, the subjects of which to be decided upon by the participants. Subsequently, reflection evaluation of the preceding discussion and its group dynamic aspects would be stimulated by the trainer. In later stages each group member was encouraged to exercise the function of discussion leader.
5. Each member in turn would also function as the group's observer, and prepare a written report on the discussion to be read and commented upon by the group and trainer in the next sessions.

The training course was organised in 3 groups, convening weekly in locations which could be reached conveniently by the members of the respective groups. Each group consisted of 6 diabetic patients, 2 or 3 family doctors and 1 or 2 medical or psychology students. The training was divided into 3 periods of 8 weeks. Trainers had 7 consecutive sessions with a group. There was then a combined session of the 3 groups together. Following this general meeting in which the trainees from the three groups exchanged and compared their experiences, the trainers switched to different groups (again for 7 consecutive sessions followed by an 8th joint meeting) and this procedure was repeated a third time. At the end of the third period, two formal instructions in group dynamics and one in the technique of diabetes management were given in general meetings.

The three groups together then discussed which of the trainees were sufficiently prepared to function as discussion leaders and/or observers to new groups. As a result of the training 10 out of 17 patients who had participated felt confident enough to fulfil one or other of these functions; they were judged so also by both the trainers and their fellow-trainees. Four of the seven family doctors fulfilled these requirements, as did 4 out of the 5 medical and psychology students.

Observations on developments during the training course

The idea of arranging the training of patients and family doctors jointly was first viewed with some hesitation and concern that both parties might find it difficult to become involved in such a novel endeavour. The proposal met with objections from neither the patients nor the doctors. At the beginning the doctors had some difficulty in adjusting to communicating with patients on an equal footing. This was especially so when patients openly criticised the behaviour of members of the medical profession which they had experienced. In later stages the doctors identified without difficulty with the group. They told the group that they had gradually developed a more empathetic attitude towards the patients in their practice.

The patients learned to appreciate better that doctors find it difficult to deal with patients for whom they can offer no cure, especially as most of these patients did not spontaneously volunteer their emotional problems. Most patients who participated in the training course improved their relationship with their own doctor.

A striking observation was that the doctors agreed that they had also learned more about the disease itself and its management than they had either in medical school or from text books on the subject. They felt better equipped to manage the treatment of their own diabetic patients and less likely to refer them to diabetic clinics. This was the more remarkable, since at the beginning of the training the doctors generally were reluctant to join in the discussions on the technical aspects of diabetes management, because they found that the patients knew more about it than they themselves. Most doctors rapidly caught up in knowledge about diabetes with the patients in their group, possibly as a result of the 'confluent learning'.

The 'tertiary' groups

In the third phase of the project the trained discussion leaders and observers who felt confident in their function, started to work with new groups of diabetic patients. They formed 'couples' consisting of a group leader and an observer. In the autumn of 1978 nine discussion groups were started, comprising altogether 73 diabetic patients. Like the previous ones, these 'tertiary' groups met in weekly sessions lasting about 90 minutes. All tertiary groups (whether guided by two patients, or by a doctor and a patient, or by two medical students) had equally high attendance rates as the primary groups, and the content of their discussions was also remarkably similar. Although the participants had committed themselves to attend the group discussions regularly only for the duration of six months, each of the groups decided to continue its sessions at the end of the term, some in weekly meetings, others with intervals of two weeks or more. Practically no group members left before the agreed term, and all participants appeared to be as satisfied with this form of education as were the members of the primary groups. Again a number of these 'next generation' diabetic patients became motivated to apply for a training to become group leaders and observers.

The guiding couples of functioning groups met about once in four weeks for supervision with one of the previous trainers, to whom the observers submitted their reports on the group discussions. In these meetings both medical issues about diabetes and group dynamic phenomena were explained and discussed. General meetings of all active participants in the project are held several times a year to discuss problems and developments, and to update developments in diabetes. These meetings take place with remarkable efficiency and reflect at the same time the general mood and understanding of a group discussion: participants speak and listen in turn, criticise each other (including the supervisors) frankly and sincerely (but always constructively), and accept criticism from each other without taking offence.

It seems as if the common group experience has induced in the participants a greater propensity to accept and respect each other's personality.

Further developments of the project

In the first five years following their joint training, most patients and some family doctors continued to function regularly as 'guiding couples' to long-term discussion groups. Each year they kept 8 or 9 groups running, comprising about 70 participants. Most groups continued in weekly sessions for two terms of 6 months, some for three terms and a few for even longer. Two of the most experienced patients functioned successfully as assistant trainers to a second training course in which 4 family doctors and a social worker were trained jointly with 14 diabetics.

From the experience of postgraduate presentations, some patients became aware that they could teach professionals in health care and public services a great deal about the practical and emotional consequences of having to live with diabetes. They accepted invitations to give talks on this subject to various health professionals. Their vivid presentations of personal experiences of living with diabetes and the restrictions attending its treatment, apparently made much more impact on the audience than the usually more formal technical lectures.

In the course of these successive activities patients gradually took more initiative and responsibility. The trainers by and by were fulfilling a less dominant and directive role. These developments illustrate what educational potentialities may be activated with diabetic patients trained in the manner described in this chapter.

As yet, this model of doctor-patient cooperation in diabetes education and treatment, possibly because it requires a new and non-traditional attitude of both doctors and patients, appears still to be insufficiently appreciated.

CONCLUSIONS

Adequate treatment of diabetes mellitus requires consistent doctor-patient cooperation in which both partners fulfil an active and mutually complementary role. In order to understand and control his metabolic regulation in line with the doctor's advice, the diabetic patient has to acquire both sufficient knowledge about diabetes and its treatment, and the skills and motivation to implement this knowledge in the daily control of his condition. The doctor has to appreciate the patient's individual personality and ways of coping with diabetes, to be able to give him the time, the technical information and the emotional support he needs. To fulfil their mutual partner role, both doctors and patients require education. We find this can best be achieved in group discussions dealing with both cognitive and emotional aspects of adequate control. Such discussion groups are also suggested as a means to train doctors and patients as diabetes educators.

REFERENCES AND FURTHER READING

Assal J P, Berger M, Gay N, Canivet J (eds) 1983 Diabetes education. Excerpta Medica, Amsterdam

Baker L, Barcai A 1970 Psychosomatic aspects of diabetes mellitus. In: Hill O W (ed) Modern trends in psychosomatic medicine 2. Butterworths, London

Berger I L 1978 Presidential address: Group psychotherapy today. International Journal of Group Psychotherapy 28: 307

Boogaard P R F van den, Boomsma A Y 1983 Machteloosheid en het effect van een gespreksgroep voor diabetes patienten. Gezondheid en Samenleving 4: 264

Diabetes Education Study Group 1986 Symposium on diabetic patients as educators in diabetes. Noordwijkerhout, Netherlands (in press)

Gfeller R, Assal J P 1980 Das Krankheitserlebnis des Diabetespatienten. In: Folia psychopractica 10 Hoffman-La Roche, Basel, p 19

Groen J J, de Loos W S 1973 Psychosomatische aspecten van diabetes mellitus (with a summarizing chapter in English). Bohn, Amsterdam

Groen J J, Pelser H E 1981 Gespreksgroepen voor patienten met diabetes mellitus. Nederlands Tijdschrift voor Geneeskunde 125: 257

Groen J J, Pelser H E 1982 Newer concepts of teaching, learning and education and their application to the patient–doctor cooperation in the treatment of diabetes mellitus. Pediatric and Adolescent Endocrinology 10: 168

Hefferman A 1959 An experiment in group therapy with the mothers of diabetic children. Acta Psychotherapeutica 7 (suppl): 155

Hinkle L E, Wolf S 1949 Experimental study of life situations, emotions and the occurrence of acidosis in a juvenile diabetic. American Journal of Medical Science 217: 130

Hinkle L E, Wolf S 1950 Studies on diabetes mellitus. Journal of Clinical Investigation 29: 754

Hinkle L E, Wolf S 1951 Studies on diabetes mellitus. Journal of Clinical Investigation 30: 818

Hinkle L E, Wolf S 1951 Studies on diabetes mellitus. Psychosomatic Medicine 13: 160–184

Hinkle L E, Wolf S 1952 Studies on diabetes mellitus. Journal Mount Sinai Hospital 19: 537

Hinkle L E, Wolf S 1952 Studies on diabetes mellitus. Diabetes 1: 383

Holmes D M 1985 Diabetes in psychosocial context. In: Joslin's Diabetes mellitus, 12th edn. Lea and Febiger, Philadelphia, pp 822–906

Holmes D M 1986 The person and diabetes in psychosocial context. Diabetes Care 9: 194

Jacobson A M, Hauser S T 1983 Behavior and psychosocial aspects of diabetes. In: Ellenberg M, Rifkin H (eds) Diabetes mellitus: theory and practice, 3rd edn Medical Examinations Publishing Co, New York, pp 1037–1052

Krall L P 1985 Education, a treatment for diabetics. In: Joslin's Diabetes mellitus, 12th edn. Lea and Febiger, Philadelphia

Kravitz A R, Isenberg P L, Shore M F, Barnett D M 1971 Emotional factors in diabetes mellitus. In: Marble A, White P, Bradley R, Krall L P (eds) Joslin's diabetes mellitus, 11th Edn. Lea and Febiger, Philadelphia, pp 767–782

Krosnick A 1970 Psychiatric aspects of diabetes. In: Ellenberg M, Rifkin H (eds) diabetes mellitus: theory and practice. McGraw-Hill Book Co, New York, pp 920–933

Laron Z (ed) 1970 Stabilization of juvenile diabetics. The Gont Beilison Symposium Stenfert Kroese, Leiden

Laron Z 1977 Psychosocial aspects of balance in juvenile diabetes. Pediatric and Adolescent Endocrinology 3: 1

Pelser H E, Groen J J 1983 How to listen better to patients. In: Assal J P, Berger M, Gay N, Canivet J (eds) Diabetes education. Excerpta Medica, Amsterdam, p 224

Pelser H E, Groen J J, Stuyling de Lange M J, Dix P G 1979 Experiences in group discussions with diabetic patients. Psychotherapy and Psychosomatics 32: 257

Simmonds J F 1976 Psychiatric status of diabetic youth in good and poor control. International Journal of Psychiatry and Medicine 7: 133

Sullivan B J 1978 Selfesteem and depression in adolescent diabetic girls. Diabetes Care 1: 18

White P 1985 Diabetic children and their later lives. In: Joslin's diabetes mellitus, 12th edn. Lea and Febiger, Philadelphia

Wilkinson D G 1981 Psychiatric aspects of diabetes mellitus. British Journal of Psychiatry 138: 1

Yalom I D 1975 The theory and practice of group psychotherapy. Basic Books, New York

14

G. H. B. Baker

Backache

INTRODUCTION

Backache is a very common condition. More than half the population will suffer a disabling attack at some time in their lives, and the condition is probably the biggest cause of absence from work. There is an extraordinary discrepancy between the wealth of evidence of the importance of psychological factors in chronic backache and the almost, or complete, ignoring of these factors in some authoritative pronouncements in the field (Jayson 1984, Waddell 1982). The complexity of pain perception is recognised by Porter (1986). Controlled trials have failed to demonstrate the value of most of the commonly used treatment approaches and there is a strong case for a major rethinking of the medical approach to the problem, with much more emphasis on the psychosocial aspects. It may be that patients will be better served in special clinics for the condition than in the busy orthopaedic, rheumatological, gynaecological, neurological and pain clinics, where persistent cases tend to be referred at present.

THEORETICAL BACKGROUND

Low back pain can be caused by inflammatory conditions (e.g. ankylosing spondylitis, rheumatoid arthritis and infections), by neoplastic disease (primary and secondary), and by metabolic disease (e.g. Paget's disease, osteoporosis, hyperparathyroidism). These causes can usually be distinguished by a careful history, examination and relevant investigation. Because back pain is so common, and these conditions are so relatively rare, they are sometimes not diagnosed as quickly as they might be. It has been suggested (Lancet leading article 1985) that a questionnaire could be developed which would enable the association between specific symptoms or syndromes with these various diagnoses to be recognised. Such a questionnaire could then be used clinically, completion by the patient ensuring a more complete survey of all the potentially relevant questions than is always possible in the clinic.

In this chapter, however, the subject is back pain in the absence of evidence of inflammatory, neoplastic or metabolic disease. Such pain may or may not be associated with clinical or radiological evidence of prolapsed or degenerated intervertebral discs, or of osteoarthrosis of the spine. It is variously described as mechanical, degenerative, or, more accurately, as 'non-specific back pain' (Jayson 1984).

The precise aetiology of many such cases is obscure. Clinical signs of paralysis, wasting or anaesthesia are evidence of pressure on a nerve root, but pain radiation into the leg is not necessarily an indication of nerve root pressure, though with radiation beyond the knee, root involvement is probable (Brewerton 1986). Radiographic evidence is very unreliable: many cases of severe chronic low back pain show no abnormality and many middle-aged people free of back pain show an abundance of changes of the sort commonly held to be causes of pain — for example, when 52 volunteers free of back pain had computer-assisted tomography of the spine, 11 showed radiological evidence of disc herniation (Wiesel et al 1984).

Purely 'mechanical' explanations of low back pain, as seen, for example, in a leading British textbook of rheumatology (Jayson 1986) which has 27 pages on low back pain without any mention of psychological factors, appear to regard pain as a simple sensory sensation. In fact, chronic pain is a complex perception in which the pain-producing stimulus is very greatly modified before reaching consciousness. Two important general factors magnify the contribution of psychological factors to the perception of pain, and especially low back pain. The first is that pain, unlike the other senses, is purely subjective. The patient cannot check his perceptions against other people's in the way that he could his perception of colour, for example. The second is the great medical uncertainty that exists about the diagnosis, treatment and prognosis of backache. The doctor's uncertainty is often conveyed to the patient and this facilitates perceptual distortion.

Among the specific factors known to affect perception are personality, mental state, cultural background, cognitive assessment of the significance of the pain, family history of painful conditions, childhood experience of pain, the response of those close to the patient to his pain, the possibility of compensation for 'injury', and resentment relating to the cause of the pain and to unsuccessful attempts to relieve it.

Much of the perceptual modification of pain probably occurs in the cerebral cortex, but Melzack & Wall (1965), in their 'gate control' theory of pain, recognising that 'the amount and quality of perceived pain are determined by many psychological variables', demonstrated that descending inhibitory impulses could prevent or reduce the transmission of pain in the spinal cord.

The major consideration in backache is the development of *chronic* pain. Acute episodes of back pain are extremely common. A general practice study (Banks et al 1975) found that a sample of 198 women on a general practitioner's list aged 20–44 years had an estimated 1095 episodes of back pain in a year and only one in 52 of these episodes resulted in the patient consulting her doctor. Another general practice study (Dillane et al 1966) found that 7.5% of their practice consulted the doctor with back pain in a period of 4 years, the maximum rate of new cases being in the 50–59 year age group. A French study (Bucquet & Colvez 1985) found that 2.5% of the population consulted their doctor with low back pain in the course of a year. Eighteen per cent of an American sample reported 'frequent back pain' during the year before interview (Reisbord & Greenland 1985). Though psychosocial factors are undoubtedly important in many of these episodes, and may be relevant to optimal management of them (Fordyce et al 1986), our main concern will be the ways in which a small minority of these acute episodes develop into chronic disabling conditions. In the absence of evidence of nerve root pressure, it is difficult to predict which acute cases will become chronic, although Keel (1984) has suggested valuable danger signs. In one study, 4% of a random sample of men aged 40–47 years reported they had been off work with low back pain for more than 3 months in the last 3 years (Svenson & Andersson 1982).

Psychosocial factors

Personality disorder can be defined as existing when, in the absence of formal psychiatric illness, there are long-standing difficulties in coping with the demands of everyday life, particularly in the formation of satisfactory relationships socially and sexually or in work. Patients with such difficulties will be predisposed to perceive back pain as more disabling than the general population because the pain is a psychologically acceptable cause of the difficulties experienced by the patient, and will sometimes induce more caring behaviour from those around him than would otherwise be available. Of patients attending a pain clinic, 37% were found to fulfil diagnostic criteria for personality disorder (Reich & Thompson 1987).

The mental state has a profound effect on perception. This can be seen very dramatically in the apparent absence of acute pain in injuries experienced in the excitement of battle or sport (Scott & Gijsbers 1981). In chronic pain the most relevant effect is depression. Among 80 patients with chronic low back pain, 21% had a major depressive disorder, 54% had an intermittent depressive disorder, and 20% were not depressed (France et al 1986). The authors recommend that rating scales for depression should be considered part of the assessment for all patients with low back pain.

Higher levels of anxiety have also been shown to be associated with more pain (Bond 1973). Increased paraspinal electromyographic activity has been shown in low back pain patients discussing personal stress (Flor et al 1985) and relaxation procedures have been shown to be beneficial (Linton & Gotestam 1984).

That cultural background affects perception of pain was first suggested by Zborowski (1952), who studied 87 hospitalised pain patients in New York, the majority of whom were suffering from 'herniated discs and spinal lesions'. He found marked differences in the experience of pain according to whether the patient's ethnic origins were Jewish, 'old American', Italian or Irish, and argued that these differences were due to cultural differences in attitude towards pain, learnt in childhood. Though the study, as reported, is methodologically unsound, the observations match clinical experience.

Marked variations are found between patients in their cognitive assessment of the significance of pain. The extremes of this variation are represented by the patients who regard an aching back as a harmless though tiresome burden, on the one hand, and those who live in daily fear that the pain indicates the imminent possibility of some much worse catastrophe (e.g. a disc 'slipping', a muscle or ligament 'tearing') on the other (Smith et al 1986). These cognitions are often founded upon discussions, perhaps poorly understood, with doctors, and doctors should be aware of the interpretations that anxious patients may put on their explanations. Another cognitive aspect is that patients with low back pain may be prone to interpret muscular pain arising from exercise of infrequently used muscles as evidence of exacerbation of their back condition (Schmidt 1985).

There is some evidence that people who have been brought up in homes where other family members have suffered chronic painful conditions are more likely to develop chronic painful conditions themselves (Hartvig & Sterner 1985).

The idea that pain is sometimes magnified or prolonged as a result of the response of other people to the patient's complaints of pain is a central concept in the behavioural approach. 'Operant conditioning' is the term used to describe the fact that behaviour which is rewarded tends to be repeated, while behaviour which is punished, or not rewarded, tends to be extinguished. The psychiatric concept of 'hysteria' is also relevant here: hysterical behaviour is defined as behaviour which is unconsciously motivated for secondary gain — usually emotional warmth or support from another person. People who have been emotionally deprived in childhood, who are currently in a state of emotional deprivation, who have acquired emotional support as a result of painful illness in childhood, or, especially, those who have any combination of these factors, are predisposed to this mechanism. If such patients then suffer an acute episode of back pain, and as a result experience an increase in the warmth and caring attention of those near them, there is a powerful inducement for the expressions of pain to continue. In the absence, or failure to respond, of close family, the same psychological mechanisms may apply to the patient's interactions with medical, nursing or other paramedical staff. It has been demonstrated (Waddell et al 1984) that the amount of physical treatment received by patients with backache is influenced more by their illness behaviour than by the actual physical disease. The leading authority in this concept of pain is Fordyce (1984), who concentrates on the observable manifestations of pain, the 'pain behaviour', and attempts to extinguish it by behavioural methods. One of the principal features of this approach is encouraging others (staff and family) not to respond to the patient's complaints, but rather to respond with attention and social feedback to the performance of treatment schedules involving increased activity. In addition, the patient's tendency to request analgesics is extinguished by providing the medication at regular intervals, rather than on request.

The issue of compensation is also easily translated into simple behavioural terms. If back pain commences as a result of an injury at work, or as a result of an accident in which another party may be responsible, then the issue of financial compensation is likely to arise. The more severe the pain, and the greater and more prolonged the disability, the more the compensation is likely to be. The patient is likely to undergo repeated questioning, examination and investigation, which tends to keep the perception of his symptoms fresh, and at the forefront of his mind. Such mechanisms will be more powerful if the patient is unemployed (whether as a result of the injury or not) as he will have more time to dwell on the symptoms, and less inducement to purposeful activity which would displace thoughts of the injury. In addition, it is much more acceptable to the patient to attribute his unemployment to the back injury, rather than to any personal inadequacy. Though compensation is seen as one of the exacerbating factors in chronic low back pain, a comparison of 47 patients involved in litigation versus 33 controls found very little difference on psychological testing and no support for the idea that litigants describe their pain as more severe than do non-litigants (Mendelson 1984). Malingering, or conscious falsification of symptoms for gain in compensation cases (as in the Jack Lemmon film 'The Fortune Cookie'), has been estimated to occur in less than 5% of cases of chronic low back pain (Leavitt & Sweet 1986). However, this must be a very insecure estimate, in view of the difficulty of knowing to what extent the indicative clinical signs are consciously or unconsciously mediated.

In some cases a profound sense of grievance towards the person or firm held by the patient to be responsible for an injury seems to be a factor in exacerbating the disability, even in the absence of a compensation factor, or after the compensation issue has been settled unfairly in the eyes of the patient. I have also seen cases in which great resentment against a surgeon responsible for an earlier, unsuccessful operation on the back seemed to have been a factor in prolonging the disability. It is as if the patient is saying 'look what you have done to me', and cannot 'forgive' the guilty party by getting better.

Lastly, in this account of the theoretical background, it may be of interest to collate some of the terms which have been used to draw attention to the fact that there are often psychological factors operating in cases with physical symptoms. Hysteria (from the Latin for the uterus) and hypochondriasis (from the name for the upper quadrant of the abdomen) are both derived from anatomical terms — *hysteria* because it was believed that physical complaint for emotional gain was an exclusively female activity, and originally was thought to be due to the womb 'wandering' and *hypochondriasis*, the excessive pre-occupation with physical symptoms and conviction of ill health, because the upper abdomen was seen as a typical region of concern. *Conversion reaction* is a psychoanalytic concept suggesting that neurotic conflict is converted into physical symptoms whereas *abnormal illness behaviour* is a behavioural psychologist's term indicating that all behaviour is learnt, that there are norms of illness behaviour (Mechanic 1977) and that abnormal illness behaviour can be understood in terms of learning theory. *Psychosomatic disease* was used to indicate those diseases in which there were clear organic and psychological dimensions (e.g. peptic ulcer) but is now more often used to emphasise that man is an inseparable unity and that to discuss somatic disease without considering its psychological aspect is to be 'a myopic mechanic . . . unable to detect the whole beyond the part' (Wall 1984). This is close to the concept of *holistic medicine*, though that seems to have come to be heavily associated with the ideas of alternative (i.e. non-medical and usually non-proven) remedies. Some robust souls will classify patients who appear to complain disproportionately as *whingers*, though, within patients hearing, this may be modified to *supratentorial disorder*. The American Diagnostic and Statistical Manual (DSMIII) refers to *somatisation disorder*, the tendency to experience and communicate psychological distress in the form of somatic symptoms that the patient misinterprets as signifying serious physical illness (Lipowski 1986), and the word *alexithymia* describes people who lack an ability to describe their feelings verbally and who report multiple somatic symptoms (Lesser 1985). The *Briquet syndrome* is a syndrome, operationally defined by the St Louis School (Guze et al 1986), of many physical complaints in the absence of objective signs, while the *pain-prone personality* (Engel 1959), and *psychogenic pain* (Jayson 1986) are other formulations.

THERAPEUTIC APPROACHES

Physical treatments

Opinions about the best treatment for cases with an acute back pain syndrome are very diverse and Nachemson (1985) summarises: 'traction, flexion and extension exercises, X-ray therapy, short-wave therapy, ultrasound, muscle relaxants, biofeedback, anti-inflammatory drugs, injections and manipulations of various types have failed to demonstrate any effect on return to work of acute patients'. The standard 'symptomatic' treatment in general practice in 1966 (Dillane et al 1966) was rest, heat, liniment and aspirin. 'Strict bed rest for three weeks' has been recommended for an 'acute flare-up of mechanical or degenerative low back pain' (Edgar 1984). On the other hand, a clinical trial involving 252 patients (Gilbert et al 1985) favoured early mobilisation over bed rest of 4 days' duration, nor was any subset of patients discovered who benefited from bed rest. Fordyce et al (1986) compared two treatments in patients with very recent onset of acute back pain. Fifty-seven patients were prescribed analgesics, activity limits and exercises on a time-based schedule, while 50 patients were advised to adjust the treatment schedule according to their pain. The two groups showed no differences 6 months later, but at 9 and 12 months later, the patients on the time-contingent schedule were better than those treated on the pain-contingent schedule. A Swedish study (Berquist-Ullman & Larsson 1977) of 217 patients with acute lumbosacral pain (median duration at entry to study 9 days) compared back school (see below), physiotherapy, and a placebo (short-wave diathermy). Eighty-seven percent were better within 3 months, though 60% had a recurrence within the year. The mean duration of symptoms after the first treatment was 14.8 days in the back school group, 15.8 days in the physiotherapy group, and 28.7 in the placebo group. However, the duration of sick leave showed little difference (20.5, 26.5 and 26.5 days respectively) and there was no difference in the number nor length of absences due to recurrences in the three groups.

The physical treatments prescribed in chronic low back pain include those already mentioned for acute pain, together with several additional modalities. They all 'tend to be unsatisfactory' (Yates 1986). Again, there is a conflict between those who seek to rest the back, for example with a brace, and those who advocate activity. Willner (1985) tried the effect of a rigid brace on 26 patients with chronic low back pain (mean duration 2.1 years) with negative myelography. Four patients had complete relief, five had reduced symptoms and 17 experienced no relief. On the other hand, 73 chronic low back pain patients, referred as failures of conventional medical or surgical care, were admitted to a very active 3-week physical rehabilitation programme, based on the theory that much of the disability in such cases is due to deconditioning caused by prolonged disuse of spinal joints and muscles (Mayer et al 1986). As well as activity, the programme included psychological treatments. Ninety-two per cent having been unemployed, 82% returned to work (perhaps there was less unemployment in Dallas than in the UK!). A less intensive rehabilitation programme emphasising activity also produced good results (Lichter et al 1984).

Coxhead et al (1981) compared treatment in 322 outpatients with a sciatic syndrome. Each treatment (traction, exercises, manipulation, corset) showed a small degree of immediate benefit, compared to a high rate of spontaneous improvement, but no benefit could be seen at 4- or 16-month follow-up.

Epidural injection of diamorphine over the nerve roots corresponding to the painful area in cases of chronic pain gave good relief in 19 of 20 patients at 24 hours: eight patients still had relief at 8 weeks, but within 6 months all had recurred (Campbell 1983). A development of this is slow continuous morphine infusion into the epidural space at the L1/T12 level, in which good results over periods of up to 2 years are claimed (Auld et al 1985). A placebo-controlled trial of epidural steroids in 73 patients with lumbar root pain failed to demonstrate efficacy (Cuckler et al 1985).

Back school is a system of treatment developed in Sweden and based on ergonomics. The aim is to teach patients with low back problems, usually in a group, to understand the mechanisms of symptom production and also the elements of prevention and self-care. A typical course has four sessions, each of 1 hour, over a period of 8 days, with sessions on (1) anatomy and pathology, (2) posture, (3) lifting, and (4) relaxation, mobilisation and strengthening. Veldman et al (1986), in Edinburgh, suggest that the multitude of other possible treatments indicates that none has become a universal success, that the effects of all treatments are usually short-lived, and that back school is the most generally appropriate. Klaber Moffett et al (1986), from Oxford, compared three 1-hour sessions of back school with three ½-hour sessions of exercise, with random allocation of 78 chronic patients. At 16-week follow-up they found functional disability and pain levels significantly better in the back-school patients and argued that this approach encourages a positive outlook and discourages a passive, dependent attitude. However, it is likely that there are patients, especially those in whom the hypochondriacal element heavily outweighs the physical, for whom back school provides material for more colourful visualisation of what might go wrong with their backs, thereby contributing to disability.

The last resort in physical treatment is operation, which may be removal of a prolapsed disc, laminectomy or spinal fusion. Weber (1983) described a study in which patients considered suitable for surgery were randomly allocated to conservative therapy or operation. At 1 year the surgically treated group were 'rather better', at 4 years the advantage was 'less clear' and at 10 years there was 'little difference'. The improvement in the majority of the conservatively treated group suggested that 60% of the surgically treated patients may have had an unnecessary operation. Glynn (1987) suggests that surgeons rarely operate for back pain, but for symptoms in the legs, bladder or bowel and says that most patients find that surgery does not relieve their back pain. Clearly the decision to operate in the absence of objective signs of anaesthesia or paralysis is a very difficult one and should never be made without careful consideration of the psychosocial and work situation (Nachemson 1985).

Psychological aspects of treatment

The principal aims of the psychological management of backache are: to limit as much as possible any inappropriate disability which may result from the condition; to prevent iatrogenic complications; and, to recognise, and if possible treat, any major psychological, social, or psychiatric factors in causation.

The author works as a psychiatrist within a hospital department of rheumatology. Over the years about 100 cases of back pain have been referred to him from orthopaedic, rheumatology or other clinics. The great majority of these cases are, and the emphasis in this chapter is on, chronic cases, but a word about acute cases is appropriate.

The acute onset of an episode of severe low back pain is, as the author and many of his readers know from personal experience, not usually regarded by the victim as a trivial event. Although common, the pain, disability and deformity caused are such that he will often believe that something fairly serious has gone wrong with the back and will probably require more than casual reassurance before being convinced that the outlook is good. This will necessitate the doctor taking a full history, including following up any clues as to recent emotional upset, and making a careful physical examination. The necessity for special investigations (of which the commonest will be erythrocyte sedimentation rate, serum calcium and alkaline phosphatase levels and radiography of the lumbar spine) will be determined by the clinical characteristics of the case, but there will be a low percentage of positive results in the absence of clinical pointers, except in the case of radiography, which, as we have seen, will often show false positive results, especially in a middle-aged or elderly subject. A careful assessment of the case, seen by the patient as careful, followed by comprehensive explanation probably using the concept of muscle spasm, confident prediction of early recovery and encouragement to remain mobile and progressively to increase activity will limit the degree of unnecessary invalidism to a minimum. Prescription of analgesics and advice as to the beneficial effects of heat (for example from warm baths) may be appropriate. 'Although physicians may be unable to assign a definite cause for back pain in many situations, they can certainly provide plausible explanations. In most cases they can also offer reassurance that serious disease is not present and that improvement is very likely' (Deyo & Diehl 1986). Detailed psychological enquiry is too time consuming to be pursued in every case, but is obviously necessary when indicated, for example by a recent history of traumatic life events, obvious emotional distress, or by the patient relating his pain to psychological stress.

Case 1

A 26-year-old secretary was referred to the rheumatology department as an emergency because of severe generalised pain in all levels of the back — cervical, dorsal and lumbar. Physical examination showed diffuse tenderness around the spine and reluctant movements, but no more specific abnormality. The history revealed that the pain had come on 12 days before, after some heavy lifting, the day after her husband's suicide. Psychiatric assessment revealed that her father was domineering and had attempted incest with her when she was 12 years old. She described her mother as very timid and blamed her father for this. She had three older sisters. A paternal uncle had committed suicide and the eldest sister had severe mental illness.

She had worked as a secretary from the age of 18 years, met her husband at 20 and married at 22. She described him as quiet, serious and very insecure. Although he was good at his skilled profession and their marital life was happy, he disliked his work very much, and been consistently depressed and often spoke of suicide. He had been seen several times by psychiatrists, but for years she felt an imminent risk of his suicide. She found his persistent misery hard to bear, thought of separation, but felt unable to leave him because she felt sure he would kill himself if she did. The week before he died, he made two serious suicide attempts and in retrospect the fatal attempt (plastic bag asphyxiation) might have been anticipated and prevented by her. Her husband had been her only confidante and after his death she felt unable to confide in anyone because of the psychological disruption and pathology in her own family. When seen 1 week after this ventilation of her traumatic story, she reported that the pain had cleared up completely over the day or two following the first interview and she returned to work with good plans for the future on the day of the second interview. She was seen on a total of four occasions and on the fourth (1 month after the first interview and 6 weeks after her husband's death and the onset of pain) reported that she now felt well, did not want to attend further, and was planning to go abroad to live with her sister. In this case it seemed that reassurance as to the absence of serious physical disease followed by ventilation of very distressing personal experience enabled the pain to settle, perhaps because of reduced muscular tension, within a day or two.

Reassurance as to the absence of serious physical disease, combined with a credible explanation of symptoms in the light of an understanding of the patient's psychological situation can be very therapeutic in the chronic case as well.

Case 2

A 29-year-old school teacher was admitted to hospital for investigation of back pain which had resulted in him being virtually confined to bed for 4 months. His father had died suddenly at the age of 70 years, 4 years before, and his mother, to whom he was very close, in a road traffic accident 1 year before. He had one sister, 10 years older, with whom there had always been a difficult relationship. He had a switchback academic career, doing badly at school until his final years, when he won a scholarship to university, where he had a disappointing career, and was not accepted for postgraduate work. He taught abroad for some years, but then found a place for postgraduate work at another university, where his thesis was ultimately rejected. He had experienced little success with girls and had been impotent on three occasions with the only girl with whom he had attempted intercourse. After his mother's death he felt 'lonely' in her flat during the Christmas vacation. He spent most of the Easter holiday in bed 'exhausted' and back pain increased during the summer term, ending in almost total disability during the summer vacation and the subsequent term. He had received conflicting advice from two general practitioners (one prescribed rest, the other swimming) and was then referred to hospital, where he had sequentially received a corset, physiotherapy, remedial gymnastics, phenylbutazone and advice to return to work, all without benefit. He was eventually admitted to hospital and while there requested psychiatric help. In addition to reviewing the psychiatric history, the investigations were discussed in detail and he was given firm reassurance as to the absence of serious physical disease. He was discharged from hospital 2 days after the interview, returned to work and was playing football the following week. He was seen again, 10 years later, because he had developed disabling back pain following his wife's desertion. He had again received divergent opinions and advice about his pain from doctors and physiotherapists, and again was relieved of pain by ventilation of the emotional situation, though he remains in psychotherapy because of the emotional reaction to his loss.

The two case histories above showed clinical improvement following psychiatric intervention, but of course this is often not the case. In some cases, the best one can do is to throw light on a difficult psychosocial situation. Its recognition will usually assist in the management of physical symptoms presenting in the future.

Case 3

A 66-year-old woman was referred from a medical outpatient clinic with a complaint of low back pain which made her unable to get about. The history revealed a life of illness, including many absences from school because of 'eye trouble', which she said was the reason why she never learnt to read or write. Her husband reported that she had been ill very frequently throughout their 44 years of married life. She had always shown little emotional response and their sexual relationship had been slight. She had never liked to mix with other people and as a result they were socially isolated. When first seen she was on eight medications for five separate conditions (osteoarthrosis, chronic respiratory disorder, angina, depression, and anxiety), the evidence for all of which was minimal in spite of attendance at many different outpatient clinics and hundreds of investigations. The medications were progressively reduced by the medical clinic and 3 months later she was reported to be symptomatically much improved and off all medication, though the underlying personality disorder and tendency to physical complaint was undoubtedly unchanged.

This patient had confined her multiple consultations to orthodox medical practitioners but some patients may be tempted to turn to alternative practitioners if medical consultation is unsatisfactory.

Case 4

A 30-year-old woman from abroad, married to a blind Englishman, was referred to the clinic because of disabling back pain of 4 months' duration. Her parents were both doctors, the father a radiologist and the mother a specialist in physical medicine. Her back pain had developed on the first day of a new job, after a long vacation in her home country, where she would rather live but her husband would not. They had married 4 years before, and since then the husband had developed Hodgkin's disease and had become sterile as a result of radiotherapy. She wanted to bear a child. She had felt her general practitioner's attitude, when she had consulted him with the pain, to be dismissive, and she had subsequently seen a cranial osteopath, an acupuncturist, a shiatzu practitioner, a psychic healer, a rheumatologist (a very brief interview), an individual psychotherapist and a marital psychotherapist (with her husband). A second rheumatologist, seen privately at her mother's expense, had curtailed the interview after about 10 minutes, prescribing a corset and saying repeatedly 'there is nothing to worry about' in the face of her questioning. The marital psychotherapy, at a centre of psychotherapeutic excellence, seemed much the most likely to be helpful and she was encouraged to persevere with that.

A frequent finding in the history of cases with chronic low back pain is evidence of problems in sexual relations before the onset of the back pain. In my own experience (Baker 1987) 52 of 72 patients (22 men, 50 women) referred for psychiatric opinion with low back pain of more than 6 months' duration, described problems in sexual relations before the onset of pain.

Among the 22 men, 14 had definite problems in sexual relationships before the onset of their back pain. The problems included impotence (three), report of uninterested or reluctant partner (three), or more often a poor or absent relationship with infrequent or no intercourse (eight). In one case, the couple had drifted apart emotionally and back pain was given as the reason why intercourse was impossible. Among the other seven men, two were divorced and remarried, two reported a satisfactory sexual life, one had sexual problems only since his back injuries and in two this detail was not recorded.

Among the 50 women, 38 had psychosexual problems existing before the onset of back pain. Sixteen reported that they had never been interested in the opposite sex, or they had never enjoyed sex, or that there was no sexual response in intercourse. Eight reported having had no sexual relationships ever, or for very many years. Four gave histories suggesting rejection of their own femaleness and probable latent homosexuality, though none described actual homosexual experiences. Eight others gave histories of various problems concerning their sexual lives — extremely restrictive parents to an age of 29 years, much older and sexually inactive husbands, a 'man-hating' mother, and sexual relations 'perfunctory' etc.

Case 5
A 38-year-old nurse was referred to orthopaedics with a 3-year history of pain following lifting a patient. Little was found in the way of physical signs, a diagnosis of hysteria was made, and she was referred for psychiatric assessment. She married at 18 years, but it proved unhappy. She disliked sexual intercourse and her husband was 'oversexed'. She had six children, but left them and him after she found her sister in his arms. Soon after she left him, she met her second husband, 22 years her senior, very kind and considerate and not at all sexually demanding. She is very happy with him, and he is very solicitous of her back. Though fully co-operative in the first psychiatric interview, this patient was very angry when seen again and refused to discuss her difficulties. Two years later she was again referred by the orthopaedic surgeons but failed to attend.

In most cases of this kind, the sexual problems will be very long-established, and the patient (and partner if there is one) will be reluctant to alter the established, if precarious, equilibrium. An occasional early case, with a co-operative partner, may be worth considering for a behavioural psychotherapy approach to the sexual problem.

In some cases the problems seem to be deep-seated neurotic problems of a kind suggesting insight-orientated psychotherapy.

Case 6
A 33-year-old man was referred with widespread pain in the neck and dorsal region which had developed from a painful thumb acquired while 'boxing' with his 6-year-old son. His own parents had separated when he himself was 6 years old and he had then been brought up as a 'second-class citizen' in his grandmother's family. He left school at 15 years and had been successful in work. He married at 25 years but had regretted that decision since before the ceremony. The relationship was very hostile, and a recent exacerbation was caused by his wife's wish to have another child and his feeling that this would be 'a final nail in my coffin'. He had a number of extramarital affairs. There was frequent talk of separation, but he did not want his son to suffer as he had. He was referred for psychotherapy.

Perhaps the most important psychiatric diagnosis to make in low back pain is that of severe depression, because the condition is life-threatening (by suicide) and treatment very likely to be effective, often with substantial relief of pain, no matter whether pain or depression seems primary.

Case 7
A 70-year-old man had suffered from recurrent back pain, necessitating 2–3 weeks off work every year for 35 years. He was the youngest, and only survivor, of seven, the last and closest sibling having died 6 weeks before our patient was seen. His first wife died by suicide 19 years before and he had remarried a woman 20 years his junior 3 years before. His mental state was one of severe depression, constantly pre-occupied by guilty thoughts and thoughts that life was not worth living. His sleep and appetite were very poor, with loss of 28 lb in 2 months. He was referred to his local psychiatric service where he was admitted for treatment of depression and had electroconvulsive therapy with substantial reduction of back pain.

Prolonged minimal support may be of considerable benefit to socially isolated patients for whom little else can be done. Fifteen to thirty minutes at intervals of 4–8 weeks can produce a sense of security and continuity for the patient out of proportion to the professional time it consumes. This support is probably dependent on a close understanding of the patient being established at the outset, so that the patient feels that the doctor understands his position, both physical and psychological, in depth. Such a relationship makes chronic pain easier to bear.

Mention should be made of a more structured psychological treatment of chronic low back pain, as described by Fordyce (1984). If the patient is on large doses of analgesic medication, this medication should be given at regular intervals, not 'as required'. The dose should be given in a uniform volume of liquid, the amount of analgesic present being progressively reduced. The patient should be given a programme of steadily increasing activity, and should win attention and feedback by fulfilling this programme, and not by complaining of pain. Alternative interests and activities should be stimulated and encouraged.

Training in progressive relaxation (Jacobson 1938) may be a valuable therapy in patients with marked muscular tension.

Case 8

A 39-year-old divorced woman had enjoyed good health until 1 year previously, when she moved to London from the north for a better job. Very soon after the move she began to experience severe tension. Contributing factors included an extremely stressful work situation, the loss of her 19-year-old daughter who did not like London and returned to their previous home town, and great anxiety about her 14-year-old daughter whose new school was very bad, so that the patient felt it necessary to put her into a boarding school. Her presenting symptom was severe and persistent low back pain of 1 year's duration. She was taught progressive muscular relaxation in the clinic — alternately contracting and relaxing the various muscle groups of the body and finishing with 10 minutes' relaxation. She practised this twice daily at home with an audio tape, with review in the clinic every 2–3 weeks, where she was encouraged to relax consciously when she felt muscular tension building up. After 6 weeks she reported substantial reduction of her back pain, both in severity and persistence.

A final difficult problem in psychological management is properly to evaluate the indications for operation in the presence of clear evidence of psychosocial problems.

Case 9

A 43-year-old woman looking younger than her years, well dressed and carefully made up, gave an 8-month history of severe back pain with sudden onset while doing heavy gardening work. She had been reared in an orphanage without any knowledge of her parents. She had trained as a children's nurse, but also worked in a pub, where she met her husband, a policeman, who proved to be a very heavy drinker, often verbally and physically violent. The relationship had been very strained, with infrequent sexual relations. She was a committed Christian, views which her husband rejected completely. Arguments were frequent and violent. She had thought of leaving, but could see no future for herself or her daughters, aged 11 and 8 years, if they did so. They lived in police accommodation. A myelogram was thought by the radiologist to show a significant disc herniation, but the surgeon decided against surgery on the grounds of her histrionic personality, the fact that some of her symptoms seemed anatomically impossible to link with the lesion, and the obvious gross psychological stress. A second orthopaedic surgeon, at a different hospital, agreed with this view but she was eventually operated on at a third hospital with great benefit.

SUMMARY

The psychological principles of management for the different professionals likely to be involved in cases of backache may be described.

The general practitioner dealing with an acute case must make an adequate assessment of the case, based on history and examination:

1. to exclude obvious evidence of inflammatory, neoplastic or metabolic disease and to exclude evidence of dangerous nerve root pressure;
2. to reassure the patient in the absence of such evidence, that the likeli-

hood of a good prognosis is high and that serious underlying disease has been excluded;
3. to persuade the patient that the case has been adequately assessed and understood so that resort to various alternative practitioners is unnecessary;
4. to give weight to a treatment programme which might include simple analgesics and advice about early mobilisation, progressing to more activity, including swimming or walking, where appropriate.

Any case with persistent pain and disability for longer than a month should have a fuller assessment, including, in most cases, a detailed psychosocial enquiry, a complete physical examination and any appropriate investigation arising from that examination (which will often include haematology, including erythrocyte sedimentation rate, calcium and alkaline phosphatase levels and radiography). In the absence of evidence of underlying disease or of operable degenerative disease (which might include muscle wasting or anaesthesia in the legs or pain radiating below the knee in the presence of computer-assisted tomographic or myelographic evidence of disc herniation or severe osteoarthrosis). In cases of doubt, operation should never be decided on without assessment of the psychosocial situation. In the absence of underlying disease, or of operable degenerative disease, referral to physiotherapy may be appropriate.

The physiotherapist should carefully review the patient's medical notes, and if possible discuss the case with doctors involved, paying particular attention to discovering what (if any) diagnostic information or advice has already been given to the patient, in the hopes of avoiding, where possible, contradictory opinions, or opinions which seem to the patient to be contradictory. The physiotherapist should then apply the chosen treatment with maximal therapeutic optimism, conveying to the patient an expectation of improvement and increased activity on the patient's part.

Where the psychosocial assessment reveals significant psychological factors, then referral may be appropriate, but will fail unless the referrer is able to explain to the patient that he accepts that the pain is real and that referral is made because psychosocial factors are contributing to the pain and will also fail unless the psychiatrist, psychologist, or social worker to whom the patient is referred understands and accepts the patient's pain and communicates that to the patient. Any suggestion by any of the professionals concerned that the pain is not believed, or is regarded as 'imaginary', will be very likely to send the patient off to an alternative practitioner with possibilities of all kinds of complication and unnecessary invalidism. Simultaneous application of physiotherapy and a psychological approach may make it easier for some patients to improve (Shofar & Ruddick 1976).

There is a good case for special clinics where cases of chronic back pain without underlying disease or operable conditions might be referred if the simple measures described above have not produced significant relief, and especially if the patient is still out of work. In these special clinics, severely disabled and chronic patients would have a more detailed assessment and a much more intensive and comprehensive rehabilitation programme, planned on principles derived from behavioural psychotherapy. Other appropriate psychiatric treatments would be available as required, in close liaison with the rehabilitation programme.

REFERENCES

Auld A W, Maki-Jakela A, Murdoch D M 1985 Intraspinal narcotic analgesia in treatment of chronic pain. Spine 10: 777–781

Baker G H B 1987 Chronic low back pain: a psychiatric assessment of 72 patients. In: Christodoulou G N C (ed) Psychomatic medicine: past and future. Plenum Press, New York

Banks M H, Beresford S H A, Morrell D C, Waller J J, Watkins C J 1975 Factors influencing demand for primary medical care in women aged 20–44 years: a preliminary report. International Journal of Epidemiology 4: 189–195

Berquist-Ullman M, Larsson U 1977 Acute low back pain in industry: a controlled prospective study with special reference to therapy and compounding factors. Acta Orthopaedica Scandinavica (suppl 170): 1–117

Bond M R 1973 Personality studies in patients with pain secondary to organic disease. Journal of Psychosomatic Research 17: 257–263

Brewerton D A 1986 The doctor's role in diagnosis and prescribing vertebral manipulation. In: Maitland D G Vertebral Manipulation 5th edn. Butterworth, London

Bucquet D, Colvez A 1985 Sciatica and low back pain in private practice: extent of the problem and therapeutic approaches. Revue Epidemiologie et Sante Publique 33: 1–8

Campbell W I 1983 Epidural opiates and degenerative back pain. Ulster Medical Journal 52: 161–163

Coxhead C E, Inskip H, Meade T W, North W R S, Troup J D G 1981 Multicentre trial of physiotherapy in the management of sciatic symptoms. Lancet 1: 1065–1068

Cuckler J M, Bernini P A, Wiesel S W, Booth R E, Rothman R H, Pickens G T 1985 The use of epidural steroids in the treatment of lumbar radicular pain. A prospective randomised double-blind trial. Journal of Bone and Joint Surgery 67AM.: 63–66

Deyo R A, Diehl A K 1986 Patient satisfaction with medical care for low back pain. Spine 11: 28–30

Dillane J B, Fry J, Kalton G 1966 Acute back syndrome — a study from general practice. British Medical Journal ii: 82–84

Edgar M A 1984 Backache. British Journal of Hospital Medicine 32: 290–301

Engel G L 1959 'Psychogenic' pain and the pain prone patient. American Journal of Medicine 26: 899–918

Flor H, Turk D C, Birbaumer N 1985 Assessment of stress-related psychophysiological reactions in chronic back pain patients. Journal of Consulting and Clinical Psychology 53: 354–364

France R D, Houpt J L, Skott A, Krishnan K R R, Varia I M 1986 Depression as a psychopathological disorder in chronic low back pain patients. Journal of Psychosomatic Research 30: 127–133

Fordyce W E 1984 Behavioural science and chronic pain. Postgraduate Medical Journal 60: 865–868

Fordyce W E, Brockway J A, Bergman J A, Spengler D 1986 Acute back pain: a control group comparison of behavioural versus traditional management methods. Journal of Behavioural Medicine 9: 127–140

Gilbert J R, Taylor D W, Hildebrand A, Evans C 1985 Clinical trial of community treatment for low back pain in family practice. British Medical Journal 291: 791–794

Glynn C 1987 Intractable pain: a problem identification and solving exercise. Hospital Update January: 44–54

Guze S B, Cloninger C R, Martin R L, Clayton P J 1986 A follow-up and family study of Briquet's syndrome. British Journal of Psychiatry 149: 17–23

Hartvig P, Sterner G 1985 Childhood psychologic environmental exposure in women with diagnosed somatoform disorder. Scandinavian Journal of Social Medicine 13: 153–157

Jacobson E 1938 Progressive relaxation. University of Chicago Press, Chicago

Jayson M I V 1984 Difficult diagnoses in back pain. British Medical Journal 288: 740–741

Jayson M I V 1986 In: Scott J T (ed) Copeman's textbook of the rheumatic diseases. Churchill Livingstone, Edinburgh, pp 1407–1434

Keel P J 1984 Psychosocial criteria for patient selection: review of studies and concepts for understanding chronic back pain. Neurosurgery 15: 935–941

Klaber Moffett J A, Chase S M, Portek I, Ennis J R 1986 A controlled prospective study to evaluate the effectiveness of a back school in the relief of chronic low back pain. Spine 11: 120–122

Lancet Leading Article 1985 Spondylitis: time for a new name and a new approach to diagnosis 2: 479–481

Leavitt F, Sweet J J 1986 Characteristics and frequency of malingering among patients with low back pain. Pain 25:357–364

Lesser I M 1985 Current concepts in psychiatry. Alexithymia. New England Journal of Medicine 312: 690–692

Lichter R L, Hewson J K, Radke S J, Blum M 1984 Treatment of chronic low back pain. A community based comprehensive return to work physical rehabilitation programme. Clinical Orthopaedics 190:115–123

Linton S J, Götestam K G 1984 A controlled study of the effects of applied relaxation plus operant procedures in the regulation of chronic pain. British Journal of Clinical Psychology 23: 291–299

Lipowski Z J 1986 Somatization: a borderland between medicine and psychiatry. Canadian Medical Association Journal 135: 609–614

Mayer T G, Gatchel R J, Kishino N, Keeley J, Mayer H, Capra P, Mooney V 1986 A prospective short-term study of chronic low back pain patients utilizing novel objective functional measurement. Pain 25: 53–68

Mechanic D 1977 Illness behaviour, social adaptation and the management of illness. A comparison of educational and medical models. Journal of Nervous and Mental Disease 165: 79–87

Melzack R, Wall P D 1965 Pain mechanisms: a new theory. A gate control system modulates sensory input from the skin before it evokes pain perception and response. Science 150: 971–978

Mendelson G 1984 Compensation, pain complaints and psychological disturbance. Pain 20: 169–177

Nachemson A L 1985 Advances in low back pain. Clinical Orthopaedics 200: 266–278

Porter R W 1986 Management of back pain. Churchill Livingstone, Edinburgh, ch. 7, pp. 43–46

Reich J, Thompson W D 1987 DSMIII personality disorder clusters in three populations. British Journal of Psychiatry 150: 471–475

Reisbord L S, Greenland S 1985 Factors associated with self-reported back pain prevalence; a population based study. Journal of Chronic Diseases 38: 691–702

Schmidt A J M 1985 Cognitive factors in the performance level of chronic low back pain patients. Journal of Psychosomatic Research 29:183–189

Scott V, Gijsbers K 1981 Pain perception in competitive swimmers. British Medical Journal 283: 91–93

Shofar S, Ruddick N 1976 Collaboration: a physiotherapist in the psychiatric team. Physiotherapy 62: 80–82

Smith T W, Aberger E W, Follick M J, Ahern D K 1986 Cognitive distortion and psychological distress in chronic low back pain. Journal of Consulting and Clinical Psychology 54: 573–575

Svenson H-O, Andersson G P J 1982 Low back pain in 40–47-year-old men. I Frequency of occurrence and impact on medical services. Scandinavian Journal of Rehabilitation Medicine 14: 47–53

Veldman H J G, Shaw P C, Thomson L C 1986 The back school. Seminars in Orthopaedics 1: 86–90

Waddell G 1982 An approach to backache. British Journal of Hospital Medicine September: 187–219

Waddell G, Bircher M, Finlayson D, Main C J 1984 Symptoms and signs: physical disease or illness behaviour. British Medical Journal 289: 739–741

Wall P D 1984 In: Wall P D, Melzack R (eds) Textbook of pain. Churchill Livingstone, Edinburgh, p 840

Weber H 1983 Lumbar disc herniation: a controlled prospective trial with 10 years of observation. Spine 8: 131–140

Wiesel S W, Tsourmas N, Feffer H I, Citrin C M, Patronas M 1984 A study of computer-assisted tomography. 1. The incidence of positive CAT scans in an asymptomatic group of patients. Spine 9: 549–551

Willner S 1985 Effect of a rigid brace on back pain. Acta Orthopaedica Scandinavica 56: 40–42

Yates A 1986 In: Currey H L F (ed) Mason and Currey's clinical rheumatology, 4th edn. Churchill Livingstone, Edinburgh, p 139

Zborowski M 1952 Cultural components in response to pain. Journal of Social Issues 8: 16–30

15
J. A. Cotterill

Eczema and psoriasis

INTRODUCTION

Both eczema and psoriasis are very common skin disorders and almost all patients are managed either by their family doctors or by dermatologists without recourse to psychiatric or psychological advice. A psychiatrist or psychologist may occasionally be involved by his dermatologist colleague in patients with various forms of neurodermatitis including pruritus ani and pruritus vulvae. However, a psychiatrist is much more likely to be involved in patients with delusions of parasitosis or more often in those presenting with dysmorphophobia.

ECZEMA

Theoretical background

There are many different types of eczema. The simplest classification is to divide this inflammatory condition of the skin into exogenous and endogenous eczema. The commonest type of endogenous eczema is atopic eczema, which is often associated with asthma and/or hay fever and a family history of one or more of these conditions in one or both parents or close relatives. The commonest type of exogenous eczema is that which arises when the skin is either irritated by primary irritants or becomes sensitised by potential allergens, such as nickel, chrome and rubber. Eczema involving the hands and feet (pompholyx) may arise as part of an atopic eczema or be precipitated by irritant or allergic contact factors. Thus, the low-grade eczematous changes due to primary irritants which develop, particularly on the hands of housewives, in men working with cutting oils in industry and in women working in hairdressing, are much more common in individuals with an atopic background and with a past history of infantile eczema in particular. Therefore, in some patients it is not possible to differentiate clearly between endogenous and exogenous factors.

Neurodermatitis may be generalised or localised (lichen simplex). It is seen particularly on the necks of women and the legs of men or can be more generalised. Pruritus ani and vulvae are examples of localised neurodermatitis.

The central clinical feature of all eczema is pruritus. There are those who believe that eczema arises only in individuals who damage their itchy skin by scratching. Pruritus and its amelioration by scratching is an everyday phenomenon which is thought to be utilised by most individuals to reduce frustration (Musaph 1983). In an eczematous patient, however, whilst immediate itching can be decreased by scratching, the lesions produced by scratching are itchy and therefore a vicious itch/scratch cycle is established. A reduction of itching by scratching serves as a strong reinforcer of further scratching behaviour (Bär & Kuypers 1973).

Atopic eczema

A classic patient with atopic eczema begins to develop dry, itchy skin at about the age of 3 months. The eruption is generally well represented in the flexures, face and nappy area. The child often becomes fretful and will not sleep. This puts a strain on the family as in severe cases no-one at home is able to sleep during the night. The natural history of atopic eczema is that in the vast majority of patients the eruption eventually disappears, but this may take several years and there may be subsequent symptom shifts into either asthma or hay fever.

From an immunological point of view atopic eczema is characterised in the majority of subjects by a very elevated serum IgE level. At the same time there is a depression of T-cell function, leading to a reduction in the ability to express delayed hypersensitivity. Prick tests and radio-allergosorbent test (RASTs) often show multiple immediate reactions to a wide range of allergens, including house dust mite, dust pollens, animal dander and occasionally to some foods such as nuts. There is evidence that the house dust mite may be an important factor in the pathogenesis of atopic eczema, in that killed house dust mites placed in contact with normal skin in subjects with raised antibodies to house dust mite antigen develop classical eczema after 48 hours of application of dead mites under occlusion (Mitchell et al 1982).

There have been claims of specific personality types in atopic eczema. It is a difficult field to evaluate as it is often difficult to know in an individual subject what effect the skin disease has had on personality development. There seems to be no doubt that eczema, particularly if it is affecting the skin of the face, can lead to a significant reduction in self-esteem and to marked depression; both are reversible after successful treatment. It has been claimed that patients with atopic eczema have a characteristic psychological profile, tending to be in a state of high manifest anxiety, depressed, neurotic and hypochondriacal (Al-Ahmar & Kurban 1976). These workers confirmed earlier work by Obermeyer (1955), who also claimed that patients with atopic eczema had an abnormal personality.

However, more recent work by Palos et al (1986), who studied 55 children with atopic eczema and 16 age-matched control children, throws some doubt on these earlier findings. Psychological examinations were also performed in both parents, using the Freiburg Personality Inventory. The children's personality profile was evaluated using the Hamburg Neuroticism and Extroversion Scale. These workers showed no significant differences between the atopic children and controls. An interesting finding was that the mothers of atopic children had been more unspontaneous and less emotional than the normal population whereas there was no significant difference for the fathers. The atopic mothers favoured adult behaviour in their children. In children's drawings there was a lack of friendly atmosphere and that the fathers of atopic children were drawn significantly smaller than the respective mothers.

One fairly consistent aspect of personality, particularly in children with atopic eczema, is hyperkinesis. This behaviour not only often wrecks the consulting room, but also exhausts the accompanying parents. This type of behaviour can dominate the clinical situation, delegating the evident eczema to a secondary role.

It is generally agreed that stress may trigger eczema in atopic individuals and Brown (1972) has highlighted the problems of assessing the part stress may play. Stress-related exacerbation of eczema is seen by dermatologists particularly in young women who are about to be married, or recently married, and in both sexes before and during examinations. The stress of taking a driving test may be sufficient to induce problems. Stress at work and at home and during marital disharmony can all play a pact in pathogenesis. The mechanism of adverse reaction of eczema to stress is not clear, but there is an increasing volume of evidence that stress, like atopic eczema, may be associated with a depression of T-cell function (Lancet Editorial 1985).

Effect of eczema on emotional and social life

The preschool life of a child with atopic eczema depends much on parental attitudes to the condition. Some children, fortunately a very small minority, are completely rejected by their parents and in this writer's experience this is more common in ethnic minority groups. Parents, and mothers in particular, can be divided into consolers and 'torturers'. Scratching may be either very firmly prohibited or made easier by the mother. Whatever the patents' attitude, however, the child has to be touched, massaged, rubbed and bandaged every day and sometimes several times a day. It is likely that this behaviour conditions the relationship between child and parent (Panconesi 1984a).

As a generalisation, it is true to say that children with eczema lose very little time at school on account of their skin problem. Indeed, it is very difficult to persuade a child to consider admission for intensive inpatient treatment during school term time. It is probably more factual to say that it is even more difficult to persuade the often dominant and demanding mother that this is the best course of action. If the eczema is complicated by asthma, then protracted periods off school may result.

In general, children with severe eczema tend to be smaller in stature than sex- and age-matched normal controls. This effect seems to be independent of whether the atopic children have been treated with local or oral steroids. Problems at school arise because their eczema sets them apart from their fellow pupils. Moreover, children with eczema are more prone to viral infections, and in particular viral infections of the skin, such as extensive warts, lesions of molluscum contagiosum or severe herpes simplex infections. Problems may arise in an atopic child who has to swim in a chlorinated pool. Immersion in this type of water often defats and degreases the skin and will usually make the eczema considerably worse. The schoolchild with eczema is unlikely to have the benefit of helpful discussions with his school about future suitable occupations and it is a matter of sadness for the writer to see potentially unsuitable candidates trying, for instance, to go into nursing or hairdressing, with subsequent disastrous results on morale. Subjects with atopic eczema have to avoid environmental conditions characterised by excessively high or low ambient temperatures or very high humidity. Dust, detergents and lipid solvents are also likely to exacerbate eczema. Excessive exposure to water should also be avoided. This can make work, for example in engineering, using water-soluble cutting oils, very difficult.

A significant proportion of patients with eczema will still experience considerable problems during adolescence. If these skin problems are expressed in potentially exposed areas of the body, such as the face and hands, there may be profound difficulties in the development of meaningful relationships, particularly with the opposite sex. It is interesting that women with mild to moderate eczema usually seem to socialise and marry without undue difficulty, whereas a significant proportion of men with moderate eczema feel unable to do so. This causes much misery and resentment and these feelings often go unexpressed. A minority of atopic individuals develop cataracts or even keratoconus and this may produce educational problems and subsequent problems with employment.

Therapeutic approaches

Most patients with eczema respond reasonably well to conventional therapy, but considerable advocacy is required for the parents of the youngster with eczema to come to terms with the skin problem. Local steroids, ointments and creams are employed most commonly to control eczema. These preparations vary widely in potency and there is a great deal of anxiety, particularly amongst the potential patients, about the damage which these agents can do to the skin if used excessively. This anxiety, if extreme in parents, may lead to a child being virtually left untreated lest he develop some thinning of the skin or some adrenal suppression at some time in the future.

It is the writer's experience that in children with moderate to severe eczema, quite potent local steroids may have to be used in the short term to bring problems under control, but once under control less potent preparations often suffice topically.

It is important to prevent nocturnal scratching. Savin et al (1973) established that an eczematous subject may spend at least 2–6% of sleeping time scratching. This activity can be abolished by the use of antihistamines at night in most subjects. However, in hyperkinetic children antihistamines often have a stimulative effect which can make problems even worse. It should be remembered that most children seem to be able to tolerate very high doses of antihistamines without undue problems. General advice about avoiding excessive exposure to potential primary skin irritants, such as water, detergents, oil, grease, dust, high and low ambient temperatures and high humidity is also proffered. An emollient oil, used either in the bath or as an after-shower, is often a useful adjunct. It is important that the subject with atopic eczema does not do too much bathing.

Patients with severe eczema or generalised eczema may require oral steroids, usually in the short term, but occasionally in the long term. Patients whose eczema fails to respond to these measures may be given in addition immunosuppressant drugs such as azathioprine.

Brown & Bettley (1971) showed the value of brief psychiatric treatment in patients with eczema who were motivated to accept this type of care. However, in the absence of such motivation, a referral to a psychiatrist may worsen eczema, especially in the short term.

As mentioned above, eczema, particularly if it involves the face, is often accompanied by considerable lowering of self-esteem, depression and anxiety. These feelings may be compounded by sleeplessness and scratching at night. The dermatologist usually has no hesitation in using tranquillisers or antidepressants in this type of clinical situation. Temazepam is a useful drug in the short term to prevent nocturnal scratching and to give the patient a reasonable night's sleep whilst allowing him to get up and work the following day. The writer has usually no preference with regard to antidepressants and usually employs amitriptyline, which seems to be well tolerated by most patients.

Psychological forms of treatment

It is a fact that patients with atopic eczema are almost never referred for psychological or psychiatric opinion. If stress or conflict has been a precipitating factor this is usually fairly self-evident and most dermatologists are quite happy to explore such stress and conflicts with the patient during a normal consultation. Most such therapy takes place in an outpatient setting on an informal basis. The writer likes to interview his patients initially fully dressed, making a note of how the patient is dressed and of general posture, particularly whether the patient shows the droop of depression or sits on the edge of the chair, or the woman fidgets with anxiety. The history is taken in the conventional way and during the history both verbal and non-verbal cues are explored further. If stress and conflict is centred around subjects such as birth, marriage, death, or work both in regard to financial reward and job satisfaction, every opportunity is given to the patient to try to talk about these problems and to indicate whether there are any other problems. There is no doubt that many patients are dissatisfied with dermatological doctor–patient relationships (Jobling 1976) and this sort of dissatisfaction may have been one stimulant to the formation of self-help societies, such as the National Eczema Society. The dermatologist in the United Kingdom is under intense pressure for time in outpatient clinics and must make maximum use of the time available with each patient. A general air of optimism is important and good relationships must be fostered to try to get the patients to come to terms with what often turn out to be chronic disorders which lower self-esteem. The dermatological consultation can be usefully examined in terms of game analysis (Cotterill 1981).

Game 1 — Diagnosis

Most patients with atopic eczema come along to the dermatologist knowing their diagnosis and looking for management. However, in young infants the diagnosis may not be clear, nor may it be clear in eczema of late onset.

Game 2 — Tests

Most patients want to know why they have developed eczema and a subgame of tests/allergy usually develops. The physician is questioned whether he thinks the patient is allergic to milk, food or some other agent. The dermatologist can respond by doing appropriate prick tests or RASTs. Patch tests are usually unhelpful in patients with atopic eczema, but useful in patients with exogenous eczema. Some patients come along with a vague feeling that they should have a blood test of some sort.

Game 3 — Prognosis

Patients and parents want to know what the outlook is. They are told that in the vast majority of affected individuals the eczema will eventually disappear, but there is no way of predicting when this will happen. There may be symptom shifts into asthma or hay fever. The patients are told that the eczema can usually be well controlled with appropriate medication which is now safe and effective.

Game 4 — Reassurance

Reassurance is most often played by doctors to reassure themselves rather than the patients, but many patients with eczema are looking for reassurance.

Game 5 — Catharsis

If psychological factors seem to be of importance, a firm game of 'Catharsis' can be played and if this is only a relative success, 'Collusion' can be played with a referral to a psychiatrist. There is evidence from the literature that a psychiatric referral can be helpful so long as the patient is motivated (Brown & Bettley 1971). It is pointless sending a patient to see a psychiatrist if the patient does not agree with this proposed course of action.

Game 6 — Admission and discharge

Patients whose skin steadfastly fails to settle with outpatient therapy are often admitted to hospital for inpatient treatment. A hard game of 'Discharge' is sometimes worth playing, particularly with difficult patients. If the patient is still having considerable difficulties they will often initiate alternative medical approaches, utilising hypnosis, acupuncture or homoeopathy.

A variety of alternative therapies have been proposed for patients who do not settle. Thus, Bär & Kuypers (1973) described the use of behaviour therapy using techniques which could be classified into four main groups. (1) Systematic desensitisation is used mainly in neurotic disorders, with anxiety as the principal clinical feature. Attempts were made to induce anxiety inhibition following repeated exposures to weak, anxiety-arousing stimuli, after which progressively stronger stimuli are introduced. (2) Aversion therapy may also be used in patients with persistent behaviour disorders, such as compulsive scratching or pathological hair pulling. In this technique, the patient is given an unpleasant stimulus, for instance electric shock, whenever the bad habit is displayed. (3) Operant techniques may be used to modify compulsive habits, where rewards are given to reinforce adapted behaviour and punishment is given for unadapted behaviour. Tokens may be employed in the token economy system. The patient, usually a child, receives a token after a short, fixed interval for good, non-scratching behaviour. (4) Assertiveness training techniques are employed in patients who are afraid of expressing their emotions and also in those who experience extreme social fear. Cataldo et al (1980) used a method of extinction, involving selective inattention to the patient during periods of compulsive scratching, to try to condition patients to stop scratching. In a recent study, a behavioural method (habit reversal) in combination with a hydrocortisone cream was compared to use of the cream alone in 17 patients with atopic dermatitis (Melin et al 1986). Habit reversal led to significantly less scratching than in the control group.

Illustrative cases

Miss L. G., aged 21 years
This patient gave a history of atopic eczema for as long as she could remember. There were exacerbations at the age of 6 years, 19 years and 21 years of age. The most recent exacerbation was very severe and the patient had to give up her work in the printing industry. During her first visit to the clinic this was the only information that could be elicited. During her second visit, when the patient was accompanied by a maternal aunt, much more information was forthcoming. It was interesting that the maternal aunt was married to an Italian and lived for most of the year in Italy. She told her niece that it was important to express her feelings, as people do in Italy. Encouraged by her aunt, the patient told me that her father had psoriasis and suffered greatly from his nerves. The patient was unable to relate to her father because of these problems. The mother was the breadwinner, but because she spent most of her time working, she did not find time to communicate with either the patient or her husband. When the patient's exacerbation of eczema began she had just finished with her boyfriend and her only brother was about to get married. In addition, her grandmother, to whom she was very attached, died suddenly. The patient had been unable to see her grandmother during her very brief illness and this made her feel very guilty. After this catharsis, the patient's skin problems settled down very rapidly. She is being encouraged to ventilate her feelings in future and behave more like an Italian rather than a Northern European!

Mrs J. J., aged 25 years
This patient had had eczema off and on ever since she was a small child, but had recently developed a severe exacerbation of her atopic eczema. During the first consultation the patient denied any particular stress problems, but returned to the clinic a month later to say that her skin was absolutely normal once more. This time she admitted that she had had severe marital problems. Her husband, whom she married about 10 months previously after knowing him several years, did not give up drinking as he had promised — in fact his alcoholism became worse. When her eczema developed she was in conflict about what to do concerning this situation. However, she had resolved her conflict by leaving her husband. These life events had been too painful to relate during her first visit.

Mr D. P., aged 27 years
This man had had atopic eczema for as long as he could remember and there had been several small outbreaks, especially during adolescence. He had recently presented with a much more extensive exacerbation, but this time denied any significant stress or conflict in his life. When seen a month later, however, the patient admitted that he had been desperately worried about his sister, who had been thought to have a brain tumour. There had been a considerable delay in making the diagnosis and it was only at operation that a vascular lesion was discovered, rather than a tumour. The neurosurgeon was able to remove the vascular lesion completely and the patient's sister made a good recovery. However, it was only during the second visit to the dermatologist that the patient was able to talk about this period of intense anxiety.

Miss S. N., aged 15 years
This young lady gave a lifelong history of eczema, but in the last year there had been severe exacerbations requiring several admissions to hospital. The patient's mother

described her daughter as extremely irritable and there had been many recent heated arguments at home over trivial matters. Stress factors were asked about during the patient's first visit to the clinic, but these were denied both by the patient and her family. However, subsequently it became evident that the patient's skin problems and her irritability had been gradually developing since her parents were divorced 3 years previously. The patient had an intense dislike of her mother's new boyfriend because she felt that this relationship was, at least in part, responsible for her parents' divorce. Moreover, her mother's boyfriend was still married and would not leave his wife. The patient was also very anxious that her mother would have a nervous breakdown and on one occasion she had to restrain her mother from taking an overdose of drugs. More recently the eczema had spread on to her face, which had depressed her considerably and increased her sense of isolation. She had recently finished with her boyfriend. Her relationship with her father was reasonably good and she felt able to talk to his new girlfriend, but only guardedly because she did not want to be disloyal to her mother.

This schoolgirl had felt the tensions at home were intolerable. She went to live with the maternal grandmother and her skin settled very rapidly. She made new friends and found a new boyfriend. However, there is still much conflict in the situation and difficulty in communicating with her mother and boyfriend.

PSORIASIS

Theoretical background

Psoriasis is a relatively common skin disorder, affecting about 2% of the population in the UK. The only predictable thing about psoriasis is its unpredictability and it can begin at any age. Classically, however, the condition begins in childhood with a characteristic involvement of the elbows, knees and scalp. Facial involvement is common in children, but rare in adults. There are many different morphological varieties, varying from follicular, guttate, through to discoid, plaque and exfoliative and pustular psoriasis. About 15% of patients may also develop arthritis. The commonest type of arthritis is a distal symmetrical arthropathy involving the distal interphalangeal joints of the hands and feet. Psoriatic arthritis may mimic rheumatoid arthritis, except that the rheumatoid factor is negative. Some patients develop the clinical features of ankylosing spondylitis. An unfortunate minority can develop a very severe destructive arthropathy with severe disability.

Cell kinetic studies have demonstrated that in psoriasis the involved areas of skin produce normal skin cells much faster than normal. These immature keratinocytes reach the skin surface in 3 or 4 days instead of maturing for over a month in normal skin. The resultant new skin is red and scaly and about 50% of patients may be itchy. The pruritus is thought by many to be associated with stress. Psoriasis is thought to be genetically determined, although the precise mechanism for genetic transmission has not been fully worked out. However, over 80% of patients give a positive family history. Many factors may precipitate psoriasis in genetically predisposed individuals, including physical trauma (Koebner's phenomenon), infective stress, e.g. streptococcal sore throat, and emotional stress. The literature on basic personality types in psoriasis is conflicting. The same can be said of the literature in regard to precipitation by stress or conflict. The difficulties of interpretation of the various studies have been well surmised by Payne et al (1985). They studied 32 patients by postal questionnaire, matching 16 patients with psoriasis for age, sex and marital status with 16 control patients suffering from cutaneous neoplasms, viral warts and fungal infections. They were unable to show that psoriasis is affected by life events, but admit, however, that their sample was small and did include patients whose psoriasis seems to have been precipitated by a streptococcal sore throat. Moreover, Payne et al selected a 1-year period prior to the development of psoriasis for study, but data from Seville (1977) would suggest that an incubation period from stress to psoriasis lies between 2 days and 1 month. These authors have also discussed the difficulties of retrospective study using a postal questionnaire. The fact that patients with psoriasis tend to be depressed may also limit the data that is forthcoming. Paljan et al (1984) in a computerised study involving 100 psoriatic patients and 100 controls, demonstrated that stress was significant not only in the initial eruption of psoriasis, but also in later stages. This series was noteworthy in containing nine psoriatic patients with a university degree and 36 with a high-school diploma. Farber et al (1968) found 30% of their patients with psoriasis developed an exacerbation during periods of stress, whilst Gilbert et al (1973) found that 80% of their psoriatic patients developed an exacerbation following stress. Seville (1977) studied 132 psoriatic patients whose skin problems were subsequently cleared using dithranol, after which the patients were followed up for 3 years. Seville demonstrated an incubation time (2 days–1 month) for psoriasis: a stressful incident within a month before an attack of psoriasis was remembered by 39% of patients. The prognosis of the patient with insight into a specific stress situation prior to the skin problems was significantly better than in the patient who had no insight.

In a study of psychological characteristics of psoriatics Goldsmith et al (1969) demonstrated a high incidence of psychiatric disorders in hospitalised psoriatic patients. Denial of disease was quite common. This was thought to explain some treatment failures with outpatient therapy. The authors felt, however, that their results should not necessarily be extrapolated to psoriatics as a group on the basis of this highly selected hospital study. Goldsmith et al found no significant difference between the psoriatics and controls in terms of neuroticism and extroversion, but the psoriatics showed a lack of confidence and self-esteem, which may be related to adverse changes in body image. Thus, Hardy & Cotterill (1982) found that patients with psoriasis were more depressed than an age- and sex-matched control population without skin disease.

Social and emotional aspects of psoriasis

Psoriasis is not usually a serious clinical problem until school age and after, but in severe instances can lead to many problems at school, not only because the rash sets the patient apart from others, but also because repeated courses of treatment need to be done on an inpatient or outpatient basis, leading to a considerable loss of school time. The older psoriatic patient with extensive disease feels set apart and has particular problems with communication, sometimes with his dermatologist (Jobling 1976). Indeed, the social and psychological problems that the psoriasis sufferer may experience in the community may have led to the formation of the Psoriasis Association, and the value of supportive group therapy for psoriasis patients has been claimed by Coles (1965, 1967). Fortunately for most adults, psoriasis does not usually occur on the face, but if it does, particularly in women, it leads to considerable cosmetic distress. Many patients carry small vacuum cleaners with them so that they can clean up the scales in hotel bedrooms etc. The psoriasis may dictate where and when patients can go on holiday, and what time of day they can swim in either the sea or a swimming pool. The leper complex is a very real entity for patients with psoriasis. There are studies to show that adult psoriatics tend to drink alcohol more heavily than controls (Monk & Neill 1986). These authors reported an excessive consumption of alcohol, especially in men with severe psoriasis when compared even with patients with severe eczema.

Panconesi (1984b) concludes: 'Unfortunately, the chronic and acute stress of daily life exacerbates or reactivates this 'healthy person's disease' [an Italian expression — *malattia dei sani*] which seems often so easily curable with an attractive prescription: avoid a hurried, stressful life, avoid work, go to the seaside and stay a long time on a stupendous sunny beach, always following summer with wisely chosen itineraries, massaged with choice unguents by someone young and lovely, who, we assure you, will have no difficulty in getting close. A rich man's disease?'

Therapeutic approaches in psoriasis

There are several effective methods of treating psoriasis. The disease can be controlled but not cured. For very small areas of psoriasis, local steroids are often employed. For the larger areas treatment is given in dermatological outpatient clinics or on an inpatient basis, using the phenolic compound dithranol in conjunction with ultraviolet light and tar baths. Older patients with difficult psoriasis may be treated with a combination of a light-sensitising drug, psoralens and ultraviolet light A (320–400 nm). This is called PUVA therapy.

More difficult psoriasis may be treated with cytotoxic drugs, such as azathioprine, hydroxyurea, methotrexate and 5-fluorouracil. When pruritus is a marked feature there are usually stress factors in the background and these must be explored and investigated. Any anxiety or depression is treated with the appropriate therapy. Some patients like to equip themselves at home with their own ultraviolet light apparatus, whilst others go on a package tour to the Dead Sea for natural phototherapy. Ultraviolet light helps almost all patients with psoriasis, the exception being those with a skin which burns easily, which usually goes with red hair and blue eyes. In younger patients who have repeated exacerbations of psoriasis following streptococcal sore throats, prophylactic penicillin may be given in the long term and occasionally tonsillectomy is performed.

Psychological aspects of treatment

As in the case of eczema, it is also true of psoriasis that frank psychiatric or psychological involvement is very rarely needed or required, except where alcoholism has become a problem. The management of the patient with psoriasis, from the psychological point of view, is identical to that of the patient with eczema. The ultimate game to be played in both conditions is time.

Illustrative case histories

Mr J. R., aged 37 years

This man presented with a severe generalised rash which developed 24 hours after he had knocked down and killed a little girl on the road. The accident was not his fault but this experience filled him with a mixture of very profound feelings, including anger that this should happen to him, and extreme sorrow that he had killed someone. On examination, the man had generalised guttate psoriasis, which completely disappeared, with very minimal local therapy, over the ensuing 4 weeks. Most outpatient attendances during this time centred around the accident and the patient's and his family's reaction to it. I saw the man again 18 months later with another severe episode of generalised guttate psoriasis. This episode developed 1 week after finding his father-in-law dead. Once more, talking about the feelings engendered by this experience led to a prompt resolution of his psoriasis. He has had no further problems.

Miss P. Y., aged 47 years

This lady was seen on exacerbation of her psoriasis which she had had off and on since the age of 7 years. Psoriasis in this patient always occasioned considerable anxiety and reactive depression which had necessitated treatment with diazepam and amitriptyline. She had also had outpatient treatment. The background to this exacerbation was explored and it became apparent that her psoriasis developed after she had been 'flashed' by a man in a shopping arcade in Leeds. This experience she found deeply frightening. The patient was unmarried and this demonstration of male sexuality engendered a mixture of conflicting emotions. This patient was managed with outpatient conventional topical treatment with dithranol for her psoriasis and frequent outpatient consultations, during which she expressed her feelings.

Mrs S. N., aged 75 years

This man had had psoriasis for most of his adult life and in the last 15 years it had become severe enough to necessitate several hospital admissions, with regular daily outpatient bathroom treatment to control his skin even in the more quiescent periods. There had been a severe exacerbation about 3 years previously, which followed the death of his wife. The patient had been very attached to his wife, but there were no children and no immediate relatives in the area. Because the patient's psoriasis became unmanageable, not only with outpatient treatment, but also with established inpatient treatment, it was decided to put him on the cytotoxic drug hydroxyurea. This drug had a dramatic effect on the patient's psoriasis, which virtually disappeared, and regular outpatient attendances to the psoriasis bathrooms became unnecessary. In fact, the psoriasis was so well controlled that the patient needed to be seen only every 6 weeks, very briefly to monitor progress and any complications of the drug therapy.

The patient failed to keep his last follow-up appointment with me and I was very saddened to learn that he had committed suicide by throwing himself in front of a train. This event led me to wonder whether I had really helped this man by virtually eliminating his psoriasis. By doing this, I had also eliminated the need for him to attend the outpatient department regularly. He had no local family and few local friends and his relationships with the nurses in the psoriasis bathrooms may have become very important to him. There may, therefore, be times when it is important that the dermatologist does not win the battle.

REFERENCES

Al-Ahmar H F, Kurban A K 1976 Psychological profile of patients with atopic dermatitis. British Journal of Dermatology 95: 373–377
Bär L H J, Kuypers B R M 1973 Behaviour therapy in dermatological practice. British Journal of Dermatology 88: 591–598
Brown D G, Bettley F R 1971 Psychiatric treatment of eczema: a controlled trial. British Medical Journal 1: 729–734
Brown D G 1972 Stress as a precipitant factor of eczema. Journal of Psychosomatic Research 16: 321–327
Cataldo M F, Varni J W, Russo D C, Estes S A 1980 Behaviour therapy techniques in treatment of exfoliative dermatitis. Archives of Dermatology 116: 919–922
Coles R B 1965 Treatment of psoriasis in groups. Medical World 2: 1
Coles R B 1967 Group therapy in the skin department. Transactions of the St John's Hospital Dermatological Society 53: 82–85
Cotterill J A 1981 Dermatological games. British Journal of Dermatology 105: 311–320
Farber E M, Bright R D, Nall M L 1968 Psoriasis. A questionnaire survey of 2,144 patients. Archives of Dermatology 98: 248–259
Gilbert A R, Rodgers D A, Roegnik H 1973 Evaluation of psoriasis. Cleveland Clinics Quarterly 40: 147–150
Goldsmith L A, Fisher M, Wacks J 1969 Psychological characteristics of psoriasis. Archives of Dermatology 100: 674–676
Hardy G E, Cotterill J A 1982 A study of depression and obsessionality in dysmorphophobic and psoriatic patients. British Journal of Psychiatry 140: 19–22
Jobling R G 1976 Psoriasis — a preliminary questionnaire study of sufferers. Subjective experiences. Clinical and Experimental Dermatology 1: 233–236
Lancet Editorial 1985 Emotion and immunity 2: 133–134
Melin L, Norén P, Frederiksen T, Swebelius B G 1986 Behavioural treatment of scratching in patients with atopic dermatitis. British Journal of Dermatology 115: 467–474
Mitchell E B, Chapman M D, Pope F M, Crow J, Jouhal S S, Platts-Mills T A 1982 Basophils in allergen-induced patch test sites in atopic dermatitis. Lancet 1: 127–130
Monk B E, Neill S M 1986 The role of alcohol consumption in the natural history of psoriasis. British Journal of Dermatology 115 (suppl 30): 11–12
Musaph H 1983 Psychogenic pruritus. Seminars in Dermatology 2: 217–222
Obermeyer M E 1955 Psychosomatic medicine. Charles C Thomas, Springfield, Illinois
Paljan B, Kinsky A, Cividina-Stranič E 1984 Psychosomatic factors influencing the course of psoriasis. Acta Dermatologica and Venerologica (Stockholm) (suppl 113): 121–122
Palos E, Ring J, Zimmermann A 1986 Psychosomatic aspects of parent/child relations in atopic eczema. Paper read at the European Society for Dermatological Research and the Society for Investigative Dermatology Fifth Joint Meeting, Geneva

Panconesi E 1984a Stress and skin diseases: psychosomatic dermatology. Clinics in
    Dermatology II 4: 110–125
Panconesi E 1984b Stress and skin diseases: psychosomatic dermatology. Clinics in
    Dermatology II 4: 131
Payne R A, Rowland-Payne C M E, Marks R 1985 Stress does not worsen psoriasis? —
    A controlled study of 32 patients. Clinical and Experimental Dermatology 10: 239–235
Savin J A, Patterson W D, Oswald I 1973 Scratching during sleep. Lancet 2: 296–297
Seville R H 1977 Psoriasis and stress. British Journal of Dermatology 97: 297–302

16

Renal failure

INTRODUCTION

Planning improvements in the psychological aspects of care for people in renal failure (or any other serious illness) takes one directly to a fundamental policy decision. There are basically two alternative approaches and, while these are not necessarily mutually exclusive, it is difficult to avoid a commitment of emphasis to one which, with limited resources, will then reduce involvement in the other. To highlight the contrasting objectives, I will term these the casualty-based and preventive approaches, with the obvious implication that the former involves assisting individuals who have become psychological casualties in illness while the latter implies the objective of preventing such casualties. Those contemplating developments in the psychological side of renal medicine are faced quite simply with a dilemma — which approach to adopt.

The casualty-based approach is familiar and clearly described by Lipowski (1982). Salmons & Blainey (1982) provide typical examples of the approach in a kidney unit. Noting the high incidence of psychological difficulties amongst people surviving by dialysis or dealing with life after a transplant, the key role they describe is that of the visiting expert in psychological matters who receives requests from the nephrologists for assistance with individual cases.

Such a system is part of the stable structure of medicine, well established and aided by decades of experience. Why then the dilemma in policy making, why change anything? If I may continue with a nautical metaphor, then I can say that during the last 10 years my sense of direction in psychological work with people suffering renal failure has changed from that of working on a constantly shifting bearing, by which I mean doing whatever psychological work seemed necessary in relation to the nature of the 'casualty' referred, to working on an alternative, constant bearing. The target of this constant bearing is a scheme of preventive psychological care which *guarantees* a sequence of stress-reducing interventions for all clients of the kidney unit and their immediate family. The change is underpinned by the conviction (supported by plenty of evidence) that many of the so-

261

called psychological casualties treated in the approach of workers like Salmons & Blainey are *needless casualties* generated not by the cruelties of renal failure itself, but by the psychological neglect and psychological stress imposed on these people by the prevailing system of care. The challenge is then that those working with a conventional, casualty-based approach spend much of their energy treating *distress which is produced by the system of care itself*. Inefficiency of this order is obviously unacceptable and, thus, commitment has to be towards a preventive style of care.

Such a commitment does require a wholly different working style to that of the conventional approach. The introduction of a programme of preventive psychological care, particularly in a general hospital setting, requires an initial phase in which the attitude, knowledge and working practices of the staff become the main objects of attention rather than those in renal failure. Hence the dilemma in policy making, since transfer of direct attention away from those with obvious needs clearly evokes difficulties for any therapist. However, without this critically important phase of education and re-orientation, experience shows that little really changes and the seriously ill not only have to contend with the stress of their illness but also to continue absorbing the hardships unwittingly created by a staff without psychological insight and objectives.

THE NEED FOR PREVENTIVE PSYCHOLOGICAL CARE

Since 1978 my brief has been that of appraising the psychological aspects of care in a typical renal unit. The basic question in mind has been 'what psychological objectives are reasonable for the staff of such a unit to hold, and what approach will best help them secure these?' This inquiry has slowly given birth to the so-called 'psychological care project', with its clear emphasis on preventive issues. The rationale involves two arguments. Firstly, and obviously, the provision of psychological care for seriously ill people and their partners is necessary since illness and handicap cause stress and, thence, distress. Failure to deal with this properly amounts to poor quality of care and probably poor quality of life for the people involved, a theme which has been expanded at length by Nichols (1984).

There is, however, an equally powerful justification for psychological care in relation to physical treatment and its outcome. Thus, secondly, preventive psychological care underpins physical treatment such that, in its absence, the efficiency of physical treatment may be seriously diminished. It is, therefore, an essential ingredient of overall care which pays for itself by maximising the potential of physical treatment.

Nowhere is this simple equation better demonstrated than in the field of renal medicine. In extreme examples which I have, sadly, witnessed on several occasions, the investment of enormous amounts of medical and nursing time, the effort of several years of physical treatment, the expense of several years of dialysis (in excess of £13 000 per year) plus various surgical interventions have been wiped out by the destructive impact of inadequate psychological care: in particular, insufficient information and education to give understanding, isolation with powerful and destructive emotional reactions, consequent high levels of stress, loss of morale and negative beliefs which are acted out in various forms of non-compliance. In other words, the risk in neglecting psychological care is that of producing a failure to maintain self-care through compliance with dietary and treatment regimes, both of which are essential for survival for those on dialysis ('dialysands'). It is in this sense that excellence in medical treatment can be neutralised by the neglect of psychological care.

Thus it is no surprise to learn that Wai et al (1981), on following the fortunes of 285 people surviving on home dialysis, found that physiological variables had little relationship to outcome, whereas certain psychosocial variables, in particular depression, discriminated clearly between survivors and non-survivors. Similarly, and reflecting the importance of the attitudes and approach of staff, Kaplan De-Nour (1983), reporting an extended study of 100 dialysands, was able to demonstrate that unrealistic expectations, denial and lack of agreement in staff had a strong relationship with poor adjustment, poor compliance and poor survival rates.

Sources of stress

Preventive psychological care depends on a thorough and honest awareness of the stressors likely to be encountered in renal failure. I say honest, because not all the information is likely to be comfortable since it may well imply deficiencies in the working practices of a unit. Also, as Kaplan De-Nour & Czackes (1974) have shown, supervising medical staff are likely to function with a personal need to see well-being where it does not exist, with a consequent denial of the hardships and distress suffered by clients.

Nichols & Springford (1984) conducted an independent survey of the stressors experienced by 34 dialysands training in the techniques of, and surviving by, haemodialysis (HD) and peritoneal dialysis (PD), the latter including some people using continuous ambulatory peritoneal dialysis (CAPD), the bag-change method which has since the time of data collection become much more prevalent in use. Clear conclusions emerged. These people and their families did have very heavy burdens to bear and often suffered much distress. Stress came from many sources but basically these sources were the system of care and the dialysis.

1. Stress related to the system of care

Abstracting from the findings of the Nichols & Springford (1984) survey, and adding some 8 years of clinical observation, the following serve as examples of powerful but wholly avoidable stressors imposed by the physically oriented approach to renal medicine.

Poor teaching. Patients and their partners have enormous amounts to learn in terms of technique and life management. For those on haemodialysis, this involves complex skills such as venepuncture and dialysis session management. Yet, although good teaching was essential, nurses had no training as teachers and teaching was non-systematic and often poor in quality, which created additional pressures and anxiety.

Inadequate general communication. There was no *scheme* for ensuring that clients were kept informed (and that they understood) in the fast flow of events. Confusion, anger or apprehension was a frequent consequence.

Staff were out of touch and lacking insight. Listening skills were poor and there was minimal effort to make contact with the real needs and experiences of clients and their relatives. Staff exerted a 'pressure to be well and not be a nuisance' and were inclined to project well-being. The sense that staff failed to comprehend the nature of the difficulties caused much distress to some clients.

Staff were ill at ease with emotional reactions. The *normal* predictable reactions by clients and partners were treated like infections, that is, as something to do battle with. Comprehension by the staff was poor and distancing was common, which caused further isolation and suffering for those in a state of reaction. Derogatory concepts such as 'making a fuss' or 'not pulling their weight' were freely used by some staff when encountering anxiety or depression.

Partners were conscripted as medical auxilliaries. There was little awareness by staff of the enormous burdens that home dialysis placed upon the partners. Social and moral pressure was exerted to ensure that partners continued in the role of dialysis assistant even in the context of marital breakdown or anxiety state. Some partners were very distressed, some trapped and desperate.

Home dialysis families were 'set adrift' on their own. The loss of contact between the unit and those who had completed their training and converted to home dialysis was marked. The experience of abandonment, although not intended, was highly stressing for some partners.

In an attempt to find a common source of these characteristics, much seems to be accounted for in the perpetuation of the role of 'a patient' as the foil to the role of the traditional doctor and nurse. Little is required of 'a patient' save passivity and a mute acceptance of whatever the medical or nursing staff think best. There is no sense of active coparticipation, no negotiation and few personal responsibilities in the patient role — people are converted into objects to which things are done. Consequently, there is no built-in *obligation* in the nursing and medical roles to monitor the personal effects of treatment decisions, to prepare people for the experiences to come or to make the same considerate provision that one would make for people in other spheres of life. For example, the essential work of keeping 'patients' properly and regularly informed of what is happening and what is going to happen reduces to a matter of personal whim on the part of a doctor. It is not a *guaranteed* component in the medical role, as studies of the woeful failure to inform people of their illness show (Elian & Dean 1985). In fact, what the Nichols & Springford (1984) study tapped into was a defective *system* of care.

Blodgett (1981), in an extensive review, allocates a substantial section to the influence that staff attitudes, both to the task of care and to their clients, can have on the well-being of the people involved. He notes that 'over time the outcome of these relationships may not only influence adjustment, but survival itself', a conclusion verified in objective studies by Kaplan De-Nour (1983) and illustrated by a personal account from a young couple in the last chapter of Nichols (1984).

2. Stress related to survival by dialysis

The vast body of the literature on renal failure echoes a recurring theme — life in renal failure is highly stress-laden for the majority of those involved. Transplantation may bring some, but not total relief, and the risk of the transplant failing always smoulders in the background. We need to encompass some aspects of the life to understand this situation and appreciate the nature of the stress.

From primitive beginnings, dialysis technology has now developed to a degree of sophistication. The techniques available are variants of either haemodialysis or peritoneal dialysis. In haemodialysis, blood is diverted from major vessels, passed through an artificial kidney which simulates some kidney functions by a complex process of hydrostatic ultrafiltration and diffusion, and returned. Access to the bloodstream is a difficulty since high flow rates are required. The standard solution is the surgical creation of a fistula, i.e. an anastomosis between a substantial artery and vein, usually in the forearm. Cannulae are then inserted to draw and return blood for the duration of a dialysis session. Dialysis sessions usually take about 5–6 hours, at a frequency of three times per week. The assistance of a partner or nurse is necessary. Training for home dialysis takes 6 months and requires the acquisition of significant skills and acceptance of consider-able responsibility. The fistula may fail and, for some, this initiates a difficult struggle for 'access'.

In peritoneal dialysis, a permanent catheter is inserted in the abdominal cavity. A fluid, termed 'dialysate', which attracts water, ions and the break-down products of metabolism from the blood, is fed into the body cavity. Osmosis and diffusion occur through the walls of the blood vessels in the peritoneum and digestive system and the fluid becomes saturated with excess or waste blood contents. The dialysate is then removed and the operation continuously recycled with fresh dialysate. A machine system can be used, with dialysis sessions on alternating nights. Usually, though, CAPD with four bag changes per day, each day, is favoured. CAPD offers the advantage of 'steady-state' as opposed to 'tidal' blood chemistry, better control of hypertension, reduced cardiovascular stress, fewer problems with anaemia and fewer dietary restrictions; it is marginally cheaper, does not need a partner's assistance and requires less training time (Burton et al 1983). Set against this is the daily monotony of four time-consuming bag changes, the disfigurement of a permanent abdominal catheter site and the ever-present risk of peritonitis should sterile technique be other than good. Shurr et al (1984) report that 56% of a sample of CAPD users had sustained one or more episodes of peritonitis with time on CAPD ranging from 1 month to 3 years. Repeated or intractable infections prevent the continued use of the system.

People in renal failure now live, whereas before they would have died. Relationships continue and some activities can be preserved which, for most clients, makes the many hardships and burdens worthwhile. There is no sense in pretending that life carries on as normal though; or that it is other than a difficult life for both the dialysand and partner. Some groups fare better than others. For example, those in partial rather than total kidney failure probably do better physically, as do younger, more resilient people who were active prior to their illness. Psychologically, older, retired people may prove more able to adapt and will settle simply for the continuation of their main relationship and the companionship therein, which allows a more positive attitude to dialysis, as a 'friend' that extends life. In comparison, younger people, at the expansive phase of life, who are attempting to start a career, make relationships or start a family, usually find the situation fraught with obstacles, which sometimes generates bitter resentment towards dialysis (Shurr et al 1984). The issue of whether those surviving by haemodialysis are better off than those using CAPD is complicated by so many situational and personality issues that it is unsafe to make generalisations.

While dialysis simulates kidney function, it does not do so perfectly and thus leaves the client in a fluctuating, toxic state of uraemia. The fluctuating nature of this uraemia is more marked with haemodialysis. For those who do less well, this produces an insidious, multisystem failure. Myopathy often becomes a major problem with consequent great loss of muscle power. This may eventually reduce walking range to about 100 yards at a time and make lifting everyday domestic objects difficult. Anaemia is another likely effect which produces great fatigue. In the Nichols & Springford (1984) survey, over 50% of sufferers complained of constant tiredness and weakness, an invisible but serious handicap. This effect may become amplified in the familiar circular effect of depression, as Cardenas & Kutner (1982) report following a study of 137 dialysands.

Many dialysands also suffer various associated minor ills. In the Nichols & Springford survey, these included itching skin (63%), cramps (50%) and jumpy legs (30%), together with a high incidence of headache and nausea. Forty-four per cent of those in their first year complained that they felt weak and ill between dialysis, and especially so just after dialysis. Uraemia also brings mood changes in the form of depression and irritability, and where antihypertensive drugs are used, these also tend to evoke depressed states. Concentration may be diminished, making intellectual tasks and reading difficult. Lastly, a proportion of both sexes are likely to suffer sexual losses in the form of partial or total impotence in men, reduced capability for sexual arousal in women and an impaired or even abandoned sexual life. The proportion affected is not firmly established since different studies produce a wide range of prevalence figures for sexual dysfunction varying between 28% and 100% (Degen et al 1983). However, as an example Levy (1973) found 49% of 202 men to have increased sexual problems while Procci & Martin (1985) found that although sexual activity did not progressively deteriorate over a period of 30 months in men undergoing haemodialysis, nevertheless, against normal populations, there were clear reductions in sexual activity with 55% of the men complaining of erectile failure. Salmons & Blainey (1982) believe that a similar proportion of women suffer failure in sexual arousal and women may find greater difficulty with the issues of disfigurement and body image.

At an individual level, these impersonal figures reduce down to the guilt of a young woman who, as well as being absent from the home 3 days a week for dialysis and training, being too weak to shop, deal with the children and cope with housework with any real degree of effectiveness, is searching for ways to explain to her husband that she cannot respond sexually any more, nor summon the physical energy for normal intercourse. Or the frightened, tearful, middle aged man who feels that having had to give up his job and the 'male tasks' in the home, his impotence will be the last straw for his wife.

Several clients have described to me how the lengthy phase of predialysis uraemic deterioration was like waiting for a sentence of punishment to begin. The visits for familiarisation and preparation of a fistula or peritoneal catheter can evoke haunting fears for those 'in waiting'. Little is written of this phase of the dialysis career but the clinical glimpses are worrying and clearly show the need for maximum support and care.

Much better known is the impact of training for home dialysis and the actual conversion to home dialysis. Haemodialysis is without doubt more demanding than CAPD since the dialysand and partner are effectively being asked to master advanced medical technology at a time of enormous personal crisis. Training to *full* self-sufficiency takes a year or more, the first 3–6 months of this being unit-based, normally occupying 3 days a week, a good proportion of which time the partner needs to be present. Between them, the couple have to learn the skills of monitoring blood pressure, preparation of the machine and lines, venepuncture, sterile technique in these procedures and the ensuing attachment of blood lines, understanding and responding correctly to machine alarms, the use of anticoagulants, the management of dialysis for 4–5 hours, ultrafiltration, coming off the machine, and dealing with problems such as blood leaks, pressure abnormalities, etc. Not surprisingly, the effect of learning these skills and the burden of responsibility for dialysis at home thereafter weighs heavily on many of those involved. The stress element was clearly revealed in the Nichols & Springford (1984) survey with 67% of dialysands in their training year reporting anxiety and tension prior to dialysis and during needling, 46% of partners worrying that they would not be able to deal with emergencies in dialysis, and over one-third of the partners feeling anxious when running a dialysis session and frightened of making a mistake which would cause serious difficulties or death.

Those who use CAPD have a less burdensome task in training, which is normally completed within 6–8 weeks. Partners do not have any essential involvement. Nevertheless, the tedious, exact and fairly lengthy procedures of a bag change, together with the ever-present risk of peritonitis, certainly cause difficulties for some of these people. In the Shurr et al (1984) study, 50% of the sample reported experiencing feelings that life was not worth living and had thought about suicide. This was more likely in younger people (mean age 41 years against a mean age of 55 years). From personal clinical experience, I find that people with somewhat obsessive personalities can struggle with this technique rather more than others, particularly after the first episode of peritonitis.

The actual conversion to home dialysis involves a significant psychological shift from the nurturing atmosphere of the unit, with staff ever present to give advice, instant medical assistance and support, to that of home, with no company and no ready support or assistance. The disorientating and alarming impact of the change is discussed by Brey & Jarvis (1983).

3. The stressful impact on life.

In general, both forms of dialysis intrude greatly into the pattern of normal life. In haemodialysis the dialysand can never be more than 2 or 3 days away from the machine. The dialysis sessions, each of 5–6 hours, must take place three times a week. Dialysis can be taken as an evening event for those who work but, even so, it is hardly welcomed as something to return home to three nights a week. It is also a physical intrusion in the sense that a room must be completely set aside to provide a suitable operating environment for the equipment. Similarly, with CAPD, the bag changes four times a day, which must be conducted with exacting care, are tedious and demanding, particularly away from home.

The requirements of dialysis and the physical changes described above inevitably lead to considerable losses in role. In the short term there is severe disruption for all in occupational, recreational, social and family roles. In the long term, whether or not these losses are sustained depends on the adjustment achieved and that in turn is determined by personality (Kaplan De-Nour 1981), family and cultural factors (Streltzer 1983, Lowry & Atcherson 1980) and the perception of the situation, particularly where this involves a sense of personal diminution (Landsman 1978) or intrusive-ness and loss of control (Devins et al 1984). Incidentally, Schreiber & Huber (1985), in a comparison of home and unit-based haemodialysis clients, concluded that although relieved of the personal responsibilities of home dialysis, those regularly having dialysis in the renal unit were more stressed, so location is also an important factor.

Kaplan De-Nour (1983) reported that only 28% of dialysands achieved full occupational rehabilitation and 35% made no progress at all. Shurr et al (1984) found CAPD clients to achieve a somewhat better level of re-habilitation, although their inclusion of house-keeping activities as a form of self-employment may have influenced figures in a positive way. Sherwood (1983) produced a useful survey, with 55 American dialysands of mixed ethnic extraction. By use of an extensive, structured interview, life domains were identified which were moderately or seriously affected by dialysis, viz.:

employment activity	66%	ability to enjoy life	40%
vocational activity	57%	social contacts	40%
leisure-time pursuits	57%	self-esteem	36%
eating habits	57%	relationships with friends	31%
sexual activity	53%	family relationships	29%

Nichols & Springford (1984) also included general life activities reflecting much the same situation as Sherwood revealed. However, of particular note was the erosion of morale and esteem in key relationships. Thus, dialysands in their first year reported:

feeling no good as a parent	60%
feeling that there is too much strain on my partner	57%
I feel I'm spoiling my partner's life	50%
I'm difficult to live with	43%
feeling no good as a husband/wife	36%

Also of significance for those of a preventive persuasion, 31% of dialy-sands reported being *ashamed* because they were depressed or anxious. This serves as a pertinent example of unnecessary stress: *because* there had been no forewarning of emotional ups and downs, no permission given for these, and no guiding intervention, these people suffered further in the experience of normal, predictable and common reactions.

Dietary restrictions for those on CAPD are relatively mild; those on haemodialysis have a stricter regime which can include fluid limits of 800 ml per day for those in complete renal failure. Thus, 43% of dialysands reported craving for liquid (Nichols & Springford 1984), evidence of a difficult daily struggle akin to that of the alcoholic. In Kaplan De-Nour's (1983) study, only 23% were able properly to comply with the required regime and 39% fell into the gross dietary abuse category. Most clients find failure to comply with fluid and dietary restrictions a stressful issue, full of conflict and guilt and a never-ending struggle which starts each day on waking up. Lastly, we should note the shortened life span and threat of death which affects those surviving by dialysis. In Kaplan De-Nour's (1983) longitudinal study of 100 dialysands, 37 died within 5 years.

The stressful impact of dialysis on partners must also concern us. Approximately half of the requests I receive for individual assistance and therapy at the Exeter unit are to do with partners. Many unwittingly foster an unnecessary dependency on the part of the dialysand and become trapped by the invalid role which they have helped create, again illustrating the need for preventive work with the family (Nichols 1986). Others slip into emotional exhaustion with the demands of dialysis, recurring physical crises for the dialysand and the greatly increased work load involved in taking on some of the dialysand's former roles. In Nichols & Springford (1984), partners responded thus:

feeling depressed at how he/she has changed	61%
feeling exhausted	54%
finding his/her depression hard to bear	31%
feeling trapped because he/she depends on me so much	27%
the staff do not realise how difficult life is	40%

I am not able to include a section on dialysis in children. It is a highly fraught and difficult experience for parents and children alike, which merits separate attention. Several chapters in Levy (1983) deal with the topic.

Evidence of the stress

Many papers chart the extent of psychological disturbance in these populations. I will select a few statistics to make this point. Kaplan De-Nour (1983) records 53% of the dialysands to be moderately or severely depressed, 30% to be moderately or severely anxious and 27% to pass through episodes of suicidal risk. Kutner et al (1985) assessed 128 dialysands using a battery of established scales. They found that over half of these people manifest signs of depression with 26.6% established as unequivocally depressed. Similarly, 45% of the sample manifest clinical anxiety. Livesley (1982), studying a group of dialysands in Scotland, employed the Symptoms of Anxiety and Depression (SAD) Scale and found that the mean anxiety and depression score for the group was significantly higher than the norm for the general population, although it was lower than the norm for the psychiatric population. Farmer et al (1979), using Goldberg's interview schedule, assessed 32 dialysands and found a point prevalence for psychiatric morbidity (i.e. proportion at any specific time) of 31%.

The partners of dialysands are known to have a prevalence of psychological disorder above that of the normal population too. Lowry & Atcherson (1986) discuss the findings in a review of various studies concerned with the psychological state of spouse-assistants involved in home haemodialysis. Some of the studies indicate that up to 75% of spouse-assistants are adversely affected, experiencing depression and anxiety at a rate which exceeds that in the dialysands. Lowry & Atcherson's own study, which was used to show the benefit of an improved training and support programme, yielded less dramatic figures. Their sample found the first few months of training and then functioning independently as a dialysis assistant to be the most demanding, with 38% reporting depressed mood and disturbed sleep, 31% reporting anxiety-related effects and 28% irritability. These proportions declined somewhat with the passage of time. The study did not involve a lengthy follow-up, however, and the authors speculate that in the longer term, problems and negative reactions increase. There was certainly some evidence to confirm this speculation in the study by Nichols & Springford (1984).

I want to close this section on stress in dialysis with a qualification. Not all dialysands and their partners become locked in such an unenviable and disheartening struggle. Some do make successful adjustment and settle to the routines of dialysis while living a life basically free of major upset, despite the stresses. Much depends on the way that the particular renal units run things.

Transplantation and stress

This, too, is a section which truly merits a separate chapter. I am, therefore, limited to a very brief indication of the psychological aspects to be considered in relation to transplants.

Some dialysands build enormous hopes on the possibility of a transplant. One or two I have met actually had difficulty leaving their house in case a call came through saying that a matching kidney had been found. For the majority, though, it is a hoped-for escape route which also carries the frightening risk of failure and disappointment. It is kept in the background unless active plans are made for a transplant from a living donor.

During the last few years, a new immunosuppressor, cyclosporin, has improved success rates and become favoured since it does not have the distressing effect of cushingoid facial disfigurement which steroid immunosuppressors produce. However, it is a difficult drug to use, is actually nephrotoxic so can lead to difficult clinical management problems and is unpleasant to take (Woodhams 1986).

Simmons (1983) offers a useful survey of 237 people receiving transplants between 1970 and 1973 and then followed through for between 5 and 9 years. Most were still alive in 1981 and 71% (related live-donor transplants) and 47% (cadaveric transplants) still had the original graft functioning. In terms of physical, psychological and social well-being, the picture was moderately good, with the exception of diabetic transplantees who generally had a much more troubled passage. Much of the negative impact of uraemia had gone and about two-thirds had improved in terms of self-image and self-esteem and were in a reasonable psychological state. Most had found that their sexual life was improved and 83% of the non-diabetic men had resumed work.

Other authors have less positive findings, although we should bear in mind that all the studies cited below refer to conventional treatment using steroid-based immunosuppression. Chambers (1983) writes: 'at some stage practically all transplant patients experience episodes of anxiety, depression and anger secondary to complications, painful treatment, drug therapy. . . .'

The first few weeks of a transplant can indeed be harrowing, particularly if there is a physical problem or rejection crisis which causes it to 'hover' for days (or weeks) on the margins of non-functioning failure. Fortunately, cyclosporin has reduced the risk of this. Muthny (1984) found that a large proportion of transplantees showed great strain during such times, particularly so if the graft eventually failed.

Chambers (1983) and also Freyberger (1983) suggest predictable stages in emotional reaction to a transplant. A period of great hope combined with fear of failure yields to a more relaxed state as the graft functions and health improves. Things then become more complicated again with fears of rejection, feelings of fragility and issues to do with acceptance of the graft itself and the new state of being. These stages are plausible but unsubstantiated. Certainly, it is a very busy time emotionally. The new kidney is sited low in the front of the abdomen, 'tapped' into the femoral artery and linked to the bladder. Chambers (1983) claims that there can be difficulties in accepting the graft as part of one's own body. There is a sense of hosting an alien presence. This is more likely if the donor was of the opposite gender. Where the organ is donated by a live relative, there can be great emotional complications, particularly in the event of a failure which is likely to evoke much guilt and self-recrimination.

With steroid immunosuppression, the facial disfigurement can lead to compliance problems. This is more likely with young people, especially women (Stewart 1983). Armstrong & Weiner (1982) offer a useful illustration of the complicated family dynamics involved and discuss several cases of active non-compliance which have led to the graft being destroyed. While, for the majority, a working kidney brings a joyous rebirth and much improved health and strength, not all clients find it so simple. Muthny (1984) comments that the transition from the invalid role, dependency and abundant care to relative health and unaccustomed independence is frightening. Several of his clients reacted with relief when their grafts failed.

Most transplantees adjust to living with the threat that their new kidney could fail at any time. However, if it does fail after a period of normal functioning, it can be a devastating blow that may lead to decline and eventual 'psychosomatic death', as described in the introduction to Nichols (1984).

A SCHEME OF PSYCHOLOGICAL CARE

Petersen (1985), in discussing the circumstances of 'dialysis families', includes a quotation from Horejsi which, for me, exactly catches the problem which we should be striving to eliminate. I can do no better than repeat it: 'We seem to be able to offer services once the family has nearly destroyed itself or is in genuine crisis, but don't do much to prevent the destruction in the first place.'

The practice of preventive psychological care seeks to assert the opposite situation. This is the scheme which has been piloted at the Exeter Renal Unit and has been described in Nichols (1984, 1985, 1987) and Woodhams (1984 a,b). It is essentially an attempt to forge a collaborative alliance between staff and clients in order to maintain a stress-reducing regime. The history of the difficulties in developing the scheme and of its central depen- dence on the nursing profession is given in Nichols (1985). The approach involves the whole staff but with the nurses as front-line workers. It involves change in both attitude and practice, as outlined below. My position is that the *psychological management* of people in renal failure must be based on a scheme of this type.

Staff objectives

The core role of the specialist in psychological work in a unit, whether it be psychologist, psychiatrist or social worker, must be that of education and leadership in psychological matters. The first priority has to be to 'market' the principles, practices and objectives of preventive psychological care so that nursing and medical staff understand, value and share these. As an example, I will list the objectives which I, as a psychologist, and the senior nurse at the Exeter Renal Unit now jointly hold and publicly declare.

1. We seek to eradicate the notion of passive 'patients'. In its place, we try to build long-term relationships with people who are seen as clients, or better, as 'associates' of the care team. (As yet, no-one has come up with a truly suitable role title.)

2. We endeavour to make a provision of psychological care that is avail- able to all clients and partners. The objective is to 'head-off' problems and minimise stress by means of a carefully planned educational and support strategy.

3. We endeavour to maintain a psychological surveillance and also encourage clients to share difficulties with us at an early stage. There is a specialist back-up service of psychological therapy and thus, when care alone is insufficient, therapy is available. We do not allow a situation where clients need the 'ticket' of a breakdown in order to attract attention and receive the benefits of this service.

4. We work to the idea that our clients are active participants with a *responsibility for self-care*. A major component of self-care is making use of

the provisions offered by the nurses and psychologist in terms of information, education, emotional support and counselling.

5. We seek, through the medium of constant training, to maintain a body of nurses who regard psychological care as a key part of their duties. In the context of a primary nursing scheme they are allocated responsibility for the educational programme and psychological well-being of specific clients. The basic provision of psychological care is thus *guaranteed* for all clients, not just those who are overtly distressed. To underpin this, we try to instil in the nurses a sense of independent accountability in relation to this guarantee of psychological care. They give the care because it feels a *necessary* part of their job, not because someone else prescribed it. Naturally, other professionals are not excluded from contributing to this care but the emphasis on the nurses arises because in a renal unit they alone have a work pattern which allows the intensive contact of the type needed for this care.

The components of psychological care

In setting up a scheme of this type, it is important to produce a structure and function that is within the capability of nursing staff and which blends with their everyday duties. It clearly cannot depend on the contribution of an outside expert who is only occasionally present. The basic structure evolved is described below.

1. Monitoring psychological state

The nurse is taught to be aware of the psychological condition of her client and to check it regularly. She uses a straightforward approach based on questions like 'how is he coping, are there signs of emotional change or distress, is he perceiving the situation in realistic terms and is the behaviour appropriate for the situation? What are the current anxieties and problems?'

A very brief written report (ideally negotiated with the client) is lodged with records every 2 weeks or so to encourage a proper formulation of observations and thoughts. Use of psychiatric nomenclature is not sought. What is sought, however, is a constructive response from the nurse in relation to her observations. She is *responsible* for ensuring that action is taken with one or more of the care strategies given below.

2. Emotional care

The nurses are taught that serious illness almost inevitably provokes emotional activity. However, in the majority of cases these responses are aspects of normal, predictable, emotional processing (e.g. a response to threat against personal security in life, or responses to loss of role and body functions). Thus, such emotional activity should be expected, valued and respected rather than construed as something alien, to be attacked and subdued by one means or another. Rather than bland reassurances, blocking strategies or immediate recourse to the drug cupboard, care procedures are taught which facilitate the expression of feeling and so aid emotional processing.

Emotional care is always available in the unit should crises occur, but its real input is at the low-key, everyday, preventive level. The nurse will take the initiative and regularly make time to ask her clients how things are and whether they have issues which they would like to share and talk through. Isolation is broken and, ideally, the shame so often evoked by intense personal feeling is displaced by the sense that this is important work to be done and that it is valued by the staff.

A small proportion of clients become disturbed by reactions which need therapy in addition to this care. These are referred to the psychologist or psychiatrist on the basis of a collective decision by the nursing and medical team.

3. Informational care

The nurses are trained to regard information exchange as having much the same character as the physical routines of nursing, that is, it cannot be done once and be considered complete. Instead, because of distortion, selective forgetting, lack of understanding and the changing nature of circumstances, information has to be continually renewed and consolidated. The objective in informational care is to maintain the information which a client and his partner hold at a level of accuracy and sufficiency such that they have *realistic* expectations of their near future. For example, if a peritoneal catheter is to be inserted, they will know why, how the surgery will be conducted and experienced, have an awareness of complications such as blockage, leaking and infection which will require further intervention and will be planning around a broad time band of possible life disruption to cater for these. No *predictable* outcome should take them by surprise because the information will have been shared in advance by the nurses. If expectations are to remain realistic, the work of correcting and updating knowledge must become a routine. Knowledge of the current clinical plan, its rationale, the likely course of medical and surgical intervention together with information on the nature and likelihood of possible setbacks, side effects and complications must be offered to clients on a very regular basis to achieve effective prevention of stress. Of course, people may worry, but if briefed in a problem-sharing/problem-solving way and with a sense of proper support, the worry is realistic and productive, allowing psychological preparation. The opposite approach, that is, the conspiratorial style, allows no preparation and renders people very vulnerable. They are required to find out on their own the negative impact of side effects, or the possibilities of surgical failure, complications and setbacks. Many find this situation highly traumatic. Informational care is primarily a matter of professional, planned information exchange to achieve maximum care. Much emphasis is put on checking exactly what people do know, a requirement captured by a phrase which we use a great deal to remind ourselves of the need, i.e. 'something told does *not* mean something heard, remembered and understood'. Supporting this effort, much work also goes into the preparation of materials for general educational purposes, so that standard information is delivered consistently and the time drain on nurses is minimised. Informational care cannot be forced on people. It is a matter of making a clear invitation to share information. Some will be in a condition where they cannot deal with it or are too ill to cope with anything much at all. Others may be in a defensive state of denial which blocks involvement. Therefore, how far to proceed has to be a matter for the sensitive judgement of the nurses. In this work, communication skills are clearly at a premium. As an aid, nurses are taught to use the IIFAC routine (Nichols 1984) whenever they are engaged in information exchange. In brief:

I   Initial check: established whether the client is in a suitable state to receive information and, by questioning, check his actual knowledge carefully before beginning

I   Information exchange: impart the necessary information in manageable packages using suitable language, notes and diagrams. Ideally, record the session so that it can be played again later by the client

FAC   final accuracy check: have the client repeat back the basic content in order to check for distortion and completeness. Correct as necessary

4. *Counselling*

As nurses become more experienced and confident with psychological work, the care role is extended by a counselling activity. Training is either internal or external by means of continuing nurse education courses. The counselling is of an elementary type and not intended as a substitute therapy. The aim in training is to shift the nurses away from giving advice to a mode of functioning in which they assist a person to talk through issues, help elaborate the perception of a situation and help clarify the options available in solving problems.

5. *Representing client's needs — Advocacy.*

Because of her knowledge of a client and the family involved, the nurse is well placed to contribute to the general case planning. She is also able to make known to her medical colleagues any particular needs or difficulties which trouble the client and family to ensure that these are taken into account and proper assistance given where this is necessary. This will include securing a referral to the psychologist or psychiatrist. Such a role is not always easy for young nurses and a degree of confidence-building and assertion training may be necessary.

6. Personal support

Finally, nurses are taught to regard support for themselves as a major professional responsibility. Involvement in this work and the regular exposure to the distress of others *without* adequate support is construed as a form of self-neglect and is much frowned upon. The support systems advised are of individual or group contact with the psychologist, a support network scheme amongst nurses for immediate response to difficulties and scheduled support meetings run by the nurses for less urgent business.

The approach seeks to provide stress-reducing care from the first moment of contact with the renal unit. However, the contact may extend for many years and it is equally important that there is no abandonment, the preventive concern must persist in the long term.

Routine medical surveillance and assistance is maintained by the doctors in the renal unit. However, the role of monitoring psychological well-being and providing care falls primarily to the home sisters. These are experienced nurses with counselling training who maintain a monitoring and support function with all clients on home dialysis. Their role is to maintain a contact with clients through periodic home visits. They operate the psychological care scheme on an extended time and extended geographical basis.

PSYCHOLOGICAL THERAPY

As you will now know, I am recommending that the first priority in the renal unit is the creation of a training apparatus and working structure to give preventive psychological care for all clients. This does not negate the value of individual or group therapy in a renal unit — that has not been my point at all. Rather, it has been to convince that limiting the provision to individual therapy alone involves collusion with institutionalised psychological neglect in that only those who manifest dramatic distress receive attention, whereas virtually *all* clients in renal failure and their partners experience much stress and merit psychological assistance and care.

However, although a care scheme such as this reduces the call for psychological therapy, it does not remove it altogether. The scheme needs to operate in relation to a psychological therapist. The remainder of the chapter should go to a review of the nature of the tasks likely to befall the psychological therapist.

Without doubt, the first task for any person offering psychological therapy in a renal unit has to be that of learning the basics of renal medicine, dialysis and transplant procedures. It is both counterproductive and unhelpful to work in an ill-informed state. It is similarly unhelpful if a therapist approaches work in a renal unit offering only a narrow speciality in therapy. On the contrary, great flexibility and an open-minded eclecticism is the ideal. This applies to psychiatrists, psychologists and social workers equally. In my experience, the psychiatrist who solely offers a diagnostic interview followed by chemotherapy is rapidly construed with the same low level of regard by the staff as, say, a psychologist who offers only family therapy, or only relaxation therapy. The situation in which people in renal failure find themselves was made clear in the earlier section on stresses in renal failure. There is clearly a broad spectrum of stress and, furthermore, there is an even broader spectrum of reactions to this stress. For this reason, it is pointless attempting to catalogue likely reactions in detail here; they are diverse, but, at the same time, will hold no surprises for the trained therapist. Rather, I will substantiate the plea for eclecticism by a review, giving examples of the relevance of different types of therapy.

Chemotherapy

There is an incidence, albeit low, of psychotic reaction and also occasional, very severe depression, anxiety state and other disabling conditions. In these circumstances there is a clear place for chemotherapy, assuming that it is well integrated with other care procedures and therapy (Salmons & Blainey 1982).

Cognitive behavioural approaches

People on dialysis programmes often run into practical problems and can benefit from the various techniques of biofeedback and cognitive behavioural therapy, for example, nervous tension or phobic reactions to the needling event. In the case of the dialysand, the tension may lead to vasoconstriction and reduction of blood flow rate in the fistula, such that dialysis becomes inadequate. In these circumstances, biofeedback based on forearm electromyelography or skin temperature measures combined with relaxation training and stress-management techniques have been found to be a great help with clients at Exeter. Similarly, anxious, tense reactions by partners attempting venepuncture can risk a damaged fistula and produce a very fraught atmosphere. Again, relaxation training and the development of a problem-solving, stress-managing style usually prove to be of considerable benefit for the partners involved. This may be usefully extended to tensions throughout the dialysis session.

The problem of fluid control is also one which the direct and practical approach may assist. Keeping to a requirement of 800 ml per day proves beyond the capability of many people and the pattern of special efforts followed by giving up and bingeing sometimes occurs, very reminiscent of addictive states. Thus, permissible between-dialysis fluid weight gains of

2–3 kg may be exceeded (with gains of 5–6 kg), which is very damaging to the cardiovascular system. Care must be taken in adopting simple behavioural techniques in these cases since there can be complex motivational issues involved. However, the problem-solving style of analysis with record keeping and graded targets for achievement in fluid intake (usually starting at 1500 ml per day) have proved effective for us on many occasions.

Sexual counselling and therapy

Some elements of sexual counselling should be included in the psychological care programme but occasional cases will need referral and therapy programmes. The normal elements of talking through problems and establishing positive attitudes together with a practical education in the best approach to intercourse and extracoital alternatives where impotence is persistent are usually sufficient. Watts (1983) gives a useful overview of strategies for sexual counselling in renal failure.

Couples' therapy and relationship problems

My personal clinical experience is that most approaches for assistance in relationship problems are unilateral. Most commonly, it is a woman partner who feels trapped in an empty and unsatisfactory relationship, seeing a destiny of years of unhappiness as a slave to haemodialysis or a support figure to an invalid towards whom she now feels great ambivalence and anger. Often these partners have experienced a long period of growing disillusionment and fatigue. Sometimes a powerful need for a sexual relationship and a yearning for children complicates things further.

I must warn you that these are difficult cases for any therapist, particularly if the dialysand refuses involvement or the partner pleads for confidentiality. The therapist is so easily caught between divided loyalties. Nevertheless, the work of examining feelings, motives and behaviour through conversation-based therapy and 'allowing' expression and existence of all thoughts and feelings is important. So, too, is expansion of insight concerning the dynamics of the situation, especially where the partner is partly responsible for maintaining the behaviour or circumstances against which she is now rebelling. In cases where the relationship has deteriorated badly, the therapist's best contribution is that of assisting with the inevitably traumatic separation. In other cases, leading the partner into a more satisfactory adaptation to the situation, particularly in terms of a guilt-free concern for greater *self*-care and more efficient ways of meeting personal needs emerges as the key contribution. When the dialysand will participate, then leading him to see that the partner has needs too and that care must be reciprocated, often leads to improved relationships and communication. If circumstances permit, joint or whole family sessions are most useful.

Individual psychotherapy

The range of possible content is vast. Mention of a few common themes must suffice. Renal failure is, in reality, a terminal illness. This process may be interrupted for a while by transplantation and slowed down by dialysis. Nevertheless, there will always be a few clients involved with a unit who are near the end. The psychological therapist may, therefore, sometimes be needed to assist a client in preparation for dying. This will involve resolving worries and relationship issues, dealing with grief and the task of letting go and saying goodbye. Very occasionally there may be a request to assist a client who wants to stop dialysis and retreat into death. In these cases, the client's needs and feelings must be explored, honoured and given priority. At the same time, the therapist must constantly liaise with staff to ensure continuing good care and help both them and the relatives when the anticipated death causes emotional upheaval.

Reaction to dialysis, a failed transplantation attempt, failure of a transplanted kidney after several years, long-term adaptation to life after renal failure, etc., will produce grief reactions, anxiety reactions, anger, self-neglect, denial, listless withdrawal and a host of other patterns. In general, the best indication for therapy is that the client actually wants therapy and has some objectives to bring to the therapy. Poor bets in therapy are people who are 'sent' to therapy by one of the staff, perhaps because they are a nuisance or a burden, and who have no motivation and no objectives in therapy.

In general, as long as the therapist remains informed and aware of the medical situation and likely outcome in the ensuing months, therapy will follow the same lines as elsewhere. The client must feel safe and valued and be able to explore feelings, motives and perceptions in the totally free manner that fosters insight and greater self-awareness. At the same time, the therapist will work towards facilitating the completion of emotional processes and helping a client achieve mastery of the situation.

Group therapy

Group techniques are helpful and relevant where circumstances permit. The encounter of dialysand with dialysand and partner with partner can be most valuable, particularly for newcomers to the situation and for long-term support. Similarly, with those involved in transplants it is also a useful medium for promoting a continued effort at self-care while offering the cohesive support and sense of accountability that membership in a group produces. With a little training and guidance, a basic support group is also an activity which a capable nurse can undertake (Payne & Harrison 1984).

REFERENCES

Amstrong S H, Weiner M F 1982 Non-compliance with post-transplant
    immunosuppression. International Journal of Psychiatry in Medicine 11: 89–95

Blodgett C 1981 A selected review of the literature of adjustment to haemodialysis. International Journal of Psychiatry in Medicine 11: 97–124

Brey H, Jarvis J 1983 Life change: adjusting to continuous ambulatory peritoneal dialysis. Health and Social Work 9: 203–209

Burton H J, Canzona L, Wai L et al 1983 Life without a machine. In:Levy N B (ed) Psychonephrology II. Plenum, New York

Cardenas D D, Kutner N G 1982 The problem of fatigue in dialysis patients. Nephron 30: 336–340

Chambers M 1983 Psychological aspects of renal transplantation. International Journal of Psychiatry in Medicine 12: 229–236

Degen K, Strain J J, Zumoff B 1983 Biosocial evaluation of sexual function in end-stage renal disease. In: Levy N B (ed) Psychonephrology II. Plenum, New York

Devins G M, Binik Y M, Hutchinson T A et al 1984 The emotional impact of end-stage renal disease: importance of patients' perceptions of intrusiveness and control. International Journal of Psychiatry in Medicine 13: 327–343

Elian M, Dean G 1985 To tell or not to tell the diagnosis of multiple sclerosis. Lancet: 27–28

Farmer C J, Snowdon S A, Parsons V 1979 The prevalence of psychiatric illness among patients on home dialysis. Psychological Medicine 9: 509–514

Freyberger H 1983 The renal transplant patient: three stage model and psychotherapeutic strategies. In: Levy N B (ed) Psychonephrology II. Plenum, New York

Kaplan De-Nour A 1981 Prediction of adjustment to chronic haemodialysis. In: Levy N B (ed) Psychonephrology I. Plenum, New York

Kaplan De-Nour A 1983 An overview of psychological problems in haemodialysis. In: Levy N B (ed) Psychonephrology II. Plenum, New York

Kaplan De-Nour A, Czackes J W 1974 Bias in assessment of patients on chronic dialysis. Journal of Psychosomatic Research 18: 217–221

Kutner N G, Fair P L, Kutner M H 1985 Assessing depression and anxiety in chronic dialysis patients. Journal of Psychosomatic Research 29: 23–31

Landsman M 1978 Adjustment to dialysis: the middle years. Dialysis and Transplant 7: 432–434

Levy N B 1973 Sexual adjustment to maintenance haemodialysis and renal transplantation. Transactions of the American Society for Artificial Internal Organs 19: 138–143

Lipowski Z J 1982 Modern meaning of the terms 'psycho-somatic' and 'liaison psychiatry'. In: Creed F, Pfeffer J M (eds) Medicine and psychiatry: A practical approach. Pitman, London

Livesley W J 1982 Symptoms of anxiety and depression in patients undergoing chronic haemodialysis. Journal of Psychosomatic Research 26: 581–584

Lowry M R, Atcherson E 1980 Home dialysis drop-outs. Journal of Psychosomatic Research 24: 173–178

Lowry M R, Atcherson E 1986 Spouse assistants' adjustment to home haemodialysis. Journal of Chronic Diseases 37: 293–300

Muthny F A 1984 Post-operative course of patients during hospitalization following renal transplantation. Psychotherapy and Psychosomatics 42: 133–142

Nichols K A 1984 Psychological care in physical illness. Croom Helm, Beckenham

Nichols K A 1985 Psychological care by nurses, paramedical and medical staff: essential developments for the general hospitals. British Journal of Medical Psychology 58: 231–240

Nichols K A 1986 Chronic physical disorder in adults. In: Orford J (ed) Coping with disorder in the family. Croom Helm, Beckenham

Nichols K A 1987 Teaching nurses psychological care. In: Muller D (ed) Teaching nurses psychological skills. British Psychological Society, Leicester

Nichols K A, Springford V 1984 The psycho-social stressors associated with survival by dialysis. Behaviour Research and Therapy 22: 563–574

Payne G M, Harrison B 1984 Reducing stress in renal patients and their families: a nurse-managed patient support group. Journal of Nephrology Nursing November/December: 138–140

Petersen K J 1985 Psychosocial adjustment of the family caregiver — home dialysis as an example. Social Work in Health Care 10: 15–31

Procci R W, Martin J D 1985 Effect of maintenance haemodialysis on male sexual performance. Journal of Nervous and Mental Diseases 173: 366–372

Salmons P, Blainey J D 1982 Psychiatric aspects of chronic renal failure. In: Creed F, Pfeffer J M (eds) Medicine and psychiatry: a practical approach. Pitman, London

Schreiber W K, Huber W 1985 Psychological situation of dialysis patients and their families. Dialysis and Transplant 14: 696–698

Sherwood R J 1983 The impact of renal failure and dialysis treatments on patients' lives and on their compliance behaviour. In: Levy N B (ed) Psychonephrology II. Plenum, New York

Shurr M, Roy C, Atcherson E 1984 CAPD: Dialysis 365 days a year. Journal of Nephrology Nursing July/August: 20–24

Simmons R G 1983 Long-term reactions of renal recipients and donors. In: Levy N B (ed) Psychonephrology II. Plenum, New York

Stewart R S 1983 Psychiatric issues in renal dialysis and transplantation. Hospital and Community Psychiatry 34: 623–626

Streltzer J 1983 Cultural aspects of adjustment to end-stage renal disease. In: Levy N B (ed) Psychonephrology II. Plenum, New York

Woodhams P 1984a Nurses and psychologists — the first-hand experience. Nursing Times January 11: 34–35

Woodhams P 1984b Information and good psychological care in renal failure. Talk given at the annual conference of the National Federation of Kidney Patient Associations, Oxford

Woodhams P 1986 Personal communication

Wai L, Richmond J, Burton H, Lindsay R M 1981 Influence of psychosocial factors on survival of home dialysis patients. Lancet 2: 1155–1156

Watts R J 1983 The patient on renal dialysis — strategies for sexual counselling. In: Levy N B (ed) Psychonephrology II. Plenum, New York

17
Geoffrey G. Lloyd

Early intervention for alcohol abuse

INTRODUCTION

Immediately after the Second World War alcohol consumption in the United Kingdom was at its lowest level for three centuries (Chick 1982). It then rose steadily during the next three decades until 1979, following which, at least temporarily, there was a modest decline. During the years of increased consumption there was also a rise in alcohol-related disabilities, including physical illness, psychiatric illness, social problems and crimes related to alcohol (Royal College of Psychiatrists 1979). Greater awareness of the range of disabilities has emphasised that the problem is more pervasive than was once realised. In the minds of some doctors the stereotype alcoholic has been the individual who exhibits loss of control, craving, increased tolerance and withdrawal symptoms in the absence of alcohol; in other words alcoholism has been equated with physical and psychological dependence. This view is now regarded as too narrow. A World Health Organization report (WHO 1977) defined alcoholism as a more inclusive term for all types of harmful drinking, whether or not the individual had symptoms of dependence. This broader definition was also followed in the Royal College of Psychiatrists' report.

PREVALENCE OF ALCOHOL PROBLEMS

The adverse effects of alcohol on physical health are well established. The clinical manifestations are multiple and virtually any organ can be affected; indeed it has been claimed that alcoholism has replaced syphilis as the great mimic of disease (Paton et al 1982). Consequently alcohol makes a substantial contribution to the demands on health service facilities, particularly within the general hospital. Prevalence figures vary from one hospital to another according to its nature and location as well as to prevailing cultural factors (Beresford 1979). However, recent British studies have consistently shown that just over a quarter of male medical inpatients have a current or previous alcohol problem and in some of these cases alcohol has contributed directly to the illness for which hospital admission has been required.

The reported rates for women are lower and more variable, reflecting both their lower consumption and greater reluctance to admit to problem drinking (Jariwalla et al 1979, Jarman & Kellett 1979, Lloyd et al 1982). Alcohol problems are also frequently encountered in accident and emergency departments, partly because of the role which alcohol plays in industrial, domestic and road traffic accidents. Holt et al (1980) estimated breath alcohol concentrations in patients attending an accident and emergency department during the evening and found that 32% had levels equivalent to blood levels in excess of the legal limit for driving a motor vehicle. In a comprehensive survey of a London general teaching hospital, Barrison et al (1982) found an overall prevalence of abnormal drinking similar to those previously reported. However, there was considerable interspecialty variation, with abnormal drinking being commonest among surgical, medical and orthopaedic patients and least common among gynaecology, ENT, dental and plastic surgery patients. The majority of patients who were abnormal drinkers had been admitted for reasons unassociated with alcohol abuse and their drinking would not have been detected unless specific enquiries had been made.

Alcohol problems are only slightly less common in general practice. Wallace & Haines (1985) conducted a questionnaire survey of two urban practices and identified 11% of men and 5% of women as excessive drinkers accordingly to previously defined consumption criteria. When wider criteria were used, including the subjects' concern about their drinking, 22% of men and 9% of women were classified as problem drinkers. In a sample of patients attending a health centre King (1986) found that 13.6% of men and 1.3% of women were drinking at levels above the Royal College of Psychiatrists' 1979 recommendations.

In purely economic terms the implications for the National Health Service are considerable. A recent survey has estimated that the social costs to the NHS are over £95 million each year in England and Wales. When the effects on industry, material damages and the costs of criminal activity are taken into account the total social cost of alcohol misuse was estimated to be in excess of £1500 million at 1983 prices (McDonnell & Maynard 1985).

EFFECTIVENESS OF TREATMENT

It is unlikely that any of the established medical facilities will be able to cope with the present level of alcohol problems. Specialised treatment has usually been delegated to psychiatrists often working in alcohol treatment units based in psychiatric hospitals, but the effects of specialised treatment are uncertain and a close scrutiny of controlled trials makes gloomy reading. Willems et al (1973) found that a lengthy admission, lasting for 3 months, to an alcoholism unit produced results which were no better than those obtained after a 3-week admission. At the Maudsley Hospital, Edwards

& Guthrie (1967) found that inpatient treatment was no more effective than outpatient treatment and in a subsequent study it was shown that for married male alcoholics a single session of direct counselling was just as effective as an extensive range of psychiatric treatment, including inpatient treatment if indicated (Orford & Edwards 1977).

It could be argued with justification that psychiatrists are referred only a small proportion of people with alcohol problems, usually those who have sustained the most serious damage to their health and social life and who are left with little or no social support after years of heavy drinking. But it has become clear that psychiatrically orientated treatment can make little impact on the alcohol problems of an entire population, even if the treatment were effective in the first place. Alcohol consumption in the community is distributed continuously and most people with alcohol problems are distinguished from the remainder simply by the fact that they drink more heavily. The majority do not have any underlying psychiatric illness and it is doubtful whether they have any particular personality abnormality.

The disappointing results of treatment and the awareness of the size of the problem have diverted attention to the possibilities of treatment at an earlier stage in the natural history of alcoholism. It makes more sense for steps to be taken to prevent problems arising in the first place or to reverse them before they have become established. Broadly speaking there are two methods which might be appropriate, one political and the other educational, but if a national policy is to be effective it will probably have to combine elements of both approaches.

EARLY RECOGNITION OF THE PROBLEM DRINKER

A policy of early intervention places much emphasis on identifying the problem at an early stage in its evolution. Several medical reports have described patients with advanced physical complications and have stressed the importance of early recognition. Doctors have been criticised for failing to detect alcohol problems among their patients. It is implied that the appropriate questions are not asked and that alcoholism is not considered sufficiently often in the differential diagnosis. One of the earliest studies on this topic was conducted in general practice by Wilkins (1974) and similar observations have been made in hospital practice by Barrison et al (1980). Saunders et al (1985) interviewed a series of patients with alcoholic liver disease and found that 35% claimed never to have received any advice about their heavy drinking. Less than half had been advised by their general practitioner to reduce or stop drinking and only 22% had been referred to a hospital clinic for specific management of a drinking problem. The authors suggested that patients escaped detection for many years because they only had a mild dependence syndrome.

Symptoms and signs

In view of the high prevalence of alcohol problems among patients in hospital or attending general practice surgeries, doctors are well placed to detect the problem drinker before irreversible physical, psychological or social changes have occurred. *A high index of suspicion is essential.* The doctor should be alert to a wide range of clues because none is diagnostic in itself. Most patients who turn out to be problem drinkers initially present with vague, multiple symptoms which do not fit any recognisable diagnostic pattern. They are frequent attenders at the general practitioner's surgery or have repeated admissions to hospital.

Certain features of the social background should increase the index of suspicion. These include repeated absences from work, accidents, marital tensions and a family history of alcoholism. Many occupations are known to be associated with an increased risk, particularly those which involve the manufacture, distribution or sale of alcohol; other high-risk groups include journalists, seamen, company directors and doctors. Indeed, occupational health screening in these groups offers a potentially high detection rate. The ethnic origin of the patient may also provide a clue; in Britain patients of Irish or Scottish descent are more likely to abuse alcohol than those of other ethnic backgrounds. The patient may complain of dyspepsia, anorexia, morning nausea or recurrent diarrhoea. There may also be impotence, infertility, depression, anxiety, insomnia, nightmares or failing memory. Characteristically these will not be linked in the patient's mind with alcohol consumption; even if they are, the link will not be volunteered.

The physical examination may show the patient to have a bloated, plethoric face with peri-orbital oedema. Obesity is common and is often accompanied by gynaecomastia. There is often poor dental hygiene, with gums which bleed easily and a smell of stale alcohol on the breath. The cardiovascular examination may reveal a sinus tachycardia, atrial fibrillation, cardiomegaly and essential hypertension which responds poorly to medication. On abdominal examination the liver may be enlarged but signs of portal hypertension or liver failure do not usually develop for many years. Central nervous system examination may uncover a marked tremor, ataxia or peripheral neuropathy and cognitive testing may show evidence of impaired concentration and poor short-term memory.

Symptoms and signs such as these should lead to specific questioning about drinking habits. It is helpful for the patient to describe the pattern of his drinking during a typical day so that the total daily and weekly consumption can be quantified. This is conventionally measured in units of alcohol, one unit being equivalent to half a pint of beer, a glass of wine or a single measure of spirits. The alcohol content of each of these drinks is approximately 9 g. As will be discussed later, there is no generally accepted safe level of drinking. The Royal College of Psychiatrists' 1979 report suggested that a regular weekly consumption above 56 units would lead to adverse consequences but a subsequent report has revised this to 21 units weekly for men and 14 units for women (Royal College of Psychiatrists 1986).

Screening tests

Special screening tests have also been advocated in the detection of problem drinkers (Lancet Leading Article 1980). Laboratory tests are an attractive option because several are affected by regular alcohol consumption. From the many tests available the two most widely used are the serum gamma glutamyl-transpeptidase (GGT) and the mean corpuscular volume (MCV). Chick et al (1981) have shown that these parameters correlate significantly with admitted alcohol consumption and that the probability of being a heavy drinker increases progressively with elevation in both these tests. However, as screening tests they were thought to lack power, a conclusion also reached in a study of patients in a psychiatric hospital (Bernadt et al 1982). They also lack sufficient sensitivity to be helpful in identifying early problem drinkers among the physically ill (Lloyd et al 1982).

Self-administered questionnaires are more promising. A shortened version of the Michigan Alcoholism Screening Test (MAST) and an even briefer questionnaire, the CAGE, have both been shown to be superior to laboratory tests in a psychiatric population (Bernadt et al 1982) but their use in general medical patients is debatable. Mayou & Hawton (1986) claim that many patients who are known by their doctors to have alcohol problems are not detected by the questionnaires which, they state, are not sensitive to early alcohol problems at a more treatable stage. Wallace & Haines (1985) have developed a self-administered questionnaire for use in general practice. This includes questions on quantity and frequency of consumption together with a modified version of the CAGE. Estimates of consumption obtained by the questionnaire have been shown to correlate highly with those obtained at a subsequent interview, except among female excessive drinkers who tended to report lower levels of consumption at interview.

Consumption and disabilities in medical patients

An alternative approach is the use of a detailed, structured interview of the type developed by Chick et al (1985) for a general hospital survey. In addition to recording consumption, this documented a wide range of medical, psychological and social consequences of alcoholism. Patients were regarded as problem drinkers if they acquired two or more points according to the criteria listed below. Patients scored one point for presence of any variable except presence of illness definitely due to alcohol which scored two points.

Consumption
Over 14 units in a day on 10 or more occasions in past year
Over 50 units in typical week
Over 12 units in 24 hours in typical week

Current medical problems
Present illness potentially related to alcohol
Present illness definitely related to alcohol
Weight problem due to alcohol

Medical problems in past 2 years
Peptic ulcer aggravated by drinking
Liver disease due to alcohol
Accident due to drinking

Social problems in past 2 years
Antisocial behaviour
Problems at work (including absence)
Domestic arguments
Violence
Family rupture (threatened or actual)
Financial
Police

Dependence on alcohol in past 2 years
Difficulty in reducing consumption
Restlessness without alcohol
Tremor (over 1 day a week)
Morning relief drinking (over 1 day a week)
Hallucinations
Withdrawal seizure

During the first 6 months of screening, 27% of male medical admissions were identified as having a current or previous alcohol problem, 23% being newly identified cases. Women had a lower prevalence: 11% had a current or previous alcohol problem but only 3% were newly identified cases (Lloyd et al 1982). A subsequent detailed study confined to male patients showed that many problem drinkers reported levels of consumption which have previously been regarded as safe (Lloyd et al 1986). The level which gave fewest misclassified cases was a weekly consumption above 39 units. It was very unlikely that patients reporting consumption above this level would not have problems related to alcohol but several problem drinkers reported drinking less than this during a typical week. Consumption levels were distributed continuously in the entire population of medical inpatients and there was no evidence of bimodality. These are shown in Figure 17.1.

It is important to realise that many patients with alcohol problems are admitted to hospital with illnesses which are not in themselves related to

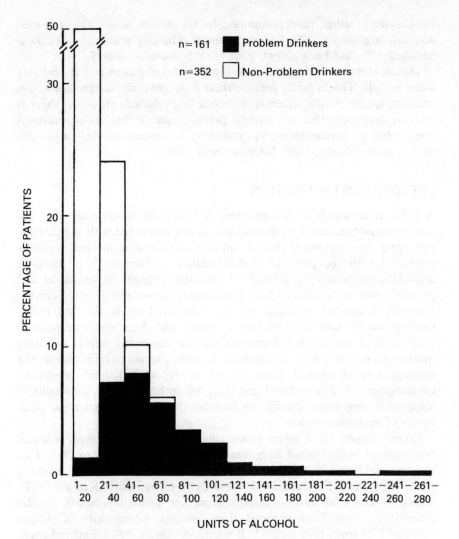

Fig. 17.1 Mean weekly consumption in a population of medical inpatients. (Reproduced with permission from Lloyd et al 1986.)

alcohol. This applied to 55% of the cases in our study. However, compared with patients without alcohol problems, the problem drinkers were more likely to have been admitted with liver, upper gastrointestinal or respiratory disorders and less likely to have had myocardial infarction or other cardiovascular disorder. Classical symptoms of dependence were infrequent at this stage. Seventeen per cent reported difficulty cutting down consumption, 12% reported restlessness or irritability when without a drink and 9% reported regular morning relief drinking. Withdrawal fits and hallucinations were reported by 5% and 7% respectively. Social problems related to alcohol were rather more common. In the above series 25% reported domestic arguments, 19% had experienced difficulty preventing drunkenness and 17% had been absent from work because of alcohol.

The ideal method of screening still awaits development and is probably some way off. This is partly because there is no generally accepted objective criterion against which screening tests can be evaluated. However, there is growing agreement that, for current practice, questioning about consumption, either by questionnaire or interview, is superior to the use of laboratory tests (Wallace 1986, Lockhart et al 1986).

POLITICAL INTERVENTION

A political approach to the problem is based on observations that the adverse consequences of alcoholism are closely correlated with the national per capita consumption of alcohol and that consumption, in turn, is closely correlated with the price of alcohol relative to income. It is therefore argued, most lucidly by Kendell (1979), that changes in legislation and general economic conditions have been largely responsible for the dramatic increases in alcohol consumption which occurred up to the late 1970s. Controls on the sale of alcohol were relaxed and there was a decrease in taxation or a failure to compensate for the combined effects of rising incomes on effective levels of taxation. Kendell goes on to claim that all the consequences of alcohol abuse would be reduced if total population consumption could be reduced and that, within broad limits, this could be achieved by legislative changes to increase the price or restrict the availability of alcoholic drinks.

Recent trends have given some support to this argument. Alcohol consumption in the United Kingdom fell by 11.4% from 1979 to 1982. This was followed by a 19% fall in drunkenness convictions, a 7% fall in drinking and driving convictions and a 4% fall in cirrhosis mortality (Kendell 1984). There was also a fall in mean disposable income during this period. Similar observations have been reported from Sweden, where sales of alcohol dropped 17% from 1976 to 1982 (Romelsjo & Agren 1985). This reduction was attributed partly to a greater awareness of alcohol problems, to raised prices and to restrictive measures introduced by the Swedish parliament. The latter included the prohibition of the sale of beers of medium and high strength and the closure of all state retail shops on Saturday. Romelsjo & Agren found that there were reductions in the mortality rates from cirrhosis and pancreatitis between 1979 and 1982 which they attributed to decreased consumption among a subgroup who had been particularly heavy drinkers. On the other hand they found no reduction in mortality from alcoholic psychosis, alcoholism or alcohol intoxication. This was explained on the grounds that these conditions occur more often in socially deteriorated, dependent alcoholics who had been unable to reduce their consumption. However, conflicting evidence on the effect of legislative change has come from a Scottish study which found that hospital admissions for alcohol-related problems actually fell following the introduction of more liberal licensing hours (Eagles & Besson 1985).

EDUCATIONAL INTERVENTION

Health education is an attractive approach to alcohol problems because it enables information to reach a large proportion of the population with the aid of mass media techniques. Despite the lack of supporting evidence Grant (1984) believes there is growing interest in alcohol education as the best available approach to minimising problems. But there will need to be careful attention to the planning and presentation of these programmes if they are to succeed. Plant et al (1979) evaluated a campaign mounted by the Scottish Health Education Unit in 1976. Using television and press advertising the main aim of the campaign was to encourage people with drinking problems to seek treatment, but it was also envisaged that it might lead to reduced alcohol consumption by the general public. The campaign reached three-quarters of the population and, although it was not possible to monitor its precise impact, it appeared that referrals to treatment agencies increased shortly after the campaign began. However, the general level of public knowledge about alcoholism did not increase nor was there any change in the general level of consumption.

As Grant (1984) has pointed out, most health education programmes assume that increasing knowledge will lead to changing attitudes and then to changing behaviour, but this sequence of relationships has not been proved. Informing people about the consequences of alcohol abuse and recommending safe levels of consumption may be ineffective unless it is accompanied by advice on dealing with social pressures to drink and how to develop alternative behaviours and lifestyle. Any large-scale programme must be carefully tailored for the audience it is intended to reach; the content must be suitable for the population and their expectations and the identity of the person doing the communicating should be appropriate. Doctors could take a leading role in such programmes particularly in schools and in industry and occupational physicians should be involved in developing an employer's policy towards alcohol in the work place. Health education obviously faces many obstacles, not least the expensive, sophisticated advertising supported by the drink industry. Education for alcohol problems is still in its infancy and better results may be obtained with more experience. Furthermore political intervention might be more readily accepted by the public if it is accompanied by information on the effects of alcohol on health (Smith 1982).

COUNSELLING THE INDIVIDUAL PROBLEM DRINKER

Once it is recognised that the patient has acquired a pattern of drinking which is damaging his health, family or social life, the doctor should be prepared to accept responsibility for attempting to modify the problem. Many doctors are pessimistic about the effects of their intervention but there is good evidence that in time problem drinkers are able to modify their drinking for the better. One of the important facts to be grasped is that although relapses are common they do not necessarily mean that all is lost from a therapeutic viewpoint. Indeed the course of the condition is characterised by relapses and remissions and each setback can be used profitably as an opportunity to identify and modify those factors which seem to trigger bouts of drinking.

The goals of intervention and the advice given will depend on the severity of the patient's drinking problem. A crucial question to be answered is whether the patient must be advised to become completely abstinent or whether he can be encouraged to resume safe levels of drinking or what some would call 'social drinking'. In the early days of alcoholism treatment abstinence was nearly always the goal, but it has become apparent that even some severe alcoholics can return to harmless drinking and several treatment programmes now encourage this, an approach which might become more appropriate if patients are to be encouraged to seek help at an earlier stage. Heather & Robertson (1981), who have reviewed the issue of controlled drinking in detail, have claimed that abstinence is an inappropriate treatment goal for most problem drinkers and that it may actually hinder reduction in consumption. They have summarised several theoretical advantages of a controlled drinking goal, including the important one that the adoption of total abstinence from alcohol places the individual in a deviant role which creates further psychological problems. After reviewing the results of treatment they conclude that controlled drinking treatments significantly reduce consumption of many problem drinkers to non-problem levels; brief interventions are effective in achieving this, especially those based on behavioural techniques including self-monitoring and self-help manuals. The value of brief counselling is exemplified by the case below.

A 53-year-old man was admitted to hospital following a first myocardial infarction. He was a hard-working, ambitious business man who had built up a company from scratch, and he was a heavy smoker; both these factors were thought to have contributed to his cardiac disease. Systematic enquiry about his alcohol consumption indicated that he drank regularly, consuming several measures of whisky most evenings after returning home from work. His average weekly consumption was in excess of 50 units and he had recently become aware of increasing irritability towards his wife, sleep disturbance and tension in the early morning. A nurse spent 1 hour with him during his admission explaining the harmful effects of alcohol on his health and pointing out that continued consumption at his previous level would almost certainly result in major medical and social complications. The patient was surprised to learn that his alcohol consumption was excessive and, although he made it clear that he would not wish to give up drinking completely, he maintained that he would be able to reduce his intake to at least half of what it had been. He was advised to reduce the number of days on which he consumed alcohol and to avoid holding business meetings at times when alcohol was readily available.

When seen 12 months later he reported that he was drinking on only 2 or 3 days each week and his mean weekly consumption had fallen to approximately 20 units. He had had no further medical illnesses, his marital relationship had improved and he reported that he was working more effectively at his business. Biochemical and haematological tests did not reveal any evidence of alcohol-related damage.

Although it can be difficult to identify those who can continue to drink at reduced levels, current opinion suggests that complete abstinence must remain the target for those with severe symptoms of dependence or physical damage from alcohol. Abstinence should also be recommended if the patient has previously tried and failed to achieve controlled drinking.

A 45-year-old woman was seen by a psychiatrist after her admission to a medical ward following the onset of jaundice which was diagnosed as being due to alcoholic hepatitis. She also had evidence of peripheral neuropathy on neurological examination. She readily admitted to an increasing alcohol consumption during the previous 5 years and she attributed this to difficulties coping with the demands of running a home, looking after two children and having to help in her husband's horticultural business. She complained that he made too many demands on her and she reported using alcohol to help her relax. Initially she had drunk only in the evenings but during the previous 6 months she had started drinking shortly after getting up in the morning, this being done to help relieve withdrawal symptoms. By the evening she had usually been intoxicated and her difficulties in running the home had escalated.

Her physical condition gradually improved and she was seen together with her husband on several occasions. She was advised that she should become completely abstinent in view of the damage to her physical health and she was encouraged to ventilate her dissatisfaction with the various roles she was expected to fulfil. In particular her husband, who was also a heavy drinker, was encouraged to take on extra staff at work so that his wife's involvement could be reduced until the children were more independent.

She was seen regularly for support after leaving hospital and she maintained abstinence, although this was initially difficult for her. Within 6 weeks of leaving hospital she became clinically depressed, with typical symptoms of guilt, hopelessness, sleep disturbance and weight loss. Her mood disturbance persisted and antidepressant medication was prescribed with a successful response. This was continued for 12 months, after which it was tailed off with no recurrence of the depressive symptoms. She remained well and completely abstinent when last seen, 2 years after her initial admission.

Initially the patient may be reluctant to change his drinking habits, minimising the extent of his consumption or even completely denying a problem. This situation is particularly likely if the initiative for referral has been taken by someone else, such as the spouse or employer. The first step therefore concerns convincing the patient that he has a problem and to this end it is helpful to draw up a weekly 'drinking diary' which records the amount of alcohol consumed and circumstances in which it was drunk. In conjunction with this the patient should be asked to construct a balance sheet indicating the beneficial and adverse consequences of his drinking. This should list the beneficial effects such as the taste, socially enhancing effects and so on, together with the drawbacks on the patient's health, occupational prospects, financial situation and family life.

A radical change in life-style is usually required, more so for those patients who need to become abstinent. The patient will have to look at factors which lead to drinking. These may include a job, social meetings after work, leisure activities, marital or family tensions. The situations where alcohol is regularly encountered should be avoided and new patterns of leisure activities developed. It may be necessary to recommend a change of job, particularly for those who are employed in the alcohol trade in some capacity. Treatment is likely to be more effective if the spouse is actively involved. Not only will she provide additional information about the drinking problems but she can help support her husband towards problem-free drinking and an alternative way of life. Conjoint sessions can also provide emotional support for the spouse in her own right and they are essential if marital tensions are causing or perpetuating the problem.

If major problems have not developed and there are no symptoms of severe dependence the patient may be advised to reduce his consumption rather than become completely abstinent. This may well be a more realistic and acceptable policy for early problem drinkers. The issue will then arise as to what levels of consumption can be considered safe. There is no consensus on this matter and a recent survey of people considered to be experts in the field of alcoholism research and treatment showed a wide variation of opinion (Anderson et al 1984). Many would now consider the limit recommended by the Royal College of Psychiatrists in 1979 of 56 units weekly to be too high. General practitioners tend to be more conservative and in a recent survey of GPs the mean recommended level of safe drinking was 18 units weekly for men and 13 units for women. This reflects the evidence that women are more susceptible to the harmful effects of alcohol (Wallace et al 1985). This has been acknowledged by the Royal College of Psychiatrists' (1986) revised report, suggesting that an acceptable weekly level of drinking is 21 units for a man and 14 units for a woman. In addition to recommending an upper limit it is necessary to advise spacing consumption; the equivalent of two or three pints of beer two or three times a week is a pattern of drinking which can be advised to most early drinkers. For women who are pregnant or trying to conceive many doctors would recommend complete abstinence in view of evidence of damage to the fetus in those who drink heavily and of increased risk of spontaneous abortion even in moderate drinkers.

Regular reviews of the patient's progress are essential. At first the patient should be seen frequently, perhaps on a weekly basis. Short-term goals should be set which the patient has a realistic chance of achieving. For example the patient should be encouraged to negotiate a forthcoming business meeting without accepting alcohol or to avoid meeting friends in a bar before a football match. Follow-up interviews enable a rapport to develop and demonstrate to the patient his doctor's interest in his problems. Laboratory tests (GGT and MCV), although less helpful in screening, are useful for monitoring progress and their results should be communicated to the patient and discussed with him as soon as possible.

Evidence is accumulating that counselling of this nature is effective for newly identified problem drinkers. In Malmö, Kristensson et al (1983) studied a cohort of apparently healthy middle-aged men who were invited to participate in a health screening programme. Heavy drinkers were identified initially on the basis of two consecutive GGT values in the top decile of the GGT distribution and were randomly allocated to either an intervention or a control group. Subjects in the intervention group were offered continuing follow-up and consultations with the same doctor every third month; they also had GGT tests and reinforcing contacts with the same nurse each month. Counselling was focused on living habits and subjects were given advice to modify their drinking although they assumed full responsibility for the outcome of their participation. Moderate drinking rather than abstinence was the agreed target and continued consumption was tolerated as long as GGT values did not rise. Information about the GGT level was given at every check up and when values had stabilised at an acceptable level the frequency of therapeutic contacts was reduced. The control group did not receive this systematic counselling but were merely advised by letter to restrict their alcohol intake and informed that they would be invited for new tests after 2 years. Two and 4 years after the initial screening the GGT values in both groups were significantly decreased. However, there were significant differences between the groups with regard to sickness absences, hospitalisations and mortality. The intervention group had fewer days off work because of sickness, less time in hospital and a mortality rate of half that of the controls after 4 years.

Less intensive counselling was evaluated by Chick et al (1985) in a group of male medical inpatients. Problem drinkers were identified using the structured interview described previously and were allocated to either an intervention or a control group. Patients in the intervention group received a single session of counselling from a nurse experienced in the treatment of alcoholism. The session lasted up to 60 minutes, during which the nurse engaged the patient in a discussion on his lifestyle and health which helped him to weigh up the disadvantages of his pattern of drinking and to come to a decision about his future consumption. The objective was to help the patient towards problem-free drinking, though abstinence was the agreed goal for some. The patient was also given a specially prepared booklet which reiterated the advice given verbally, encouraged the maintenance of a drinking diary and listed the addresses of local agencies which could be contacted. Control patients received no such advice and no comment was made about the content of the screening interview. The physician in charge, however, may have advised the patient to modify his alcohol consumption, according to his normal practice.

Patients were not interviewed again until 12 months later. On that occasion they were interviewed by an independent nurse who was unaware of the design of the study. Both groups had reduced their mean weekly consumption to a similar degree but the counselled group had a significantly better outcome when a global measure was used which took into account problems related to alcohol. They also had a significant reduction in GGT values.

THE ROLE OF DRUGS IN MANAGEMENT

Drugs have a limited role in long-term management but there are some specific indications when they are helpful.

Detoxification

Some problem drinkers continue to drink heavily because they are physically dependent and are unable to cope with withdrawal symptoms when they attempt to stop or cut down. For them detoxification is necessary and drugs play an important part in this. Benzodiazepines are the drugs of choice and have several advantages over chlormethiazole. A suitable regime would be to give 20 mg of chlordiazepoxide four times daily to start with and tail this off over a 6-day period. Equivalent doses of other benzodiazepines can also be used. If withdrawal symptoms are particularly severe larger doses can be given with safety. It is usual to give vitamin supplements in the form of Parenterovite injections to prevent the development of Wernicke's encephalopathy.

Alcohol sensitisation

For long-term treatment some patients benefit from taking one of the drugs which sensitise the body to alcohol. Disulfiram (Antabuse) 200 mg daily can be used to this effect. If a patient taking this drug also drinks alcohol there follows a very unpleasant reaction which includes flushing, headache, palpitation, nausea and vomiting. Knowledge that this will occur can have a deterrent effect, preventing a sudden impulse to drink. To be successful the drug has to be taken regularly and some doctors enlist the supervision of spouse or employer to ensure compliance. The drug should not be given to patients with heart disease or those with suicidal tendencies. Antabuse appears to be particularly suitable for alcoholics who drink impulsively in bouts and those who drink heavily only in certain situations, for example at office parties. Some doctors arrange for it to be given by a nurse at work, continued employment being made conditional on regular taking of Antabuse.

Psychotropic drugs

Psychotropic drugs, apart from benzodiazepines, are useful for the small proportion of alcoholics who have an underlying psychiatric disorder, which is usually an anxiety syndrome or depression. It should be remembered that in most depressed alcoholics the mood disturbance is a direct or indirect consequence of drinking and improves after stopping drinking. A decision about antidepressant treatment should therefore be made only after detoxification and a period of abstinence. Antidepressants should not be prescribed to those who are likely to continue drinking heavily, because of the dangers of drug interactions. Neuroleptic drugs are required for schizophrenia and alcoholic hallucinations and their prescription should be supervised by a psychiatrist.

REFERRAL TO OTHER AGENCIES

A general practitioner or hospital doctor can achieve good results with many alcoholic patients but in some cases the level of support required is more intensive than can be given by one doctor. Referral to other agencies should then be considered but it is best if the doctor continues to keep contact with the patient. In many areas local councils on alcoholism have been established. These voluntary bodies organise the training of counsellors and provide free advice to alcoholics and their families. Some patients benefit from groups run by Alcoholics Anonymous (AA), which has branches throughout Britain. Other patients however find the quasireligious approach of AA difficult to accept and drop out after their first meeting. It is impossible to predict who will do well at AA, especially because groups vary in terms of the personalities of their active members. However, doctors should know how to put patients in touch with groups in their area and also be aware of Al-Anon and Al-Alteen groups which respectively provide support for the spouses and teenage children of alcoholics. A newer organisation, ACCEPT, may be suitable for those who dislike the AA approach.

   If referral to a psychiatrist is contemplated it is important to know which of the local specialists is interested in treating patients with alcohol problems and it helps if there is an accessible alcohol treatment unit with a full range of therapeutic facilities. Although the efficacy of these units is not established most doctors are glad to be able to call on expert advice for their more difficult patients. The best results are likely to be achieved if the GP or physician refers the patient before severe physical, psychiatric or social complications have occurred. As a rough guide, referral should be considered if an under-lying psychiatric illness is suspected, the patient shows evidence of a personality disorder, there is major breakdown in family support or the patient has failed to respond to the type of counselling outlined previously. Referral to hospital is also required for patients with severe withdrawal symptoms, particularly epilepsy or delirium tremens.

CONCLUSIONS

There is now evidence that simple counselling measures improve the prognosis of problem drinkers particularly if patients are identified before serious complications have developed. Doctors are uniquely placed to identify early problem drinkers and should have a high index of suspicion for alcohol-related disorders among patients consulting them with recurrent, multiple or poorly defined symptoms. Specific questions about alcohol consumption are superior to the use of laboratory tests as screening procedures although the latter are useful to monitor the effects of treatment. The results of recent controlled studies should do much to reverse the pessimism associated with treatment of alcoholics and provide a rationale for systematic screening for patients at risk. Detailed enquiry into alcohol consumption and related problems should now form a routine part of medical assessment.

REFERENCES

Anderson P, Cremona A, Wallace P 1984 What are safe levels of alcohol consumption. British Medical Journal 289: 1657–1658

Barrison I G, Viola L, Mumford J, Murray R M, Gordon M, Murray-Lyon I M 1982 Detecting excessive drinking among admissions to a general hospital. Health Trends 14: 80–83

Barrison I G, Viola L, Murray-Lyon I M 1980. Do housemen take an adequate drinking history? British Medical Journal 281: 1040

Beresford T P 1979 Alcoholism consultation and general hospital psychiatry. General Hospital Psychiatry 1: 293–300

Bernadt M, Taylor C, Mumford J, Smith B, Murray R 1982 Comparison of questionnaire and laboratory tests in the detection of excessive drinking and alcoholism. Lancet 1: 325–328

Chick J 1982 Epidemiology of alcohol use and its hazards: with a note on screening methods. British Medical Bulletin 38: 3–8

Chick J, Kreitman N, Plant M 1981 Mean cell volume and gamma-glutamyl transpeptidase as markers of drinking in working men. Lancet 1: 1249–1251

Chick J, Lloyd G, Crombie E 1985 Counselling problem drinkers in medical wards: a controlled study. British Medical Journal 290: 965–967

Eagles J M, Besson J A O 1985 Changes in the incidence of alcohol-related problems in North-East Scotland, 1974–1982. British Journal of Psychiatry 147: 39–43

Edwards G, Guthrie S 1967 A controlled trial of in-patient and out-patient treatment of alcohol dependence. Lancet 1: 555–559

Grant M 1984 In Krasner N, Madden J S, Walker R J (eds) Alcohol related problems: room for manoeuvre. Wiley, Chichester

Heather N, Robertson I 1981 Controlled drinking. Methuen, London

Holt S, Stewart I C, Dixon J M J, Elton R A, Taylor T V, Little K 1980 Alcohol and the emergency service patient. British Medical Journal 281: 638–640

Jariwalla A G, Adams P H, Hore B D 1979 Alcohol and acute general medical admissions to hospital. Health Trends 11: 95–97

Jarman C M B, Kellett J M 1979 Alcoholism in the general hospital. British Medical Journal 2: 469–472

Kendell R E 1979 Alcoholism: a medical or a political problem? British Medical Journal 1: 367–371

Kendell R E 1984 The beneficial consequences of the United Kingdom's declining per capita consumption of alcohol in 1979–82. Alcohol and Alcoholism 19: 271–276

King M 1986 At risk drinking among general practice attenders: prevalence, characteristics and alcohol-related problems. British Journal of Psychiatry 148: 533–540

Kristensson H, Ohlin H, Hulten-Nosslin M B, Trell E, Hood B 1983 Identification and intervention of heavy drinking in middle-aged men: results and follow-up of 24–60 months of long-term study with randomised controls. Alcoholism 7: 203–209

Lancet Leading Article 1980 Screening tests for alcoholism. 2: 1117–1118

Lloyd G, Chick J, Crombie E 1982 Screening for problem drinkers among medical in-patients. Drug and Alcohol Dependence 10: 355–359

Lloyd G, Chick J, Crombie E, Anderson S 1986 Problem drinkers in medical wards: consumption patterns and disabilities in newly identified male cases. British Journal of Addiction 81: 789–795

Lockhart S P, Carter Y H, Straffen A M, Pang K K, McLoughlin J, Baron J H 1986 Detecting alcohol consumption as a cause of emergency general medical admissions. Journal of the Royal Society of Medicine 79: 132–136

McDonnell R, Maynard A 1985 The costs of alcohol misuse. British Journal of Addiction 80: 27–35

Mayou R, Hawton K 1986 Psychiatric disorder in the general hospital. British Journal of Psychiatry 149: 172–190

Orford J, Edwards G 1977 Alcoholism. Oxford University Press, Oxford

Paton A, Potter J F, Saunders J B 1982 Detection in hospital. In Alcohol Problems. BMJ, London

Plant M A, Pirie F, Kreitman N 1979 Evaluation of the Scottish Health Education Unit's 1976 campaign on alcoholism. Social Psychiatry 14: 11–24

Romelsjo A, Agren G 1985 Has mortality related to alcohol declined in Sweden? British Medical Journal 291: 167–170

Royal College of Psychiatrists 1979 Alcohol and alcoholism. Tavistock London

Royal College of psychiatrists 1986 Alcohol: our favourite drug. Tavistock, London

Saunders J B, Wodak A, Williams R 1985 Past experience of advice and treatment for drinking problems of patients with alcoholic liver disease. British Journal of Addiction 80: 51–56

Smith R 1982 Preventing alcohol problems: a job for Canute? In Alcohol Problems. BMJ, London

Wallace P 1986 Looking for patients at risk because of their drinking. Journal of the Royal Society of Medicine 79: 129–130

Wallace P, Cremona A, Anderson P 1985 Safe limits of drinking: general practitioner's views. British Medical Journal 290: 1875–1876

Wallace P, Haines A 1985 Use of a questionnaire in general practice to increase the recognition of patients with excessive alcohol consumption. British Medical Journal 290: 1949–1953

Wilkins R H 1974 The hidden alcoholic in general practice. Eleck Science, London

Willems P, Letemendia F J J, Arroyave F 1973 A two-year follow-up study comparing short with long-stay inpatient treatment of alcoholics. British Journal of Psychiatry 122: 637–648

World Health Organization 1977 Alcohol-related disabilities. WHO, Geneva

18

Jenifer Wilson-Barnett

Distressing hospital procedures

INTRODUCTION

Apart from being hospitalised, with all the attendant inconvenience and associated fears, there are several events which cause additional distress for many patients. Surgery has been deemed one of the most stressful. Patients frequently talk about this as *the* most feared and dramatic event, but other procedures such as certain diagnostic tests also cause much anxiety, discomfort and sometimes embarrassment. However, there is much research, published over the last 20 years, which has evaluated specific interventions aimed at alleviating this distress, both psychological and physical. As this work has shown some very positive advantages from such preparatory interventions, it is appropriate to review the relevant studies for their practical implications.

In this chapter some of the descriptive work will be reviewed first as it explores the scale and nature of the problem. The giving of information and its relationship to anxiety will then be discussed as it is fundamental to the effects of many of the psychological experiments. Following this the most usual interventions will be compared and principles for their practical application outlined.

Benefits of these specific approaches will be discussed, as these justify the effort which should be given to this type of treatment. Although much of the routine explanation and information may be given by nurses, the guidelines should be seen as relevant to all staff in all their interactions with patients. Wider implications will therefore be emphasised in the concluding section.

It is rare to find an area in which so many experimental studies reveal such consistent findings which have direct indications for practice. As so many patients have surgery and other invasive procedures and their recovery is influenced by their feelings about such events the subject should be relevant to many health workers. Skills in giving information and in listening are basic to so many therapies. For this reason also this work adds to our knowledge in general care and should contribute to good practice.

PATIENTS' EMOTIONAL REACTIONS TO SURGERY

There is overwhelming evidence that most patients feel apprehensive or nervous about surgery. A few patients certainly claim not to feel this but they are rare and usually men. Anxiety has normally been found to peak just before surgery (Johnston 1978) but may be elevated for a few days before and after. Although anxiety is found to be the most usual emotion, Ridgeway & Mathews (1982) discuss the idea that specific worries rather than generalised anxieties are typical for many patients. Despite this most people cope well with surgery, although clinicians are constantly surprised by the variation in recovery rates and psychological responses to such treatments (Wilson-Barnett & Fordham 1983).

Reasons given for this fear of surgery are many and, of course, depend on the individuals' circumstances and their own interpretation and meaning of the event. Carnevali (1966) interviewed surgical patients to identify the source of their fears and found that the anaesthetic was mentioned by a majority. They were worried that they might wake too soon during the procedure or that they might die under the anaesthetic. Fear of 'being cut' and of 'mutilation' also affected many, as did the fear of pain and discomfort afterwards.

Although there is a certain similarity between individuals' main fears, it is interesting and important to note that rather idiosyncratic concerns can also be expressed. For instance, elderly people sometimes fear being incontinent during surgery and a few patients loathe the idea of having an intravenous infusion.

Deep-seated fears of dying, explored by Ramsay (1972), are not often expressed by patients but when asked specifically many admit that they have thought about this at times. The idea of being 'put to sleep' is sometimes likened to what happens with pets who have to be 'put down'.

One of the most dreaded diseases (or disease complexes) is cancer. Researchers (French 1979, Ramsay 1972) have found that many patients fear the discovery of a malignancy during surgery and associated with this is the concern about whether they would be told if this was the case. Euphemistic language employed by staff to avoid distress sometimes compounds this problem. Patients and staff talk about 'the operation being successful', which can mean different things. To some patients this can mean that there was no cancer and to others that it has all been removed.

Description of patients' fears and the level of their emotional response is often dependent on the skill in and length of interview. Most researchers would agree that it is sometimes very difficult to explore this with patients. Men are particularly reluctant to admit they are afraid whereas women seem to be more aware of their own feelings and more willing to discuss them. It is essential for both research and clinical purposes to establish rapport with patients and appear relaxed, in order to avoid inhibiting the subject.

This is certainly the case when one is exploring a concern which is personal and possibly of an intimate nature. Individuals do have different perspectives and concerns about surgery. Perhaps the easiest mistake that staff can make is to assume they know what makes patients afraid.

SPECIAL TESTS

Although surgery is widely recognised as a major stressful event other procedures undertaken, usually for diagnostic purposes, may be equally anxiety-evoking for some patients. In a survey (Wilson-Barnett & Carrigy 1978) of medical ward patients we found that nearly half had experienced an invasive or special test which involved the patient in a lengthy procedure, usually done by a specialist from a different department. A vast majority of patients expressed a negative view about such tests, using such terms as 'frightening', 'painful', 'exhausting' or 'embarrassing'.

Discussion of these tests is perhaps merited because strategies for alleviating anxieties are similar to those evaluated for surgical patients and because patients are generally more neglected prior to these tests and less informed about them. Such diagnostic tests include special radiographs, biopsies and endoscopies. Many involve specific physical preparation, take more than an hour to complete and several hours for recovery.

In contrast to surgery, patients are found to be apprehensive about special tests because they will be awake and expected to follow instructions from staff. They therefore feel what is being done and are fully involved, although sometimes sedated. Commonly patients who anticipate such tests admit to having a 'fear of the unknown' and are rarely provided with a detailed account of what is done. Because diagnostic techniques are developing so rapidly it is also difficult for staff to keep fully informed of the procedure.

Another factor which mitigates against patients' preparation for these tests is their routine nature. Because patients are scheduled for special radiographs so frequently, staff seem to become complacent about their effects. For instance, a barium meal or enema is really commonplace for general medical and surgical wards, although, of course, not so for the individual patients. In one study (Wilson-Barnett 1978) for two-thirds of patients scheduled for a barium enema this was their first. After rather vigorous preparation which at times included an evacuation enema, patients were often tired and deprived of sleep. Many were rather elderly and emaciated and felt uncomfortable and very anxious during the procedure. Such experiences should not be forgotten and indeed the situation is improving in most general hospitals. For outpatients, of course, there is little opportunity for discussion and preparation.

Other diagnostic tests are even more akin to surgery. Cardiac catheterisation and angiography, for instance, involve a sterile procedure which is extremely invasive and at times 'desperately uncomfortable'. Finesilver's

(1979) study showed that despite patients acceptance of this test many were distressed before and during the procedure.

Compounding anxiety over the experience of the test is the patients' concern about the results or diagnosis which will follow. Many are very worried about the possibility of cancer and some researchers (Wilson-Barnett 1978) have found that those who are subsequently found to have cancer are much more anxious during the test and prior to their diagnosis. This may indicate that those with more serious illnesses are indeed likely to suffer from more severe emotional disturbance (see Moffic & Paykel 1975).

Researchers in this field recommend that patients should be told that their diagnosis will usually be discussed with them after the test is done. In reality, and where possible, it is common for non-serious diagnoses to be made and relayed to the patient during the procedure, whereas a suspected malignancy is rarely disclosed at this time.

Nurse researchers have contributed to experimental work in this field and this may be because they witness and are sometimes surprised by patients' reactions. Once more it is difficut to predict which type of test will elicit most distress. In one study Wilson-Barnett (1979) found that producing a urine specimen was more stressful for an elderly lady than having a cardiac catheter!

COMMUNICATION WITH PATIENTS TO ALLEVIATE ANXIETY

A generally open and friendly approach is seen to be very helpful to patients. It apparently gives them confidence that they can ask for information if they require it. Open communication is fundamental to professional practice (Macleod Clark 1983) and seems to effect a more relaxed atmosphere. Seen as the background to more specific communications, it serves to provide staff with more disclosures from patients which can then help to direct therapy and the giving of information.

If one defines anxiety as 'fear of the unknown', as an unrealistic fear orientated to the future with an uncertain cause (Marks & Lader 1972), it is not surprising that giving information should help to reduce it. The exact mechanism for this is hypothesised. Patients themselves say that they no longer fantasise or imagine dreadful experiences when they receive a realistic account. Even though many do not remember every detail it reassures them generally. Forewarning of what will happen also avoids surprises or shocks which are unpleasant and lead to a nervous anticipation of what else might ensue.

There is, however, some validity to the fact that giving specific information about a particular stressor may increase anxiety. Andrew (1970) and De Long (1970) found that those patients who did not prefer to use information as a coping resource and were, in fact, given this tended to do less well than similar subjects who did not receive this pre-operative information. Sensitive and individual approaches to communication are essential in practice. Although such patients are in the minority it is important to assess what types of coping strategies tend to be used by each one. There are approximately 10–20% who tend to refuse specific offers of preparatory information (Ridgeway & Mathews 1982).

In practice it is obviously best to get to know individual patients prior to (what is usually seen as) a stressful event. By talking with them, and assessing their emotional and cognitive needs and usual coping strategies, appropriate interventions can be selected. Currently this has to be planned quite carefully in view of the rapid turnover of patients. Staff must therefore schedule a preprocedural visit for someone who is already assigned to that patient's care.

Providing fairly comprehensive information about a surgical or diagnostic procedure allows the patient to discuss concerns or questions and plan ahead. Hopefully they will then realise that questions are encouraged, that staff are trying to help them relax and prepare them to be involved in their own care. Patients may use this opportunity in different ways. They may reveal their own strategies or exercises or plan to use diversional tactics.

Complaints about the lack of information given in hospital are still common. Studies undertaken for the Royal Commission on the NHS (1979) reflect this. Yet by providing an environment which maximises opportunities to assess needs and provide continuity of psychological care it should be possible to reduce complaints as well as anxiety.

RESEARCH BASE

Since the early study of Egbert et al (1964) which demonstrated how information on anaesthesia breathing exercises and pain relief helped patients to make a more speedy recovery, psychologists and nurses have been refining the interventions and the experimental designs. Research in the late 1960s and early 1970s tended to compare two groups of subjects, one group receiving a package of information about surgery and early recovery and the other (controls) receiving 'usual care'. As it became evident from other studies, particularly on nurse communication (Wilson-Barnett 1979, Macleod Clark 1983) that 'usual care' did not involve very much systematic information giving, results were very impressive. Experimental patients were shown to have a shorter length of stay, require less pain medication and have fewer complications (see Wilson-Barnett 1984).

Most studies tended to compare a standardised package of intervention and few attempted to identify whether any type of personality or coping strategy interacted more favourably with the intervention (Andrew (1970) and De Long (1970) mentioned previously were exceptions). Individual preference was therefore not catered for.

Studies tended to be fairly small and samples were mixed in terms of sex and type of operation. Many did not assess outcome measures blind to

Table 18.1   Different interventions designed to reduce stress

Surgery	Tests
Procedural and physical coping: information vs controls	
Dumas & Leonard (1963)	Tryon & Leonard (1965)
Egbert et al (1964)	Wilson-Barnett (1978)
Lindeman (1972)	
Leigh et al (1977)	
Procedural and physical coping: sensory information vs controls	
Hayward (1975)	Finesilver (1979)
Boore (1978)	Karlsson (1980)
Procedural vs sensory	
Johnson et al (1977)	
	Johnson et al (1973)
	Johanson Hartfield & Cason (1981)
Procedural and sensory information vs 'coping' advice	
Langer et al (1975)	Fuller et al (1978)
Ridgeway & Mathews (1982)	

experiment grouping and researchers did not publish their intervention in detail. Despite this, the volume of research grew, encouraged by the positive findings (Table 18.1).

PROCEDURAL INFORMATION

Most early studies were designed to evaluate information which was presented verbally and included an account of the procedure, with when and what would be done by whom. Few included a placebo intervention relying on a control group but when this was included results have been slightly less significant (Devine & Cook 1983). Even so, this type of intervention was generally seen to improve patients' reports of their experiences and physical outcome.

Details of physical pre-operative preparation (bathing and shaving) and the premedication were included in all. They also explained where the wound would be sited and the type of dressing to be applied. Intravenous infusions or wound drains would be discussed and usually patients would be told about what pain medication they could expect and ask for. Length of bed rest and plans for mobilisation were also included.

One study which compared the benefits of an interview with those of a booklet about the anaesthetic (Leigh et al 1977) found that the booklet was less effective in reducing anxiety than the interview. These researchers, who were anaesthetists, discussed the pressure of time which may prevent the pre-operative visit; they advise that an interview should be held, but possibly carried out by the anaesthetic nurse.

Patients undergoing tests appreciate details of the procedures involved. Schuster & Jones (1982) found that patients particularly appreciated information on the purpose of the test and when they would hear the results.

Patients are usually conscious during many tests and would therefore welcome being told the length of the procedure, which helps them to endure any discomfort (Wilson-Barnett 1979).

A typical intervention is given below. This leaflet was left for the patient to read, or not, at leisure.

Explanation to patients for a barium enema

The purpose of this procedure is to X-ray the bowels and back passage. By passing barium into the bowels through the back passage an outline of the lower bowel can be seen. If there is anything wrong with these parts it may show up on these X-rays.

In order for the bowel or intestines to show clearly, they must be completely empty of waste materials. So the day before you must eat food that has little waste materials in it, such as dry biscuits, plain bread, lean meat, clear fruit jelly and clear soup. All this food will be sent from the diet kitchen. Also to clear the tubes you should drink plenty of water, at least a glass full at 1 p.m., 3 p.m., 7 p.m., and one before bed on the day before your X-ray. Also on the night before your X-ray, at about 8 p.m., the ward nurse will give you a glass of specially prepared solution to drink. This will be followed at 10 p.m. by three tablets to be swallowed with a glass or more of water. All this preparation is to ensure the bowel is empty, but you can have a light breakfast on the morning of your X-ray.

On the morning of your X-ray the ward staff will give you a suppository, which is to be inserted into your back passage as high as possible. This procedure is slightly uncomfortable, but not painful. It is important for you to try to retain the suppository for about 15 minutes, if possible, before going to the toilet. Prior to your X-ray you will be given a gown by the ward staff and you may also wear your dressing gown and slippers when the porter comes to collect you and take you to the X-ray department. On arrival at the department you may be required to wait for a short time before being shown into the X-ray room. In this room, where the main lights are turned off at the start of the procedure, there will be odd trolleys and pieces of X-ray equipment. The main X-ray camera, which takes films shown on a television and ordinary X-rays, is a solid box suspended from the ceiling. It moves up and down and along the length of the table. The X-ray table, where the patient lies, is metal and solid and feels rather hard, but is covered by a paper cloth and pad in case any barium is spilt. The camera is worked from behind a screen by the wall and by a foot pedal near the table by the doctor. The doctor stands beside the table and directs the procedure and takes films, and the radiographer takes the permanent 'still' X-rays from behind the screen. She also changes the film plates in the camera. The staff all wear special aprons to protect them from too much X-ray.

When the doctor comes, he may ask you a few questions about your illness and look at your X-rays. With you lying on your front he will then insert a plastic enema tube into your back passage, which may be a little uncomfortable, but you will get used to it. This tube is closed off or opened to let in the barium, by the doctor. The doctor may also pump in a little air so this shows up more of the bowels for the X-rays. You may now be asked to change your position, from side to side, and on to your back, and periodically to hold your breath. The table may be tilted head down or feet down, and this makes a slight noise, as does the movement of the camera. In all, the procedure will take 30–40 minutes. When all the X-rays are taken you may have to wait for the doctor to see the last pictures. He may not be able to tell you straight away what he has found as he needs to study them very carefully.

Before you empty your bowels, the radiographer may want to take a few more shots with you on your side, leaning against a side support fixed to the table. She will then guide you to the nearest toilet. For these last few minutes you may feel rather blown-out and also eager to empty your bowel. If you can, you should hold your muscles tight before and after the tube is removed and you are then shown to the toilet. If you cannot hold it do not worry, it sometimes leaks and it will only spill on to the paper covering on the floor. After this, you will then be taken back to the ward. You may expect to feel a little uncomfortable until your bowels are back to normal. This should take an hour or two, but you can eat and drink normally as soon as you want to. Your stools will be whitish for a day or two until all the barium is completely evacuated.

PHYSICAL COPING ADVICE

On general wards advice on breathing and leg exercises is commonly given by physiotherapists and nurses. This type of information can be incorporated in pre-operative experimental interventions. Lindeman's (1972) study evaluated group teaching for a 'stir-up regime', of deep breathing, coughing and bed exercises. Advice was given in a classroom setting or individually and exercises and moving 'skills' were demonstrated. Both groups of patients benefited equally from these interventions, as measured by shortened length of hospital stay and improved ventilatory function.

Further studies (Boore 1978, Hayward 1975) have included other aspects of pre-operative teaching. Advice on moving and coughing while supporting the wound, on sitting up and turning over in bed, and on getting out of bed, was thought to be particularly helpful in reducing discomfort after surgery. Most researchers comment that practising such techniques before surgery facilitates earlier mobilisation postoperatively.

Patients undergoing certain special tests welcome advice on coping with the attendant physical distress and physical coping advice is well received. For example, patients undergoing cardiac catheterisation were advised to tighten and relax the muscles in their legs and back in turn (Finesilver 1979). This helped them cope with discomfort and boredom and prevented stiffness.

In a careful study of women undergoing gynaecological examinations, Fuller et al (1978) compared the effect of physical coping advice with other interventions. Clenching the hands together, deep breathing and relaxation were all found to be helpful. Patients who have mastered certain techniques such as yoga and relaxation, should be encouraged to employ them. Relaxation was specifically compared with an information giving intervention for 70 surgical patients (Wilson 1981). The relaxation group benefited by reduced hospital stay, less medication and pain, whilst reporting increased strength and energy. For the future, when more staff are trained in relaxation methods, such interventions may be used more routinely to alleviate fear, although for most patients, they would mainly be used as an adjunct to giving clear information.

SENSORY INFORMATION

Information interventions need to be accurate accounts of what the patient will experience and need to reflect the patients' perspectives. Johnson (1983) established that information on what patients feel, see, and even smell is more influential in alleviating their distress and promoting their recovery than other types of information. In a study with patients scheduled for gastroscopy Johnson et al (1973) demonstrated that information on sensations experienced during this investigation was associated with more co-operative behaviour and reduced discomfort when compared with procedural information or a control condition. A taped message was played to the experimental group of patients before the procedure. Photographs of the equipment and how it was used were also shown to the patients. The taped message included sounds of the suction and details of how it felt to have the throat sprayed and the gastroscope passed into the pharynx and oesophagus. Johnson has explained that the aim of this type of intervention is to help the patient have an accurate expectation and to have a 'cognitive map' which will guide their experience in terms of timing and the nature of events. Similar work with children having a plaster of paris cast removed (Johnson et al 1975) also showed this principle could apply for non-surgical yet frightening events. Several surgical studies (Johnson 1983) have also shown the superiority of this type of information over procedural information and have provided reliable evidence on the type of sensations, experienced. Physical sensations, temporal and spatial orientation require the use of objective language, not evaluative terms. Only sensations that are experienced by at least 50% of patients should be explained.

Careful descriptions of each test or surgical procedure from patients' accounts are necessary before an intervention can be designed. Patients must be asked to recount what happened and how it felt so that their terminology can be used for the benefit of others. Several patients should be interviewed in this way in order to establish the most common sensations. For instance 'aching', 'pressure', 'pulling', 'sharp', 'sore' and 'tender' are the most commonly used words to describe sensations felt in an abdominal incision. An accurate preparatory explanation might therefore be: 'When you return from the recovery room to the ward the anaesthetic will be wearing off and you may start to feel your incision. You may feel a pulling sensation with pressure around the area from the dressing. It may also start to feel sore and tender to touch, sensations which become sharper over time. Remember you can always ask for a pain killer so that you feel more able to cough and move about.'

PRACTICAL ISSUES IN PREPARATORY INTERVENTIONS

Adequate time to provide information prior to a procedure is essential and this should be planned systematically by nurses and doctors or others with a caring role. Patients may prefer to have a relative with them at this time and this has certainly been recommended for teaching sessions, such as hospital discharge planning (Wilson-Barnett & Oborne 1983) and certain advantages accrue. For instance, relatives may remind patients of some aspects or encourage patients to practise exercises. If more than one patient is scheduled for the same procedure a joint session would seem appropriate. Interactive sessions are considered more helpful and staff should ensure that requisite details are to hand and if necessary the patient's notes, or photographs of equipment or other pictures.

Certain principles should be adhered to and staff should avoid giving too much information too rapidly or using unfamiliar or semitechnical language. Sessions should really not continue for longer than 20 minutes without pause, an overall plan for the explanation should be used and illustrative materials may be needed for clarification at times.

Most staff have difficulty in explaining procedures without employing specific terminology which may be unfamiliar to patients. Cosper (1967) found that several terms such as 'nil by mouth', 'premedication', 'incision', 'infusion', 'drain', and 'void' were not understood by a majority of patients. It is therefore important to provide opportunities to practise by role playing and video feedback.

Hayward (1975) and Johnson (1983) advise that sessions should be informal and interactive. Preferably the staff member should be known by the patient and be someone he trusts. Questions should be invited initially and throughout the session and if the answers are not known the information should be sought from a reliable source. Co-ordination of such information giving is important to ensure it is reliable and not contradictory.

For those patients who appear rather nervous it is essential to explore particular worries initially. Information should be selected accordingly and more than one session may be required in order to include topics on sensations and exercises.

Evidence that one in seven patients choose not to be informed about forthcoming events demonstrates that blanket guidelines are problematic (Ridgeway & Mathews 1982). Patients who do not seem to want information should certainly not be forced to receive it. They may appreciate a discussion about something other than the impending event and relaxation or diversional approaches. This may utilise non-cognitive mechanisms of stress reduction.

Researcher's notes form Hayward's (1975) experimental intervention are provided below, as they pinpoint the danger of information overload. Pre- and postoperative information on sensations and recommended exercises can be seen as being most useful to a majority of patients.

1. Pre-operative nursing information
   a. Impressed on patient that specific medical information will be given by the doctors. We are merely giving general information about pre- and post-operative care.

    b. Reinforcement of patient's decision to undergo surgery. Stressing of long-term benefits.

    c. Relevant selection from following items of nursing care. This will obviously vary according to the type of operation.

      (i) Who to ask for information, i.e. ward sister, who will then arrange other appointments if appropriate.

      (ii) Idea of pre-operative care. Why following may be necessary (selected for relevance of operation type):

        medical examination

        consent form

        dietary restrictions (if any)

        laboratory specimens

        pre-operative shaving

        premedication, and other pre-anaesthetic procedures

        may have blood transfusion or intravenous fluids

        may recover in recovery room, or intensive care unit

2. Postoperative pain and discomfort aspects

    a. Pain is a normal reaction to an operation, but its severity can often be affected by the patient's attitudes.

    b. Pain is amplified by muscle spasm or tenseness in the muscles surrounding the operation site — the tighter these are, the more it hurts.

    c. Therefore, relaxation of the immediate area and of the whole body may help the pain. Practice beforehand.

    d. Avoid strain on the injured part by rehearsing changes of position etc.

    e. Information on physiotherapist and early ambulation.

    f. Patient is told about any item of postoperative care specific to his/her operation, e.g. infusions, tubes, diet.

WRITTEN MATERIAL

Most research in this area indicates that a simple written account prior to surgery or another procedure can be useful for both patients and staff. Vocabulary and style of prose should be assessed carefully, most material produced in hospital being inaccessible for a majority of patients (Cosper 1967). It is important that the size of print is larger than that in most textbooks as patients are likely to be elderly and unable to see print easily. Diagrams or illustrations are important. Where there is enough information to fill more than one side of paper it is advisable to leave spaces in order to add personalised comments or answers to patients' questions. A typical pre-operative booklet would be about 10 pages long, as designed by Leigh et al (1977), with 75 words per page. Such material should not replace an interview but can usefully augment and provide structure for this. It serves as an aide-memoir for the staff member and can be used for later reference by the patient.

There are disadvantages to producing printed accounts. It is difficult to make them universally applicable yet useful and they tend to become out-dated rapidly as surgical and diagnostic techniques develop and change. However, they can provide a valuable source of information for staff who are unfamiliar with some of the details of surgical treatment or diagnostic procedures.

Summary guidelines are provided below using elements of interventions which have been shown to be beneficial for patients prior to special tests or surgery.

1. Sessions should be interactive but provide a chronological account of the procedure and its efforts.
2. Major queries or concerns should be explored initially.
3. All information should be given in everyday language.
4. Sessions should not be longer than 20 minutes.
5. Patients should be encouraged to ask questions and write things down if they wish.
6. A written account can be used to guide the session and left with the patient for future reference.
7. Information which relates the patients experience and sensations is most important.
8. Advice on physical coping is particularly useful if the patient is conscious during a procedure.
9. The patient should be constantly assessed for signs of fatigue or fear.
10. If information does not appear to be relevant to the patient a different approach should be tried, e.g. exercises or relaxation.

INFORMATION VERSUS SPECIFIC WORRIES AND COPING ADVICE

Studies by Langer et al (1975) and Ridgeway & Mathews (1982) have shown that it may be more effective to focus on major worries rather than give a comprehensive account of what a patient will experience during the pre-operative period. Common fears mentioned in the early part of this chapter were explored in these studies and patients were encouraged to view them more positively with the aid of specific information. In Ridgeway & Mathews' study a booklet was designed to help patients control negative feelings about certain events. Major worries were listed and followed by statements minimising the worry by providing realistic information. Active participation in this process was encouraged, patients were asked to supply their own positive thoughts about a common worry and then to produce a negative one which was reappraised positively. Female patients in this study were able to do this effectively and benefited more from this, on certain measures of recovery, than males, given information on procedural and sensory aspects of surgery.

Positive reappraisal has to be practised by patients and most ward staff are unfamiliar with this technique. It is sometimes quite difficult to employ this realistically when patients are very nervous and unable to discuss specific worries. However, positive findings on the use of this approach justify further research and staff training.

AN INTEGRATED APPROACH

In the clinical setting staff should aim to maximise the possible benefits of different interventions by using a combined approach. This is obviously indicated only where patients accept it readily or when they are in a condition to understand and use information.

For those patients reluctant or unable to identify their particular worries initially a conversation providing them with an account of the procedure may facilitate more focused discussion on the topics as raised. This approach should incorporate the benefits of a comprehensive description and an exploration of specific worries. If positive reappraisal can be employed for these worries this can be an additional strength. Advice can be interspersed with demonstration and discussion of diagrams or pictures, to avoid loss of concentration and when patients appear to respond positively to one type of presentation this can then be exploited fully throughout the session.

A summary of this more combined approach, particularly relevant to patients undergoing surgery, would require five more preliminary steps before using those previously listed.

1. Discuss with patients how they feel about surgery.
2. Identify specific worries.
3. Explore these worries and their perceived cause.
4. Provide realistic information about these aspects of surgery.
5. Encourage one or more positive statements on each topic.

POSITIVE EFFECTS OF PREPARATION: SURGERY

Planned information giving has been shown to provide psychological and physical benefits. Patients have reported that they feel more prepared and knowledgeable and they have the opportunity to rehearse various strategies and methods of coping. Anxiety reduction is more marked for patients undergoing tests but surgical patients report that they feel less worried and more capable when prepared in this way (Johnson 1983).

There have been consistent reports of shorter hospital stay, fewer complications and a more rapid recovery from surgical intervention studies (see Wilson-Barnett 1984). One of the greatest challenges for those working in general hospitals is to plan for and give time to psychological care. This is underemphasised in practice, despite overwhelming evidence of the benefits. It may be that increased participation by the patient both in mental planning and physical practice makes patients more capable during the postoperative period. Reduced levels of catecholamines (Boore 1978) may also result in greater immune competence, preventing infection and thrombosis.

Patients observed while undergoing tests in intervention studies by Johnson et al (1973) and Finesilver (1979) tended to have an 'easier' procedure. Patients require less sedation when prepared in this way, which enables them to be more alert, respond to instructions and practise physical coping methods. They therefore take a shorter time to recover.

In whatever ways patients use the information and advice, it seems that the majority find this helpful and now seem to complain when they remain uninformed. It is therefore clear that these sessions should become part of their treatment plan, in the interests of both politeness and prevention of unnecessary complications.

APPROPRIATE PERSONNEL

For everyday occurrences of routine surgery and tests it is probably the nurse who can establish a relationship with the patient and provide information. However he needs to be a skilled, sensitive and properly trained communicator, who feels committed to this approach as a useful and important aspect of care. Such staff need to be able to recognise signs of anxiety, distraction or fatigue and be a patient and active listener. Knowledge of procedures and patients' experiences must be correct and up to date.

Physicians and psychologists may also be involved in this type of intervention either before the patient is admitted and nurses are not available or when patients specifically ask them for guidance. Ward records should be kept to ensure that one member of staff has been assigned to this task and where a doctor wishes to undertake this particular care he should obviously let nursing staff know.

In the case of very distressed patients, special attention or a referral may be indicated. Where major surgery is planned, possibly necessitating treatment in the intensive care unit, a distressed pre-operative patient should be considered 'at risk'. For such patients a psychologist or psychiatrist may need to engage in rather more protracted psychotherapy which could mean delaying surgery. Anxiolytics are sometimes prescribed but they should not replace discussion with the patient to explore fears and provide some useful guidance for coping with surgery.

Those who refuse to accept psychological interventions such as specific information may prefer diversional tactics through 'keeping busy'. They often respond to a schedule of exercises or relaxation. Here nurses and physiotherapists should work together. Relaxation and preparatory tapes are rarely used on general wards but they should be a more commonly accepted form of treatment. However, it is never wise to persuade a patient who is denying the need to face up to or adjust to the situation to listen to any type of preparation. Evidence suggests they fare worse with than without preoperative information (Andrew 1970).

CONCLUSION

One of the greatest challenges for those working in general hospitals is to plan for and devote time to giving psychological care. This is underrepresented despite the overwhelming evidence that it has great therapeutic value, particularly when patients are anticipating a 'stressful' event. Pressure to give physical care appears so great in the hurly-burly of ward activities that other aspects of care have to be explicity scheduled and assigned.

It is also self-evident that providing psychological care is not something we can all do solely with a caring approach and strong motivation. Communication skills can be learned and improved through a range of processes, such as role play and video feedback. This type of skills training is very effective and of such wide relevance to professional practice that all health carers could benefit from this during and after training. Resources such as illustrative materials, booklets and accurate reports of sensations experienced need to be available in the settings where patients should receive psychological preparation.

Patients are now becoming more involved in their care to their clear advantage and with scarce resources they need to engage in preventative and positive coping behaviour in order to suffer less and benefit more from other treatments. This chapter has focused on research-based interventions which help a great many patients at stressful times. Hopefully in the next decade these will be a fundamental part of practice for all nurses and other members of the health care team.

REFERENCES

Andrew J M 1970 Recovery from surgery with and without preparatory instruction for three coping styles. Journal of Personality and Social Psychology 15: 223–226
Boore J 1978 Prescription for recovery. Royal College of Nursing, London
Carnevali D L 1986 Pre-operative anxiety. Americal Journal of Nursing 66: 1536–1529
Cosper B 1967 How well do patients understand hospital jargon? American Journal of Nursing 1932–1934
De Long R D 1970 Individual differences in patterns of anxiety arousal, stress-relevant information and recovery from surgery. PhD thesis, University of California
Devine E C, Cook T D 1983 A meta-analytic analysis of effects of psycho-educational interventions on length of post-surgical hospital stay. Nursing Research 32: 267–274
Dumas R G, Leonard R C 1963 The effect of nursing on the incidence of post-operative vomiting. Nursing Research 21: 12–15
Egbert L D, Battit G E, Welch C E, Bartlett M K 1964 Reduction of postoperative pain by encouragement and instruction of patients: a study of doctor patient rapport. New England Journal of Medicine 270: 822–27

Finesilver C 1979 Preparation of adult patients for cardiac catheterisation and coronary cineangiography. International Journal of Nursing Studies 16: 211–221

French K 1979 Some anxieties of elective surgery patients and the desire for reassurance and information. In Oborne D J, Gruneberg M M, Eiser T R (eds) Research in psychology and Medicine vol. 2. Academic Press, London

Fuller S S, Endress M P, Johnson J E 1978 The effects of cognitive and behavioural control on coping with an aversive health examination. Journal of Human Stress 4: 18–25

Hayward J 1975 Information — a prescription against pain. Royal College of Nursing, London

Johansen Hartfield M, Cason C L 1981 Effects of information on emotional responses during barium enema. Nursing Research 30: 151–155

Johnson J E 1983 Preparing patients to cope with stress while hospitalised. In Wilson Barnett J (ed) Patient teaching. Churchill Livingstone, Edinburgh, pp 19–33

Johnson J E, Morrissey J E, Leventhal H 1973 Psychological preparation for an endoscopic examination. Gastrointestinal Endoscopy 19: 180–182

Johnson J E, Kirchoff K T, Endress M P 1975 Altering children's distress behaviour during orthopaedic cast removal. Nursing Research 24: 404–410

Johnson J E, Riche V H, Fuller S S, Endress M P 1977 Sensory information, instruction in coping strategy and recovery from surgery. Research in Nursing and Health 1: 4–17

Johnston M 1978 Anxiety in surgical patients. Psychological Medicine 10: 145–152

Karlsson K 1980 The effect of information on patients undergoing intravenous pyelography. Internal report. University Hospital of Uppsala, Department of Radiology

Langer E J, Janis I L, Wolfer J A 1975 Reduction of psychological stress in surgical patients. Journal of Social Psychology 11: 155–165

Leigh J M, Walker J, Janaganathan P 1977 Effect of pre-operative anaesthetic visit on anxiety. British Medical Journal 2: 978–989

Lindeman C A 1972 Nursing intervention with the presurgical patient. Nursing Research 21: 196–209

Macleod Clark J 1983 Nurse–patient communication — an analysis of conversations from surgical wards. In Wilson-Barnett J (ed) Nursing research: ten studies in patient care. Wiley, Chichester

Marks I, Lader M 1972 Clinical anxiety. Heinemann, London

Moffic H S, Paykel G S 1975 Depression in medical in-patients. British Journal of Psychiatry 126: 346–353

Ramsay M A E 1972 A survey of pre-operative fear. Anaesthesia 27: 396–402

Ridgeway V, Mathews A 1982 Psychological preparation of surgery: a comparison of methods. British Journal of Clinical Psychology 21: 271–280

Royal Commission on the NHS 1979 Report No 5. HMSO, London

Schuster P, Jones S 1982 Preparing the patient for a barium enema: a comparison of nurse and patient opinions. Journal of Advanced Nursing 7: 523–527

Tryon P A, Leonard R C 1965 Giving the patient an active role. In Skipper J K, Leonard R C (eds) Social interaction and patient care. Lippincott, Philadelphia pp 120–127

Wilson J F 1981 Behavioural preparation for surgery: benefit or harm. Journal of Behavioural Medicine 4: 79–102

Wilson-Barnett J 1978 Patient's emotional responses to barium X-rays. Journal of Advanced Nursing 3: 37–46

Wilson-Barnett J 1979 Stress in hospital. Churchill Livingstone, Edinburgh

Wilson-Barnett J 1984 Interventions to alleviate patients' stress: a review. Journal of Psychosomatic Research 28: 63–72

Wilson-Barnett J, Carrigy A 1978 Factors influencing patients' emotional reaction to hospitalisation. Journal of Advanced Nursing 3: 221–229

Wilson-Barnett J, Fordham M 1983 Recovery from illness. Wiley, Chichester

Wilson-Barnett J, Oborne J 1983 Studies evaluating patient teaching: implications for practice. International Journal of Nursing Studies 20: 33–44

J. A. Kohler, M. Radford

The dying child

CAUSES OF DEATH

Death in childhood was commonplace a hundred years ago in Britain and former generations of parents were to some extent prepared to lose a child during his early years. Nowadays, mainly because of the decrease in mortality from infective illness, childhood death is uncommon after the newborn period and a rarity after the age of 1 year. As a society, we are inexperienced in dealing with death in children, and community and religious support are not readily available. Whatever the age, duration of illness, or cause, the ending of a child's life is both a tragedy for the parents and a deeply distressing event for medical, nursing and paramedical staff who cared for him.

The commonest cause of death in the 1–14 year age group is accidental death. Although there may be a brief period of intensive care following the traumatic event, there is usually no recognisable period when the child is 'dying'. Hence there is usually little or no time to prepare the family for such a catastrophe.

Children dying of chronic disorders have been more closely studied. Cancer is the commonest fatal disease of children, and although 50% of all children with cancer can be cured, the remainder will die. Some deaths will occur before the disease is brought under control and a few will result from treatment-related conditions. In these cases death will probably not be accepted as inevitable until it occurs, and the concept of a 'dying' child is inappropriate. The majority of cancer deaths, however, are caused by recurrent or uncontrollable disease. A first or second recurrence will probably be treated with curative intent, but eventually a decision may be made that further aggressive treatment is not justified. Treatment is changed from curative to palliative and this change marks the beginning of a defined period of terminal care (Wilkes 1980).

For children with chronic progressive disorders such as cystic fibrosis or muscular dystrophy, a period of terminal care may be difficult to define. Active intervention during an exacerbation of the disease may prolong the child's life for a few more months, but as the quality of life between hospital admissions deteriorates, the decision to withhold treatment may become necessary.

MEDICAL TREATMENT

The aim of any treatment given during the terminal phase is to ensure a pain-free and dignified death.

Pain relief is normally provided by gradually increasing doses of oral opiates, diamorphine syrup commonly being used. The analgesics need to be given early and regularly, before any pain has the chance to return, so that the anticipation of pain is eliminated and the patient maintains a sense of control over his symptoms. For children at home, very careful instruction must be given to both parents and family doctors, since there is often a reluctance to increase the daily dose because of misconceptions concerning addiction or overdose.

Anorexia, constipation and insomnia are also common problems, and depression is likely to be present, particularly in the older age group. There may be a specific role for drugs such as tricyclic antidepressants, but time spent talking with the child is often more effective.

PLACE OF DEATH

Just as home is the natural place for a child to live, so it seems to be the natural place for a child to die. Various studies on home care for children dying of cancer have suggested that not only do the children themselves feel happier at home, but that their parents cope better with bereavement if they have been able to care for their child during the terminal illness (Martinson et al 1978, Lauer et al 1983).

Using the Minnesota Multiphasic Personality Inventory, Mulhern et al (1983) assessed the psychological adjustment of the family following the death of a child at home or in hospital. Following a hospital death, parents were more anxious, depressed and defensive. Siblings were more emotionally inhibited, withdrawn and tearful.

In a typical hospital setting, there is no privacy for parents and they have no control over their child's immediate environment. They cannot prevent noise or interruption and there is little that they can provide for their child without someone else's permission. These parents suffer the negative psychological consequences of helplessness.

If a dying child is hospitalised, one parent is normally resident, leaving the other struggling at home with the healthy siblings. The family is divided at a time when the need to be together is greatest.

We recently interviewed parents of 18 children dying of cancer following a defined period of terminal care, to discover the practical and emotional problems encountered by these families (Kohler & Radford 1985). They were all quick to recognise the advantages to the whole family of having the dying child at home, but did not express their negative feelings unless specifically given the opportunity to do so. We found that 80% of parents were afraid that their child would suffer uncontrollable symptoms, especially pain, and more than half admitted to extreme anxiety over the moment of death. They dreaded a painful, undignified death, and were particularly afraid it would be sudden, finding one parent alone and unprepared for its occurrence.

A hospital bed was always available for the dying child, and the parents were reassured that readmission was no reflection of failure on their part. Five children were eventually readmitted; four to hospital and one to a local hospice. Three of the children had uncontrollable symptoms and two were admitted at the parents' request.

Few children die in a hospice. Helen House, the first hospice for children, was opened in Oxford in 1982, but although priority has been given to children with a terminal illness, the aim has always been to offer respite care rather than to be a place where children die (Dominica 1982). Children are physically easier to care for at home than adults, and have parents to look after them. With support and encouragement this is usually possible. A hospice should perhaps be regarded more as 'a philosophy rather than a facility' (Corr & Corr 1983), or an approach to the giving of care rather than simply a place in which services are offered. As the service grows, instead of a few children being admitted to hospice beds, nurses from the hospice may be available to offer domiciliary care to many children dying at home.

PREPARING THE CHILD FOR DEATH

Children of less than 6 years of age have a limited capacity to appreciate the permanence and irreversibility of death. Very young children have no fear of death, but as they grow older they naturally become afraid of separation from their parents. Some understanding of death may have been gained by the experience of losing a grandparent or other close family member, or even by the loss of a family pet.

In our study, only one family discussed death with their child. Three children, however, talked openly of death in the last 24 hours, even though it had never been mentioned. Two of these asked for 'last trips' to a certain place, and one commented that 'there would be no more holidays'. It seems that, like adults, many children know intuitively when they are going to die, even occasionally when death is sudden and entirely unexpected (Kübler-Ross 1983). The difficulty lies in finding someone in whom to confide. They are often aware of their parents' grief and are afraid to say anything which might further upset them. Thus these children can be lonely with everyone around knowing that death is imminent but pretending it is not going to happen. Parents naturally wish to protect their children from knowledge which may frighten them, and fear the child will 'give up' if he knows there is no hope of cure. By avoiding all discussion on the subject they may actually increase the child's distress. Parents may end up using all their available emotional energy in the negative and largely unsuccessful pursuit of hiding the diagnosis, rather than in the more positive task of supporting the child (Vernick & Karon 1965).

It is not only a fear of the unknown which causes distress. Children, like adults, need the opportunity to put their lives in order and say goodbye. We recently looked after a 14-year-old boy with relapsed leukaemia. He was in hospital for several months receiving different toxic courses of treatment and became gradually more depressed and withdrawn. We were sure that he knew that time was running out, but his parents were anxious to keep fighting the disease and would not discuss the possibility of failure. Eventually a bone marrow aspiration was planned to see if the final choice of drugs was working. The day of the test came and the poor lad lay curled up, half hiding under the sheets all morning whilst his parents chatted brightly. The result was conclusive: the treatment had failed. There was no point in giving any more drugs and the option of taking him home was discussed with his parents. At their request, we simply told the young man that the treatment was not working and that we wanted him to have a few days at home. He looked long and hard at us, and as soon as we had gone, he said to his parents: 'So that means I'm going to die'. They wept together, but it was an immense relief that all pretence was over. The next day the patient was a changed person. He was sitting up in bed, writing letters, making lists of people he wanted to see and deciding which possessions should be given to whom. He went home and carried out all his plans in a week. He then announced that he had had enough and was ready to die. He did so within 24 hours.

Even quite young children 'drop hints' that they know of their approaching death, and these may be picked up by visitors other than parents. In hospital, nursing staff are often aware of this happening, and are naturally unsure how to respond, especially if the parents have specifically banned the topic of death from discussion. One of our patients kept reporting his nightmares to the nurses. He repeatedly dreamt that he was in a long, dark tunnel and that a variety of frightening animals were trying to catch him. He would then ask if he was ever going to get better, but only if his mother was not in the room. We longed to talk to him about his fears and to try to reassure him, but we also felt we had to respect his mother's wish for silence. She would have the rest of her life to remember his last few days and we wanted her to look back without regrets or anger. In paediatrics above all other hospital specialties, it is impossible to deal with any patient in isolation.

It is often easier for families with a strong religious faith to accept death, since they can look forward to a spiritual life after death and ultimate reunion with their dying child. If a child is familiar with the concept of a god or a heaven, it is very comforting if death is discussed in these terms

(Burton 1974). It is clear that only parents who have a firm conviction of a life after death can pass on that reassurance to their children.

All families are different and will deal with death in their own individual way. We believe strongly, however, that each child should be given the opportunity to discuss the subject, although not every one will choose to take it up.

COUNSELLING PARENTS

When parents are told that their child is going to die, the questions most frequently asked are 'How long will it be?' and 'How will he die?' Even if these are not voiced, they normally require some sort of answer.

The duration of the terminal phase is very variable and often unpredictable. In cases of 'sudden' death, where ventilatory support is being withdrawn following a period of intensive care for example, one may be talking in terms of hours or days. In chronic diseases, the terminal phase may last weeks or months. However vague the answer, doctors still have a better idea than a lay person, and some estimate helps the family to make appropriate plans. In our study of children dying of cancer (Kohler & Radford 1985), the mean duration of terminal care was 5.6 weeks. This mean was increased by four children who died at 2 months, 3 months and two at 5 months respectively. The median time was only 2 weeks.

The question 'How will he die?' is asked with particular anxiety by parents opting for home care. Hospital deaths are clean and clinical, with staff available to control unpleasant symptoms and share the burden of responsibility. At home, parents have the enormous strain of coping with the uncertainty and fear of the end. Those caring for adults dying at home have expressed similar fears (Reilly & Patten 1981).

When interviewing bereaved parents, we were told by one couple how, shortly before their child died of leukaemia, they had been visited by another well-meaning bereaved parent bearing 'the wadding'. This had apparently not been necessary after all for their child, but they thought it might be useful for someone else. This naturally struck horror into the recipients, who assumed that torrential haemorrhage was likely to occur. This fear dominated their last few days with their child. When she eventually died peacefully, they carefully put 'the wadding' aside, and some months later passed it on in the same way. How easily a myth is perpetuated, and how damaging it can be. Unless one tries to discuss what may or may not happen, parents will usually imagine something far worse.

In our study, of 17 witnessed deaths, 14 were described as peaceful. In the 17 cases, the child had shown a steady deterioration in the days preceding death so that the event was entirely expected. This is not only reassuring information, but is vital in counselling other families facing a similar situation.

Linked to the fear of death itself is the anxiety over the practical arrangements which must be made after death. Although these are difficult to discuss in advance, especially when the child is relatively well, lack of specific guidance can lead to further distress. Parents often say that they wished that their child's body could have stayed longer in the house after death, and that events moved too quickly once the funeral director was contacted. They also worry about contacting a doctor in the middle of the night, but rumours of rigor mortis or other postmortem phenomena dominate their thinking. Ideally there should be a doctor or nurse well known to the family available at all times during terminal care, anticipating problems of this kind and expecting to attend when the child dies. A useful handbook *What To Do When Someone Dies* is available (Rudinger 1967).

Friction all too often arises between parents during the terminal phase. Usually the wife has borne the brunt of hospital visits and she may resent her total responsibility. The husband may have to work overtime to help meet extra expenses, and is seen as hiding away at work. When the situation at home is very painful, this may also be true. The husband may rightly feel neglected by his wife as their child assumes the central role in the family. Disagreements arise as to how the sick child should be treated, especially if he misbehaves, and how much he should be allowed to do. Parents feel guilty if they go out and enjoy themselves, and most totally abandon any kind of social life. This may continue after the child's death, since they feel in some way disloyal if they forget to grieve, however briefly. By encouraging parents to talk and by discussing some of these differing attitudes it may be possible to help them to support each other at a time when they desperately need mutual comfort.

The only people who really know how it feels to lose a child are those who have been through the same experience. There are many support groups for families with children with specific diseases and for those with progressive disorders. These cater for parents of living children and of those who have died. The Compassionate Friends is a society which produces excellent literature for bereaved parents and has volunteers all over the UK and in many other countries ready to talk to or visit such parents. Most parents of dying children prefer to wait until after the death before making contact with outsiders, and often have to be encouraged to do so even then. It is often more helpful than they imagined.

We have an oncology parents' support group lead by our social workers. This group comprises parents of children currently receiving treatment, parents of those who have completed treatment successfully, and bereaved parents. In addition to organising informal talks and social evenings, these parents provide support for each other. When parents lose a child, they often want to talk to someone who knew their child when he was well, and it is therefore easier for them to relate to someone within the local group.

COPING WITH SIBLINGS

Although it may be possible to keep a diagnosis or prognosis from a young child, it is much harder to hide it from older siblings. If the child is going to die, they will inevitably find out eventually. Children have access to far more information now than even a few years ago, and television, newspapers and advertising posters tell them about a variety of life-threatening diseases. There are many examples of sick children or their siblings hearing the diagnosis from class mates, often accompanied by very inaccurate statements (Parker & Mauger 1979). It is much better if they have been told by their own parents in an atmosphere of trust and security. Withholding information from children seems to be unsuccessful in reducing their anxiety since they clearly sense that something is seriously amiss. If they are not given age-appropriate explanations, they are prone to fantasise. A disease that everyone is afraid to talk about always seems more frightening than one which can be named and discussed openly.

Children experience very mixed feelings about their dying brother or sister. Their pity for the suffering child is mixed with envy, since such a child becomes the focus of family attention. Often there is also guilt: a child may fear that he is in some way responsible for his sibling's illness, perhaps through previous aggressive behaviour. There may also be anxiety that he too could die. This is particularly difficult to cope with when it is a real possibility, as in the case of genetically inherited disorders where more than one child in the family is affected. The healthier child needs special support when his sibling's condition starts to deteriorate.

Young siblings are particularly vulnerable since they are most dependent on their mother. She may be anxious to spend most of her time with the sick child, but frustrated by lack of time for the baby. The relationship suffers if the baby has to be with someone else for any length of time. Although provision is always made for a baby to stay with the mother and sick child in hospital, we find that most mothers feel that they cannot divide themselves between the two children and want to give the patient their total devotion. Toddlers and young children who feel rejected may externalise their resentment by difficult behaviour, or may accept events with passive resignation, and become withdrawn and miserable. Older children may develop psychosomatic symptoms or find other attention-seeking ploys. Older girls are often given the responsibility for looking after younger children, which they may do very competently, but often at the expense of their school work or own social lives.

These age-related differences in measures of adaptation to living with a sick sibling have been studied in detail by Spinetta (1981). Professionals must be aware of the needs of siblings and continually remind families of these needs. Through active and continued communication siblings can express and resolve issues related to the disease and its treatment.

We encourage parents to try to involve the other children in their sick sibling's care. They can accompany them to hospital and see what treatment entails and meet the doctors and nurses on the ward. Treats and outings can be planned around all the children. If the sick child is at home, small jobs can be found for each sibling to do for him.

A recent study of adjustment to the death of a sibling, using behaviour checklists and self-concept scales, showed that even 2 or 3 years after the death, a high percentage of children show sufficient difficulties to warrant psychiatric help (Pettle Michael & Lansdown 1986). Events experienced by the child which made adjustment more likely included: having knowledge of the diagnosis and likely fatal outcome; participating in the child's care; having the opportunity to 'say goodbye' near the time of death; attending the service or being with the rest of the family on the day of the funeral; being able to have some of the patient's possessions; and previously experiencing the death of a relative or pet. Two other experiences, the sibling dying at home and seeing the dead body, were found in this study to be of questionable benefit. Low self-esteem among surviving children was found to be very common, and there was often idealisation of the dead sibling. In general, the self-esteem was higher when there had been a long illness, perhaps reflecting a greater opportunity for parents to prepare themselves and their children for the forthcoming loss.

Some siblings show little grief at the time of death, but it comes out later at the time of some trivial loss or when something reminds them of the patient. Other children use substitution to keep the relationship alive: they may fantasise about the dead sibling, press their mother to have another baby, or endow a friend with the lost child's characteristics (Lindsay & MacCarthy 1974).

It is important that teachers both of the dying child and of his siblings are aware of the situation. For the sick child, attending school for as long as possible, even on a part-time basis, is a normal activity and therefore reassuring. School combats boredom, and abandoning learning in effect tells the child that there is no future and no hope. Written information is welcomed by most teachers, since they themselves will be coping with their own fears and preconceived ideas of sickness and death. For children with cancer, we provide an information sheet for schools. This deals not only with the child's illness in general terms, but also offers suggestions as to how to talk to the rest of the class before and after the child's death.

ROLE OF DIFFERENT PROFESSIONALS

Most children with life-threatening conditions are looked after by a hospital specialist, often a consultant whom they have known for a long time. When a decision not to give further active treatment is made, the family may feel that further visits to the hospital are unnecessary, especially if long distances are involved. The main responsibility for medical care then falls on the general practitioner. His ability and willingness to take over care at that crucial stage depends on his involvement with the family during the child's illness. If communication between the specialist and the GP has been good, and the GP has continued to act as doctor for the rest of the family, the parents are more likely to have confidence in him, and not feel that a comparative stranger is taking over at an emotionally critical stage.

Contact with the hospital team can be maintained by regular telephone calls, or occasional visits to the home by arrangement with the family doctor. An appointment with the specialist at the hospital following the child's death is also appreciated by the family, both to discuss any aspects of the child's disease or last illness, and also to talk over family problems and difficulties with siblings. Medical representatives at the funeral are also welcomed since their presence adds credibility to the sense of worth that family members gather about their loved one (Irvine 1985). It is also a final opportunity to demonstrate care for the person who died and often helps to resolve the doctor's feelings of sadness and failure. Society's rituals serve a useful function.

Nurses who visit dying children at home similarly build up a relationship with the family over a period of time. We have a growing team of paediatric district nurses who visit our oncology children regularly at home throughout treatment, giving occasional injections, monitoring side effects of treatment and generally supporting the families. They are in an ideal position to take on terminal care should the need arise. A social worker is also attached to each of our families at diagnosis both to act in a generally supportive role and to provide practical and financial help.

A patient's failure to get well frustrates one of the primary goals and needs of a health care worker, and this often leads to feelings of anger and guilt (Rothenberg 1967). Care of dying children is stressful and the carers themselves need support to prevent emotional exhaustion. This is best achieved in a professional environment in which the physician and other members of the health care team trust each other and feel safe to discuss their problems of coping with the stress (Koenig 1981). Professional 'burn-out' is less likely to occur if the individual leads a balanced life-style. Professionally this may mean involvement with children with routine illnesses, research or teaching activities. On a personal level, a stable home life and recreational pursuits are also important.

We hold a weekly psychosocial meeting comprising doctors, nurses, social workers, play therapists and a psychologist, all caring for oncology patients. Not only can we co-ordinate our therapeutic approach, but we can openly discuss our own feelings and ways of handling certain problems. Few spouses understand the pressures of working with these families, and discussion with other professionals may protect our own family lives.

Care of the dying is not a subject taught in medical schools. It requires a different approach to teaching, with the involvement of experienced psychotherapists or psychiatrists (Goldie 1983). Students could be encouraged to consider their feelings about their own death; what they would wish for when dying; who they would want to speak to and what they would want for themselves by way of information and pain relief. This may have great benefit both for the future doctors themselves, and for their future patients.

CONCLUSION

Death in childhood will remain a reality for the foreseeable future. Medical expertise should ensure a pain-free and dignified death, but an understanding of the complex psychological factors surrounding a grieving family is essential if each member is to come to terms with his loss. The goal for the child, the family and the health care team is the same: to cope successfully with living with dying.

REFERENCES

Burton L 1974 Tolerating the intolerable. In Burton L (ed) Care of the child facing death. Routledge and Keegan Paul, London, pp. 16–38

Corr C A G, Corr D M 1983 Hospice care principles and practice. Faber and Faber, London

Dominica F 1982 Helen House — a hospice for children. Maternal and Child Health 7: 355–359

Goldie L 1983 Doctors in training and the dying patient. Journal of the Royal Society of Medicine 76: 995

Irvine P 1985 The attending at the funeral. New England Journal of Medicine 312: 1704–1705

Koenig H M 1981 Reflections of a pediatric cancer specialist. In: Spinetta J J, Deasy-Spinetta P (eds) Living with Childhood Cancer. C V Mosby, St Louis, p. 223–229

Kohler J A, Radford M 1985 Terminal care for children dying of cancer: quantity and quality of life. British Medical Journal 291: 115–116

Kübler-Ross E 1983 On children and dying. Macmillan, New York

Lauer M E, Mulhern R K, Wallskog J M, Camitta B M 1983 A comparison study of parental adaptation following a child's death at home or in the hospital. Pediatrics 71: 107–112

Lindsay M, MacCarthy D 1974 Caring for the brothers and sisters of a dying child. In Burton L (ed) Care of the child facing death. Routledge and Keegan Paul, London

Martinson I M, Armstrong G D, Gers D P 1978 Home care for children dying of cancer. Pediatrics 62: 106–113

Mulhern R K, Lauer M E, Hoffmann R G 1983 Death of a child at home or in the hospital: subsequent psychological adjustment of the family. Pediatrics 71: 743–747

Parker M, Mauger D 1979 Children with cancer. Cassell, London

Pettle Michael S A, Lansdown R G 1986 Adjustment to the death of a sibling. Archives of Disease in Childhood 61: 278–283

Reilly P M, Patten M P 1981 Terminal care in the home. Journal of the Royal College of General Practitioners 31: 531–537

Rothenberg M B 1967 Reactions of those who treat children with cancer. Pediatrics 40 (suppl): 507–510

Rudinger E (ed) 1967 What to do when someone dies. Consumers' Association, London

Spinetta J J 1981 The sibling of the child with cancer. In Spinetta J J, Deasy-Spinetta P (eds) Living with childhood cancer. C V Mosby, St Louis

Vernick J, Karon M 1965 Who's afraid of death on a leukaemia ward? American Journal of Diseases of Children 109: 393–397

Wilkes E 1980 Chairman's Report. Department of Health and Social Security Working Party on terminal care. HMSO, London

Liaison psychiatry

INTRODUCTION

The foundations of liaison psychiatry can be traced to the 'psychobiological' theories of Adolf Meyer (Lief 1948) which were so influential in American psychiatry. The psychosomatic approach championed by the analysts; e.g. Dunbar (1935) and Alexander (1950), gave liaison psychiatry its impetus with their characterisation of the psychological mechanisms in the genesis of physical disease (e.g. difficulty in handling hostility leading to hypertension, conflict over dependency needs in peptic ulceration etc. — the so-called 'Chicago Seven'). Whilst of only historical interest now, these ideas had considerable influence in their time. The first liaison psychiatry service, identified as such, was established in Colorado before the Second World War (Billings 1939) and the early history of liaison psychiatry is essentially North American (Lipowski 1974) with a later start in the UK (Fleminger & Mallett 1962, Crisp 1968).

The influence of the early psychoanalytical ideas has declined markedly, owing mainly to a failure to establish disease specificity of the described personality characteristics or to demonstrate the physiological mechanisms postulated. The awareness, however, that different temperaments are more common in some disorders is obvious to observant clinicians. Newer classifications have been generated to highlight possible causative connections. One of the most widely quoted of these is, of course, Friedman & Rosenman's (1971) 'Type A coronary prone' personality. Other, more controversial, studies (e.g. Greer et al 1979) on the relationship of emotional expression and the genesis and course of various malignancies focus attention on the immune system as a possible mediator between emotional state and physical health. Investigation of such hypotheses has ensured a continuing relationship between psychiatrists and their general hospital colleagues.

The last 20 years has seen a significant expansion in liaison psychiatry in the US and even the establishment of the first few NHS liaison psychiatry posts in Britain. The main stimulus for this growth has been the accumulating body of research (e.g. Shepperd et al 1960, Maguire et al

1974) which has documented the high proportion of patients consulting non-psychiatric doctors for what were essentially psychiatric disorders. These disorders often went untreated, frequently unrecognised, while the patient was extensively investigated and treated for apparently physical causes of their discomfort.

American literature highlights the misuse of inpatient facilities. Moffic & Paykel (1975) showed that 30% of medical inpatients in Boston wards were suffering from psychiatric, predominantly affective, disorders and that for most of them this went unrecognised. Presumably in the third who were recognised as such, this was either judged to be additional to a physical disorder or treatment in the medical ward was considered appropriate for the patient's emotional state. This latter is undoubtedly a widespread practice among clinicians, and carefully used may prove a powerful and efficient intervention in chronic maladaptive life-styles. It is possible that the proportion of inpatients with purely emotional disorders is lower in Britain because of the filtering effect of primary care. Studies here show clearly how heavy the burden of minor psychiatric mordibity is in primary care (Shepperd 1966).

Postgraduate training to enable GPs to recognise the somatic presentation of psychiatric disorders is now well established (Royal College of General Practitioners 1972). More importantly, adequate emphasis is at last being laid on training general practitioners in the necessary interventions to treat these disorders. This includes short-term counselling (Gath & Catalan 1986) and increasingly direct access to psychological management resources (e.g. clinical psychology sessions, social workers and community psychiatric nurses attached to health centres) (Freeling & Fitton 1983).

Whilst awareness of the need to recognise and treat correctly patients with psychiatric disorders who have become involved in the general health care systems is undoubtedly the most important motivation for liaison psychiatry's present vigour, there are other issues. The value of proper psychological management of patients with serious physical illnesses or undergoing surgery has been highlighted. In surgical patients its value has even been demonstrated financially with studies (e.g. Wilson 1981 Mathews & Ridgeway 1984) showing that careful psychological preparation for surgery both reduces postoperative anxiety and distress and can even reduce the length of hospital stay by a number of days.

Liaison psychiatrists have also found themselves in demand to help deal with the complex emotional issues which arise among staff members (particularly nurses) in high-stress areas of modern medicine. This is particularly so in areas such as medical oncology, obstetrics and intensive care. Here, the specific goals of treatment may be unclear — is this distressing cytotoxic regime really treatment for this individual or part of a trial of the drug? How does one emotionally relate to issues of a statistically better prognosis when treating an individual? In obstetrics and gynaecology the continuing paradox of dealing simultaneously with distressed infertile patients whilst assisting at the termination of pregnancies of equally distressed women can generate staff stress and conflict which needs skilled handling. Liaison psychiatrists have often been asked to find ways of resolving some of these issues and developing support systems for staff which reduce stress while permitting essential and important medical work to continue.

Poor communication within large medical teams, especially with patients suffering grave and often terminal disorders, has received much attention in the mass media. A paternalistic approach from doctors is less readily accepted by an educated and health-conscious population. Psychiatrists have been involved in teaching communication skills at both undergraduate and postgraduate levels and have conducted much of the research into the wishes of patients concerning how much they want to be told about their illness.

Two other features of present-day medicine have undoubtedly contributed towards liaison psychiatry's present position. Firstly, an international epidemic of self-poisoning has forced an awareness of psychological issues upon medical wards. The sheer volume of hospital admissions (the commonest cause of female medical admission in Britain — Hawton & Catalan 1983) for a deliberately self-inflicted disorder has ensured the regular presence of psychiatrists on the wards. Indeed it has been considered mandatory for all these patients to be assessed by a psychiatrist (HMSO 1968) before discharge. Whilst this policy is now under review, and alternative solutions to the problem of assessing self-harm patients are being sought, it has served to ensure that psychiatrists and physicians know each other. Secondly, in the USA a backlash against the diminished role of the doctor in psychiatric practice in the 1960s and 1970s (especially in the community mental health centres generated by Kennedy's reforms) has led to active 'remedicalisation', with psychiatrists keen to emphasise their links with general medicine and to focus on the interplay of physical and psychological ill-health.

FUNCTION OF THE LIAISON PSYCHIATRIST

The last 15 years has seen the establishment of a handful of full-time and part-time consultant posts dedicated to liaison psychiatry. These have arisen from local initiative rather than central planning. Consequently they are individual in their nature, the distribution of emphasis between clinical service, research and teaching has varied according to the situation and the special interests of the post-holder.

It is generally agreed that postgraduate teaching and the support of general ward staff is a most important part of the liaison psychiatrist's brief. It is obvious that liaison psychiatry can never be responsible for all the psychological management of general patients. It must strive, therefore, to raise the awareness and competence of the general staff in handling the psychological disturbances which accompany somatic disorders. The diagnosis and treatment of co-existing psychiatric disorders remains a small, but vital, facet of the job. It is essential for the liaison psychiatrist's face validity both with colleagues and with students. Through it he can often demonstrate his specific skills and, through managing severely disturbed patients, defend his status within the unofficial medical hierarchy. The various components of a liaison psychiatrist's role will be considered in greater detail.

1. Co-existing psychiatric illness

Serious psychiatric disorders are common. Some 3–4% of the population suffers from long-standing psychiatric problems (Cooper 1966). It is not surprising therefore that general doctors have to take this into account. In addition the stress of physical illness can destabilise a carefully achieved psychological equilibrium, and the interactions of drugs used in psychiatric and somatic treatments may also give rise to problems. Liaison psychiatrists usually develop special expertise in this overlap of treatments for physical and psychiatric disorders. Where patients are under the care of catchment area psychiatric teams it is often best to involve them in the psychiatric management during inpatient somatic treatment, as familiarity with the patient's normal functioning is the best guide in monitoring progress. The liaison psychiatrist needs, however, to offer availability and strenuously to avoid demarcation disputes in such issues, as such considerations are alien to most physicians and surgeons.

2. Psychiatric complications of physical illnesses and their treatment

The management of the psychological and psychiatric consequences of physical illness are the subject matter of this book. The liaison psychiatrist needs to be familiar with these areas and endeavour to raise his physician colleagues' awareness of them. As will be obvious from this book's contents, this is predominantly an empirical activity and demands a flexible and individually tailored approach to the various disorders. There is little room for adherence to rigid doctrinal approaches.

3. Behavioural and psychiatric problems as causes of physical illness

The liaison psychiatrist will often be involved in helping general teams develop programmes to modify clinically detrimental life-styles. Often these programmes are aimed at reducing stress or encouraging changes in diet or exercise patterns. Whilst cardiac, diabetic, rheumatology etc. teams are best placed for this counselling, achieving such changes in habits is often complex and may require acquiring skills which are often the province of psychiatrists and psychologists.

The importance of alcohol and drug usage must be borne in mind. As Dr Lloyd (Ch.18) points out, the opportunity for counselling patients with early signs of alcohol abuse should never be missed in the medical ward. To do so one needs to see beyond the stereotype of the down and out alcoholic. It is alertness to the possibility of the problem, rather than sophisticated treatment interventions, which is needed. The same applies to the more dramatic consequences of stopping alcohol or hypnotic usage on admission to hospital. Often their use is so routine that active enquiry is required for elucidation. Sometimes their use is denied or misrepresented out of embarrassment. Questioning the patient who begins to become overanxious and irritable a couple of days after admission can often lead to simple reinstatement or replacement treatments which pre-empt the development of full-blown delirium tremens or abstinence syndromes.

This heightened awareness of psychological causation can also prevent repetitive and fruitless investigation of conversion disorders and also of such conditions as Munchausen's syndrome, dermatitis artefacta or even the various physical complications of chronic anorexia nervosa. These are conditions in which the patient will undoubtedly deny the connection between behaviour and illness and in which, unfortunately, simple treatments do not necessarily follow. Recognising them does, however, offer the possibility of developing an appropriate psychiatric strategy and certainly reduces the risk of further entrenchment of the patient's behaviour.

Case History

A 58-year-old married woman who ran a small hotel and restaurant with her husband was repeatedly admitted for investigation of malabsorption syndrome. She had had over 14 admissions during the preceding 12 years. Her complaints were of weakness, weight loss, abdominal pain and loose stools. More recently she had also been noted to be anaemic and to have developed a polyneuritis. It had been recorded on previous admissions that her bowel looseness rapidly improved but that her weight did not increase although treatment of her iron deficiency anaemia was successful. She was a pleasant, co-operative patient who impressed her doctors by her stoical, uncomplaining acceptance of her disorder.

At a grand round her full history was presented and the possibility of atypical anorexia nervosa raised by the liaison psychiatrist. An interview with the patient and her husband easily confirmed the diagnosis. She had married early and borne her only child at the age of 19 years. This child, a daughter, died when only a few weeks old. During her grief she had lost weight which she had never regained and she had developed a classic anorexic life style. There had been no sexual contact with her husband, a gentle, avuncular man, over whom she fussed and for whom she prepared elaborate meals which she herself never ate. She confined herself to health foods 'because of my weak stomach'. She used considerable quantities of senna. Whilst in hospital it was clear that she disposed of much of her food in the lavatory but never vomited.

She was utterly impervious to any attempt at psychological understanding of her disorder. Careful dietary advice involving the husband's help enabled her to maintain her weight without developing anaemia. A modest reduction in her laxative abuse resulted in the disappearance of her abdominal discomfort and looseness of stool. Follow-up via her GP at 2 years revealed that she continued her regular, somewhat restricted, life-style. She was very thin but felt well and had required no further intervention.

4. Deliberate self-harm

As mentioned above, deliberate self-harm (DSH) is one of the commonest causes for medical admission in Britain. Most of these patients are relatively young, more often female and only exceptionally suffering from any form of psychiatric illness. The Government policy that all such patients should be assessed by a psychiatrist in addition to their medical assessment and treatment, was to ensure that the patient's psychosocial state received adequate attention and that the overdose (as it most often was) was not judged purely on the grounds of potential lethality.

In the light of the epidemic of DSH which developed in the 1970s (and appears at present to have peaked), these strictures seem utopian, and indeed, excessive. It has become increasingly recognised that psychiatric manpower is not only in too short supply to ensure this service, but also that other professional groups (appropriately trained social workers, psychiatric nurses) are equally able to assess and counsel such patients. Indeed it has been suggested that psychiatrists, by their style of work and professional training, are poorly equipped to help these patients. What is so often needed is short-term, problem-based counselling and support, at which non-medical personnel clearly seem to excel (Hawton & Catalan 1987).

The liaison psychiatrist still has an important role in this service. Often he is responsible for managing it and ensuring the initial training of the counsellors. He needs, also, to be on hand to advise on the management of those patients who are suffering from a psychiatric disorder. Responsibilities for such assessments and treatment must not become the sole prerogative of the counsellors. If so, trainee doctors and psychiatrists would fail to develop their capacity to judge the seriousness of DSH attempts necessary in situations where the full specialised services are not always at hand. Attitudes towards DHS patients are variable and not always positive. Ensuring that they are dealt with efficiently and in a way which is made meaningful to both doctors and nurses on the medical wards helps mitigate these negative attitudes and foster a more general acceptance of the importance of emotional factors and individual motivation in patients. It has also been suggested (Ramon et al 1975) that there is considerable divergence in attitude towards DSH patients between doctors as a group and nurses as a group. There is a value, therefore, in a medically based perspective in training general staff. Excellent, thoroughly practical handbooks on the assessment and counselling of DSH patients are available (e.g. Hawton & Catalan 1987), so the subject will not be dealt with in further detail here.

5. Psychological responses to illness

Falling ill can be a major crisis for many patients, generating anxiety and despair and leading to far-reaching reappraisals of their lives (Caplan 1964). This is not so for all individuals. Many patients accept the occurrence of their ill-health with courage and realism. More often this is so when they are older or when they have had earlier warning signs of their approaching illness and have had time to adjust their expectations.

Becoming seriously ill often involves giving up long-held (although perhaps rarely articulated) ambitions and hopes for the future. These are brought into question, reviewed and modified in the aftermath of the diagnosis. For some patients this crisis is an important, creative time.

Case History
A business man, admitted with crescendo angina, was noted to be tearful in the early mornings and withdrawn during the day. On the fifth day after admission he talked to the houseman about how envious he felt over the fuss being made over a nursing auxillary's birthday. It was dawning on him how much his whole life had been increasingly taken over by his pursuit of success and in the process how he was missing out on the very things that his money ought to have been giving him. He never became fully involved with the small group of men on the ward who had also suffered angina or coronaries. He remained quiet and somewhat of a loner. On follow-up, however, he seemed increasingly relaxed, had sold off part of his business and referred to his chest pain as 'the best thing that had happened to me for a long time'. He remarked that talking it over with the house officer had helped inordinately (it had been a brief conversation of 15–20 minutes) and he was particularly glad that nobody had 'preached at him'.

Grieving for lost hopes is a normal and healthy aspect of adapting to illness. Given some gentle support most patients will come through this particular crisis, often sadder but wiser.

6. Pathological responses

Personal vulnerability or even misunderstanding of the nature and implications of a diagnosis may lead to catastrophic responses to illness. In particular, terms such as 'cancer' or 'multiple sclerosis' may be so emotionally charged for patients that they decompensate totally when confronted by them. Treatable psychiatric disorders, such as anxiety states and depression, are common in the course of serious physical illness (Maguire et al 1978). Patients may respond to their illnesses in ways which leave the staff treating them baffled and concerned

The range of responses is wide, from rage and hostility through total collapse and regression to apparently blissful denial. Most of these responses are well displayed in normal grief (Parkes 1986) and patients often shift from one to another. Only when they become entrenched or overpowering do they interfere with the patient's resolution of his crisis or with effective management. Staff members can also be overwhelmed by these strong, primitive emotions, especially when mechanisms such as 'projection' or 'splitting' are employed. Most often this happens when a patient's sense of hopelessness infects the staff treating him. In such cases the liaison psychiatrist's outside status may help restore a more realistic assessment. By encouraging the staff to step back he can balance their empathic response to the patient with knowledge and experience. In more complicated situations the liaison psychiatrist may have to work with both staff and patient to help unravel confused emotions.

Case History
A 7-year-old girl was dying from aplastic anaemia. She was often in considerable pain and was being reverse barrier nursed. This tragic situation was complicated by the parents' response, which was so extreme that nursing staff were going off sick. They could not bear the tension and dreaded being on the shift when the girl would eventually die. Her mother voiced clear and repeated suicidal intent and the father was abusive and critical to the staff. In particular, he undermined nurses' morale by making unfavourable comparisons between them: 'Oh it's you — we'd hoped Nurse A would be on as she is so much better with Jane'. After a few weeks of this the parents were viewed as utterly bad people by the staff, who were both frightened of them and disliked them intensely.

The Liaison Senior Registrar was involved with the parents only after preparatory work with the staff who had requested a session together to work out 'what was to be done'. This session ranged far beyond this particular family and nurses talked about the awful stresses of caring for young, dying children. It became clear that, at one level, it was almost a relief to have someone (the girl's parents) to feel angry at and blame. It appeared to discharge some of their bitterness at the unfairness of their young patients' fates.

The Senior Registrar did not make any links but allowed them to talk about how unfair their job often seemed. An interview with the parents was arranged and proved to be productive. The father readily acknowledged that his fury reflected his impotence and he was able to contain it better after talking. His wife, it transpired, had often threatened suicide in the past. Taking responsibility for her helped the father feel he had some practical role to play and relieved the nurses and doctors of one more burden which they felt 'unfairly' loaded with. A degree of calm was achieved and Jane's death was not accompanied by the feared consequences.

In this situation the Senior Registrar had recognised how the projection on to the parents of the staff's feelings about illnesses was preventing them tackling the undoubtedly difficult issue of the parents' emotional decompensation. He had been asked to help with the situation, not to make observations on it, and quite rightly refrained from linking the two in an interpretation.

Denial poses particular problems for psychiatrists who may have acquired, in their professional contact with neurotic patients, an understandable wish to facilitate conscious awareness of denied conflicts. Working with the seriously physically ill teaches one a healthy respect for such defence mechanisms. They can often provide the patient with brief periods of efficient functioning whilst they confront their dilemma in small doses.

7. The Unco-operative patient

Of all the different responses to illness, the one which usually causes greatest incredulity is the patient who refuses the treatment offered. There are socially acceptable and readily understood reasons in some cases, such as religious dictates for Jehovah's Witnesses or the elderly patient who says 'enough is enough'. Where patients seem unable to explain their refusal or the explanation seems hopelessly inadequate, a psychiatric opinion is often requested. The attending team usually suspect an affective disorder (depression or anxiety) as the cause of the refusal. The patient's evaluation of the benefits of treatment is thought to be distorted by his despair or fear. This may be so, in which case appropriate specific treatments may be indicated and medical or surgical intervention may have to be delayed.

Quite often, however, the refusal or poor co-operation arises out of the different views held by the patient and his doctors of his illness. Tuckett et al (1985), medical sociologists, referred to the medical consultation as a 'meeting between experts'. The doctor is an expert on medical knowledge and the patient an expert on himself. Tuckett points out that this ideal is rarely met in practice and the doctors (and many patients) consider that only one view of the situation, the doctor's, has any relevance. General practitioners have a long tradition of Balint (1964) groups which emphasise the personal nature and significance of a patient's illness and the need for doctors to take account of this. The liaison psychiatrist's contribution to helping with the non-co-operative patient on the wards is often to explore and make clear these differences so that the patient and doctor cease to talk past one another. A useful structure for exploring non-compliance in patients is to screen four levels.

a. The personal (intrapsychic) meaning of the illness for the patient is what he or she understands the diagnostic term to imply. This is often based partly on popular misconceptions ('all cancer is incurable', 'all cancer patients die in agony' etc.) and partly on personal experience.

Case History

An otherwise co-operative and calm nun refused radiotherapy after an operation for carcinoma of the breast. The doctor explained at length that it was the best chance of halting the spread of the cancer and prolonging her life. She thanked him politely but declined the offer. He assumed she was depressed and asked the psychiatrist to assess her. The psychiatrist experienced the same bland refusal and was puzzled as there was nothing in her mental state to suggest depression or any other psychiatric disorder. Suggesting that 'It would be useful to know more about you' he took a standard history, during which she mentioned an aunt who had died some years previously from carcinoma of the breast. The aunt had also had radiotherapy and had died 15 months after operation. It became clear that the patient assumed that her aunt's treatment had been successful and that when the surgeon had talked of extending her life expectancy he meant for about 6–15 months. She had not considered this extra 9 months worth the sickness and lethargy she knew to be associated with the radiotherapy. Once she realised the extent of the possible gains she readily consented to treatment. The surgeon considered it remarkable that an otherwise well educated and sensible woman should make important life decisions on such 'irrational premises'.

b. *The interpersonal* significance of the illness and treatment, and its impact on others, is particularly important in palliative measures. Patients may refuse because they see treatment as prolonging their demise and casting an impossible burden on their carers — usually their spouses or children. Again, they may harbour misconceptions about the facts — usually surrounding the difficulties of pain control or managing colostomies etc. These need to be dealt with as in (a). More often talking it over with the family is needed. This does not need to be a long-winded procedure and often a $\frac{1}{2}$-hour single meeting can sort out many problems. The commonest scenario is that the family share the patient's concerns, though to a much lesser degree. Having faced it, however, they insist that their wish to be involved and make the most of the remaining time with the patient is far more important to them. Sometimes small practical issues may need sorting out and compromises found.

Case History
An elderly diabetic man was refusing an essential above-knee amputation for gangrene. Direct exploration by both the surgeon and psychiatrist yielded nothing. In a less structured family discussion it became clear that the patient's house, a suburban Edwardian villa, was a powerful symbol for everything he had achieved. It was the product of his hard work as a shopkeeper and also the home in which he had brought up his three daughters. He regularly consoled himself at times of despair by daydreaming of future generations of his family growing up in the gardens of his house. It was immediately obvious to the family that he was convinced that they would sell the house to buy a bungalow if he returned unable to manage stairs. Arrangements were discussed to convert one of the downstairs rooms into a bedroom and he readily acceded to the amputation.

c. *Resistance in the doctor–patient relationship*, perhaps based on a past misunderstanding, can lead to poor compliance. This situation is more often characterised by irritation and bad feeling on both sides rather than the perplexity which is common in (a) and (b). The patient may harbour resentment that the present treatment is needed because the doctor 'got it wrong' or missed the diagnosis earlier. His failure to co-operate properly is partly because of damaged trust in the doctor and partly a most effective means of punishing him. The only way forward is to tease out what the resentment originates from. If it is based on fact, then an honest acknowledgement and simple explanations can often clear the air. Usually the delay in diagnosis can be shown to have little importance for the prognosis.

Gaining a proper sense of proportion about the error requires that the patient feels safe enough to disclose his concerns. This may be helped by a neutral (though medically trained) outsider. If the patient's ideas are totally wrong then the psychiatrist can confront them then and there, e.g. 'I had a persistent cough 2 years ago — if they had X-rayed me then I wouldn't be in this mess now'. In situations where no resolution is obtained, it may be necessary for the patient's management to be transferred to another doctor.

d. *Team communication issues* are much more likely to cause problems in modern hospitals. Seriously ill patients are usually managed by an extensive team — nurses, house officers, senior registrars and consultants, etc. The relationship to each of these members is different and that, along with the differences of temperament and personal styles of staff members, can often lead to the patient feeling confused and occasionally misled. The likelihood of dialogue decreases as status within the team increases. It is not just that the consultant is busy but also that the patient is less likely to question him. All those questions which are not asked on the round (despite the consultant asking directly 'Is there anything more you would like me to explain?') are asked of the nurses and house officers straight afterwards. Usually this causes no problems. Problems arise, however, if there is no consensus in the team about what the patient should be told and especially so if senior members are either inconsistent or unapproachable.

A commonly reported scenario is the consultant implying a more favourable outcome which is ostensibly accepted by the patient. He then confronts the house officer with 'He was just saying that to spare me, wasn't he?'. The house officer's position is wretched. He is being asked directly for the truth. which involves him in apparent disloyalty to his chief. If the system starts to go wrong patients become confused and distressed and the liaison psychiatrist may be called. His position is delicate. It is not his job to tell a surgeon or physician how to run his team. Usually what can be achieved is to identify the silent rules which regulate the team. It may be, for example, that the consultant wishes his staff to be frank with the patient but does not want to deal with these issues on a busy ward round. Talking it over with the house officer, sister or senior registrar may reveal that a new team member is unaware of this, hence the flurry of distress.

A common misunderstanding about the role of the liaison psychiatrist concerns the use of the compulsory powers under the Mental Health Act 1983. The Act relates only to the detention and treatment of people suffering from severe mental illness and its powers only extend to the treatment of mental illness. It cannot be used to authorise the treatment of a physical illness (especially a surgical operation) against the wishes of a patient. Operating on a patient who, for instance, is confused and unable to give consent but is desperately ill is governed by common law and dictated by the doctor's 'duty of care'. Treating a confused patient's heart failure, where that confusion is the result of his heart failure, neither requires the use of the Mental Health Act nor acquires any protection by its use. A willingness patiently and repeatedly to explain this issue to generations of house officers is an essential requirement for a liaison psychiatrist. The circumstances of the request are invariably unique, the experience always stressful and the undergraduate lectures on the Mental Health Act always long forgotten.

8. Staff support

High-technology medicine imposes considerable strains on the staff responsible for it. Some wards, e.g. oncology and intensive care, can be filled exclusively with desperately ill patients. Not only is the degree of pathology overwhelming but sometimes the rationale for different procedures is hard to grasp or ambiguous. Devolution of responsibility is an inevitable feature of sophisticated team work and a consequence of the increasing technical demands on nursing staff. Alongside this the loosening of hierarchical structures can remove the ready defence of 'It's not my decision. I'm only doing what I'm told' from those who are nearest the patient.

In some ward situations there may be a willingness to acknowledge stresses and ask for help with them. Often this comes from the nursing staff. Denial of stress, 'looking on the bright side', is the commonest defensive style in medical and surgical wards. Where it is the chosen method it is probably fruitless for the liaison psychiatrist to attempt any other approach.

Where help is requested the commonest response is some form of staff support group. This involves setting aside an hour a week at a regular time, usually during shift overlap, for the nurses. The liaison psychiatrist may be asked to conduct the group (others such as hospital chaplain, social worker, etc., are also perfectly capable). It seems important to have an outsider who is not involved in the ward hierarchy. Each group is different and will reflect the idiosyncracies of the ward. The liaison psychiatrist's role utilises general skills from group therapy.

The group needs firm boundaries. It must not spill over into the rest of the day and so the therapist must ensure that it resolves what is brought up in it. Time must be spent examining the worries which do come up, thinking about their source and how they could be reduced. He needs to ensure that the atmosphere is safe. This means gauging sensitively the degree of challenge to accepted roles which is tolerable and encouraging consensus about it.

Members of a staff support group are colleagues, *not patients*. The leader should model an equal, respectful response to others' difficulties and not interpret unconscious conflicts which he thinks may be contributing to them. Similarly, he will gently interrupt and contain any new, overenthusiastic group member who may, relieved to feel that he can let his guard down, start to 'reveal' all. The aim is to recognise and share common stresses and thereby encourage the members' abilities to empathise and more effectively support each other. This is rarely helped by concentrating exclusively on the individual characteristics of members.

The 'outsider' status of the therapist is soon compromised, though not lost. As he comes to know the realities of the ward work he will acquire greater flexibility in his responses. Sometimes he will respond to complaints of how difficult it is on the ward by agreeing and commiserating. Another time he might wonder aloud why everyone is so down as things do not seem any worse than usual.

Staff support groups seem successful. It is doubtful, however, whether they should be pushed against any great resistance. If a ward is ready for one it will probably ask. A group which is accepted against mild resistance often flourishes when anxieties about the therapist 'analysing' them or about the release of uncontrollable emotions have been dispelled.

CONCLUSIONS

There is great scope for liaison psychiatry in helping ward staff deal effectively with patients' psychological and emotional problems. There is probably also a place in many wards for the liaison psychiatrist to help the staff directly. To be helpful it is vital that he is not dogmatic and that he is prepared to see patients whom he does not consider necessarily to need his intervention. His role will remain predominantly educational and facilitative.

REFERENCES

Alexander F 1950 Psychosomatic medicine. Norton, New York
Balint M 1964 The doctor, his patient and the illness, 2nd edn. Churchill Livingstone, Edinburgh
Billings E G 1939 Liaison psychiatry and intern instruction. Journal of the Association of the American Medical College, 14: 375–385
Caplan G 1964 Principles of preventive psychiatry. Basic Books, New York
Cooper B 1966 Psychiatric disorder in hospital and general practice. Social Psychiatry 1: 7–10
Crisp A H 1968 The role of the psychiatrist in the general hospital. Postgraduate Medical Journal 44: 267–276
Dunbar F 1935 Emotions and bodily changes. Columbia University Press, New York
Fleminger J J, Mallett B L 1962 Psychiatric referrals from medical and surgical wards. Journal of Mental Science 108: 183–190
Freeling P, Fitton P 1983 Teaching practices revisited. British Medical Journal 287: 535–537
Friedman M, Rosenman R H 1971 Type A behaviour pattern: its association with coronary heart disease. Annals of Clinical Research 3: 300–312
Gath D, Catalan J 1986 The treatment of emotional disorders in general practice: psychological methods versus medication. Journal of Psychosomatic Research 30: 381–386
Greer S, Morris T, Pettingdale K W 1979 Psychological responses to breast cancer: effect on outcome. Lancet 2: 785–787
Hawton K, Catalan J 1987 Attempted suicide. A practical guide to its nature and management, 2nd edn. Oxford Medical Publications, Oxford
HMSO 1968 Hospital treatment of acute poisoning. London
Lief A 1948 The commonsense psychiatry of Dr Adolph Meyer. McGraw-Hill, New York
Lipowski Z J 1974 Consultation liaison psychiatry: an overview. American Journal of Psychiatry 131: 623–630

Maguire G P, Julier D L, Hawton K E, Bancroft J H J 1974 Psychiatric morbidity and referral on two general medical wards. British Medical Journal 1: 268–270

Maguire G P, Lee E G, Bevington D J, Kucheman C S, Crabtree R J, Cornill C E 1978 Psychiatric problems in the first year after mastectomy. British Medical Journal 1: 963–965

Mathews A, Ridgeway V 1984 Psychological preparation for surgery. In: Steptoe A & Mathews A (eds) health care and human behaviour. Academic Press, London: pp. 231–259

Moffic H S, Paykel E S 1975 Depression in medical inpatients. British Journal of Psychiatry 126: 346–353

Parkes C M 1986 Bereavement: studies of grief in adult life. Tavistock Publications, London

Ramon S, Bancroft J H J, Skrimshire A M 1975 Attitudes towards self-poisoning among physicians and nurses in a general hospital. British Journal of Psychiatry 127: 257–264

Royal College of General Practitioners 1972 The future general practitioner, learning and teaching. London BMJ

Shepherd M, Davies B, Culpan R H 1960 Psychiatric illness in the general hospital. Acta Psychiatrica and Neurologica Scandinavica 35: 518–525

Shepherd M 1966 Psychiatric illness in general practice. Oxford Medical Publications, Oxford

Tuckett D, Bolton M, Olson C, Williams A 1985 Meetings between experts. Tavistock Publications, London

Wilson J F 1981 Behavioural preparations for surgery: benefit or harm? Journal of Behavioral Medicine 4: 79–102

Index